Teaching Chinese, Japanese, and Korean Heritage Language Students

Curriculum Needs, Materials, and Assessment

ESL & Applied Linguistics Professional Series
Eli Hinkel, Series Editor

Visit www.routledge.com for additional information on titles in the ESL & Applied Linguistics Professional Series

Teaching Chinese, Japanese, and Korean Heritage Language Students

Curriculum Needs, Materials, and Assessment

Edited by

Kimmi Kondo-Brown
James Dean Brown

Lawrence Erlbaum Associates
Taylor & Francis Group

New York   London

Lawrence Erlbaum Associates
Taylor & Francis Group
270 Madison Avenue
New York, NY 10016

Lawrence Erlbaum Associates
Taylor & Francis Group
2 Park Square
Milton Park, Abingdon
Oxon OX14 4RN

© 2008 by Taylor & Francis Group, LLC
Lawrence Erlbaum Associates is an imprint of Taylor & Francis Group, an Informa business

Printed in the United States of America on acid-free paper
10 9 8 7 6 5 4 3 2 1

International Standard Book Number-13: 978-0-8058-5878-5 (Softcover) 978-0-8058-5877-8 (Hardcover)

Library of Congress Cataloging-in-Publication Data

Teaching Chinese, Japanese, and Korean heritage language students : curriculum
   needs, materials, and assessment / edited by Kimi Kondo-Brown, James Dean
   Brown.
      p. cm.
   Includes bibliographical references and index.
   ISBN-13: 987-0-8058-5877-8 (c : alk. paper)
   ISBN-10: 0-8058-5877-6 (c : alk. paper)
   ISBN-13: 978-0-8058-5878-5 (p : alk. paper)
   ISBN-10: 0-8058-5878-4 (p : alk. paper) 1. Chinese Americans--Education. 2.
   Japanese Americans--Education. 3. Korean Americans--Education. 4. Schools,
   Chinese--United States. 5. Schools, Japanese--United States. 6. Schools,
   Korean--United States. 7. Native language and education--United States. I.
   Kondo-Brown, Kimi. II. Brown, James Dean.

   LC3071.T43 2007
   371.97'951073--dc22   2006034316

Visit the Taylor & Francis Web site at
http://www.taylorandfrancis.com

This book is dedicated with love and appreciation to our
mothers, Mitsuko Kondo and Jeanne Y. Brown

CONTENTS

PREFACE

This edited book aims at further promoting and improving HL instruction by providing a collection of theoretical and practical papers about HL curriculum design, learner needs, materials development, and assessment procedures. Heritage language (HL) learners are defined in this book as "any learners who have acquired their cultural and linguistic competence in a nondominant language primarily through contact at home with foreign-born parents and/or other family members" (see first sentence of chap. 1 for source). Interest in HL students defined as such is growing by leaps and bounds. Indeed, HL instruction is increasingly becoming a "hot topic" in the field and may even be said to be a burgeoning subdiscipline within the fields of foreign language (FL) education and applied linguistics.

The target language groups in this collection are Chinese, Japanese, and Korean. In countries like the Unites States and Canada, speakers of East Asian languages are among the fastest growing populations. School and adult children from this growing immigrant population are studying their HLs in a variety of settings at different stages of their lives. In the United States, for example, there are numerous community-based HL and supplementary schools where school-age HL children study their HLs. At the university level, HL students from East Asian backgrounds are becoming more visible than ever in language courses, where they study their HLs in either traditional FL classes in a single-track system, or special heritage or bilingual courses in a multitrack system.

The authors in this collection have worked with school-age and/or university HL students from East Asian backgrounds as teachers and researchers. Most of them are themselves from East Asian immigrant backgrounds. The work collected in this book not only makes references to the existing learning and curriculum theories but also generates new ideas and questions based on previous and new empirical data about East Asian HL students learning experiences and outcomes.

We hope that this book will prove useful to applied linguists, educators, and graduate students who are interested in FL curriculum, pedagogy, and assessment studies; HL development and instruction; and East Asian language learning and teaching. The book may also prove useful as a primary text or reference for researchers, educators, and students for instructional and research purposes in departments concerned with East Asian language students, or as a main or supplementary text in FL curriculum development and pedagogy courses. To these ends, chapters on the following topics have been included:

Chapter 1—Kondo-Brown and Brown provide a detailed overview of the aim and scope of the entire book, with a special focus on pedagogical and curriculum issues involved, and detailed descriptions of the chapters and how they are organized.

Chapter 2—Kondo-Brown provides a literature review of recent empirical studies that deal with needs analysis, curriculum innovations, as well as instructional and assessment activities for heritage learners in East Asian languages.

Chapter 3—Kataoka, Koshiyama, and Shibata report on a study of approximately 1,600 first- to ninth-grade Japanese *hoshuukoo* students' performances on assorted Japanese and English proficiency tests with the goal of determining their language and curricular needs.

Chapter 4—Hasegawa examines the validity of various Japanese proficiency measures used in empirical studies to study Japanese heritage learners with the goal of examining the needs for developing specific proficiency measurement instruments for child HL learners.

Chapter 5—H.-S. Kim reports on a study of two groups of nonheritage learners and three groups of heritage learners with the goals of identifying the differences in their language transfer and strategies when processing Korean relative clauses and providing pedagogical implications for HL instruction.

Chapter 6—Kondo-Brown and Fukuda investigate how language background factors such as heritage background and study/living abroad experiences influence the intersentential referencing of Japanese texts and lead to implications for teaching reading in the single-track program where HL and non-HL university students study together.

Chapter 7—Lee and Kim examine second-generation Korean American college students' language attitudes with a focus on their motivational orientations, learning situation, and self-efficacy, as well as applications of these concepts to curriculum design.

Chapter 8—Yu proposes "a compromise curriculum" that simultaneously attends to the language needs of university heritage and nonheritage learners of Korean at the beginning and intermediate levels.

Chapter 9—Weger-Guntharp investigates the language and affective needs of university heritage and nonheritage learners of Chinese in the regular track designed primarily for the nonheritage learners.

Chapter 10—Drawing on empirical evidence about child Japanese HL learners as well as educational and instructional theories for child learners, Douglas provides a model for developing curriculum and implementing pedagogical strategies for young HL learners.

Chapter 11—Wu discusses the motivations and linguistic needs of Chinese heritage learners, and then explores ways to blend technology, a learner-centered approach, and the 5 Cs principles of the National Standards for Foreign Language Education into a curriculum that meets their needs.

Chapter 12—Zhang and Davis report on an action-oriented interpretative case study that examines the effects of online chats in developing Chinese literacy skills of university heritage learners in an experimental class.

Before the publication of this book, curriculum developers who wished to focus on HL learners had to rely largely on general second language (L2) curriculum books. However, this is the first curriculum development book for child and adult HL students in which the implications and recommendations are not only connected to L2 curriculum models and learning theories but also specifically founded on evidence from empirical studies about HL students. We hope that this book will promote research about heritage students in East Asian languages and provide ideas and inspiration that will help improve the teaching of HL students in various educational settings all over the world.

ACKNOWLEDGMENTS

We would like to thank the reviewers commissioned by LEA for their thorough and valuable feedback as well as the LEA editorial and production staff, especially Dr. Eli Hinkel and Naomi Silverman, for their creativity and professionalism in helping us to produce this book. We would also like to thank all of the authors for their outstanding contributions.

Kimi Kondo-Brown and J.D. Brown
Kane'ohe, Hawai`i

LIST OF CONTRIBUTORS

James Dean Brown
Department of Second Language Studies
University of Hawai`i at Mānoa
Honolulu, Hawai`i

Niki Davis
Center for Technology in Learning and Teaching
Iowa State University
Ames, Iowa

Masako O. Douglas
Department of Asian & Asian American Studies
California State University, Long Beach
Long Beach, California

Chie Fukuda
Department of East Asian Languages & Literatures
University of Hawai`i at Mānoa
Honolulu, Hawai`i

Tomomi Hasegawa
Department of Second Language Studies
University of Hawai`i at Mānoa
Honolulu, Hawai`i

Hiroko C. Kataoka
Department of Asian & Asian American Studies
California State University, Long Beach
Long Beach, California

Hae-Young Kim
Department of Asian & African Languages & Literature
Duke University
Durham, North Carolina

Hi-Sun Helen Kim
Department of East Asian Languages & Civilization
University of Chicago
Chicago, Illinois

Kimi Kondo-Brown
Department of East Asian Languages and Literatures
University of Hawai`i at Mānoa
Honolulu, Hawai`i

Yasuko Koshiyama
International Studies & Languages Division
Pepperdine University
Malibu, California

Jin Sook Lee
Department of Education
University of California, Santa Barbara
Santa Barbara, California

Setsue Shibata
Department of Modern Languages & Literatures
California State University, Fullerton
Fullerton, California

Heather Dawn Weger-Guntharp
Department of Linguistics
Georgetown University
Washington, D.C.

Sue-mei Wu
Department of Modern Languages
Carnegie Mellon University
Pittsburgh, Pennsylvania

William H. Yu
Department of East Asian Languages & Literatures
University of Hawai`i at Mānoa
Honolulu, Hawai`i

De Zhang
Center for Technology in Learning and Teaching
Iowa State University
Ames, Iowa

I

Overview

Chapter 1

INTRODUCTION

Kimi Kondo-Brown
James Dean Brown
University of Hawai'i at Mānoa

THE AIM AND SCOPE OF THIS BOOK

Heritage language (HL) learners are defined in this book as any learners who have acquired their cultural and linguistic competence in a nondominant language primarily through contact at home with foreign-born parents and/or other family members (The UCLA Steering Committee, 2000; Valdés, 1995). For example, Jon in Kondo's (1997) study was a 19-year-old Japanese American who had the bilingual and bicultural capacity to go between Japanese-speaking immigrant parents and English-speaking peers and others in the community. Jon was born and raised in a middle-class, multi-ethnic community in Honolulu, where he was immersed in English throughout his K–12 years. Jon spoke only Japanese at home until he started going to an English-speaking kindergarten. In kindergarten, Jon learned English quickly, and in elementary school, he was the top of his class. Although Jon used English exclusively outside home, he continued to use Japanese at home with his mother. At the time of data collection, Jon was an English-dominant high achieving college student who could speak Japanese comfortably and used the language regularly with his mother. Because of his fluency in speaking Japanese, people sometimes labelled him as a native speaker of Japanese or a bilingual student.[1] However, Jon was not satisfied with his Japanese proficiency, especially his *keigo* (formal language) and literacy skills. As an ambitious student with an international business major who dreamed of having a bilingual career, Jon was studying Japanese in the university's Japanese language program.

Jon's parents are among the growing foreign-born population in the United States. For example, in 2004, there were 34.2 million foreign-born U.S. residents, accounting for 12% of the total U.S. population, which was 2.3% higher than the previous year (Bernstein, 2005). Within the foreign-born population, about half were born in Latin America, and a quarter were born in Asia. Among those who came from Asia, populations of East Asian immigrants are notably expanding. For example, according to recent immigration statistics, between 1990 and 2000, the foreign-born population from China increased by 87%, and it is now the fourth-largest immigrant group in the United States (Grieco, 2004). During the same period, the foreign-born population from Korea increased by 52%, and it is now the seventh-largest immigrant group (Yau, 2004). Compared to immigrants from Korea and China, immigrants from Japan are fewer, but during the same period, approximately 6,800 Japanese arrived annually as permanent residents (The Office of Immigration Statistics, 2006).

Heritage language students from East Asian backgrounds like Jon are studying their HL in a variety of settings at different stages of their lives. In the United States, for example, there are numerous community-based and often religious-affiliated HL schools for school-age children. In different parts of the nation, more than 1,000 Korean HL schools (Shin, 2005), more than 600 Chinese HL schools (Chao, 1996), and 50 Japanese HL schools (Douglas, 2006) are offering weekend, after-school, or summer programs. Compared to Chinese and Korean HL schools, Japanese HL schools may seem far less numerous. However, this figure does not include the nation's approximately 84 *hoshuukoo* (supplementary Japanese schools) where children from Japanese speaking families—who may be permanent residents of the United States—study Japanese (see Kataoka et al., this volume). Young HL learners may also study in various two-way immersion or mother-tongue maintenance programs in Chinese (e.g., Lao, 2004), Japanese (e.g., Hayashi, 2006), and Korean (e.g., Shin, 2005; Sohn &

---

[1]Jon's oral Japanese proficiency was judged to be "advanced" on an oral proficiency test (OPI) with an ACTFL (the American Council on the Teaching of Foreign Languages) tester.

Merrill, forthcoming). These immersion and maintenance programs are integrated into regular school-day curricula in American schools.[2]

Furthermore, according to a recent Modern Language Association report (Welles, 2004) on foreign language (FL) enrollments at the postsecondary college levels, in 2002, Chinese and Japanese were among the seven most commonly taught languages in the U.S. institutions of higher education. During the same year, Korean ranked lower at 14th in enrollments, and yet it was the most rapidly expanding language with an amazing increase of 128% since 1990. Clearly, HL students of Chinese, Japanese, and Korean are becoming more visible than ever in courses that teach these languages (Kondo-Brown, 2003; Shirane, 2003). They study their HLs in traditional FL classes either in a single-track system or in special HL or bilingual courses in a multitrack system (Kondo-Brown, 2003; see also Yu, this volume; Zang & Davis, this volume; Wager-Guntharp, this volume; Wu, this volume).

This edited book with a focus on East Asian HL students was conceived to promote and improve HL instruction in Chinese, Japanese, and Korean by providing a collection of theoretical and practical papers about such instruction in terms of curriculum design, learner needs, materials development, teacher support, and assessment procedures. A curriculum development book like this one seems very timely. First, interest among researchers and practitioners in providing better HL instruction has grown rapidly in recent years (e.g., Brinton & Kagan, forthcoming; Campbell, 2003; Krashen, Tse, & McQuillian, 1998; Peyton, Ranard, & McGinnis, 2001; The UCLA Steering Committee, 2000; Valdés, 1995; Van Deusen-Scholl, 2003; Webb & Miller, 2000). Second, the latest sociological and social-psychological HL studies dealing with East Asian HL immigrants in the United States and Canada indicate that (a) HL development should be understood in its many layers of interconnected contexts of micropsychological and macrosocietal factors, and (b) proper and effective HL instruction in various educational settings is much desired by East Asian immigrant communities (Kondo-Brown, 2006). Such studies clearly indicate the need for curriculum development books intended to improve East Asian HL instruction in various school settings. This edited collection does just that.

In the past, work on HL instruction in the United States has mostly focused on speakers of Spanish, the nation's largest immigrant population

---

[2]To date, the counts of young HL learners enrolled in all of these HL schools or special language maintenance programs are not available, except rough estimations given for Chinese HL schools. According to McGinnis (2005), as of early 2005, student enrollments in two types of Chinese HL schools—one has connections with Taiwanese, and the other mainland Chinese immigrant communities—are estimated to be 100,000 and 60,000, respectively.

(Lewelling & Peyton, 1999). Researchers of Spanish HL instruction have proposed theoretical frameworks and approaches for ways to design and implement such instruction (e.g., Faltis, 1990; McQuillan, 1996; Merino, Trueba, Samaniego, 1993; Valdés, 1995; Valdés, Lozano, & Garcia-Moya, 1981). However, in their work, little empirical evidence of the effectiveness of these proposed teaching ideas has been produced (with the notable exception of McQuillan, 1996). The work collected in this book not only adopts the existing general learning and curriculum theories but also generates new ideas and agendas based on previous and new empirical data, data about East Asian HL students' learning needs and motivations as well as about the effectiveness of given East Asian HL programs or instructional strategies.

As such, our work may have valuable implications for other HL populations including speakers of Spanish because certain characteristics of these speakers seem common across languages. For example, HL students of Spanish may: speak fluent Spanish but not be able to read and write it (Valdés, 1995); demonstrate varying levels of both oral and written Spanish proficiency (Aparicio, 1983; Garcia & Diaz, 1992); thus, indicating a need for developing HL curriculum with individual differences in mind (McQuillan, 1996). These issues previously raised for Spanish HL learners are further examined in East Asian HL settings with relatively large-scale empirical data (Kim, this volume; Kataoka, Koshiyama, & Shibata, this volume), as well as practical instructional examples (Wu, this volume; Zang & Davis, this volume).

We also point out that, before this book, curriculum developers who wished to focus on HL learners in East Asian languages had to rely on general language curriculum books (e.g., J. D. Brown, 1995; Clark, 1987; Dubin & Olshtain, 1986; Johnson, 1989; Nunan, 1987, 1991; Richards, 2001; White, 1988; Yalden, 1985), on nonspecific communicative language curriculum books (e.g., Finocchiaro & Brumfit, 1983; Johnson, 1982; Munby, 1978; Yalden, 1983, 1988), or on generic books about language materials development (e.g., McDonough & Shaw, 2003; Tomlinson, 1998, 2002).

In this chapter, we adapt the curriculum framework from the first of the books listed in the previous paragraph (J.D. Brown, 1995) to structure our discussion of curriculum issues as they relate specifically to HL learners. The elements of language curriculum from that book are given in Figure 1.1. They include needs analysis, objectives, testing, materials, teaching, and program evaluation with arrows connecting each of the five main elements consecutively forward and backward, but also relating each of the five main elements to program evaluation. We feel that, in general, this model will work not only for most language curriculum development, but also for HL curriculum. However, some aspects of HL instruction make curriculum design and implementation different from other sorts of curriculum projects.

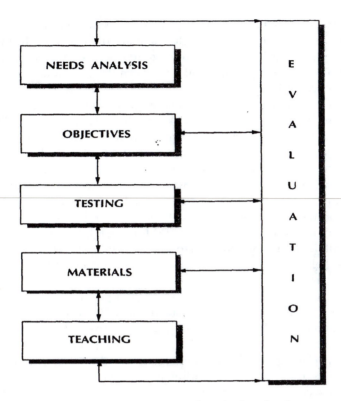

Figure 1.1. The six components of curriculum development
(J. D. Brown, 1995).

What makes HL curriculum development different from other curriculum is not the elements involved but rather the fact that the curriculum must be designed so specifically for the particular population of HL students. As a result, HL curriculum development has very special purposes more akin to language for specific purposes curriculum (as described in Hutchinson & Waters, 1987) than any other existing approach. In addition, because most HL curriculum development projects are on-going, rather than starting from scratch, the five main components of the model shown in Figure 1.1 can all be viewed as inputs for an ongoing formative evaluation project that addresses the following questions:

1. To what degree is the curriculum meeting the linguistic and situational needs of the HL learners? How have the HL learners' language learning needs changed recently? How can the perceptions of HL learners' language learning needs be improved?

2. How well do the curriculum goals and objectives match the perceived needs of the HL learners? How well are the objectives formulated, sequenced across levels, and integrated across the reading, writing, listening, and speaking skills? How can the goals and objectives be revised and improved?

3. How well do the diagnostic, progress, and achievement tests/ assessments provide feedback on the HL learners' abilities to perform the objectives at various points of time? How can the tests/assessment procedures be revised and improved?

4. How well do the existing materials match the objectives and the curriculum as a whole? How well do the textbooks match, that is, how well do they explain the material and provide practice so HL learners can achieve the objectives? To what degree are supplementary materials necessary in order for the HL learners to learn the curriculum objectives? How effective and efficient are the supplementary materials. How can the materials be revised and improved?

5. What teacher development and support policies are in place? How well do the teachers understand the differences and similarities between HL learners and regular FL learners? How adequate are the teacher-centered policies for fostering good language teaching, especially good HL teaching? How can the teacher development and support policies be revised and improved?

6. How can the information in 1–5 that was just discussed be used to demonstrate the effectiveness, efficiency, and relevant attitudes of stakeholders in the event of a summative evaluation required by a program external evaluation? Also, coming full circle, to what degree is the curriculum meeting the needs of the students and other stakeholders? In particular, what are the attitudes, beliefs, preferences, and so on of the appropriate groups of stakeholders (e.g., students, teachers, administrators, parents, politicians, etc.) toward all the curriculum components listed in the previous five points. How can the entire curriculum be revised and improved?

Note that a number of features make each of the elements of HL curriculum development somewhat different from all of the generic curriculum development approaches mentioned earlier.

1. Needs analysis: Because of the nature of HL learners, needs assessment may be a particularly important, indeed a crucial, aspect of work in HL curriculum, especially because less is known about HL learners' needs than those of FL learners (Kondo-Brown, 2003). Also, given the various definitions of HL students, it is particularly

important to decide which definition of HL learners is being applied in a given curriculum needs analysis.

2. Goals and objectives: Greater than normal individual differences among HL students will probably lead to tracking of such students into special courses or even more individualized instruction, which may in turn necessitate greater than normal variation in the goals and objectives that must be developed.

3. Testing: Test performances of some HL students may be quite different from the FL students (even creating bimodal distributions, as seen in Kondo-Brown, 2004). In addition, when tested before instruction, some HL students will have strong oral skills that may give an overall impression of high proficiency—proficiency that is not matched in their written skills.

4. Materials: A general lack of readily available materials specifically designed for HL learners may make it more difficult to find suitable materials, and may indeed, necessitate developing materials from scratch.

5. Teaching: Little in the way of teacher support and/or teacher training has been developed to date to deal with the special issues involved for HL students.

6. Program evaluation: Because of the current state of knowledge about HL learners, evaluation may not be terribly different from needs analysis at least in the early years of curriculum development.

In short, developing HL curriculum will typically require language professionals to address at least the following questions: How adequately will all the HL students' needs be met? How adequately will those HL needs be represented in the program goals and objectives? How well will the curriculum outcomes be assessed or tested for the HL students? How will HL materials be adopted, adapted, and/or developed from scratch? How will teachers be trained and supported in the process of developing new HL curriculum? And ultimately, how will program evaluation serve to renew and revise all of the other elements of the HL curriculum? Thus, this book will necessarily bring a new perspective to the existing second language curriculum and materials development projects.

One additional issue addressed by this book is the fact that currently available second/foreign language teacher training books tend to focus primarily on the development of language curriculum and materials for (and show examples from) the various European languages, but rarely deal with East Asian language students, much less East Asian HL students (e.g., H. D. Brown, 2000, 2001; Omaggio Hadly, 2001). We believe that this book will help overcome the apparent deficiencies and under-representations of East Asian curriculum studies in the existing language curriculum and pedagogy books.

HOW ARE THE BOOK CHAPTERS ORGANIZED?

Kondo-Brown's study in chapter 2 provides a literature review that examines recent trends and developments in needs analysis, curriculum innovations, instructional and assessment activities for HL learners in East Asian languages. On the basis of this review, Kondo-Brown recommends future curriculum and pedagogical research agendas that need to be investigated in order to effectively teach such students.

Kataoka, Koshiyama, and Shibata's large-scale study in chapter 3 that involves approximately 1,600 child Japanese heritage language learners (JHLLs) specifically examines this relatively unexplored issue among young HL learners based on first- to ninth-grade *hoshuukoo* students' performances on various Japanese and English proficiency tests. The study identifies the special language needs of *hoshuukoo* students and make recommendations for developing better HL curriculum for these students.

In conducting language needs analysis for young HL learners, one issue that remains uninvestigated is the appropriateness of proficiency measures employed in needs analysis. Hasegawa's study in chapter 4 deals with this issue by examining the validity of Japanese proficiency measures employed in empirical studies that involve young JHLLs. On the basis of what was learned, Hasegawa makes recommendations for assessing young JHLLs' Japanese language skills for research and instruction purposes.

As for the language needs of university-level HL learners, certain assumptions are made when comparing the language behaviors of these learners' to those of non-HL learners. For example, some authors in the HL literature appear to accept the belief that HLs' linguistic skills are superior to those of non-HL learners (e.g., Campbell & Rosenthal, 2000; Pino & Pino, 2000), whereas others seem to emphasize the notion that HL learners' learning problems are rooted in their exposure to informal varieties at home (e.g., C.-B. Lee, 2001; Ree, 1998). However, these assumptions, which are often based only on personal observations, need to be validated using empirical data (Kondo-Brown, 2003). Such studies are emerging, but they seem limited in scope (e.g., very small n-size studies with a focus on university Korean heritage language learners [KHLLs]; see Kondo-Brown, this volume).

Chapters 5 and 6 extend this line of research by comparing the specific linguistic abilities of university HL learners to those of non-HL equivalents in order to provide fine-tuned pedagogical implications for teaching both types of students, but most especially HL learners. Studies in these chapters also address the issue of individual differences within each of the HL and non-HL groups (see Kondo-Brown, this volume). H.-S. Kim's study ($N = 128$) in chapter 5 suggests that two subgroups of non-HL learners (with different first language [L1] backgrounds) and three subgroups of HL learners (with varying degrees of language exposure and use of Korean at early ages) may employ different language transfer and strategies when processing Korean relative clauses. Based on the study's findings, Kim emphasizes the need for instruction that assists HL learners notice their input-output deficiencies with intra-group differences in mind.

Kondo-Brown and Fukuda's study in chapter 6 identifies differences in referential processing when reading a Japanese narrative text among three subgroups of learners of advanced Japanese: JHLLs who grew up in a bilingual environment; non-JHLLs have studied and/or worked in Japan for 6 months or longer; and non-JHLLs without such experience. The study suggests potential instructional problems for teaching reading in a single-track advanced Japanese class, where students from different language backgrounds study together.

In planning for language instruction, consideration for affective variables is required for successful second language (L2) instruction in general (e.g., H. D. Brown, 2000; Dornyei, 2001; Dörnyei & Schmidt, 2001), and HL instruction is no exception. Indeed, a growing number of studies dealing with East Asian HL learners suggests that HL proficiency or use is predicted by or at least associated with a number of affective factors such as motivation, attitude, identity, and instructional preferences (e.g., Chinen & Tucker, 2006; Cho, 2000; Cho & Krashen, 2000; Kim, Y .G., 1992; Kondo, 1997; Kondo-Brown, 1999, 2000, 2001; J. S. Lee, 2002; Luo & Wiseman, 2000; Oketani, 1997a, 1997b; Shibata & Koshiyama, 2001).

Chapters 7, 8, and 9 make recommendations for curriculum design and pedagogical strategies based on their examinations of university HL learners' attitudes, motivation, and instructional preferences. Lee and Kim's survey study in chapter 7 examines second-generation Korean American college students' (N = 115) language attitudes with a focus on their motivational orientations, learning situation, and self-efficacy. The chapter suggests that the curricula for HL learners need to expand sociocultural components to address their integrative orientation and also provide more specific and concrete learning goals to augment their self-efficacy.

Although an increasing number of university FL programs with HLs offer multitrack systems (Kondo-Brown, 2003), for many others, this does not seem to be a realistic option (e.g., C.-B. Lee, 2000; Ree, 1998). Yu's study in chapter 8 addresses this issue with a focus on KHLLs. He proposed to create 'a compromise curriculum' that may simultaneously attend to the language needs of HL and non-HL learners at the beginning and intermediate levels. Yu's proposal is a survey-based needs analysis that identified both common and different instructional preferences and needs between university KHLLs and non-KHLLs (N = 43).

Another uninvestigated issue is that, if a university FL program establishes a two-track system that separates HL learners and non-HL learners, there will still be a subgroup of HL learners who will opt into or be placed into the traditional FL track due to limited proficiency in their HL or due to other reasons. Weger-Guntharp's study in chapter 9 specifically focuses on investigating the language and affective needs of a subgroup of Chinese heritage language learners (CHLLs) who study in the Chinese regular track designed primarily for non-CHLLs. This study indicates the importance of instructor awareness of the HL learners' sensitivity about teachers' pedagogical choices as well as non-HL learners' mixed feelings toward the presence of HL learners.

The remaining chapters (10–12) present curriculum development studies for East Asian HL learners in different settings. Each chapter examines some of the most important curriculum issues for teaching these students. The first issue is the lack of appropriate curriculum and teacher training for teaching young HL learners at community-based heritage schools (e.g., Kataoka, Furuyama, & Koshiyama, 2000; J. S. Lee, 2002; Li, 2005; Sasaki, 2001; Usui, 1996; Wang, 2003). In response to this problem, Douglas' study in chapter 10 provides a theoretical model for developing curricula as well as pedagogical strategies for young HL learners. The chapter presents steps for developing a theoretically sound curriculum for teaching young JHLLs with examples for instruction and assessment.

The second issue is that of literacy instruction, especially for university HL learners. As mentioned earlier, an increasing number of postsecondary institutions offer special HL programs. These programs often place an emphasis on literacy development for HL learners who may have unbalanced aural/oral and reading/writing skills (Kondo-Brown, 2003). Chapters 11 and 12 present recent pedagogical innovations in teaching Chinese literacy skills at the university level. Chapter 11 by Wu reports on an online literacy program developed at Carnegie Mellon University for a group of CHLLs who have functional oral/aural skills but limited literacy skills. Wu first examines the motivation and language needs of CHLLs, and then discusses how to integrate technology into learner-centered, standards-based curriculum to provide robust literacy education for university CHLLs. Chapter 12 by Zhang and Davis presents an evaluative study that examines the effect of an online chat program designed to teach basic Chinese literacy skills to university CHLLs, which was part of the class activities of regular Chinese classes where both HL and non-HL students were present. The study demonstrates that the integration of an online chat program as a regular part of instruction can enhance CHLLs' interest in and motivation for improving their Chinese literacy skills and enhance such skills as well.

Thus, by providing both theoretical and practical chapters concerning curriculum design, this book provides at least a starting point for dealing fairly, effectively, and efficiently with the very special learning needs of East Asian HL students. We hope this book will not only promote research about HL learners in East Asian languages but also encourage and foster responsible curriculum development for these learners.

REFERENCES

Aparicio, F. R. (1983). Teaching Spanish to the native speaker at the college level. *Hispania, 66,* 232–238.

Bernstein, R. (2005, February). *Foreign-born population tops 34 million, Census Bureau estimates.* U.S. Census Bureau News. U.S. Department of Commerce. Retrieved April 3, 2006, from http://www.census.gov/Press-Release/www/releases/archives/foreignbornpopulation/003969.html

Brinton, D. M., & Kagan, O. & S. Baucks (Eds.). (forthcoming). *Heritage language education: A new field emerging.* Mahwah, NJ: Lawrence Erlbaum Associates.

Brown, H. D. (2000). *Principles of language learning and teaching* (4th ed.). New York: Longman.

Brown, H. D. (2001). *Teaching by principles: An interactive approach to language pedagogy* (2nd ed.). Upper Saddle River, NJ: Prentice Hall.

Brown, J. D. (1995). *The elements of language curriculum: A systematic approach to program development.* New York: Heinle & Heinle Publishers.

Campbell, R. N. (2003). Directions in research: Intergenerational transmission of heritage languages. *Heritage Language Journal, 1.* Retrieved January 1, 2004, from http://www.heritagelanguages.org/

Campbell, R. N., & Rosenthal, J. W. (2000). Heritage languages. In J. W. Rosenthal (Ed.), *Handbook of undergraduate second language education* (pp. 165–184). Mahwah, NJ: Lawrence Erlbaum Associates.

Chao, T. (1996). Chinese heritage community language schools in the United States. In X. Wang (Ed.), *A view from within: A case study of Chinese heritage community language schools in the United States* (pp. 7–14). Washington, DC: The National Foreign Language Center at the John Hopkins University.

Chinen, K., & Tucker, G. R. (2006). Heritage language development: Understanding the roles of ethnic identity, schooling and community. In K. Kondo-Brown (Ed.), *Heritage language development: Focus on East Asian immigrants* (pp. 89–126). Amsterdam, the Netherlands: John Benjamins.

Cho, G. (2000). The role of heritage language in social interactions and relationships: Reflections from a language minority group. *Bilingual Research Journal, 24.* Retrieved May 10 2005, from http://brj.asu.edu/

Cho, G., & Krashen, S. D. (2000). The role of voluntary factors in heritage language development: How speakers can develop the heritage language on their own. *ITL Review of Applied Linguistics, 127–128,* 127–140.

Clark, J. L. (1987). *Curriculum renewal in school foreign language learning.* Oxford: Oxford University Press.

Dörnyei, Z. (2001). *Motivational strategies in the language classroom.* Cambridge University Press.

Dörnyei, Z., & Schmidt, R. (2001). *Motivation and second language acquisition.* Honolulu: Second Language Teaching & Curriculum Center at the University of Hawai´i at Mānoa.

Douglas, M. O. (2006). Pedagogical theories and approaches to teach young learners of Japanese as a heritage language. *Heritage Language Journal, 3.* Retrieved March, 2006, from ftp: http://www.heritagelanguages.org/

Dubin, F., & Olshtain, E. (1986). *Course design.* Cambridge: Cambridge University Press.

Faltis, C. (1990). Spanish for native speakers: Freirian and Vygotskian perspectives. *Foreign Language Annals, 23,* 117–126.

Finocchiaro, M., & Brumfit, C. (1983). *The functional-notional approach: From theory to pratice.* Oxford: Oxford University Press.

Garcia, R., & Diaz, C. (1992). The status and use of Spanish and English among Hispanic youth in Dade County (Miami), Florida: A sociolinguistic study, 1989–1991. *Language and Education, 6,* 13–32.

Grieco, E. (2004, January). *The foreign born from China in the United States* [Migration Information Source]. Retrieved March 25, 2006, from ftp: http://www.migrationinformation.org/archives.cfm

Hayashi, A. (2006). Japanese English bilingual children in three different educational environments. In K. Kondo-Brown (Ed.), *Heritage language development: Focus on East Asian immigrants* (pp. 145–171). Amsterdam, the Netherlands: John Benjamins.

Hutchinson, T., & Waters, A. (1987). *English for specific purposes*. Cambridge: Cambridge University Press.

Johnson, K. (1982). *Communicative syllabus design and methodology*. Oxford: Pergamon.

Johnson, R. K. (Ed.). (1989). *The second language curriculum*. Cambridge: Cambridge University Press.

Kataoka, H., Furuyama, H., & Koshiyama, Y. (2000). *Minami Kariforunia nihongo gakuen kyooshi ankeeto kekka bunseki hookokusho* [Report on the Southern California Japanese language school teacher survey results]. Retrieved May 10, 2005 from http://www.jflalc.org/teaching/jflc/fclty_rpt/jpz_kyoushi/heritage2.html.

Kim, Y. G. (1992). *The role of attitudes and motivation in learning a heritage language: A study of Korean language maintenance in Toronto*. Unpublished doctoral dissertation, University of Toronto, Canada.

Kondo, K. (1997). Social-psychological factors affecting language maintenance: Interviews with Shin Nisei University students. *Linguistics and Education, 9,* 369–408.

Kondo, K. (1999). Motivating bilingual and semibilingual university students of Japanese: An analysis of language learning persistence and intensity among students from immigrant backgrounds. *Foreign Language Annals, 32,* 77–88.

Kondo-Brown, K. (2000). Acculturation and identity of bilingual heritage students of Japanese in Hawai`i. *The Japan Journal of Multilingualism and Multiculturalism, 6,* 1–19.

Kondo-Brown, K. (2001). Bilingual heritage students' language contact and motivation. In Z. Dornyei & R. Schmidt (Eds.), *Motivation and second language acquisition* (pp. 425–451). Honolulu: Second Language Teaching & Curriculum Center.

Kondo-Brown, K. (2003). Heritage language instruction for post-secondary students from immigrant backgrounds. *Heritage Language Journal, 1.* Retrieved May 10, 2005, from http://www.heritagelanguages.org/

Kondo-Brown, K. (2004). Do background variables predict students' scores on a Japanese placement test?: Implications for placing heritage language learners. *Journal of the National Council of Less Commonly Taught Languages, 1,* 1–19.

Kondo-Brown, K. (Ed.). (2006). *Heritage language development: Focus on East Asian immigrants*. Amsterdam, Netherlands: John Benjamins.

Krashen, S. D., Tse, L., & McQuillan, J. (Eds.). (1998). *Heritage language development*. Culver City, CA: Language Education Associates.

Lao, C. (2004). Parents' attitudes toward Chinese-English bilingual education and Chinese-language use. *Bilingual Research Journal, 28,* 99–121. Retrieved May 10, 2005, from http://brj.asu.edu/

Lee, C.-B. (2000). Two-track curriculum system for university Korean language programs. In J. S. King (Ed.), *Korean language in America, 5: Papers from the Sixth Annual Conference and Professional Development Workshop* (pp. 3–11). Honolulu: American Association of Teachers of Korea.

Lee, J. S. (2002). The Korean language in America: The role of cultural identity in heritage language learning. *Language, Culture, and Curriculum, 15,* 117–133.

Lewelling, V. W., & Peyton, J. K. (1999). *Spanish for native speakers: Developing dual language proficiency* [ERIC Digest]. Retrieved March 1, 2003, http://www.cal.org/resources/digest/spanish_native.html

Li, M. (2005) The role of parents in Chinese heritage language schools. *Bilingual Research Journal 29,* 1. Retrieved March 15, 2006, from http://brj.asu.edu/

Luo, S.H., & Wiseman, R. L. (2000). Ethnic language maintenance among Chinese immigrant children in the United States. *International Journal of Intercultural Relations, 24,* 307–324.

McDonough, J., & Shaw, C. (2003). *Materials and methods in ELT: A teachers guide* (2nd ed.). Oxford, UK: Blackwell.

McGinnis, S. (2005). *Statistics on Chinese language enrollment.* Chinese Language Teachers Association. Retrieved April 3, 2006, from http://clta.osu.edu/flyers/enrollment_stats.htm

McQuillan, J. (1996). How should heritage languages be taught?: The effects of a free voluntary reading program. *Foreign Language Annals, 29,* 56–72.

Merino, B., Trueba, H., & Samaniego, F. (1993). Toward a framework for the study of the maintenance of the home language in language minority students. In B. Merino, H. Trueba, & F. Samaniegom, (Eds.), *Language and culture in learning: Teaching Spanish to native speakers of Spanish* (pp. 5–25). Washington, DC: The Falmer Press.

Munby, J. (1978). *Communicative syllabus design.* Cambridge: Cambridge University Press.

Nunan, D. (1987). *The teacher as curriculum developer.* Adelaide, South Australia: National Curriculum Resource Centre.

Nunan, D. (1991). *Syllabus design.* Oxford: Oxford University Press.

Oketani, H. (1997a). Additive bilinguals: The case of post-war second-generation Japanese Canadian youths. *Bilingual Research Journal, 21,* 15–35. Retrieved January 1, 2003, from http://brj.asu.edu/

Oketani, H. (1997b). Japanese-Canadian youths as additive bilinguals: A case study. *MOSAIC, 4,* 2, 14–18.

Omaggio Hadley, A. (2001). *Teaching language in context* (3rd ed.). Boston, MA: Heinle & Heinle.

Peyton, J. K., Ranard, D. A., & McGinnis, S. (Eds). (2001). *Heritage languages in America: Preserving a national resource.* McHenry, IL: The Center for Applied Linguistics and Delta Systems.

Pino, B. G., & Pino, P. (2000). Serving the heritage speaker across a five-year program. *ADFL Bulletin, 32,* 27–35.

Ree, J. (1998). Korean as a second language: How should it be taught. *ACTA Koreana, 1,* 85–100.

Richards, J. C. (2001). *Curriculum development in language teaching.* Cambridge: Cambridge University.

Sasaki, M. (2001, March). *Japanese as a heritage language class in Hawai`i and Brazil: Their differences and similarities.* Paper presented at the 2001 Association of Teachers of Japanese. Retrieved May 10, 2005, from http://www.colorado.edu/ealld/atj/SIG/heritage/sasaki.html

Shibata, S., & Koshiyama, Y. (2001). Social influences in the acquisition and maintenance of spoken Japanese as a heritage language. *The Japan Journal of Multilingualism and Multiculturalism, 7,* 18–37.

Shin, S. J. (2005). *Developing in two languages: Korean Children in America.* Clevedon, UK: Multilingual Matters.

Shirane, H. (2003). Attraction and isolation: The past and future of east Asian languages and cultures. *ADFL Bulletin, 34,* 2, 15–19.

Sohn, S., & Merrill, C. (forthcoming). The Korean/English dual language program in the Los Angles unified school district. In D. Brinton, O. Kagan, & S. Baucks (Eds.), *Heritage language education: A new field emerging.* Mahwah, NJ: Lawrence Erlbaum Associates.

The Office of Immigration Statistics. (2006). *Yearbook of immigration statistics, 2004.* Retrieved March 25, 2006, from ftp: http://uscis.gov/graphics/shared/statistics/yearbook/yrbk04im.htm

The UCLA Steering Committee. (2000). Heritage language research priorities conference report. *Bilingual Research Journal, 24,* 333–346. Retrieved January 2005, from http://brj.asu.edu/

Tomlinson, B. (1998). *Materials development for language teaching.* Cambridge: Cambridge University Press.

Tomlinson, B. (Ed.). (2002). *Developing materials for language teaching.* New York: Continuum International Publishing.

Usui, Y. (1996). *An ethnographic perspective on language shift, maintenance, and revitalization: Japanese in Hawai`i.* Unpublished master's thesis, University of Hawai`i at Mānoa, United States.

Valdés, G. (1995). The teaching of minority languages as academic subjects: Pedagogical and theoretical challenges. *The Modern Language Journal, 79,* 299–328.

Valdés, G., Lozano, A., & Garcia-Moya, R. (1981). *Teaching Spanish to the Hispanic bilingual: Issues, aims, and methods.* New York: Teachers College Press.

Van Deusen-Scholl, N. (2003). Toward a definition of heritage language: Sociopolitical and pedagogical considerations. *Journal of Language, Identity, & Education, 2,* 211–230.

Wang, M. (2003). An ethnographic study of Chinese heritage language education and technological innovations. *Journal of National Council of Less Commonly Taught Languages, 1,* 69–94.

Webb, J. B., & Miller, B. L. (2000). *Teaching heritage language learners: Voices from the classroom.* New York: American Council on the Teaching of Foreign Languages.

Wells, E. B. (2004). Foreign Language enrollments in United States institutions of higher education, Fall 2002. *ADFL Bulletin, 35,* 2–3. Retrieved March 31, 2006, from http://www.wisitalia.org/web/data/MLAtext.pdf

White, R. V. (1988). *The ELT curriculum.* Oxford: Blackwell.

Yalden, J. (1983). *The communicative syllabus: Evolution, design and implementation.* Oxford: Pergamon.

Yalden, J. (1985). *Principles of course design for language teaching.* Cambridge: Cambridge University Press.

Yalden, J. (1988). *The communicative syllabus.* Cambridge: Cambridge University Press.

Yau, J. (2004, December). *The foreign born from China in the United States.* Retrieved March 25, 2006, from ftp: http://www.migrationinformation.org/archives.cfm

Issues and Future Agendas for Teaching Chinese, Japanese, and Korean Heritage Students*

Kimi Kondo-Brown
University of Hawai`i at Mānoa

ANALYZING LANGUAGE AND SITUATIONAL NEEDS

As discussed in chapter 1, needs assessment is a critical aspect of work in heritage language (HL) curriculum development and instruction because we know less about HL learners than we do about foreign language (FL) learners. This chapter starts by examining the methodologies and findings of recent needs analysis studies with a focus on heritage students in East Asian languages. When one conducts needs analysis of a given group of language learners, one approach to conceptualize this work is to differentiate

---

*An earlier version of this chapter was presented as part of plenary paper at the U.S. Consortium for Language Learning & Teaching Heritage Language Workshop on May 1, 2005, in Los Angeles, California.

(a) language needs analysis from (b) situational needs analysis. *Language needs* analysis involves the investigation of "the circumstances in which the language will be used, the dimensions of language competence involved, the learners' reasons for studying the language, and their present abilities with respect to those reasons," whereas *situational needs* analysis examines "any administrative, logistical, manpower, pedagogic, religious, cultural, personal, or other factors that might have an impact on the program" (Brown, 1995, p. 40). Needs in either category can be objectively measured needs (i.e., needs determined based on observable data such as language behavior) or subjectively measured needs (needs determined on the basis of non-observable data such as wants or desires). This section examines language needs analysis studies first and then situational needs analysis.

Language Needs Analysis

A number of recent studies investigated the language needs of HL learners in East Asian languages. Table 2.1 lists these studies by the language group. As the table shows, the data used in these studies were largely quantitative, obtained mostly from university HL learners. The table also shows that the existing language needs analysis studies mostly attempted to identify the language behavior of HL learners using various performance data obtained through tests, focused-skill samples, observations, and/or self-ratings. Several other language needs analysis studies investigated HL learners' reasons for learning the language or their instructional preferences (e.g., preference of scripts to be taught or tasks to be able to perform) based on self-reports. The studies listed in the table are discussed in the following section in different language groups starting with the Chinese group.

Language Needs of Chinese Heritage Language Learners. In teaching Chinese to HL learners, one important curriculum issue is how to deal with the highly heterogeneous Chinese heritage language learner (CHLL) population within a given program/course. In order to attend to CHLLs' individual needs, some university programs have attempted to identify CHLL subgroups in their programs using tests and/or questionnaires and recommend or even offer separate tracks for these subgroups. For example, in McGinnis' (1996) study, the Chinese placement and proficiency test scores were collected from the first-year CHLLs and non-CHLLs ($N = 20$) at the University of Maryland. The descriptive analysis of three sets of test scores (listening, grammar, and reading) identified two CHLL subgroups in the program, namely "true native" and "seminative" who are mostly speakers of non-Mandarin dialects (Cantonese or Taiwanese dialect) with strong aural/oral skills but "almost non-existent" literacy skills (p. 114). Based on this analysis, McGinnis recommended a two-track system for CHLLs that separates "true-native" CHLLs from "seminative" CHLLs.

TABLE 2.1
Empirical Studies Investigating Language
Needs of Heritage Students in East Asian Languages

Study (Year)	Participants	Analysis (Main Instrument, N= size)	Language Behavior	Motives & Preference
CHINESE				
Baista Buteri (2003)	High school[a]	Qualitative (interview, $N = 72$)		X
Ke (1998)	University[b]	Quantitative (Chinese character test, $N = 85$)	X	
D. Li (2004)	University	Quantitative (survey, $N = 656$)		X
McGinnis (1996)	University	Qualitative (reading & listening tests, $N = 22$)	X	
Weger-Guntharp (this volume)	University	Qualitative (survey & interview, $N = 8$)		X
Wu (2002)	University	Qualitative (observation)	X	
JAPANESE				
Kanno et al. (forthcoming)	University	Quantitative (OPI, grammar & speaking tests, $N = 15$)	X	
Kataoka et al. (this volume)	1st to 9th grade (hoshuukoo)	Quantitative (vocab, grammar, kanji tests, $N = 1600$)	X	
Kondo-Brown (2001)	University	Quantitative (questionnaire, $N = 145$)		X
Kondo-Brown (2005)	University	Quantitative (grammar, reading, & listening tests, oral self-ratings, $N = 185$)	X	
Kondo-Brown (2006a)	University	Quantitative (reading & kanji tests, $N = 42$)	X	
Kondo-Brown et al. (this volume)	University	Quantitative (reading test, read/think-aloud data, $N = 42$)	X	
Matsunaga (2003)	University	Quantitative (Reading & kanji tests, $N = 28$)	X	
Nagaoka (1998)	9th grade (hoshuukoo)	Qualitative (Survey, $N = 4$)	X	
Nagasawa (1995)	8–10 yr old (hoshuukoo)	Quantitative (grammar test, $N = 85$)	X	

(Continued)

TABLE 2.1 (*Continued*)

Study (Year)	Participants	Analysis (Main Instrument, N = size)	Language Behavior	Motives & Preference
KOREAN				
Au & Romo (1997)	University	Quantitative (grammar & listening tests, N = 18)	X	
Cho et al. (1997)	University	Qualitative (survey, N = 24)		X
Jo (2001)	University	Qualitative/ethnography (multiple instruments)		
E. J. Kim (2003)	University	Quantitative (writing sample, N = 21)	X	
H.-Y. Kim (2003)	University	Qualitative (survey, N = 20)		X
H.-S. Kim (this volume)	University	Quantitative (listening test, N = 128)	X	
H.-S. Kim (2001)	University	Qualitative (listening test, N = 26)	X	
J.-T. Kim (2001)	University	Quantitative (writing sample, N = 9)	X	
Lee et al. (2005)	University	Quantitative (OPI, grammar & speaking tests, N = 27)	X	
O'Grady et al. (2001)	University	Quantitative (listening test, N = 36)	X	
Yu (this volume)	University	Quantitative (survey, N = 43)		X

Notes: [a]High school, High school students; [b]University, University students.

Similarly, according to Wu's (2002) qualitative case study, the Chinese program at Carnegie Mellon University has faced a pedagogical challenge due to CHLLs' highly heterogeneous language backgrounds (e.g., Mandarin vs. non-Mandarin dialect background, the length of formal instruction in Chinese, etc.) as well as differences in the demonstrated proficiency levels in spoken and written Chinese. As a first step to deal with this problem, the university's Chinese program started offering a new track for a subgroup of CHLLs who had little or no formal instruction in Chinese but speak Mandarin at home (Wu, this volume).

Even if a university FL program establishes a two-track system that separates HL learners and non-HL learners as described in the studies just mentioned by McGinnis (1996) and Wu (this volume), there will still be a subgroup of HL learners who will opt into or be placed into the traditional

FL track due to limited proficiency and exposure to the target HLs at home (Kondo, 1998). Weger-Guntharp's (this volume) qualitative study specifically focuses on investigating the language needs of this subgroup of HL learners who study in the regular track primarily for non-HL learners. The study suggests that, regardless of their dialect backgrounds, they chose to study Chinese not only because the development of Chinese is central to their identity formation, but also it is an important part of economic and academic investment. The study also indicated the importance of instructor awareness of the HL learners' sensitivity about the teachers' pedagogical choices (e.g., range of vocabulary permitted to use in classroom, discrepancies between classroom Chinese and home varieties) as well as non-HL learners' mixed feelings toward the presence of HL learners, especially during pair/group work activities.

Another important curriculum issue concerning the teaching of CHLLs is Chinese character instruction, specifically, preferences between traditional versus simplified characters. Two studies based in Canada (Baista Buteri, 2003; D. Li, 2004) suggested that CHLL preference between the two different script systems is closely related to their countries of origin. For example, as part of Baista Buteri's (2004) qualitative study, this issue was investigated based on interview data collected from high school CHLLs of Mandarin Chinese ($N = 72$, average age $= 15$). The analysis suggested that, although only simplified Chinese characters are taught in school, the CHLLs of Taiwanese background demanded that the class should use traditional characters, the characters used in Taiwan. Similarly, D. Li's (2004) survey data collected from university CHLLs ($N = 656$) indicated that, although more non-CHLLs prefer simplified characters, the majority of CHLLs, who were largely from Hong Kong or Taiwan, prefer original/ traditional characters, the characters used in these countries.

One study by Ke (1998) compared Chinese character knowledge between first-year bilingual CHLLs who speak Mandarin Chinese or one of the Chinese dialects (e.g., Cantonese, Hakka) and non-CHLLs ($N = 150$). Ke's (1998) statistical analysis of traditional Chinese character test data indicated no statistically significant differences between the groups in either recognition or production Chinese character tests. Although no follow-up study seems to be available, CHLLs' potential advantage in learning Chinese characters such as phonological familiarity may need to be further investigated because L1 and L2 reading research has suggested that phonological activation may play an important role in learning Chinese characters (e.g., Everson, 1998; Flores d'Arcasis, Saito, & Kawakami, 1995).

Language Needs of Japanese Heritage Learners. Several studies investigated the language needs of university Japanese heritage language learners (JHLLs). One survey study by Kondo-Brown (2001) asked Hawai`i-based

JHLLs about their motives for studying Japanese ($N = 145$). The descriptive analysis suggested that JHLLs at any level (from first-year to fourth-year college Japanese) have both instrumental and integrative reasons for learning Japanese. Most JHLLs at all levels seem to learn Japanese so they can use it in their immediate environments (e.g., use of Japanese for their current jobs or for communication with Japanese-speaking people in the community) rather than for use in social settings remote to them (e.g., study in Japan).

Two studies (Kondo-Brown, 2005; Matusnaga, 2003) compared Japanese proficiency levels between JHLLs and English L1 non-JHLLs using various measures (e.g., listening/reading comprehension test, grammar test, etc.) and suggested that the former scored significantly higher than the latter on these measures. For example, Kondo-Brown (2005) compared incoming university JHLLs' and English L1 non-JHLLs' ($N = 185$) Japanese competence using three proficiency measures (grammar, listening, and reading). A MANOVA analysis indicated that a subgroup of JHLLs with at least one Japanese parent scored significantly higher on all three measures than non-JHLLs as well as other subgroups of JHLLs who had hardly any exposure to Japanese outside of classrooms (e.g., HL students of Japanese descent without a Japanese-speaking parent). The result of the reading comprehension test was consistent with the result reported by Matsunaga (2003): the statistical analysis of reading comprehension data indicated that JHLLs in advanced/intermediate-level courses outperformed the English L1 non-JHLL equivalents ($N = 28$).

In Kondo-Brown's (2005) study just discussed, a profie analysis (for this statistical procedure, see Tabachnick & Fidell, 2001, pp. 391–455) was also performed on self-ratings of oral tasks, which were highly intercorrelated with the demonstrated proficiency measures. The results suggested that JHLLs (a) assess their ability to perform a variety of oral tasks significantly higher than non-JHLLs, (b) can easily carry out simple interpersonal communicative tasks as well as extended narrative tasks on personal topics, but (c) experience difficulty with prolonged conversations in formal Japanese and explanatory speeches on abstract/impersonal topics.

Kondo-Brown's (2006a) and Kondo-Brown and Fukuda's (this volume) studies compared one specific aspect of reading comprehension processes focusing on JHLLs in advanced-level courses. Kondo-Brown's (2006a) study investigated the ability to infer unknown *kanji* (Chinese character) words while reading authentic Japanese texts. The statistical analyses indicated that, first, considerable individual differences may exist *within* each of the JHLL and non-JHLL groups ($N = 42$) in terms of reading comprehension ability as well as *kanji* inferencing ability. Second, when reading comprehension ability was controlled, there was no statistically significant difference in *kanji* inferencing ability between JHLLs and non-JHLLs. Thus, as long as the students demonstrated comparable reading comprehension levels, difference in HL background did not seem to be a major concern in teaching how to infer *kanji* words in context.

Kondo-Brown and Fukuda's study (this volume), on the other hand, compared referential ability (e.g., the ability to monitor and recover unstated referents or zero pronouns) between JHLLs and two groups of non-JHLLs (with different living abroad experiences, $N = 42$). The statistical analyses indicated that, first, the ability to identify zero pronouns was strongly correlated with the ability to identify the connected predicates as well as with their overall reading comprehension ability. Second, JHLLs' ability to identify zero anaphors was significantly better than non-JHLLs who have never or only briefly visited Japan, but no better than non-JHLLs who lived in Japan for a substantial period. Thus, findings from Kondo-Brown (2006a) and Kondo-Brown and Fukuda (this volume) suggest that teachers in the single-track advanced Japanese class who use the same instructional materials for the teaching of reading may inevitably create a situation where the abilities of some learners and the difficulty of the materials will be mismatched.

One study focusing on university JHLLs (Kanno, Hasegawa, Ikeda, Ito, & Long, forthcoming) also suggested that further distinctions may need to be made within advanced-level HL learners for instructional purposes. In Kanno et al.'s study, JHLLs and non-JHLLs ($N = 15$), who were judged to be "advanced" or "superior" levels on the American Council on the Teaching of Foreign Languages (ACTFL) Oral Proficiency Interview (OPI) scale, took various oral and written tests (e.g., multiple-choice tests that deal with lexical structural knowledge and idiomatic expressions, "guided narratives" to test ability to narrate in major time/aspect frames, etc.). The descriptive analyses indicated that there are considerable intragroup differences. For example, a subgroup of "balanced" bilingual JHLLs, who happened to be all *hoshuukoo* graduates, performed better than the remaining JHLLs in terms of accuracy and complexity on oral and written tests, but they were generally weak with lexis (especially, nonbasic *kango* [Chinese character compounds]) and collocation.

A few other studies examined the language needs of younger JHLLs who were *hoshuukoo* students in the United States (Kataoka, Koshiyama, & Shibata, this volume; Nagaoka, 1998; Nagasawa, 1995). For example, Nagasawa's (1995) study ($N = 85$) compared grammatical knowledge (using a closed-response grammar test) among three groups: (a) 8- to 10-year old Japanese as a first language (L1) children, (b) 8- to 10-year old bilingual *hoshuukoo* students, and (c) English L1 university non-JHLLs who had received 300–600 hours of instruction in Japanese. The descriptive analyses indicated that child JHLLs generally scored higher than the adult non-JHLLs but lower than Japanese L1 children in most categories. It also indicated that child JHLLs performed significantly lower than Japanese L1 children on the items infrequently used at home such as *keigo* (formal Japanese) and causatives.

In Nagaoka's (1998) study, the data were collected from in-depth interviews with four Japan-born ninth-grade JHLLs, who had studied Japanese for more than 5 years at a *hoshuukoo*, and their teachers. A qualitative analysis of the student data suggested that Japanese proficiency is an important part of their identity as well as their personal and career goals. The study also indicated that these *hushukoo* students had experienced difficulties in learning Japanese because of: (a) English transfer to Japanese writing, (b) decreased Japanese vocabulary and background knowledge, (c) insufficient kanji knowledge, and (d) the challenge of keeping up the study in Japanese. The teacher data indicated that the teachers observed similar problems with regard to the learning experiences of JHLLs.

Kataoka et al.'s (this volume) study extends this line of research with a much larger sample size ($N = 1591$). In that study, the first-to-ninth-grade *hoshuukoo* students took four Japanese proficiency tests (vocabulary, particles, structural patterns, and *kanji*). Their descriptive analysis suggested that (a) Japanese proficiency levels may be polarized when the students reach the fourth grade, and (b) this polarization is the most evident in the acquisition of particles and structural patterns.

Language Needs of Korean Heritage Language Learners. A number of recent Korean heritage language learner (KHLL)-related studies compared the linguistic skills between university KHLLs and non-KHLLs (see Table 2.2). As shown in the table, most of these studies were small-scale studies (with notable exception of H.-S. Kim, this volume), and they examined specific target items using different data collection and analysis procedures. The table also shows that most of these studies identified some differences between KHLLs and non-KHLLs, but two studies did not (see also Kim, this volume). This section will discuss all of these studies listed in the table first.

Two studies (E. J. Kim, 2003; H.-S. Kim, 2001), which compared errors found in KHLLs versus non-KHLLs' speaking and/or writing samples, identified somewhat different error patterns between the groups. In H.-S. Kim's (2001) study, the speaking and writing samples were collected from university KHLLs and non-KHLLs. The linguistic errors found only from the KHLL data included consistent errors with verb conjugations due to the lack of knowledge of the Korean verb stem, and the habit of "writing as it sounds." On the other hand, non-KHLLs tended to speak as they write, and they made frequent particle-related errors such as inconsistent use of particles and the over use of one particle over others (e.g., the over use of subjective normative particle *ka*). In E. J. Kim's (2003) study, the writing samples were collected from intermediate-level KHLLs and non-KHLLs. The descriptive analyses suggested that both groups made the most errors with case particles, but non-KHLLs had more difficulty in using discourse-related particles than KHLLs.

TABLE 2.2
Studies Comparing Linguistic Behavior between University
Heritage and Nonheritage Students in Korean

Study	Analysis	Subjects (N)	Data Collection Method (Target Items)	Results
Au & Romo (1997)	Quantitative (Statistical)	Beginning (18)	Listening test (tense vs. lax consonants); Grammaticality judgment test (subject & object case markers)	Identified differences
E. J. Kim (2003)	Quantitative (Descriptive)	Intermediate (21)	Writing samples (particle errors)	Identified differences
H.-S. Kim (2001)	Qualitative	Mixed (26)	Speaking and writing samples (types of errors)	Identified differences
H.-S. Kim (this volume)	Quantitative (Statistical)	Mixed (128)	Picture-selection listening comprehension task (case markers in interpreting relative clauses)	Identified differences
J.-T. Kim (2001)	Quantitative (Descriptive)	Beginning (9)	Writing samples (null subject and whole sentence construction)	No differences
O'Grady et al. (2001)	Quantitative (Statistical)	Beginning/ Intermediate (36)	Picture-selection listening comprehension task (case markers in interpreting relative clauses)	No differences
Lee et al. (2005)	Quantitative (Statistical)	Advanced (27)	Guided narrative task (complexity and accuracy); Multiple choice grammar test (idiomatic expressions, connectives, honorifics, etc)	Identified differences

Two other studies (Au & Romo, 1997; Lee, Kim, Kong, Hong, & Long, 2005) also identified some differences between KHLLs and non-KHLLs. In Lee et al.'s study, the collection instruments and procedures were identical to those used in the previously discussed Kanno et al. (forthcoming) study, namely, guided narrative tasks and a multiple-choice grammar test. Lee et al.'s descriptive analysis indicated that (a) KHLLs performed better than non-KHLLs on all areas of the grammar test, (b) idiomatic expressions and passive constructions were the most difficult for both groups, (c) the use of connectives seemed easy for KHLLs, but not for non-KHLLs, and (d) among KHLLs, the easiness of honorifics is associated with their overall Korean proficiency.

Au and Romo's (1997) study also identified differences between KHLLs and non-KHLLs. First-year university KHLLs and non-KHLLs were tested on their listening comprehension ability to distinguish tense versus lax consonants in Korean words and on their grammaticality judgments about the use of subject and object case markers. The results suggest that three subgroups of KHLLs (students who spoke Korean regularly since childhood, students who spoke Korean only during childhood, and students who had been exposed to Korean since childhood) performed better than non-KHLLs who had no exposure to Korean until college.

Two studies (J.-T. Kim, 2001; O'Grady, Lee, & Choo, 2001), on the other hand, suggested that KHLLs may not be advantaged in Korean morphology and syntax. For example, J.-T. Kim's (2001) descriptive analysis of writing samples collected from first-year university KHLLs and non-KHLLs indicated no notable difference between these two groups in terms of null subject and wh-sentence construction. O'Grady et al. (2001) compared the ability to utilize morphosyntactic clues (i.e., case markers) in interpreting relative clauses between university KHLLs and non-KHLLs enrolled in beginning or intermediate level courses. A statistical analysis of data collected from the picture-selection listening comprehension task indicated that KHLLs are not advantaged in the target Korean morphosyntax.

H.-S. Kim (this volume) investigated this issue further with a larger sample size ($N = 128$) using a revised version of the picture-selection listening comprehension task used in the O'Grady et al. (2001) study. In Kim's study, the university KHLLs were divided into three subgroups based on the reported L1 language used at early ages (i.e., Korean as L1 [HL-KL1], both English and Korean as L1 [HL-BL1], and English as L1 [HL-EL1]). The non-KHLL group was also divided into two subgroups depending on whether the subjects' L1 were Japanese (SOV language) or English/Chinese/Russian (SVO language). The study indicated that the overall accuracy scores on the listening task were the highest among the HL KL1 and non-HL SOV groups, followed by the HL-BL1 and HL-EL1 groups. Based on this finding, Kim suggested that, first, simple dichotomous comparison between HL versus non-HL learners without controlling the L1 variable may be problematic. Second, KHLLs in general, especially those in the HL EL1 group, may not have fully acquired Korean syntax for accurately processing relative clauses, but may have sufficient semantics and inferencing ability to comprehend them.

Other KHLL-related studies investigated KHLLs' language needs based on self-reports by adult KHLLs (mostly university KHLLs; Cho, Cho, & Tse, 1997; H.-Y. Kim, 2003; Lee & Kim, this volume, Yu, this volume). These studies suggested that, first of all, adult KHLLs study Korean mainly for integrative reasons. For example, Lee and Kim's (this volume) analysis of questionnaire and interview data collected from university KHLLs ($N = 111$) suggested that KHLLs' main reason for learning Korean was integrative, such as knowing more about their Korean heritage through communication with parents. Similarly, in Cho et al. (1997) survey study, many of the adult KHLLs ($N = 24$) reported that they wanted to develop Korean to improve communication with parents and relatives and to develop closer associations with the Korean-speaking community.

Furthermore, Yu's (this volume) descriptive analysis of questionnaire data collected from beginning or intermediate-level university KHLLs and non-KHLLs ($N = 43$) suggested that both groups are interested in improving their spoken Korean in social and domestic situations, but have somewhat different priorities. For example, KHLLs strongly desire to improve their pragmatic skills to use appropriate speech levels towards the addressee (e.g., use of the honorific form with grandparents),whereas non-KHLLs want be able to understand Korean for entertainment purposes and to socialize with Korean-speaking friends. Yu's finding of KHLLs' needs to improve their ability to speak Korean with appropriate registers seems consistent with other self-reported studies (Cho et al., 1997; H.-S. Kim, this volume; H.-Y. Kim, 2003; Lee & Kim, this volume). These studies emphasize that many adult KHLLs (mostly university students) are not confident in speaking Korean and therefore, desire to improve their oral communication skills. For example, according to Lee and Kim (this volume), the university KHLLs in their study reported that they cannot meet the high expectations of native Korean speakers, especially in formal Korean. In Lee and Kim's study, the university KHLLs also expressed their desire to enhance cultural literacy so that they can appreciate the use of Korean in wider contexts.

In H.-Y. Kim's (2003) study discussed earlier, three subgroups of KHLLs were also asked to rate their confidence levels in specific Korean language skills (four skills and honorific/casual forms). The results suggested that KHLLs are generally confident in their listening ability, but the confidence levels in speaking skills and in the use of honorific/causal forms seemed to vary considerably among KHLLs. Similarly, in Cho et al.'s (1997) study discussed earlier, the adult KHLLs reported difficulty in achieving satisfying higher levels of oral proficiency in Korean. Cho et al. explained that this was partly due to low confidence in speaking Korean, which discouraged them from using the language with family and community members.

Thus, the acquisition of the formal variety seems to be a priority for KHLLs. One question is, when KHLLs study formal/academic Korean, how do childhood language linguistic variations (syntactic, lexical, phonological), developed in informal home contexts, transfer into the formal context of learning "standard" Korean? Jo's (2001) ethnographic study dealt with this issue based on the data collected over a 1-year period at two university Korean classes (basic and intermediate levels) largely populated by KHLLs. The study suggested that KHLLs have great difficulty in learning the complex Korean honorifics (see H.-M. Sohn, 1999, for a discussion of the complexity of Korean honorifics), and suffer from discrepancies between "standard/academic" versus "marginalized/parental" varieties of Korean pronunciation, vocabulary, and grammar. Jo also pointed out KHLLs' potentially poor spelling due to their habits in writing the oral version of Korean, an issue that has been largely non-investigated to date.

Summary and Future Directions:
Language Needs Analysis Studies

This section has shown that there a number of language needs analysis studies involving HL learners, especially university HL learners, in East Asian languages. Some of these studies have attempted to identify the language behavior of HL learners, and others have investigated HL learners' motivations and instructional preferences. With CHLLs, one central curriculum issue is how to deal with diverse needs and preferences among CHLLs who speak different Chinese dialects (e.g., Mandarin, Cantonese, Hakka, etc.) at various proficiency levels. In addition, the fact that many of these CHLLs are actually studying Chinese with non-CHLLs in the same classrooms appears to make the instruction more challenging, an issue explored in Weger-Guntharp's chapter. The present collection offers two curriculum innovation projects (by Wu and by Zhang and Davis) that deal with diverse learner backgrounds in beginning- or intermediate-level Chinese classrooms. This line of curriculum development studies should be much encouraged in future research.

With JHLLs, a focus has been placed on investigating language behavior of advanced-level university JHLLs and non-JHLLs. In the studies that deal with this issue, it became evident that there are considerable intragroup differences in the demonstrated receptive and production skills of students within each of the JHLL and non-JHLL groups. This may follow that, although many American universities offer separate tracks for HL learners and non-HL learners at the beginning and intermediate levels only, as Kondo-Brown and Fukuda (this volume) suggest, multitrack systems may also be needed at the advanced level given the considerable individual differences at that level. At very least, efforts are needed to develop instructional strategies that adequately consider linguistic and affective needs of subgroups of advanced students in the same track.

With KHLLs, several previous studies compared linguistic behavior between university KHLLs and non-KHLLs. However, the results seem inconclusive: Some identified differences between these groups, but others did not. For example, some studies suggest that KHLLs may be advantaged in morphology and syntax, but others do not. However, because these previous studies were mostly small-scale studies, it may not be appropriate to make definitive recommendations for curriculum and materials development based on these findings. Second, in these previous studies that compared specific language behaviors, an issue of intragroup differences within each of the HL and non-HL groups did not seem to be adequately raised. H.-S. Kim's study (this volume) is the first that has investigated the language behaviors of learners of Korean with this particular issue in mind. Kim's study, which has a relatively large sample, has adopted a more fine-tuned definition for subgroups of HL and non-HL learners, and has revealed considerable inter- and intragroup differences in Korean sentence processing. The author recommends instruction that helps learners of Korean, especially HL learners, notice their input–output deficiencies with intragroup differences in mind. This line of research seems to be fruitful for future HL materials development studies.

With university/adult KHLLs, one consistent finding is their low confidence in their ability to speak Korean and their strong interest in improving their spoken Korean, especially, the formal variety of Korean (Cho et al., 1997; Kim, this volume; Lee & Kim, this volume). The need for developing university Korean language curriculum that considers KHLLs' particular learning needs has clearly been raised (Lee & Kim, this volume; Yu, this volume). Naturally, future efforts for developing effective pedagogical strategies to better address KHLLs' needs for learning the formal variety of Korean language would be helpful. Also, the HL learners' needs for learning formal spoken language should also be investigated for the Chinese and Japanese groups. In doing so, even though most studies (previous and present) have adopted indirect measurements of spoken language (e.g., self-ratings of their own skills), the use of direct measurements (e.g., recorded natural conversation between the HL learner and another HL speaker, oral performance test, etc.) may also prove useful.

In contrast to a large number of language needs studies focusing on university HL learners, much less attention seems to have been paid to the language needs of younger HL learners, especially those who attend community-based heritage schools. In this sense, the present large-scale study by Kataoka et al. (this volume) that examines the Japanese and English abilities of school-age *hoshuukoo* students seems to be a welcome addition to this relatively unexplored area of studies about HL instruction. Future research is recommended to investigate younger HL learners' language needs in JHLLs in other educational settings as well as younger HL learners in other language groups.

Situational Needs Analysis

Situational needs dealing with East Asian HL learners seem to have been investigated mostly for students attending community-based HL schools. Table 2.3 summarizes studies focusing on the situational needs of these schools. These studies were relatively small-scale qualitative studies, and as

TABLE 2.3
Empirical Studies Investigating Situational Needs of Students at Heritage Schools

Study (Year)	Language/ Main Data	Parental Community Support	Student Use of English	Need for Teacher Training	Problem with Curriculum	Low Student Motivation
Chow (2004)	Chinese/ questionnaire				X	X
Curdit-Christiansen (1999)	Chinese/ observation		X			
Douglas (2002)	Japanese/ textbook				X	
Kataoka et al. (2000)	Japanese/ questionnaire			X	X	X
J. S. Lee (2002)	Korean/ questionnaire			X	X	
Lepore (2004)	Chinese/ Interview					X
M. Li (2005)	Chinese/ interview	X	X	X	X	
Sasaki (2001)	Japanese/ observation		X	X	X	
Usui (1996)	Japanese/ observation		X	X	X	X
Wang (2003)	Chinese/ observation	X	X	X	X	

Table 2.3 shows, they identified various instructional and curriculum problems, which seem common across Chinese, Japanese, and Korean schools. These problems include students' dominant use of English (Curdit-Christiansen, 1999; M. Li, 2005; Sasaki, 2001; Usui, 1996; Wang, 2003), low student motivation (Chow, 2004; Kataoka, Furuyama, & Koshiyama, 2000; Lepore, 2004; Usui, 1996), curriculum and instructional problems as well as the lack of teacher training (Douglas, 2002; Kataoka et al., 2000; J. S. Lee, 2002; M. Li, 2005; Sasaki, 2001; Usui, 1996; Wang, 2003). This section discusses studies listed in Table 2.3 in different language groups.

Situational Needs of Chinese Heritage Learners. Two U.S.-based studies (M. Li, 2005; Wang, 2003) emphasized the central role that Chinese parents may take in the operation of Chinese schools. Both studies suggested that teacher training and professional expertise help the teachers improve their instructional skills, and recommend collaboration between Chinese schools and universities to improve the quality of HL instruction. For example, in Wang's (2003) ethnographic study, two after-school programs at a Chinese school (where both CHLLs and non-CHLLs attend) were observed. During the 3-week observation, several characteristics common to both programs were identified: (a) the parents were very supportive, which was indispensable for the success of the programs, (b) the teachers had generally received little training in teaching methodology, and (c) the students predominantly used English. In M. Li's (2005) qualitative study, interview data were obtained from four administers and two teachers at two different Chinese schools. Like Wang's study, Li's report suggested that the school operation was largely dependent on volunteer parents and the quality of classroom instruction was low because qualified instructors and quality instructional materials were lacking.

In Curdit-Christiansen's (1999) study, classroom observation data were collected at a Chinese school in Canada. The study indicated that, whereas Chinese was used predominantly in teacher-student interactions, English and French were used predominantly in student–student interactions. According to Curdit-Christiansen, major reasons for the dominant use of English and French between students include (a) the students' desire of being identified with the mainstream culture, and (b) a considerable diversity in "Chinese" dialects used at home (e.g., Mandarin, Hakka, Wu, and Hunan). Thus, for those from non-Mandarin dialect backgrounds, Mandarin was just another unfamiliar language, and the students opted to use English and French that they are already familiar with.

Two studies (Chow, 2004; Lepore, 2004) reported low motivation among CHLLs who were attending community-based Chinese schools. In Lepore 's (2004) case study, qualitative analysis of interview data collected from students, teachers, and administrators ($N = 19$) at Chinese schools suggested that, although the CHLLs see the future value of learning Chinese, they are not highly motivated. Similarly, Chow's (2004) descriptive analysis of questionnaire data collected from CHLLs ($N = 515$) attending Canadian CHLL schools indicated that (a) their main reason for attending the school was "parents," (b) the most satisfying aspect of attending the Chinese HL programs was the opportunity to become friends with other CHLLs and (c) they were not generally motivated to do the school assignments.

Situational Needs of Japanese Heritage Learners.   A number of concerns about Japanese heritage schools in the United States or Canada have been addressed in literature-based studies (e.g., Douglas, 2006; Furuyama, 1997; Kondo, 1997; Nakajima, 2003a). These concerns include the lack of (a) proper teaching methodologies, (b) instructional and assessment materials, (c) student motivation, (d) teacher training opportunities, and (e) financial support from government sectors. Kataoka et al.'s (2000) survey data obtained from Japanese heritage school teachers ($N = 34$) confirmed these problems. Kataoka et al. also emphasized that these teachers experience difficulty in teaching partly because of the heterogeneous nature of their classes in terms of the learner's family backgrounds and proficiency levels. A recent survey obtained from 63 *hoshuukoo* also reported similar pedagogical problems in teaching students from diverse family backgrounds and at different proficiency levels (Fujimori, Kashiwazaki, Nakamura, & Ito, 2006).

Usui (1996) observed a Hawai`i-based Japanese heritage school and emphasized that the curriculum placed an emphasis on basic literacy skills only (i.e., the teaching of *kana* syllabaries) and that the students predominantly spoke English in class due to low motivation and strong peer pressure as well. Sasaki's (2001) classroom observation data, which were also collected at a Japanese school in Hawai`i, further suggested that teacher-centered activities were dominant: Learner-centered activities that encourage student-student interaction were rarely observed.

Furthermore, Douglas (2002) and Nakajima (2003b) emphasized the problem of prevalent use of *kokugo* textbooks, the Japanese language arts textbooks for Japanese L1 children in Japan, among *hoshuukoo* as well as Japanese heritage schools. Based on oral reading miscue analysis, Douglas (2002) argued that *kokugo* textbooks do not consider young JHLLs' need to acquire reading strategies to cope with various types of miscue errors. Nakajima (2003b), on the other hand, pointed out that the use of *kokugo* textbooks may demotivate JHLLs to learn Japanese partly because, due to extremely limited instructional hours, JHLLs normally use cognitively unmatched *kokugo* textbooks (e.g., the tenth-grade JHLLs use the third-grade textbooks).

Situational Needs of Korean Heritage Learners.   As part of J.-S. Lee's (2002) qualitative analysis of survey data collected from university KHLLs ($N = 40$), the study examined these students' experiences at the Korean schools they had attended. The study suggested that their untrained Korean teachers did not meet the language learning needs of KHLLs. For example, some students reported that their teachers taught the languages based on their own experiences of learning Korean as their L1 and demanded bilingual teachers who understand the learning of Korean as a heritage language. The recruitment of bilingual and bicultural teachers who may better bridge first and second generations was also recommended by Shin (2005).

Summary and Future Directions:
Situational Needs Analysis Studies

Although language needs analysis studies have focused more on university HL learners, situational needs analysis studies have mostly dealt with young

HL learners at community-based heritage schools. These studies have revealed a number of serious instructional and curriculum problems, which may explain at least partly why no relationship has been identified between the length of attendance to these schools and the students' demonstrated proficiency levels (e.g., Kondo-Brown, 2006b). Although most studies investigating heritage schools' accountability issues are small-scale, the consistency of unfavorable findings across three language groups is quite alarming and disturbing; these schools seem to need substantial community support, especially assistance in curriculum and materials development from university professionals with expertise. A good model, where university professionals and community resource persons actively assist in community-based HL schools' curriculum development and teacher training, seems to be urgently needed. Without such coordinated community support, many HL schools in any language group may remain ineffective in providing instruction for HL learners.

DEVELOPMENTS IN CURRICULUM, MATERIALS, AND ASSESSMENT

This section examines HL instruction studies reporting on the actual developments in curriculum, materials, and assessment. To date, developments in HL instruction can be seen in the areas of (a) curriculum innovations to cope with heterogeneous HL classrooms, (b) oral assessment materials development for child HL learners, (c) placement procedures for university HL learners, and (d) program evaluations. This section discusses these developments.

Curriculum Innovations to Cope with Heterogeneous Heritage Language Classrooms

One common issue in needs analysis studies in all three languages is the need for developing instructional strategies to cope with the heterogeneous HL population in a given instructional setting (e.g., Au & Romo, 1997; Kanno et al., forthcoming; H.-S. Kim, this volume, McGinnis, 1996; Ryu Yang, 2003; Weger-Guntharp, this volume; Wu, 2002). Some researchers have attempted to cope with this issue. For example, as discussed earlier, Wu (2002) identified subgroups of CHLLs at Carnegie Mellon University (CMU) who demonstrated considerably different levels of oral and written skills in Chinese. In order to meet the needs of one of the CHLL subgroups at CMU, those who typically demonstrated minimal literacy skills but higher oral/aural skills, a technology-assisted, learner-centered, standards-based curriculum for these students ("Intensive Elementary Chinese for Heritage learners") has been developed (Wu, this volume).

At the University of California Los Angeles (UCLA), Douglas (1999, 2001) developed a leaner-centered, computer-assisted curriculum for intermediate-level JHLLs whose demonstrated Japanese proficiency levels were considerably different, especially literacy skills. The program placed an emphasis on (a) self-directed study, (b) *kanji* learning strategies, (c) individualized online reading activities, and (d) the learning of formal Japanese through oral activities (e.g., presentation) as well as literacy activities (e.g., e-mail exchanges).

Curriculum innovations that consider individual differences among younger JHLLs are also emerging. For example, Douglas' work in this collection proposes a model for developing curricula and pedagogical strategies with examples for instruction and assessment in order to effectively deal with heterogeneity in the language development of young HL learners. Her work draws not only on a number of educational and learning theories about child learners, but also on empirical evidence about child Japanese heritage students. At the United Nation International School (UNIS), a multi-proficiency, multi-age curriculum has been developed in order to respond to the language needs of the students from diverse backgrounds and expectations (Ohyama, 2004; Tusda, 2001). For example, Ohyama (2004) developed a "three-stages teaching system," which consists of the foundation, developmental, and synthesis stages of learning Japanese.

Oral Assessment Materials
Development for Child Heritage Learners

The Canadian Association for Japanese Language Education (CAJLE, 2000) developed a Japanese oral proficiency test that can be used for child learners of Japanese including JHLLs aged between 6 and 15 (Nakajima, Oketani, & Suzuki, 1994). The test, which was developed based on the learning need analysis of JHLLs, utilizes picture cards in three categories as major prompts: basic vocabulary practice (e.g., family, food, sport), conversational role play (e.g., engage in child–child or child–adult conversation), and presentational role play (e.g., story retelling, speech).

Carpenter, Fujii, and Kataoka (1995) developed an oral test for children aged between 5 and 10, including child JHLLs, who attend Japanese immersion programs. The oral test consists of five sections: (a) a vocabulary-based toy box game (warm-up activity); (b) a "natural conversation" with the tester about various topics such as favorite food, family, and so on; (c) information gap tasks using picture prompts; (d) "categorization" (explain and discuss pictures); (e) the retelling of a story; and (f) classroom role-plays (formal and informal situations; pp. 165–167).

Thus, some advances seem to have been made in developing oral assessment tools for child JHLLs suggesting a number of useful techniques for eliciting oral performance samples. In future studies, as Hasegawa (this volume) suggests, the reliability and validity of these newly developed instruments and procedures may need to be further investigated.

Placement Procedures for University Heritage Learners

Various placement procedures have been adopted for university programs in order to identify HL learners who may not fit into a traditional FL instructional sequence. Some institutions may place students by measuring receptive skills only (e.g., McGinnis 1996), but others may give additional performance-based tests (e.g., S.-O. Sohn, 1995). Two studies (Kondo-Brown, 2004; Sohn & Shin, 2003) recommended the inclusion of performance-based tests into placement procedures. In Kondo-Brown's (2004) study, placement data were collected from a pool of university JHLLs and non-JHLLs ($N = 932$). The study suggested that the multiple-choice listening and reading tests effectively discriminated non-JHLLs and less proficient JHLLs into various levels. However, the same placement procedures were not effective for proficient JHLLs (most of those students' parents were both Japanese L1 speakers). On the other hand, a simple descriptive essay writing task proved to be an effective placement tool for discriminating JHLLs at any proficiency level. Similarly, Sohn and Shin's (2003) descriptive analysis of Korean placement test data collected from incoming students of Korean at UCLA ($N = 110$) suggested that standard listening/reading multiple-choice tests may not be effective in discriminating among KHLLs.

Program Evaluation Studies

Evaluating University Programs for Heritage Learners. A number of Korean HL educators have discussed the benefits of a two-track system for university KHLLs as well as non-KHLLs in terms of proficiency development and/or motivation (e.g., C.-B. Lee, 2000; Ree, 1998; Ryu Yang, 2002, 2003; Shin & Kim, 2000; S.-O. Sohn, 1995, 1997; Stomberg, 1997). For example, S.-O. Sohn (1997), who had developed a two-track Korean curriculum at UCLA, reported that the existing two-track system helped increase enrollments and retention rates. Based on this observation, Sohn suggested that multitrack system may provide both types of students with optimal opportunities to improve their Korean language skills.

A few empirical studies have actually evaluated the effect of an existing two-track system or special accelerated program for university HL learners(Douglas, 2001; Shen, 2003). For example, Shen's (2003) longitudinal pre–post test design evaluation study ($N = 32$) suggested that a homogeneous accelerated special class may offer superior instruction for university

CHLLs than regular heterogeneous Chinese classes. In this study, both courses used the same textbook but the instructional pace and activities were considerably different. The baseline data (i.e., Chinese proficiency and motivation data) collected prior to the first-year courses indicated that students in different tracks had similar Chinese proficiency as well as motivational levels. The ANOVA analyses on SATII and Vocabulary test scores collected at the end of the second-year courses indicated that CHLLs in homogeneous class outperformed those in the heterogeneous class.

Douglas (1999, 2001, forthcoming), on the other hand, evaluated the effect of a leaner-centered, computer-assisted curriculum for intermediate-level JHLLs. Although Douglas' evaluation studies were small-scale, the results consistently indicated positive program outcomes such as increases in *kanji* knowledge and *kanji* learning strategies. At the same time, a comparison of reading comprehension cloze tests at two different times turned out to be nonsignificant (2001).

Although researchers and practitioners may recommend a two-track system for programs where both HL and non-HL learners attend, many such programs do not seem to be able to afford to establish such system (Yu, this volume). Zhang and Davis' (this volume) evaluation study examined the effect of using an online chat program for university CHLLs who studied Chinese together with non-CHLLs in a single-track system. With this program, the students are required to type in Pinyin to write Chinese characters to chat with classroom peers in Chinese. The qualitative analysis of interviews and other supporting data collected from intermediate-level CHLLs indicated the positive effects of the online-based Chinese program: it not only helped the students learn Pinyin and Chinese characters but also enhanced the students' motivation and interest.

Evaluation for Programs for Child Heritage Learners. Sohn and Merrill's (forthcoming) cross-sectional study compared four-skill Korean proficiency test scores as well as standardized English test scores among fourth- and fifth-grade KHLLs who had attended three different educational settings: (a) an English immersion program with no support for Korean L1 maintenance (all-English program), (b) a transitional bilingual program where Korean-speaking teachers are allowed to use Korean to support instruction conducted primarily in English, and (c) the Korean/English Dual Language Program (KDLP), a two-way immersion program. The results indicated that KHLLs in the KDLP group: (a) performed significantly better than the other groups in Korean, and (b) performed significantly better than the transitional bilingual group in English, but compared to the English only group, no significant difference was found.

Lim and Cole (2002), on the other hand, evaluated the effect of parental communication strategy training on children's performance in

Korean. The data were collected from Korean-speaking children (aged from 2–4, $N = 21$) and their mothers. Mothers in the experimental group were trained in the use of a number of techniques to facilitate communication with children while reading a Korean book (e.g., how to comment, ask questions, wait, etc.), whereas mothers in the control group received only general information about the value of L1 reading and bilingualism. Various evaluation measures were used to evaluate mother's use of the instructed techniques (e.g., number of comments, questions, etc.) as well as children's oral performance (e.g., MLU, numbers of utterances). The ANOVA analyses indicated the positive and significant effects of the parental training on both mother's use of techniques and children's oral performance in Korean.

Summary and Future Directions:
Developments in Curriculum, Materials, and Assessment

Compared to the expanding number of needs analysis studies dealing with East Asian HL learners, there seem only a limited number of curriculum studies that document curriculum innovations and instructional materials developments for these students. Future research efforts in this area should be definitely encouraged. In doing so, curriculum innovations and materials development efforts seem to be particularly needed to cope with considerable individual differences in any program where HL learners are present. Some previous and present studies have proposed innovative online programs at the university levels (e.g., Douglas, 1999, 2001; Wu, this volume; Zhang & Davis, this volume), and others have developed instructional and assessment strategies for younger HL learners (e.g., Douglas, this volume; Ohyama, 2004). We need to continue documenting such curricular innovations and their learning outcomes so that successful instructional strategies can be adopted in other programs.

In terms of assessment studies concerning HL learners, several issues have been raised. First, research suggests that incoming university HL learners' placement decisions solely based on multiple-choice tests may not be sufficient; such decisions need to be reconfirmed using performance-based proficiency measures such as oral interview and essay writing (Kondo-Brown, 2004; Sohn & Shin, 2003). Second, some advances seem to have been made in developing oral assessment tools for child JHLLs (e.g., CAJLE, 2000; Carpenter et al., 1995). However, as Hasegawa (this volume) argues, the reliability and validity of these assessment instruments and procedures do not seem to be adequately reported, and therefore, they need to be further investigated. Furthermore, the applicability of these instruments (which were developed primarily for child JHLLs) to child CHLLs and KHLLs may also be explored. Third, evaluation studies that analyzed the effect of given HL programs or instructional strategies are not numerous either. Future research should also prioritize the need to measure the linguistic and other outcomes of the existing special language programs or instructional strategies for HL learners in various settings. Zhang and Davis's (this volume) action-oriented interpretative case study, an attempt to conduct a evaluation study by the teacher–researcher of HL instructional innovations, may become a useful model for other classroom-based HL instruction evaluation studies

CONCLUSION

This chapter has shown that, first, considerable variation exists among the empirical language needs analysis studies on university HL students across the three language groups. One consistent recommendation across languages is the need for developing institutional policies and instructional strategies that cope with sizable individual differences in demonstrated proficiency levels, which were observed not only between HL and non-HL learners but also within the HL group. Inter- and intragroup differences in performing specific receptive and production tasks have been observed in the sentence- and discourse-level processing (H.-S. Kim, this volume; Kondo-Brown & Fukuda, this volume) as well as in the use of vocabulary and expressions in spoken language (Kanno et al., forthcoming). Such studies should continue so that program developers and teachers can determine what specific curriculum goals and objectives are needed for college HL learners.

The language needs for college HL students have also been investigated from the learner perspective, based on interviews and questionnaires. Current investigations of KHLLs indicate that their affective and language needs for receiving adequate instruction in spoken Korean, particularly formal Korean (Kim & Lee, this volume; Yu, this volume). Although previous HL studies generally report a gap between advanced spoken skills and underdeveloped written skills (Campbell & Rosenthal, 2001; Wu, 2002), the work reported in this collection suggests that HL learners may not be satisfied with their spoken skills, especially their formal speech. Research conducted from the learner perspective among college HL students of Chinese further indicates a potential conflict in instructional preferences between traditional versus simplified characters among the learners themselves, depending on their heritage connections (e.g., D. Li, 2004).

All of these findings concerning university HL learners should be considered in future curriculum and materials development for university-level programs where HL students are present. For example, two of the curriculum development studies in this book (Wu, this volume; Zhang & Davis, this volume) are good examples of how to deal with the specific needs of HL students: Wu has documented a curriculum innovation process and outcomes for a subgroup of HL students whose gap between spoken and written Chinese is problematic, whereas Zhang and Davis have developed a program useful for HL students enrolled in regular Chinese class. This line of research should continue in the future. At the same time, evaluation studies that report the effect of new innovations should also be much expanded. As discussed in chapter 1, curriculum development should be viewed as a dynamic process. In viewing curriculum development as such, program evaluation is an indispensable component necessary for keeping existing and new programs improving.

Compared to university HL learners, much less attention seems to have been paid to language needs of younger HL learners. One notable exception is the work in this book of Kataoka et al. (this volume) that reports on the widening ability in morpho-syntactic knowledge that appears to be notable among fourth-grade *hoshuukoo* students. This line of research should be much expanded in all three languages in order to create defensible curriculum recommendations for younger HL learners in community-based HL schools. Given the little attention currently paid to these HL schools, it is not surprising that a number of previous situational needs analysis studies for community-based HL schools have revealed various serious instructional problems common to all three language groups. Support from universities, professionals, and community resource people for these schools is critically needed. Douglas' work in this collection is probably the first to provide steps for developing a theoretically sound curriculum for teaching heterogeneous young JHLLs. Future work that examines the applicability and effect of a proposed model for child HL learners like this one should be followed.

REFERENCES

Au, T. K., & Romo, L. (1997). Does childhood language experience help adult learners? In H. C. Chen (Ed.), *The cognitive processing of Chinese and related Asian languages* (pp. 417–441). Hong Kong: Chinese University Press.

Batista Buteri, B. (2003). *Studying a heritage language: Perception of identity and language among high school students taking Mandarin.* Unpublished master's thesis, Simon Fraser University, CA.

Brown, J. D. (1995). *The elements of language curriculum: A systematic approach to program development.* Boston, MA: Heinle & Heinle.

Canadian Association for Japanese Language Education. (CAJLE). (2000). *Kodomo no kaiwaryoku no mikata to hyooka: bairingaru kaiwa test (OBC) no kaihatsu* [Oral proficiency assessment for bilingual children]. Welland, Canada: Soleil.

Campbell, R. N., & Rosenthal, J. W. (2001). Heritage languages. In J. W. Rosenthal (Ed.), *Handbook of undergraduate second language education* (pp. 165–184). Mahwah, NJ: Lawrence Erlbaum Associates.

Carpenter, K., Fujii, N., & Kataoka, H. (1995). An oral interview procedure for assessing second language abilities in children. *Language Testing, 12,* 167–181.

Cho, G., Cho, K.-S., & Tse, L. (1997). Why ethnic minorities want to develop their heritage language: The case of Korean-Americans. *Language, Culture and Curriculum, 10,* 106–112.

Chow, H. P. H. (2004). *Heritage language learning and ethnic identity maintenance: A case study of the Chinese-Canadian Adolescents.* PCERLL Funded Research Final Report. Retrieved May 10, 2005, from http://pcerii.metropolis.net/Virtual%20Library/FinalReports/Final%20 Report%20Chow.pdf

Curdit-Christiansen, X. L. (1999). *Understanding the patterns of language use of Chinese children in Montreal community school.* Unpublished master's thesis, McGill University, Canada.

Douglas, M. O. (1999, August). *Individualized learning utilizing the Internet and JWPce computer program: A case study of heritage Japanese language learners.* Paper presented at the International Conference on Computer Assisted System for Teaching & Learning/Japanese, Toronto, Canada.

Douglas, M. O. (2001, March). *Individualized learning: A course for Japanese heritage learners at the college level.* Paper presented at the meeting of the Association of Teachers of Japanese. Retrieved May 10, 2005, from http://www.colorado.edu/ealld/atj/SIG/heritage/douglas. html

Douglas, M. O. (2002, March). *Kokugo kyookasho no gakushuu mokuhyoo bunseki* [A Japanese language textbook analysis: Learning goals]. Paper presented at the meeting of the Association of Teachers of Japanese, Washington DC. Retrieved May 10, 2005, from http://www.colorado.edu/ealld/atj/SIG/heritage/douglas_kyokasho.html

Douglas, M. O. (2006). Pedagogical theories and approaches to teach young learners of Japanese as a heritage language. *Heritage Language Journal, 3.* Retrieved March 2006, from ftp: http://www.heritagelanguages.org/

Douglas, M. O. (forthcoming). A profile of Japanese heritage learners and individualized curriculum. In D. M. Brinton, O. Kagan, & S. Baucks (Eds.), *Heritage language education: A new field emerging.* Mahwah, NJ: Lawrence Erlbaum Associates.

Everson, M. E. (1998). Word recognition among learners of Chinese as a foreign language: Investigating the relationship between naming and knowing. *The Modern Language Journal, 82,* 191–204.

Flores d'Arcais, G. B., Saito, H., & Kawakami, M. (1995). Phonological and semantic activation in reading kanji characters. *Journal of Experimental Psychology: Learning, Memory and Cognition, 21,* 34–42.

Fujimori, H., Kashiwazaki, M. Nakamura, A., & Ito, S. (2006). The current state of and demand for Japanese language education in Japanese schools and supplementary education schools. *Journal of Japanese Language Teaching, 128,* 80–89.

Furuyama, H. (1997). The future of language education in community schools: Japanese as a case study. In H.-Y. Kim (Ed.), *Korean Language in America 2: Papers from the Second Annual Conference and Professional Development Workshop* (pp.131–138). Honolulu: American Association of Teachers of Korean.

Jo, H.-Y. (2001). 'Heritage' language learning and ethnic identity: Korean Americans' struggle with language authorities. *Language, Culture, and Curriculum, 14,* 26–41.

Kanno, K., Hasegawa, T., Ikeda, K., Ito, Y., & Long, M. H. (forthcoming). Prior language—learning experience and variation in the linguistic profiles of advanced English-speaking learners of Japanese. In D. M. Brinton, O. Kagan, & S. Baucks (Eds.), *Heritage language education: A new field emerging.* Mahwah, NJ: Lawrence Erlbaum Associates.

Kataoka, H., Furuyama, H., & Koshiyama, Y. (2000). *Minami kariforunia ninongo gakuen kyooshi ankeeto kekka bunseki hookokusho* [Report on the Southern California Japanese language school teacher survey results]. Retrieved May 10, 2005, from http://www.jflalc.org/teaching/ jflc/fclty_rpt/jpz_kyoushi/heritage2.html

Ke, C. (1998). Effects of language background on the learning of Chinese characters among foreign language students. *Foreign Language Annals, 31,* 91–100.

Kim, E. J. (2003). An analysis of particle errors by heritage and non-heritage learners of Korean. In C. You (Ed.), *Korean Language in America 8: Papers from the Eighth Annual Conference and Professional Development Workshop* (pp. 37–50). Honolulu: American Association of Teachers of Korean

Kim, H.-S. H. (2001). Issues of heritage learners in Korean language classes. In J. Ree (Ed.), *Korean Language in America 6: Papers from the Sixth Annual Conference and Professional Development Workshop* (pp. 257–273). Honolulu: American Association of Teachers of Korean.

Kim, H.-Y. (2003, June). *Profiles and perspectives of heritage Korean learners.* Paper presented at the Conference and Professional Development Workshop of the American Association of Teachers of Korean, Berkeley, CA. Retrieved May 10, 2005, from http://www.duke.edu/web/aall/aallpresentation.pdf

Kim, J.-T. (2001). The degree of L1 interference among heritage and non-heritage learners of Korean: Do heritage students have advantages over non-heritage students? In J. Ree (Ed.), *Korean Language in America 6: Papers from the Sixth Annual Conference and Professional Development Workshop* (pp. 285–296). Honolulu: American Association of Teachers of Korean.

Kondo, K. (1998). The paradox of U.S. language policy and Japanese language education in Hawai`i. *International Journal of Bilingual Education and Bilingualism, 1,* 47–64.

Kondo-Brown, K. (2001). Bilingual heritage students' language contact and motivation. In Z. Dornyei & R. Schmidt (Eds.), *Motivation and second language acquisition* (pp. 425–451). Honolulu: Second Language Teaching & Curriculum Center/University of Hawai`i Press.

Kondo-Brown, K. (2004). Do background variables predict students' scores on a proficiency test?: Implications for placing heritage language learners. *Journal of the National Council of Less Commonly Taught Languages, 1,* 1–19.

Kondo-Brown, K. (2005). Differences in language skills: Heritage language learner subgroups and foreign language learners. *The Modern Language Journal, 89,* 563–581.

Kondo-Brown, K. (2006a). How do English L1 learners of advanced Japanese infer unknown kanji words in authentic texts? *Language Learning, 56,* 109–153.

Kondo-Brown, K. (2006b). East Asian heritage language proficiency development. In K. Kondo-Brown (Ed.), *Heritage language development: Focus on East Asian immigrants* (pp. 243–258). Amsterdam, Netherlands: John Benjamins.

Lee, C.-B. (2000). Two-track curriculum system for university Korean language programs. In J. S. King (Ed.), *Korean Language in America, 5: Papers from the Sixth Annual Conference and Professional Development Workshop* (pp. 3–11). Honolulu: American Association of Teachers of Korean.

Lee, J. S. (2002). The Korean language in America: The role of cultural identity in heritage language learning. *Language, Culture, and Curriculum, 15,* 117–133.

Lee, Y.-G., Kim, H.-S. H., Kong, D.-K., Hong, J.-M., & Long, M. H. (2005). Variation in the linguistic profiles of advanced English-speaking learners of Korean. *Language Research 41, 2,* 437–456.

Lepore. J. (2004, September). *Chinese school attendance and its effect on language maintenance attitudes: An exploratory case study in two Minnesota schools.* Paper presented at the Cultural Diversity and Language Education Conference, Honolulu, Hawai`i.

Li, D. (2004, May). *Setting a research agenda for teaching Chinese as a heritage language at the postsecondary level.* Paper presented at the Conference of the American Association for Applied Linguistics, Portland, OR.

Li, M. (2005). The role of parents in Chinese heritage-language schools. *Bilingual Research Journal 29, 1.* Retrieved from http://brj.asu.edu/

Lim, Y.-S., & Cole, K. N. (2002). Facilitating first language development in young Korean children through parent training in picture book interactions. *Bilingual Research Journal, 26,* 213–227.

Matsunaga, S. (2003). Instructional needs of college-level learners of Japanese as a heritage language: Performance-based analyses. *Heritage Language Journal, 1.* Retrieved December 30, 2003, from http://www.heritagelanguages.org/

McGinnis, S. (1996). Teaching Chinese to the Chinese: The development of an assessment and instructional model. In J. E. Liskin-Gasparro (Ed.), *Patterns and policies: The Changing demographics of foreign language instruction* (pp. 107–121). Boston, MA: Heinle and Heinle.

Nagaoka, Y. (1998). *A descriptive study of Japanese biliterate students in the United States: Bilingualism, language-minority education, and teachers' role.* Unpublished doctoral dissertation, University of Massachusetts, Amherst.

Nagasawa, F. (1995). *L1, L2, bairingaru no nihongo bunpoo nooryoku* [Comparative grammatical competence among L1, L2, and bilingual speakers of Japanese]. *Nohongo Kyooiku* [Journal of Japanese Language Teaching], *86,* 173–89.

Nakajima, K. (2003a). *Mondai teiki: JHL no wakugumi to kadai-JSL/JFL to doo chigaku ka* [A framework and theme for JHL: How does it differ from JSL/JFL?]. Retrieved May 10, 2005, from http://www.notredame.ac.jp/~eyukawa/heritage/papers 2003/Nakajima2003.html

Nakajima, K. (2003b). *Keishoo nihongo gakushuusha no kanji shuutoku to kokugo kyookasho* [The role of kokugo textbooks in kanji instruction for heritage Japanese students]. *Obirin Synergy, 1,* 1–21.

Nakajima, K., Oketani, H., & Suzuki, M. (1994). *Seisyoonen no tame no kaiwaryoku tesuto kaihatsu* [Development of oral proficient test for children]. *Nihongo kyooiku* [Journal of Teaching of Japanese Language], *83,* 40–58.

O'Grady, W., Lee, M., & Choo, M. (2001). The acquisition of relative clauses by heritage and non-heritage learners of Korean as a second language: A comparative study. In J. Ree (Ed.), *Korean Language in America 6: Papers from the Sixth Annual Conference and Professional Development Workshop* (pp. 345–356). Honolulu: American Association of Teachers of Korean.

Ohyama, M. (2004, March). *Multilevel/multiage curriculum at high school level: Creating a classroom environment based on diversity.* Paper presented at the meeting of the Association of Teachers of Japanese, San Diego, CA.

Ree, J. (1998). Korean as a second language: How should it be taught? *ACTA Koreana, 1,* 85–100.

Ryu Yang, J. S. R. (2002, August). *Motivational and de-motivational factors of Korean language learners at an American university: A case study.* Paper presented at the Conference and Professional Development Workshop of the American Association of Teachers of Korean, Orlando, FL

Ryu Yang, J. S. R. (2003). Motivational orientations and selected learner variables of east Asian language learners in the United States. *Foreign Language Annals, 36,* 44–56.

Sasaki, M. (2001, March). *Japanese as a heritage language classes in Hawai`i and Brazil: Their differences and similarities.* Paper presented at the meeting of Association of Teachers of Japanese [online]. Retrieved May 10, 2005, from http://www.colorado.edu/ealld/atj/SIG/heritage/sasaki.html

Shen, H. H. (2003). A comparison of written Chinese achievement among heritage learners in homogeneous and heterogeneous groups. *Foreign Language Annals, 36,* 258–266.

Shin, S., & Kim, S. (2000). The introduction of context-based language teaching to college-level Korean program for heritage learners. In S.-O. Sohn (Ed.), *Korean language in America 5: Papers from the Fifth Annual Conference and Professional Development Workshop* (pp. 167–179). Honolulu: American Association of Teachers of Korean.

Shin, S. J. (2005). *Developing in two languages: Korean children in America.* Clevedon, UK: Multilingual Matters.

Sohn, H.-M. (1999). *The Korean language.* Cambridge: Cambridge University Press.

Sohn, S.-O. (1995). The design of curriculum for teaching Korean as a heritage language. In H.-M. Sohn, (Ed.), *Korean language in America 1: Papers from the Second Annual Conference and Professional Development Workshop* (pp. 19–35). Honolulu: American Association of Teachers of Korean.

Sohn, S.-O. (1997). Issues and concerns in teaching multi-level classes: Syllabus design for heritage and non-heritage learners. In H.-Y. Kim (Ed.), *Korean language in America 2: Papers from the Second Annual Conference and Professional Development Workshop* (pp. 139–158). Honolulu: American Association of Teachers of Korean.

Sohn, S.-O & Merrill, C. (in press). The Korean/English dual language program in the Los Angles unified school district. In D. Brinton, O. Kagan, & S. Baucks (Eds.), *Heritage language education: A new field emerging.* Mahwah, NJ: Lawrence Erlbaum Association.

Sohn, S.-O., & Shin, S.-K. (2003, May). *Assessment and placement for Korean heritage speakers.* Paper presented at the conference of the National Council of Organizations of Less Commonly Taught Languages, Los Angeles, CA.

Stomberg, C. (1997). Breaking the mold: A non-heritage learner's experience in a multi-level Korean class. In H.-Y. Kim (Ed.), *Korean Language in America 2: Papers from the Second Annual Conference and Professional Development Workshop* (pp. 159–165). Honolulu: American Association of Teachers of Korean.

Tabachnick, B. G., & Fidell, L. S. (2001). *Using multivariate statistics* (4th ed.). Upper Saddle River, NJ: Pearson Allyn & Bacon.

Tsuda, K. (2001, March). *Interpretation, presentation and dramatization skills in secondary school heritage language classes.* Paper presented at the meeting of the Association of Teachers of Japanese; Chicago, IL [online]. Retrieved May 10, 2005, from http://www.colorado.edu/ealld/atj/SIG/heritage/tsuda.html

Usui, Y. (1996). *An ethnographic perspective on language shift, maintenance, and revitalization: Japanese in* Hawai`i. Unpublished master thesis, University of Hawai`i at Mānoa, Honolulu, HI.

Wang, M. (2003). An ethnographic study of Chinese heritage language education and technological innovations. *Journal of National Council of less Commonly Taught Languages, 1,* 69–94.

Wu, S. (2002). Integrating learner-centered and technology strategies for heritage students. In W. Li & C. Lee (Eds.), *Proceedings of the Southeast Conference on Chinese Language Teaching* (pp. 90–95). Duke University and University of North Carolina at Chapel Hill.

Language Needs Analysis

Japanese and English Language Ability of Students at Supplementary Japanese Schools in the United States[*]

Hiroko C. Kataoka
California State University, Long Beach

Yasuko Koshiyama
Pepperdine University

Setsue Shibata
California State University, Fullerton

BACKGROUND

Responding to Japan's international expansion since the 1970s, *hoshuukoo*, Japanese language supplementary schools, have been established outside

---

[*]This chapter is an English translation of a revised version of the original paper (in Japanese) published in *Kokusai Kyooiku Hyooron* (2005). Reprinted with permission from *CRIE Review of International Education*, 2, 1–19.

of Japan to help support the education of Japanese children living over-seas. Statistical data gathered in 2003 indicate that there are 184 *hoshuukoo* worldwide and, among them, 84 in North America (Ministry of Education and Science, 2003a).[1] There are, as of 2003, 20,848 Japanese students in elementary and junior high schools in North America. Among them, 508 attend full-day Japanese schools and 8,438 attend local schools only, but as many as 11,098, more than a half of the whole population, are enrolled in *hoshuukoo* while attending local schools (Ministry of Education and Science, 2003b). The data attest to the importance of *hoshuukoo* in educat-ing Japanese youths residing outside of Japan.

The original purpose for establishing *hoshuukoo*, according to the Ministry of Education (currently the Ministry of Education and Science), was "to pro-vide educational opportunities for Japanese children living abroad equal to those for Japanese children living in Japan" (Kaigai Shijo Kyooiku, 2003, p. 5). According to data collected in 1984, almost three fourths (72.2%) of par-ents chose *hoshuukoo* for their children so that they would not lose their Japanese language ability, and about two thirds (67.7%) chose *hoshuukoo* so their children would be able to re-enter the Japanese educational system smoothly when they returned home. Although parents stated other factors that emphasized their children's bicultural and bilingual experiences through schooling such as "promoting international identity and ways of thinking" and "acquiring foreign languages," *hoshuukoo* were fundamentally expected to teach the Japanese language as "a national tongue," and students learning the language as a heritage or foreign language were excluded in the process (Yamamoto, 1991, p. 114).

A 2003 Ministry of Foreign Affairs study, however, indicates that an increasing population of Japanese stayed in the United States for an extended period of time. Long-term residents numbered approximately 240,000 and permanent residents, 130,000.[2] As a result, despite the fact that *hoshuukoo* were originally established to educate Japanese children eventually returning home after several years of stay in the United States, these schools now have a higher enrollment ratio of children of long-term U.S. residents, and therefore need to accommodate these children who

---

[1]According to the Ministry of Education and Science (2003a), among the 84 schools in North America (31 schools with teachers dispatched from the Japanese government and 53 schools without them), 76 are in the United States, and eight are in Canada.

[2]The Ministry of Foreign Affairs (2004) defines long-term residents as individuals staying longer than 3 months but not residing as permanent residents (225,589 in the United States; 14,444 in Canada). Permanent residents are individuals allowed by the government to reside permanently in their countries of residence (106,088 in the United States; 23,511 in Canada; seven in Greenland). In this chapter, we are not bound by these legal definitions of the terms. Instead, we defined as temporary residents those whom Minoura (1991) defined as *karizumai* or "short-term residents" and those whose lifestyle is more firmly situated in American society as "long-term residents."

have different language backgrounds and learning needs (*The U.S. Frontline*, 2003, p. 5; *Lighthouse*, 2000, pp. 15–22). According to the survey conducted by Douglas et al. (2003), 27% of all students at seven *hoshuukoo* in the United States were the children of permanent residents from Japan, contradicting the primary purpose of the establishment of *hoshuukoo*, which was to provide Japanese education for the children of temporary residents. Sato (2003) identified two sources of change in the *hoshuukoo*: decline in the function of *hoshuukoo* as a symbol of the homeland for Japanese nationals and a conflict between temporary residents and permanent residents from Japan. Koshiyama (2000) indicated that parents might feel superior by sending their children to *hoshuukoo*, not to Japanese language schools, regardless of their future intentions with regard to returning to Japan or staying in the United States. Unless *hoshuukoo* offer different curricula, two different groups of students, that is, children of temporary residents who study Japanese as their native language and children of permanent residents who study Japanese as their heritage language (HL), will continue to occupy the same classroom under the same curriculum.

These *hoshuukoo* are numerous and successful in the United States, which makes it all the more important to reexamine the content of *hoshuukoo* curricula so they can meet the ever-changing educational needs of students. Reexamination also requires a concrete understanding of student backgrounds and language levels. Therefore, in order to provide such information, this study presents relevant data collected from approximately 1,600 elementary and junior high students currently attending four *hoshuukoo* in the United States and analyzed their language background and ability. The study focuses on Japanese ability, English ability, length of stay in the United States, and age at time of entry into the United States.

PREVIOUS STUDIES

Previous studies of Japanese-English bilinguals indicate that *proficient bilingualism* is rare among children who are speakers of Japanese and English: Most cases are likely to fall in the category of *partial bilingual* or *high proficiency in only one language* (Nakajima, 1998; Ono, 2002).[3] One example of this category are Japanese-speaking students who were born in the United

---

[3]Cummins (1979, p. 230) originally used the terms *balanced bilingual, dominant bilingual*, and *double-limited bilingual*. Cummins (1984, p. 59) renamed the three categories just noted as *proficient bilingualism, partial bilingualism*, and *limited bilingualism*, respectively. *Proficient bilingualism* refers to students who acquire age-appropriate level of proficiency in both communicative

States or who came to the United States at an early age, for whom English is more likely to become their primary language although Japanese is the first language of their parents (Minoura, 1991; Nakajima, 1998). In such cases, Japanese should be regarded as a "heritage language" rather than "first language" (L1) for them, which more accurately reflect their linguistic and cultural background.

Regarding linguistic differences between the students who study Japanese as their L1 and those who study it as a HL, researchers have conducted various studies. For example, there are differences in the choice of expression at the end of sentences (Kubo, 2003), choice of vocabulary (Oketani, 1991), choice of sentence pattern (Nagasawa, 1995; Nakajima, 1988; Oketani, 1991), choice of particles and verbs (Kado, Serizawa, Nakanishi, & Sakai, 1988; Koshiyama & Shibata, 2002; Yamashita, 2003), and choice of expressions in storytelling (Minami, Fukuda, & Fujiyama, 2002). It is also reported that proficiency in reading and writing *kanji* (Chinese characters) among HL learners of Japanese is lower than that for those who learn Japanese as their L1 (Matsunaga, 2003; Nakajima, 1988). Douglas (2002) and Nakajima (2002) observed that the textbooks used in *hoshuukoo*, which are adopted by the Ministry of Education, may not be appropriate for students who grow up in non-*kanji*-language environments.

Douglas, Kataoka, and Kishimoto (2003) compared the academic Japanese proficiency levels between students in *hoshuukoo* and those who were in Japanese language schools (based on survey data from their parents). In the area of parental expectations towards *hoshuukoo*, Douglas et al. (2003) found that parents of the students in *hoshuukoo* evaluate their children's academic Japanese proficiency significantly

---

and cognitive-academic aspects of both languages. *Partial bilingualism* refers to students who acquire age-appropriate level of proficiency in one language only. *Limited bilingualism* refers to students who do not acquire age-appropriate level of proficiency in either language (Cummins, 1984, p. 59). Cummins mentioned that children should become at least "partial bilinguals" for their cognitive and mental development. Ono (1989) studied the relationship between Japanese proficiency as an academic language and the academic success in Japan of Japanese children who had returned from living overseas. He found that children, on returning to Japan, are unlikely to attain the academic knowledge and skills needed to succeed in their current grade level unless they have Japanese proficiency no lower than two grade levels beneath their current grade. Ono refers to children who do not possess language ability at least two grade levels lower than their current grade as *semi-linguals*, and warns that semi-lingualism negatively affects children's cognitive and mental development. Nakajima (1998) refers to Cummins' three categories just described as *high proficiency in both languages, high proficiency in only one language,* and *insufficient proficiency in both languages,* respectively. Cummins' "limited bilingualism," Ono's "semi-lingualism," and Nakajima's "insufficient proficiency in both languages" are semantically different, but concern the same issue: if children do not possess a native-like proficiency of at least one academic language equivalent to children of their own age, their cognitive and mental development is endangered (Cummins, 1984, 1991, 1996; Nakajima, 1998; Ono, 1989, 2002).

higher in all areas of Japanese language skills, that is, reading, writing, speaking, and listening, than those whose children attended Japanese language schools. They also found that the parents' expectations for their children to obtain higher levels of proficiency in Japanese are stronger among the parents of children in *hoshuukoo* than among the parents of children in Japanese language schools. They suggest that this last expectation may be inversely related to the length of stay in the United States: The average number of years in the United States of the students in *hoshuukoo* is also significantly shorter than that of the students in Japanese language schools.

PURPOSE OF THE PRESENT STUDY

With the drastic increase in the number of students who study Japanese as a HL in *hoshuukoo,* many researchers and educators of Japanese have begun to recognize the need for special instruction for Japanese HL learners (e.g., Douglas, 2002; Sato, 2003). Classroom teachers of *hoshuukoo* also express concern about student motivation to learn under the current curricula (see Kondo-Brown, this volume). A number of specialists have called for a critical review of Japanese pedagogy and for curricula that take into account the students' language background and their purpose for studying (Calder, 2003; Fujioka, 2003; Furuya-Wise, 1999; Igawa, 1999; Kataoka, Koshiyama, & Shibata, 2003; Kishimoto, 2003).

In our view, assessing the language abilities of the students in *hoshuukoo* is the first step in establishing more appropriate Japanese language curricula and instruction. Few studies have appeared regarding the Japanese and English abilities of the students in *hoshuukoo* with a large number of students. One exception is Nakajima's 1988 small-scale study, which merely investigated Japanese and English abilities and their relation to the number of years in *hoshuukoo* in Canada. The current large-scale study is offered to inform the discussion of various expectations towards *hoshuukoo.* Specifically, the present study will examine the following issues to better understand the current Japanese and English abilities of students at *hoshuukoo:*

1. Length of stay in the United States
2. Acquisition of Japanese and English languages as academic language
3. Relationship between Japanese and English abilities
4. Relationship between the length of stay in the United States and proficiency in the two languages
5. Relationship between age of entry into the United States and proficiency in the two languages

METHOD

Participants

The participants in this study were 1,591 students from Grades 1 through 9 who enrolled in four *hoshuukoo* in the United States and took Japanese and English proficiency tests as part of their school curriculum.[4]

Japanese and English Proficiency Tests

The Japanese proficiency test and English vocabulary test developed by Ono et al. (1989) were used to measure the students' Japanese and English abilities. In that study, the Japanese test was administered over 3 years to more than 200,000 elementary and middle school students in Japan and is currently the most reliable among the tests for this purpose (for more on validity and reliability with regard to Japanese proficiency tests for child HL learners, see Hasegawa, this volume). The Japanese test includes four sub-tests, that is, vocabulary, sentence patterns, particles, and *kanji*. The sub-tests are described in the following paragraphs. Table 3.1 displays the tests administered for each grade.[5]

Japanese Vocabulary Test

This test uses different sets of vocabulary items for different grade levels. The test contains multiple-choice questions with five possible answers. In addition to the items appropriate for the grade level, each test includes items appropriate for the adjacent higher and lower grades. Each test contains 45 questions for the first grade and 30 questions for the second grade and higher. More of the items use drawings as cues in the tests for the lower graders.[6]

---

[4]The participating *hoshuukoo* schools were selected through personal contacts. These schools are probably more or less "typical" *hoshuukoo* because they are (a) supported by the Japanese government, and (b) located in urban and suburban areas with a concentration of Japanese companies and Japanese and/or Japanese-American communities. Students enrolled in these schools numbered 1,730; among these students, complete data (as shown in the grid) were available for 1,591 students.

[5]In a number of previous studies, Ono, Hayashibe, and others reported that language proficiency is highly correlated with the vocabulary test score, so that a vocabulary test can be used to determine overall language proficiency (Hayashibe, 1999; Hayashibe, Shigemasu, Ichikawa, Makino, & Ono, 1988; Ono, 2002; Ono et al., 1989). Although we considered this option seriously, we also used the results of the other Japanese subtests to determine overall Japanese proficiency as a precaution to account for the varied populations in our study.

[6]Each vocabulary test covered two grade levels, such as Grades 1 and 2 and Grades 3 and 4. One may speculate that students in even-numbered grades, for example, second and fourth grades, might have advantages resulting in higher scores. However, because the tests were

Table 3.1
Japanese Displays the Tests Administered for Each Grade

	1st Grade	2nd Grade	3rd Grade and up
Japanese vocabulary	X	X	X
Sentence pattern	X	X	X
Particles		X	X
Kanji		X	X
English vocabulary			X

Sentence Patterns

The sentence pattern test contains the same items for all grade levels. Thirty-nine questions measure the level of understanding of the sentence patterns (e.g., simple sentences, sentences with giving/receiving verbs, causative sentences, causative sentences with giving/receiving verbs, etc). Students choose one, drawing out of two that better describe the sentence.

Particles

The particles test contains the same questions for all grade levels. Sixty multiple-choice questions offer four possible answers. Students choose the most appropriate particle for the blank in a sentence.

Kanji

The *kanji* test contains 20 items for each grade level. Students are required to write *hiragana* (Japanese basic syllabaries) for *kanji* underlined in a short sentence. A number of questions for adjacent higher and lower grade levels are included in addition to the grade-level questions.

English Vocabulary

An English vocabulary test was administered to the third grade and up. For each grade-level test there are 20 multiple-choice questions with three possible answers. In addition to the questions for that grade level, a number of higher and lower grade levels are included. Each student took all questions from the third-grade level up to his or her grade level (e.g., fifth-graders

administered only a few months after the new school year began in April, the testing was conducted using the test for one grade level lower than the students' actual grade, giving students in odd-numbered grades (e.g., third and fifth grades), an advantage. As a result, the possibility that students in even-numbered grades might do better than students in odd-numbered grades should have been mediated.

answered the 60 questions for three grade levels, made up of 20 questions for each of third, fourth, and fifth grade).

Administering the Tests

Japanese and English proficiency tests were administered to the students in June, 2003. Because the tests were administered only 2 months after the new school year started, the tests administered were one grade level lower than their actual grade level (e.g., fifth-graders took the fourth grade's level).[7]

The tests were administered under the supervision of each classroom teacher. Prior to administration, the format of the test was revised by enlarging the characters and adding extra spaces between the words so that the students, especially in the lower grades, could read them more easily. Colored pages were used for the sample questions so that teachers could give instructions easily. Because not all first-graders had mastered *hiragana* at the time of testing, classroom teachers read the questions and all the choices of answers. The first-graders were instructed to write answers directly on the question sheets under the teacher's supervision. Bubble sheets were used except for the *kanji* test for students in the second grade and higher.

Age at Entry and Length of Stay in the United States

Data on the number of years of stay in the United States of the students were obtained from the participating *hoshuukoo*. Age at time of entry to the United States was calculated by subtracting the number of years in the United States from the students' ages (determined by grade level as of April 1, 2003). For instance, if a fifth-grader has stayed in the United States for 7 years, his age at time of entry was calculated to be three (10–7 = 3).[8]

---

[7]Previous research showed that almost all of the students who live in Japan have acquired basic Japanese grammar such as sentence patterns and use of particles without any special instruction by the time they reach the sixth grade. Therefore, giving a grammar test to junior high school students has generally been considered unnecessary (Ono et al., 1989). However, given the possibility that acquisition of sentence patterns and use of particles by long-term overseas residents might take a different path, we included these tests. It should be noted that because measurable levels were unavailable below the first grade in Japan, it was difficult to ascertain if proficiency among the first- and second-graders had actually reached their expected grade levels. Similarly, because testing did not go beyond the sixth grade in Japan, it was not possible to compare the eighth- and ninth-graders' levels of proficiency with those of students at the same grade level in Japan because there were no previous Japanese data with which to compare scores.

[8]There are some students who went back and forth between foreign countries and Japan repeatedly, and in these cases, the number of years in the United States may not be accurate. However, such cases are extremely rare and should not greatly affect the results of our study.

Data Analysis

Each test score for the Japanese subtests was compared with those of students in the same grade level in Japan (age level rather than the grade level for the first-graders), and grade level was determined based on the scale developed by Ono (1989). See Ono et al. (1989) for detailed information regarding the contents, scoring, and assessment procedures of these various tests. As explained earlier, the tests administered were one grade lower than the participants' grade level at the time of testing in June. Therefore, "grade-level ability" was defined as a score equivalent to the average score of students one grade lower. The English vocabulary test results were also compared with the previous test results of native English-speaking students in the United States at the same grade level.

RESULTS

The results of Japanese and English proficiency tests as well as the length of stay in the United States and students' ages at the time of entry the United States were analyzed. The fourth-graders represented the largest group with 219 students, and the smallest was the ninth-graders with 148.

Length of Stay in the United States

Table 3.2 provides the average length of stay in the United States by those children in each grade level in June of 2003. Clearly, the older the students are, the longer they have been in the United States (note especially that ninth-graders averaged more than 11 years in the United States). Table 3.3 shows the age at which these children entered the United States. Evidently, the majority

TABLE 3.2
Number of Students and Average Number of Years of Stay
in the U.S. by Grade Level

Grade Level	Number of Students	Average Years in U.S.
1	100	3.94
2	198	5.24
3	212	5.92
4	219	6.28
5	191	7.42
6	196	7.84
7	171	8.86
8	156	9.29
9	134	11.21

TABLE 3.3
Age at Time of Entering the U.S. by Grade Level ($N = 1591$)

	Age 0[a]		1		2		3		4		5		6		7		8		9		10		11		12		13+		Total	
Grade	n	%	n	%	n	%	n	%	n	%	n	%	n	%	n	%	n	%	n	%	n	%	n	%	n	%	n	%	n	%
1	44	44	6	6	5	5	13	13	13	13	10	10	9	9															100	6
2	116	59	7	4	11	6	9	5	14	7	18	9	11	6	12	6													198	12
3	116	55	10	5	10	5	12	6	15	7	8	4	16	8	19	9	6	3											212	13
4	104	48	11	5	13	6	11	5	6	3	18	8	10	5	21	10	16	7	9	4									219	14
5	103	54	8	4	5	3	10	5	7	4	10	5	9	5	12	6	13	7	9	5	5	3							191	12
6	91	46	15	8	7	4	10	5	7	4	7	4	9	5	9	5	10	5	11	6	12	6	8	4					196	12
7	87	51	6	4	9	5	4	2	8	5	6	4	5	3	10	6	10	6	8	5	9	5	7	4	2	1			171	11
8	79	51	3	2	6	4	8	5	3	2	3	2	7	5	11	7	3	2	2	1	7	5	10	6	9	6	5	3	156	10
9	88	60	7	5	10	7	4	3	3	2	1	1	3	2	4	3	1	1	5	3	4	3	5	3	6	4	7	5	148	9
Total	828	52	73	5	76	5	81	5	76	5	81	5	79	5	98	6	59	4	44	3	37	2	30	2	17	1	12	1	1591	100

[a] Age "0" indicates that those students were born in the U.S.

of the students at all grade levels were either born in the United States or entered the country when they were younger than 1 year of age (note especially that more than 75% of ninth-graders have been in the United States for more than 10 years, making them the largest group of long-term residents).

Proficiency Levels of Japanese and English Languages as Academic Languages

We first analyzed the results of each subtest by grade level. The resulting tables require some additional information to help readers interpret it. As mentioned earlier, because the tests were administered in early June, which was shortly after the new school year started, the reference grade level of attainment, which is equivalent to Japanese students in Japan, should be one grade level lower than their grade level at the time of testing. Thus, for example, expected performance of the fifth-graders in the present study is that of fourth-graders in Japan. Distributions of students' performances in each Japanese subtest and English vocabulary test are described as follows.

Japanese Vocabulary.   Table 3.4 shows the results of the Japanese vocabulary test for all grades (indicated as "Grade" across the top of the table). The shaded cells mark the expected grade level for each respective grade. Recall that the expected grade level is one grade level lower than the students' actual grade level for the reason just explained. With the exception of the first-grade students ("Grade 1"), which instead has the mean performance age level, the bottom row shows the means of performance grade levels attained by the students at various levels (e.g., the mean performance level of the second-year students [Grade 2] is 1.21, which means that the average performance level of these students is equivalent to that of Grade 1.21 students in Japan). Table 3.4 indicates that the mean performance grade levels for the Japanese vocabulary test attained by the second-, fourth-, sixth-, and eighth-graders (1.21, 3.18, 5,14, and 5.78, respectively) reached the expected grade levels (1, 3, 5, and 7, respectively). For example, approximately 84% of the second-graders and 74% of the fourth-graders had reached the expected or higher grade level performance. The third-, fifth-, and seventh-graders almost reached the expected grade levels defined by the Japanese cohort. The first-graders were expected to perform at the 5-year-old level, but their average score was that of a child of 4.17 years, making them about one grade level behind those in Japan. The ninth-graders averaged a grade of 6.88, giving them scores more than one grade level lower than the average for students in Japan.

Sentence Patterns.   Table 3.5 shows the results of the sentence patterns test (with "Grade" indicated across the top of the table), and Appendix A shows the results visually. The highest grade level attainable in this test is

TABLE 3.4
Japanese Vocabulary Ability: Grade Level
by Performance Grade Level

Grade	1		2		3		4		5		6		7		8		9	
Level	n	%	n	%	n	%	n	%	n	%	n	%	n	%	n	%	n	%
3 yrs.	37	21.6																
4 yrs.	68	39.8																
5 yrs.	**66**	**38.6**																
N/A[a]			28	15.6	23	12.2			1	.6			1	.6				
1			**99**	**55.3**	80	42.3	6	3.1	6	3.4								
2			38	21.2	**52**	**27.5**	45	23.1	23	13.1	1	.6						
3			14	7.8	22	11.6	**77**	**39.5**	58	33.1	24	13.9	8	5.0	1	.8	1	.7
4					8	4.2	50	25.6	**49**	**28.9**	62	35.8	48	30.2	11	8.4	14	10.3
5					4	2.1	12	6.2	18	10.3	**28**	**16.2**	28	17.6	21	16.0	28	20.6
6							2	1.0	10	5.7	19	11.0	**18**	**11.3**	25	19.1	22	16.2
7							2	1.0	1	.6	11	6.4	23	14.5	**14**	**10.7**	20	14.7
8							1	.5	3	1.7	21	12.1	17	10.7	28	21.4	**16**	**11.8**
9									6	3.4	2	1.2	2	1.3	14	10.7	14	10.3
10+											5	2.9	14	8.8	17	13.0	21	15.4
Total	171	100.0	179	100.0	189	100.0	195	100.0	175	100.0	173	100.0	159	100.0	162	100.0	136	100.0
Mean	4.17 (yrs. old)		1.21		1.60		3.18		3.75		5.14		5.78		7.02		6.88	

[a] "N/A" indicates that test results are immeasurable due to the fact that there is no scoring scale or for other reasons. For example, in the case of 2nd graders, if their scores were below the 1st grade level, they were categorized as N/A "immeasurable."

TABLE 3.5
Sentence Pattern Comprehension: Grade Level
by Performance Grade Level

Grade Level	1 n	1 %	2 n	2 %	3 n	3 %	4 n	4 %	5 n	5 %	6 n	6 %	7 n	7 %	8 n	8 %	9 n	9 %
N/A[a]							4	2.1									1	.7
1	150	88.2	163	91.1	148	78.3	114	58.5	87	49.7	74	42.8	49	30.8	26	19.8	29	21.3
2	4	2.4	4	2.2	14	7.9	15	7.7	4	2.3	8	4.6	12	7.5	5	3.8	2	1.5
3	7	4.1	5	2.8	7	3.7	22	11.3	25	14.3	24	13.9	22	13.8	14	10.7	17	12.5
4	1	.6	2	1.1	4	2.1	13	6.7	18	10.3	13	7.5	11	6.9	6	4.6	6	4.4
5	2	1.2	1	.6	4	2.1	8	4.1	9	5.1	8	4.6	4	2.5	10	7.6	12	8.8
6+	6	3.5	4	2.2	11	5.8	19	9.7	32	18.3	46	26.6	61	38.4	70	53.4	69	50.7
TOTAL	191	100.0	179	100.0	189	100.0	195	100.0	175	100.0	173	100.0	159	100.0	131	100.0	136	100.0
Mean	1.35		1.25		1.59		2.13		2.74		3.06		3.59		4.37		4.28	

[a]"N/A" indicates that the test scores were not measurable due to incorrect use of the answer sheet or not completing the test.

the sixth grade level. Therefore, even junior high school students who obtain a perfect score are still categorized as sixth grade level. As Table 3.5 and Appendix A indicate, the great majority of the lower elementary level students (i.e., first-, second-, and third-graders) scored at the first grade level, although some of them reached higher levels. As the students advanced in grade level, their understanding of the sentence patterns increased gradually. However, there were quite a few junior high students (seventh-, eighth-, and ninth-graders) whose scores were still at the lower grade levels, creating a bimodal distribution.

Particles.   Table 3.6 shows the results of the particles test (with "Grade" indicated across the top of the table), and Appendix B shows the results visually. As in the case of sentence patterns, the measurable levels were limited from the first grade to the sixth grade for this test. Therefore, it was not possible to judge the exact levels of the second-graders whose levels were below their expected grade levels, and the junior high students' performances could be compared only with those of the sixth-graders' average in Japan. Nevertheless, it was clear that the majority of the students' abilities to use particles remained at the first and the second grade levels until they were in the fifth grade. When they reached the sixth grade, students made a dramatic leap and nearly one half of the students (46.8%) reached the fifth grade level or higher, the expected grade level for this group. It should be noted, however, that 17 out of 136 students (12.5%) among the ninth-graders still remained at the first and second grade levels of proficiency for their use of particles.

Kanji.   Table 3.7 shows the results of the *kanji* test (with "Grade" indicated across the top of the table), and Appendix C is a visual representation of the results in terms of three performance levels (i.e., above the expected level, the expected level, and below the expected level) for each grade level. Table 3.7 and Appendix C indicate that the great majority of the students up to the fourth grade maintained their expected grade level or above in *kanji* learning (e.g., third-graders, 90.9% and fourth-graders, 80.4%). It is also apparent that the fifth-graders who were at the expected fourth grade level or above dropped to 55.2%. By the sixth grade and above, around half of the students had reached their expected grade levels or above. However, in the ninth grade, only slightly more than one third of the students had reached that level. At the same time, there were quite a few students whose *kanji* abilities remained at two or more grade levels lower than their expected ones, polarizing their distributions.

English Vocabulary.   Table 3.8 shows the results of the English vocabulary test (with "Grade" indicated across the top of the table). The English

TABLE 3.6
Correct Particle Selection: Grade Level
by Performance Grade Level

Grade Level	2[a]		3		4		5		6		7		8		9	
Level	n	%	n	%	n	%	n	%	n	%	n	%	n	%	n	%
N/A[b]					1	.5										
1	167	93.3	159	84.1	91	46.7	63	36.0	28	16.2	20	12.6	10	7.6	11	8.1
2	8	4.5	12	6.3	38	19.5	25	14.3	21	12.1	18	11.3	5	3.8	6	4.4
3	3	1.7	9	4.8	26	13.3	20	11.4	28	16.2	17	10.7	15	11.5	8	5.9
4	1	.6	5	2.6	16	8.2	22	12.6	15	8.7	15	9.4	11	8.4	19	14.0
5			2	1.1	11	5.6	18	10.3	21	12.1	19	11.9	13	9.9	14	10.3
6+			2	1.1	12	.5	27	15.4	60	34.7	70	44.0	77	58.8	78	57.4
Total	179	100.0	189	100.0	195	100.0	175	100.0	173	100.0	159	100.0	131	100.0	136	100.0
Mean	1.10		1.33		2.25		2.93		3.92		4.29		4.85		4.86	

[a]As discussed in the main text, the particle test was administered to the students in the 2nd grade and up.
[b]"N/A" indicates that the test score was not measurable because the student used the answer sheet incorrectly.

proficiency levels of the students at *hoshuukoo* as measured by an English vocabulary test were quite high but the distributions varied. This tendency was most evident among upper elementary and junior high students. English proficiency at grade level or above was the case for 82.1% of the seventh-graders, 83.5% of the eighth-graders, and 89.6% of the ninth-graders. The main reason for such variation probably lies in the students' arrival in the United States at various stages of their lives.

Relationship Between Japanese and English Academic Language Abilities. It is imperative that elementary and junior high school students acquire academic language ability appropriate to grade level in order to absorb knowledge and develop the critical thinking skills appropriate to their age. Table 3.9 shows the degree of "bilingual-ness" of the students at *hoshuukoo* based on their Japanese and English proficiency. Japanese or English ability no lower than two grade levels below their grade level is considered as having "sufficient proficiency" in academic language, and Japanese or English ability lower than three grade levels below grade level is regarded as having "insufficient proficiency" in academic language.[9]

Table 3.10 shows the distribution of students when divided according to Cummins' (1979, 1984) categories discussed earlier. The divisions include: (a) "proficient bilingual" (those who possess grade appropriate level or higher proficiency in both languages); (b) "partial bilingual" (those whose proficiency in one language is at the appropriate grade level or higher but the proficiency of the other language is lower than the grade-appropriate level); and, (c) "limited bilingual" (those whose language proficiencies in both languages are lower than the grade-appropriate level).

Tables 3.9 and 3.10 show that the ratio of partial bilinguals who are stronger in English increases as the grade level advances, and that the ratio of partial bilinguals who are stronger in Japanese is small throughout all grade levels.

Table 3.9 indicates that only 1% of students had not acquired either language at the grade-appropriate level, that is, only six students out of 597 students from Grades 6 to 9. However, this number does not include borderline cases whose proficiency in one language was rated at more than two grade levels below and in the other language, at one or two grade levels below. On the other hand, Table 3.9 shows that almost 7% of fourth-graders (and higher grades) were judged to have lower proficiencies than that of their grade level in both languages.

---

[9]This division was made following the observation by Ono (2002) that students whose academic language ability stays at a level no more than two grades lower than their own (e.g., the language ability of the third grade and above for students at the fifth grade) are able to keep up with the academic work at school.

TABLE 3.7

Ability to Read Kanji: Grade Level by Performance Grade Level

Grade	2[a]		3		4[b]		5		6		7		8		9	
Level	n	%	n	%	n	%	n	%	n	%	n	%	n	%	n	%
N/A[c]					2	1.0	2	1.1	52	30.1	15	9.6	27	20.3	31	23.1
1	70	39.1	17	9.1												
2	105	58.7	120	64.5	36	18.6	22	12.6								
3	4	2.2	34	18.3	107	55.2	54	31.0	28	16.2	27	17.2				
4			14	7.5	34	17.5	53	30.5	43	24.9	38	24.2	18	13.5	25	18.7
5			1	.5	10	5.2	29	16.7	32	18.5	36	22.8	30	22.6	14	10.4
6					4	2.1	11	6.3	10	5.8	24	15.3	17	12.8	18	13.4
7					1	.5	0	0	8	4.6	11	7.0	22	16.5	13	9.7
8							3	1.7			5	3.2	8	6.0	8	6.0
9											1	.6	11	8.3	25	18.7
10+																
Total	179	100.00	186	100.0	194	100.0	174	100.0	173	100.0	157	100.0	133	100.0	134	100.0
Mean Grade Level	1.63		2.26		3.14		3.75		3.77		5.25		5.62		5.68	

[a]As discussed in the main text, the kanji test was administered to the students in the 2nd grade and up.

[b]In this table, for 4th-graders and above, students whose performance grade levels were two grade levels below the expected grade (grades 4, 6, and 8) or three levels below the expected grade (grades 5, 7, and 9) were grouped together. For instance, for 6th-graders, 52 students, 30.1% of the 6th-graders, were at the performance grade levels 3 or below.

[c]A few students whose performance was not measurable due to mistaken use of the answer sheet or incomplete tests are also included in this group.

TABLE 3.8
English Vocabulary Ability: Grade Level
by Performance Grade Level

Grade Level	3[a] N	%	4 N	%	5 N	%	6 N	%	7 N	%	8 N	%	9 N	%
N/A[b]	53	28.2	28	14.4	25	14.4	11	6.4	8	5.1	7	5.3	3	2.2
3	56	29.8	36	18.6	19	10.9	12	6.9	12	7.6	6	4.5	3	2.2
4	22	11.7	14	7.2	11	6.3	7	4.0	1	.6	0	0	0	0
5	24	12.8	22	11.3	12	6.9	4	2.3	7	4.5	4	3.0	2	1.5
6	33	17.6	34	17.5	18	10.3	11	6.4	12	7.6	5	3.8	2	1.5
7			60	30.9	24	13.8	24	13.9	15	9.6	8	6.0	4	3.0
8					65	37.4	60	34.7	31	19.7	22	16.5	20	14.9
9							44	25.4	21	13.4	9	6.8	10	7.5
10									50	31.8	11	8.3	16	11.9
11											61	45.9	49	36.6
12+													25	18.7
Total	188	100.0	194	100.0	174	100.0	173	100.0	157	100.0	133	100.0	134	100.0
Mean	3.05		4.63		5.50		6.90		7.57		8.74		9.76	

[a]As discussed in the main text, the particle test was administered to the students in the 3rd grade and up.
[b]"NA" indicates that the test scores were either below the lowest measurable grade level or other problems (e.g., incomplete tests). In this test, the lowest English performance grade level is the 3rd grade and below it is immeasurable (N/A). For instance, in the case of 5th graders, they can be measured as "sufficient as an academic language" if their scores are at the 3rd performance grade level, but below it all becomes "immeasurable."

TABLE 3.9
Level of Bilingualism for English and Japanese as
Academic Languages, by Grade Level J = Japanese; E = English

Category[a] Grade Level	J / E n	%	J / e n	%	j / E n	%	j / e n	%	J/ (N/A) n	%	j / (N/A) n	%
6–9	440	73.3	46	7.7	105	17.6	6	1.0				
9	71	53.0	7	5.2	55	41.0	1	0.7				
8	101	75.9	12	9.0	19	14.3	1	0.8				
7	122	77.7	18	11.5	15	9.6	2	1.3				
6	145	84.4	9	5.2	16	9.2	2	1.2				
5	132	75.9			15	7.7			18	10.3	9	5.2
4	161	82.6			4	2.1			29	14.9	1	9.4
3	130	69.1			5	2.7			46	24.5	7	3.7

[a]J and E refer to sufficient proficiency in Japanese and English, respectively, in terms of academic language (no lower than two grade levels below grade level), and j and e refer to insufficient proficiency as academic language (lower than three grade levels below grade level). Thus, J/E indicates sufficient proficiency in both languages, J/e indicates sufficient proficiency in Japanese but insufficient proficiency in English, j/E indicates sufficient proficiency in English but insufficient proficiency in Japanese, and j/e indicates insufficient proficiency in both Japanese and English. N/A refers to nonmeasurable proficiency in English (see footnote 9).

TABLE 3.10
Types of Bilingualism

Grade	4		5		6		7		8		9		Total	
Type	n	%	n	%	n	%	n	%	n	%	n	%	n	%
PB	121	62.1	65	36.9	66	38.2	59	37.6	56	42.1	45	33.3	412	42.5
EB	45	23.1	65	36.9	77	44.5	70	44.6	55	41.4	75	55.6	387	39.5
JB	23	11.8	22	12.5	20	11.6	15	9.5	17	12.8	6	4.4	103	10.6
LB	6	3.1	24	13.6	10	5.8	13	8.3	5	3.8	9	6.7	67	6.9
Total	195	100.1	176	99.9	173	100.1	157	100.0	133	100.1	135	100.0	969	99.9

PB = Proficient Bilingual (attained age-appropriate level or higher proficiency in both English and Japanese)

EB = English Dominant Partial Bilingual (attained age-appropriate level or higher proficiency in English, but not in Japanese)

JB = Japanese Dominant Partial Bilingual (attained age-appropriate level or higher proficiency in Japanese, but not in English)

LB = Limited Bilingual (attained age-appropriate level of proficiency in neither English nor Japanese) Categorization devised by Cummins (1984, p. 59).

Relationship Between the Length of Stay in the United States and Proficiency in the Two Languages

Table 3.11 shows, for each grade level, the correlations between the length of stay in the United States and scores of Japanese and English tests (for example, for the first graders, the correlation coefficient between the Japanese vocabulary test scores and the length of the stay in the United States was – .34). The test scores for Japanese vocabulary and *kanji* have a negative correlation with length of stay in the United States, and a positive correlation with English vocabulary. In all the subtests, the correlations became higher at the middle elementary grades. It is also interesting to note that the negative correlations between the length of stay in the United States and acquisition of Japanese grammar (sentence patterns and particles) were highest in the upper elementary grades. These results strongly suggest that the mid- to upper-elementary years are a crucial time for supplementary school students.[10]

Relationship Between Age of Entry into the United States and Proficiency in the Two Languages

Appendix D compares performance grade level means of Japanese and English vocabulary tests at various grade levels for different age-of-entry

---

[10]One of the assumptions of correlational analysis is that two sets of correlated data are normally distributed. As shown earlier, certain sets of data in the present study were not normally distributed (e.g., bimodal distributions, positively or negatively skewed distributions), which may have influenced the present results.

TABLE 3.11
Correlations between Length of Stay in the U.S. and
Language Ability for Each Grade Level

Grade Level	Japanese Vocabulary	Particles	Sentence Structure	Kanji	English Vocabulary
1	−.34**	—	−.18	—	—
2	−.31**	−.07	−.18*	−.20**	—
3	−.25**	−.11	−.17*	−.18*	.27**
4	−.47**	−.35**	−.31**	−.41**	.47**
5	−.46**	−.52**	−.33**	−.47**	.21**
6	−.47**	−.42**	−.40**	−.52**	.42**
7	−.52**	−.26**	−.31**	−.48**	.35**
8	−.40**	−.27**	−.23**	−.45**	.61**
9	−.50**	−.24**	−.30**	−.39**	.42**

**p<0.01, * p<0.05

groups, in order to investigate how the age of entry into the United States (or departure from Japan) influenced their language acquisition development. As shown in Appendix D, the English ability of the children who were raised in Japan and entered the United States when they were 5 or 6 years old exceeded their Japanese ability in the third grade. Those children's Japanese ability did not exceed that for English despite their study at *hoshuukoo*. Those who entered the United States between the ages of 7 and 9 possessed a higher level of English ability than their Japanese ability within 2 years of entry into the United States. Those who entered the United States at the age of 10 or 11 caught up in their English ability by the time they were in the ninth grade, that is, in 3 to 4 years after entry. On the other hand, those who entered the United States after 12 years of age did not improve their English ability to equal their Japanese ability by the time they graduated from junior high school. It is also clear that the higher the age at the time of entry into the United States, the wider the difference between English and Japanese abilities.

DISCUSSION

The current study generated several significant findings. Among all the students in our study, more than half were either American-born or less than 1 year old when they moved to the United States. The majority of students attending the participating *hoshuukoo* proved to be English-dominant bilinguals at the present time.

From about the fifth or sixth grade in elementary school, the levels of Japanese tended to separate into both high and low extremes. Students at the low extreme were mainly American-born or long-term residents who grew up in the English-speaking environment. Because these students are found to possess equal or higher English ability compared to the general English-speaking population in the United States, they would presumably have no problem acquiring necessary academic information using English, but some of them do have problems with their Japanese. Therefore, based on these findings, it is reasonable to assume that the content of current *hoshuukoo* curricula and instruction may not be appropriate for these English-dominant students.

Japanese ability started to differentiate approximately from the fourth grade, and the difference became more pronounced as the grade level increased. On the whole, at lower grades, both Japanese and English abilities were at adequate levels for their age or grade with minor differences, but from the fourth grade on, the differences in their abilities became increasingly obvious. It may be the case that the content of school materials requires more abstract cognitive skills and becomes linguistically demanding from around this age period, and that the amount of studying, reading, and Japanese usage at home is directly affecting the language levels of students.

Although the acquisition levels of particles and sentence patterns differ more and more significantly in the later grades, some junior high school students remain as low as the first or second grade. Although Japanese students living in Japan normally acquire grammatical skills such as particles and sentence patterns by the end of the sixth grade, some students at *hoshuukoo* have not acquired them even at the junior high level. This clearly requires that they be treated as speakers of Japanese as a heritage or foreign language and not so-called native speakers. This consequently means that the current *hoshuukoo* curricula to teach Japanese as a national language are not appropriate for them to achieve higher proficiency levels in Japanese, and instruction to teach Japanese as a second or foreign language including Japanese grammar is necessary.

Based on her research into the Japanese and English abilities of students at *hoshuukoo* in Canada, Nakajima (1998) found that the students who entered Canada between the ages of 7 and 9 acquired English faster than any other group, and those who went overseas between ages of 10 and 12 took longer to reach the grade-appropriate level. The performance data collected in the present study from English and Japanese vocabulary tests from the equivalent age groups (7–9 years old, and 10–12 years at the time of entry) tend to support her findings (see Appendix D). There are two possible explanations for these results: First, it was more difficult for the 10–12 year old entry group to obtain higher test scores in English than the 7- to 9-year-old entry group because the older students were expected to perform tasks that require higher linguistic skills (Nakajima, 1998, p. 136). Second, the 7- to 9-year old entry group was probably first exposed to English during the critical period of learning a language, which occurs around 8–9 years of age (Groater, 1976). For this reason, it is possible that the 7- to 9-year old entry group could learn English as a second language faster than the 10–12-year-old entry group.

Generally speaking, students in our research had high English ability. There were many proficient bilinguals with both English and Japanese ability adequate for their grade level, although their ability in both languages may not be equally high. On the other hand, there were a small number of students who may be categorized as "limited bilingual" (or "semi-lingual") or who appeared on the verge of becoming such. Students in this category urgently need some kind of supplementary instruction or assistance.

There is a growing call to shift from the "the national language" to the Japanese language as a heritage or second language and also to revise *hoshuukoo* curricula to meet the needs of learners. We believe that this study sufficiently supports that assertion with concrete data concerning the language background and levels of students. Some *hoshuukoo* are already undertaking curricular modification in an effort to accommodate the needs of students (e.g., Calder, 2003; Sato, 2003).

CONCLUSION AND IMPLICATIONS

The *hoshuukoo* has an important mission to teach subjects using Japanese as a native tongue to prepare students for the time when they return home. Our analysis revealed that students have a good chance of remaining reasonably bilingual if they continue to study Japanese at *hoshuukoo*. We believe that our study also reaffirms another important mission of *hoshuukoo* to train English-dominant students to become "internationalized" citizens by improving their Japanese as a HL. At the same time, our study suggests that *hoshuukoo* need to deal effectively with students who have not acquired Japanese or English to a level sufficient for them to use either as an academic language.

We should not underestimate the significance of understanding basic language ability among students who are living in an English–Japanese bilingual environment if we want them to progress normally. It would be a good idea to continue this kind of study longitudinally at regular intervals for a better understanding of the most salient problems and their solutions. Moreover, additional tests focusing on other language functions, such as demonstratives, presupposition, or sentence comprehension, would be helpful for providing more appropriate language training to students.

We hope that this study provides some direction in formulating future educational policy and choosing appropriate curricula and instruction for students at *hoshuukoo*. We would also like to add that educational support should be considered not only the school's responsibility but the home's responsibility as well. The language environment at home and the students' own motivation and willingness to learn are also integral parts of language learning. These critical dimensions of language acquisition call for detailed discussion among specialists in the future.

ACKNOWLEDGMENTS

We would like to show our deepest gratitude to Professor Hiroshi Ono of the Educational Media Center, who graciously approved our use of the tests developed by his team. We would also like to thank the participating *hoshuukoo* that shared their valuable data with us for this study.

APPENDICES

APPENDIX A

Sentence Pattern Comprehension by Grade Level

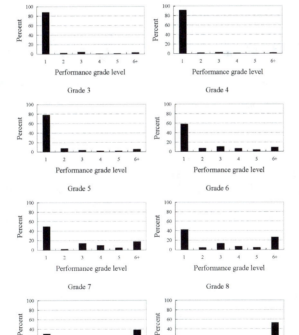

APPENDIX B
Ability to Choose Correct Particles by Grade Level

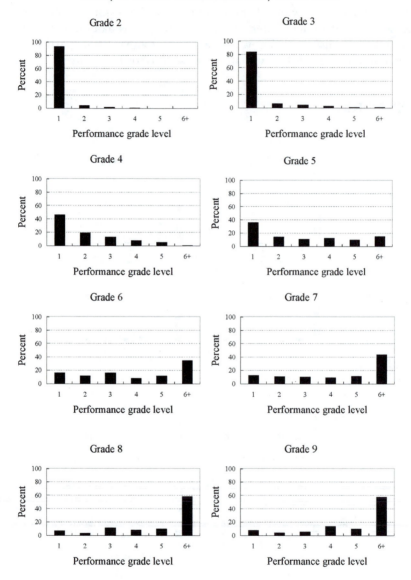

APPENDIX C
Ability to Read Kanji by Grade Level

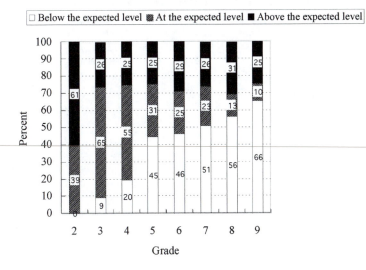

APPENDIX D
Comparison of Performance Grade Level Means for Japanese and English Vocabulary Tests at Various Grades by Age-of-Entry Groups

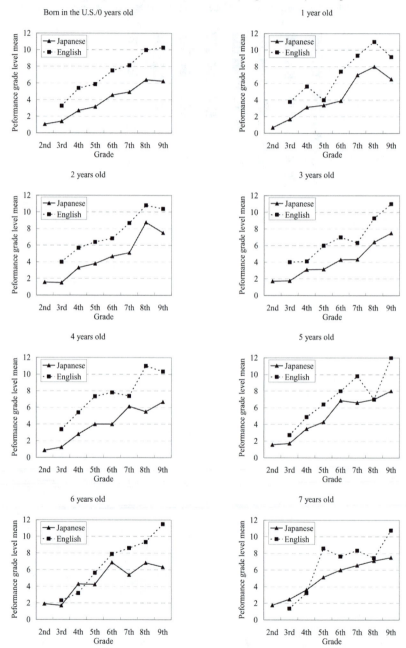

Appendix D   *(Continued)*

8 years old

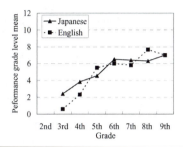

9 years old

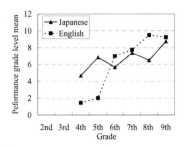

10 years old

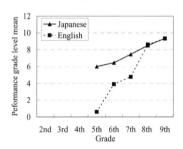

11 years old

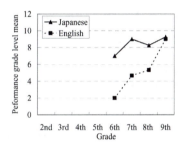

12 years old

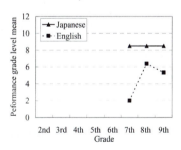

REFERENCES

Calder, Y. (2003, October). *Hoshuukoo ni okeru keishoogo kyooiku–Purinsuton nihongo gakkoo karikyuramu no nagare* [Curriculum building at Princeton community Japanese language school]. Paper presented at the conference of Japanese language schools in the United States, Los Angeles.

Cummins, J. (1979). Linguistic interdependence and the educational development of bilingual children. *Review of Educational Research, 49*, 222–251.

Cummins, J. (1984). Bilingualism and cognitive functioning. In S. Shapson & V. D'Oyley (Eds.), *Bilingual and multicultural education: Canadian perspectives* (pp. 55–67). Clevedon, UK: Multilingual Matters.

Cummins, J. (1991). Language development and academic learning. In L. Malave & G. Duquette (Eds.), *Language, culture, and cognition* (pp. 161–175). Clevendon, UK: Multilingual Matters.

Cummins, J. (1996). *Negotiating identities: Education for empowerment in a diverse society.* Los Angeles, CA: California Association for Bilingual Education.

Douglas, M. (2002). *Analyses of learning goals of Japanese language textbooks for native speakers.* Retrieved April 6, 2005, from http://www.colorado.edu/ealld/atj/SIG/heritage/douglas_kyokasho.html

Douglas, M., Kataoka, H., & Kishimoto, T. (2003). *Keishoogokoo to nihongo hoshuukoo ni okeru gakushuusha no gengo haikei choosa* [Survey of the language background of students at hoshuukoo and Japanese language schools]. *CRIE Review of International Education, 1*, 1–13.

Fujioka, N. (2003). *Keishoogo gakushuusha no hoshuu jugyookoo seikatsu ni kansuru iken to nihongo deno gakushuu seiseki* [Heritage learners' opinions of their experience at hoshuukoo and their academic performance in Japanese language]. *CAJLE, 5*, 89–102.

Furuya-Wise, E. (1999). Roles and responsibilities, and the special context of the Japanese Saturday school. In A. Yamada-Yamamoto & B. Richards (Eds.), *Japanese children abroad–Cultural, educational, and language issues* (pp. 101–105). Clevedon, UK: Multilingual Matters.

Groater, W. A. (1976). *Bairingarizumu ni tsuite* [About bilingualism]. *Gengo, 10*, 2–8.

Hayashibe, H. (1999). *Gengoryoku no hyooka to tesuto no kaihatsu* [Language assessment and test development]. In H. Ono (Ed.), *Bairingaru no kenkyuu* (pp. 29–37). Tokyo, Japan: Center for College Entrance Examination.

Hayashibe, H., Shigemasu, M., Ichikawa, M. Makino, Y., & Ono, H. (1988). *Nihongoryoku no tagenteki hyooka no kokoromi* [Trial of multi-perspective assessment of Japanese language proficiency]. *Proceedings of the 30th Conference of Japan Psychology Association.*

Igawa, C. (1999, November). *Reports on National Conference of Japanese Heritage Language Education in the U.S.* Paper presented at TJSC Workshop, Santa Monica, CA.

Japan Ministry of Foreign Affairs. (2004). *Kaigai zairyuu-hoojin ninzuu kensa tookee* [Statistics of number of Japanese residents living overseas]. Retrieved December 28, 2004, from http://www.mofa.go.jp

Kado, Y., Serizawa, C., Nakanishi, Y., & Sakai, A. (1988). *Kikokushijo to nihongo kyooiku* [Japanese children who have returned from living overseas and their Japanese language education]. *Nihongo kyooiku, 66*, 110–119.

Kaigaishijo kyooiku. (2003). *Tokushuu: Hoshuu jugyookoo no genten to tenboo* [A special issue: The essence and prospect of hoshuukoo]. *Gengo, 9*, 4–9.

Kataoka, H., Koshiyama, Y., & Shibata, S. (2003, October). *Keishoo nihongo washa no gengoteki tokuchoo towa: Yori kookateki na karikyuramu no hensee ni mukete* [Language characteristics of Japanese heritage speakers: Moving towards more effective language curriculum development]. Paper presented at the Conference of Japanese Language Schools in the U.S., Los Angeles, CA.

Kishimoto, T. (2003). *Hoshukoo ni okeru keishoogo kyooiku: Greenville hoshuukoo no rei* [Heritage language education at hoshuukoo: Case study of Greenville hoshuukoo]. *ATJ Occasional Paper*, 23–24.

Koshiyama, Y. (2000, October). *Japanization through Americanization: Acculturation of shin-issei, post-war Japanese immigrants in the U.S.* Paper presented at the Annual Western Conference of the Association for Asian Studies, Long Beach, CA.

Koshiyama Y., & Shibata S. (2002, November). *Characteristics and salient factors related to the acquisition and maintenance of Japanese as a heritage language.* Paper presented at the ACTFL Convention, Boston, MA.

Kubo, K. (2003). *Nichi-ei bairingaru oyobi nihongo monoringaru kookoosei no setsumeibun ni okeru "ta"-kei no yoosoo* [An aspect of "ta"-pattern in explanatory sentences of Japanese-English bilingual and Japanese monolingual high school students]. *CRIE Review of International Education, 1,* 44–54.

Lighthouse. (2000). *Tokushuu: Nihongo no keishoogo kyooiku* [Special issue: Japanese heritage language education], *265,* 15–22.

Matsunaga, S. (2003). Instructional needs of college-level learners of Japanese as a heritage language: Performance-based analyses. *Heritage Language Journal, 1*(1). Retrieved December 30, 2004, from http://www.heritagelanguages.org

Minami, M., Fukuda, S., & Fujiyama, E. (2002). *Goi kakutoku tassei reberu ni okeru dai-ichi gengo to dai-ni gengo no sookansei: Keishoo nihongo no kanten kara no koosatsu* [The relationship between L1 vocabulary acquisition and L2 vocabulary acquisition: From the perspective of Japanese as a heritage language]. Retrieved January 8, 2004, from http://www.colorado.edu/ealld/atj/SIG/heritage/fujiyama.html

Ministry of Education and Science. (2003a). *List of hoshuukoo in North America.* Retrieved January 14, 2004, from http://www.mext.go.jp/a_menu/shotou/clarinet/hschool.html

Ministry of Education and Science. (2003b). *Kaigai no kodomo (gakurei dankai) shuugaku jookyoo* [Japanese school-aged children enrolled overseas at hoshuukoo by region]. Retrieved January 14, 2004, from http://www.mext.go.jp/a_menu/shotou/clarinet/g5.html

Minoura, Y. (1991). *Kodomo no ibunka taiken* [Children's experience in a foreign cultures]. Tokyo: Soosakusha.

Nagasawa, F. (1995). *L1, L2 bairingaru no nihongo bunpoo nooryoku* [Knowledge and skills in Japanese grammar of L1, L2 bilinguals]. *Nihongo kyooiku, 86,* 173–189.

Nakajima, K. (1988). *Nikkei shijo no nihongo kyooiku* [Japanese education for the children of Japanese heritage speakers]. *Nihongo kyooiku, 66,* 137–150.

Nakajima, K. (1998). *Bairingaru kyooiku no hoohoo* [Methods of bilingual education]. Tokyo: Arc.

Nakajima, K. (2002, November). *Keishoo nihongo gakushuusha no kanji shuutoku to kokugo kyookasho* [Acquisition of *kanji* by Japanese heritage learners and Japanese textbooks]. Paper presented at ATJ Seminar, New York, NY.

Oketani, H. (1991). *Bairingaru ni sodatsu nikkei shijo no tame no nihongo kyooiku: Goyoo o megutte* [Japanese education for raising Japanese heritage learners to be bilingual in English-Japanese: Error analyses]. In *Nihongo kyooiku ronsyuu* (pp. 44–53). Tokyo: Gakushuu kenkyuu-usha.

Ono, H. (1989). *Kaigai kikoku jidoo seito no eigo to nihongo goiryoku no henka* [Shift of English and Japanese vocabulary skills among Japanese children and students returning from overseas]. *Ibunkakan kyooiku, 3,* 35–51.

Ono, H. (2002, November). *Nihonjin no bairingaru ikusei ni kansuru bunseki kenkyuu* [Analyses of Japanese bilingual education]. Paper presented at workshop of Teachers of Japanese in Southern California; Santa Monica, CA.

Ono, H., Shigemasu, M., Hayashibe, H., Okazaki, T., Ichikawa, M., & Kinoshita, H. (1989). *Nihongoryoku kensa no kaihatsu* [Development of a Japanese language assessment test]. (Tech. Rep. 6181003). Tokyo: Tokyo Gakugei University.

Sato, G. (2003, November). *Kaigai nihonjin gakkoo/hoshuukoo no kyooiku ni miru "nihonjin" towa* [Considering "Japanese people" in Japanese language schools and hoshuukoo overseas]. Paper presented at Public Symposium of Cultural Research Center of Wako University, Tokyo. Retrieved June 25, 2005, from www.u-gadegei.ac.jp/~sato

The U.S. Frontline. (2003). *Kodomo no kotoba o kangaeru* [Thinking of children's language], *195*, 9–22.

Yamamoto, M. (1991). *Bairingaru: Sono jitsuzoo to mondaiten* [Bilingualism: Its reality and problems]. Tokyo: Taishuukan.

Yamashita, Y. (2003). *Gankyuu idoo to misukyuu ga shimesu nihongo monogatari rikai ni okeru joshi "wa" to "ga" no purosesu ni tsuite: bairingaru no keesu sutadii o tooshite* [Understanding of reading process of particles "wa" and "ga" through eye-movements and miscues: A case study of bilinguals]. *CAJLE, 5*, 103–116.

Chapter 4

Measuring the Japanese Proficiency of Heritage Language Children

Tomomi Hasegawa
University of Hawai`i at Mānoa

WHY DO WE CARE ABOUT LANGUAGE PROFICIENCY MEASUREMENT?

Target language proficiency is often a key variable in many language learning studies (Thomas, 1994). Heritage language (HL) learning studies are no exception and whether proficiency is appropriately measured in those studies needs to be investigated, including the adequacy of using existing proficiency measurement instruments that are not necessarily developed for HL learners (Kondo-Brown, 2003). The same concern applies to HL teaching. Knowing our students' proficiency is important for understanding our students' needs and for designing our curricula and lessons.

In this chapter, I discuss some important issues in HL proficiency measurement, focusing on children who are learning Japanese-as-a-heritage language (JHL). My task presents a challenge because this single topic can be separated into at least three different parts, each of which has not been sufficiently discussed in the proficiency measurement context. First, the degree of bilingualism of heritage learners varies extensively, which creates problems in HL proficiency measurement. Some learners have native-like proficiency in their HL, whereas others have very limited communication skills. HL learners also have language knowledge and abilities that are different from typical classroom language learners (Campbell & Rosenthal, 2000; Kondo-Brown, 2003; Nakajima, 1988; Valdés, 1995). Thus, in measuring HL proficiency, the target population is by no means homogeneous, and in addition, characteristics of HL proficiency may be different from those of second and/or foreign language proficiency (Nakajima, 1988). This discussion of HL proficiency will be relevant for both child and adult HL learners. Second, measuring children's language proficiency is another big challenge. This includes methodological concerns as well as theoretical concerns in defining target language proficiency for children and adolescents of varying ages. The articles reviewed in this chapter target learners from kindergarten through high school.[1] Third, the theories and assumptions about proficiency measurement for English or other European languages may need modification when administered in Japanese, where linguistic and sociolinguistic systems considerably differ from European languages (Tsujimura, 1996). This chapter reviews existing instruments for measuring the Japanese proficiency of Japanese HL children, focusing on the heritage and foreign/second language differences as well as methodological concerns in measuring child language proficiency.

The purposes of this chapter are as follows: (a) to review the available proficiency measurement instruments for JHL children; (b) to report how the reliability and validity of those instruments have been reported; and (c) to discuss possible improvements that could be made in the future.

WHAT IS PROFICIENCY MEASUREMENT?

This chapter focuses on any kind of Japanese language test or assessment procedure designed to tap learners' language knowledge and/or abilities to use the language. This focus also means that I will not limit "proficiency tests" to those that are developed for norm-referenced purposes. In any kind of language proficiency measurement, our two central concerns are whether the measurement is consistent, taking unsystematic measurement

---

[1]It is probably more relevant to refer to high school students as "adolescents" or "young adults" rather than "children"; however, for the sake of simplicity, I use "children" to refer to children and adolescents in kindergarten through high school in this chapter.

errors into account, and whether we are measuring what we are supposed to be measuring and not something else. These two concerns are called reliability and validity, respectively (for more understanding on these two concepts, see Bachman, 1990; Brown, 2005). The reliability and validity of testing instruments are important measurement quality characteristics that we should always keep in mind when developing proficiency measurement instruments or when adopting existing instruments for our own studies. Indeed, we are always responsible for reporting reliability and validity of such instruments when we develop/adopt them.

The articles reviewed in this chapter were selected based on the following two criteria: (a) Japanese language proficiency is measured in some way, and (b) the examinees are children and/or adolescents who are learning JHL[2] (see the Appendix for a table listing the articles and assessment types). Some of the proficiency measurement instruments were not developed originally for measuring HL proficiency, an issue that is taken up in the discussion section.

The articles can be categorized into two types. The first type reports the process and the outcome of the instrument development. The second type reports proficiency as one of the research variables in the studies, for example, correlating proficiency with a psychological factor or length of HL learning. I review these two types of articles, separately, because they differ in the extent to which they discuss the proficiency measurement instrument itself, including instrument descriptions and reliability. The validity of the instruments from both types of the articles will be discussed together in the discussion section.

DEVELOPING PROFICIENCY MEASUREMENT INSTRUMENTS

The articles discussed in this section describe the process and the outcome of developing new proficiency measurement instruments. The three instruments reviewed in this section were developed for children from different learning contexts. The instrument developed by Carpenter, Fujii, and Kataoka (1995) was designed to measure Japanese proficiency of Japanese-as-a-foreign language (JFL) children in Japanese immersion programs; the one by the Canadian Association for Japanese Language Education (CAJLE) targeted JHL children; and the one by Ono et al. (1989) was developed for *kaigai-kikokushijo,* or Japanese overseas and returnee children, who

---

[2]The participants in Ikuta (2001) and Nakajima and Nunes (2001) were Brazilian children who were attending school in Japan and learning Japanese as a second language. In their studies, Portuguese was the HL. Both studies measure Japanese and Portuguese proficiency.

speak Japanese as their native language. If JHL proficiency shares some characteristics with JFL proficiency as well as with the proficiency of native Japanese speakers, all of the three instruments just discussed can potentially serve for the purpose of measuring HL proficiency.

Carpenter et al. (1995) developed and piloted an oral interview procedure for children whose ages were between 5 and 10. Their primary purpose was to assess innovative language programs for children, such as immersion programs. In developing the interview procedure, the authors were extremely careful with child-specific concerns, such as talking with an adult stranger or employing unnatural display questions, for which the interviewer already knows the answer. With these child-specific problems in mind (see Carpenter et al., 1995, for more details), they designed the interview with six subtests: (a) Toybox (3 to 4 minutes), as a warm-up activity and to test comprehension and physical responses; (b) conversation (2 to 3 minutes); (c) information gap (5 to 7 minutes); (d) categorization (2 to 4 minutes), which is intended to elicit language in abstract context; (e) storytelling (0 to 4 minutes); and (f) a classroom role play (2 to 4 minutes) for testing formal and informal use of language. Carpenter et al.'s work seems to be promising; however, it is still a work in progress, and their rating scale still needs development.

The oral interview procedure by CAJLE (2000) was developed for JHL children between 6 and 15 years of age. The interim report for this project can be found in Nakajima, Oketani, and Suzuki (1994). The interview starts with an introduction, and, depending on how the interviewer perceives the child's proficiency level, the interviewer decides how to proceed: if the child seems to be too nervous and/or his/her proficiency is too low to continue the subsequent tasks, activities such as a vocabulary game designed to facilitate relaxation follows. Otherwise, there are three different types of tasks that follow the introduction phase: (a) a task for examining basic listening and response patterns; (b) a role play in which the child's ability to carry on conversation and exchange information is examined; and (c) a cognitive task, which demands explanation and opinion statement. The interviewer uses these activities/tasks in combination, adapting to each child's age and language background, and keeping track of whether the child is or is not able to answer each item. For example, during the introduction phase, if the child is able to greet and say his/her name, the interviewer marks "O (good)," or "X (not good)" if the child fails, or sometimes "◎ (very good)" if the child not only provides an answer but also provides additional information related to the answer. For overall evaluation, the interviewer reports scores in percentage for different types of tasks as well as analytical rating for basic language skills, interaction skills, and cognitive skills. The interview lasts for about 10 minutes, and the results are reported as scores and detailed written evaluation. Both

Carpenter et al. (1995) and CAJLE (2000) failed to report the reliability[3] of their interview procedures.

Whereas the two interview procedures just discussed target oral communication skills, the Japanese test developed by Ono et al. (1989)[4] tests written language knowledge. The test includes the following seven subcategories: vocabulary, Chinese characters (*yomigana*, or how to pronounce Chinese characters), particles, sentence patterns, demonstrative pronouns, understanding presuppositions, and implications. According to Kataoka, Koshiyama, and Shibata (this volume), who used four of the subtests from Ono et al. (1989): the vocabulary section consists of 30 questions (or 45 for Grade 1 children); the sentence pattern section, 39 questions; the particle section, 60 questions; and the Chinese character section, 20 questions. The vocabulary and Chinese character sections have different versions for different grade levels, whereas the sentence pattern and particle sections have only one version across the grade levels. The test format is mostly multiple-choice, as in the following examples from Hayashibe (1999):

Particle (multiple-choice, choose a correct particle)

Panda-( ) akachan-wa totemo chiisai. [Panda-( ) baby-TOPIC very small.]

1. wa, 2. no, 3. o, 4. ni

Sentence pattern (choose a correct picture that the sentence describes.)

One of the pictures shows a raccoon dog that is patting a rabbit and the other shows a rabbit that is patting a raccoon dog.

Tanuki-ga usagi-ni kata-o tatakasete ageta.

[A raccoon dog[5] let a rabbit pat his shoulder.]

The test was originally developed to measure the language proficiency of Japanese children, who have spent significant time outside Japan. Most of

---

[3]Carpenter et al. (1995) is apparently a work in progress. CAJLE (2000) presents complete and detailed interview procedures; however, the authors are not clear about whether or not they are still in the process of analyzing interview rating data in order to report reliability.

[4]Because the original report was not available, information about this instrument is from a preliminary report (Ono et al., 1987); see summaries by Hayashibe (1999) and Kataoka et al. (this volume).

[5]The underlined phrase and word refer to the same entity. Coindexing is very obvious in the Japanese sentence, but not in the English translation.

these children were born to Japanese parents and were planning to come back to Japan, so in that sense we can claim that the test intends to measure Japanese proficiency as a first language (L1). In describing the test by Ono et al. (1989), Kataoka et al. (this volume) say that the test was developed based on Japanese language test data from about 200,000 elementary and junior high school students in Japan and is the most reliable Japanese language proficiency test that is available; however, because the original report was not available for this review, the actual reliability estimate is unknown.

MEASURING PROFICIENCY AS A RESEARCH VARIABLE

In the second type of article, researchers report Japanese language proficiency as a variable in order to examine the relationship between proficiency in Japanese and another language within the same individual (Ikuta, 2001; Kataoka et al., this volume; Minami, Fukuda & Fujiyama, 2002; Nakajima & Nunes, 2001), or to measure the Japanese language proficiency of a specific group of learners (Nakajima, 1988; Nakajima, 2003), or to compare Japanese proficiency between or among different groups of learners (Hayashi, 2003; Nagasawa, 1995; Noro, 1990; Oriyama, 2001), or to relate Japanese proficiency with social and psychological variables (Chinen, 2004). The type(s) of proficiency measurement used in each article and information regarding the reliability of the instruments are summarized in the Appendix. Some of these studies use the instruments introduced in the previous section.

Depending on their research questions, the studies use various numbers of instruments, testing different aspects of language knowledge and/or abilities. Minami et al. (2002) investigated the relationship between L1 and second language (L2) vocabulary knowledge, using the Bilingual Verbal Ability Tests (BVAT; Muños-Sandoval, Cummins, Alvarado & Ruef, 1998). Kataoka et al. (this volume) and Nagasawa (1995) use written Japanese grammar tests. In examining bilingual literacy development, Ikuta (2001) reports developmental indices of writing from Wolfe-Quintero, Inagaki, and Kim (1998). Many of the articles measure multiple aspects of language proficiency. For example, Nakajima (1988) examines the four skills, using the tests that were developed for L1 and L2 Japanese speakers and involving Japanese teachers for L1 and L2 speakers of Japanese for essay rating, and concludes that HL proficiency might be qualitatively different from JFL proficiency. Nakajima and Nunes (2001) use the oral interview procedure developed by CAJLE (2000) and the Test of Acquisition and Maintenance (TOAM), which is reported in Okazaki (2002). Hayashi (2003) reports a writing sample rating, student self-evaluations of the four skills in Japanese and English, as well as the researcher's class observation record; however, the method for quantifying her proficiency data is not clear in the article. Chinen (2004) asks about the four skills in Japanese in her self-assessment questionnaire.

Among the 11 studies reviewed in this section, the studies that report reliability in some way within the articles are Nagasawa (1995) and Nakajima and Nunes (2001). Nagasawa reports split-half reliability (r = .81) for her written grammar test. In reporting interrater reliability for interview rating, Nakajima and Nunes (2001) report correlation coefficients (type not specified; r = .369 ~ .984). It was somewhat disappointing to find that only two studies report the reliability of their proficiency measurements.[6]

One controversial way of proficiency measurement is self-assessment, which is used in Hayashi (2003) and Chinen (2004). The question we need to raise is whether such assessment is a reliable and valid measurement of one's proficiency. Hayashi's self-assessment for English proficiency is from O'Malley and Valdez-Pierce (1996); however, it is not clear what the Japanese version is like.[7] Chinen (2004) includes 19 questions in her proficiency questionnaire asking about her participants' self-perceived Japanese proficiency and makes the questionnaire available as an appendix in her dissertation. The major problems in using self-assessment are that it is not easy to make sure that participants' reports are accurate, especially when used with young children (Valdés & Figueroa, 1994). In Hayashi's case, self-assessment is not the only tool for measuring proficiency, which makes the entire set of proficiency measures more valid than solely relying on self-assessment. Chinen administered the proficiency questionnaire twice with a 6-month interval and reports that there was no significant group mean difference in proficiency self-assessment between the two administrations. However, this does not guarantee consistent self-assessment of individual participants. At any rate, when self-assessment is used, we also need to report the reliability of the instrument and discuss its validity. In addition, we have to ask ourselves how important a proficiency variable is to our research questions and decide if proficiency reported in the form of self-assessment would be good enough to convince readers that our research findings are really trustworthy. When correlating self-assessed proficiency variables and psychological attitudinal variables, they might show high correlations because learners with stronger psychological attitudes such as motivation or ethnic identity are more likely to rate their own proficiency higher, or vice versa, regardless of their actual proficiency.

---

[6]BVAT reliability may be found somewhere; however, because the instrument and its related information were not available, I was not able to track down this information. Minami et al. (2002) do not provide information on BVAT reliability.

[7]The author states that the Japanese version conforms to the guidelines of the Japanese Ministry of Education; however, it is not clear which guidelines she is referring to and how the guidelines were applied to the proficiency self-assessment instrument.

One more issue that has to be taken into consideration is practicality. When we have to measure the language proficiency of hundreds or thousands of participants, as Kataoka et al. (this volume) did, rating each participants' essay and interview is too time consuming, and using multiple-choice and/or fill-in formats of proficiency measurement can save a lot of time.

DISCUSSION

Based on the information just noted about the existing instruments that have been used to measure Japanese language proficiency of Japanese heritage children, I discuss the issues that were raised at the beginning of this chapter. I start with the discussion of the reliability and validity of the instruments, and conclude the chapter by discussing possibilities in HL and child proficiency measurement.

Reliability

Just like any language proficiency measurement, child HL proficiency measurement needs to be reliable. Unfortunately, little information was available for examining the reliability of the instruments utilized in the research reviewed here. Although we have to acknowledge difficulty in administering child proficiency measurement as well as controlling factors that usually do not influence adult proficiency measurement, child proficiency measurements should be as reliable as adult proficiency measurements, and such information should be made available to readers.

Test reliability can be reported in different ways, many of which are introduced in Brown (2005). Closed-response tests, such as the written grammar test used in Nagasawa (1995) and the Japanese test developed by Ono et al. (1989), do not require subjective judgment, because the items in these types of tests force test takers to choose the answers that they think are correct. In other words, teachers and researchers have answer keys and just need to check whether the answers are correct or incorrect. Split-half reliability reported in Nagasawa (1995) is one way of reporting internal-consistency reliability of such instruments. Other types of instruments require more subjective judgments, such as ratings of oral interviews or writing samples. Nakajima and Nunes (2001) report interrater reliability to offer evidence of the consistency of their raters' ratings.

It is important that researchers report the reliability of their instruments from their own administrations. When adopting a standardized test or a previously developed and administered test (e.g., Ono et al.'s [1989] test used in Kataoka et al., this volume), the reliability estimates from the original administration are worth reporting; however, we should also keep in mind that test reliability and validity are not about the test itself, but about the test when administered to a specific population (Brown, 2005). Thus, reliable and valid tests for native speakers of Japanese or JFL learners may not be reliable and valid for the HL learner population.

Validity

Reliability is important, but is not enough. We also need to think about the validity of our proficiency measurement instruments. For example, the reliability estimates which are typically above .95 for the *Nihongo Nooryoku Shiken,* or Japanese Language Proficiency Test,[8] seems to be high enough to call it a reliable test; however, is it a valid instrument for testing the Japanese proficiency of a child HL learner who has good oral communication skills but has never learned how to read and write in Japanese? The answer is obviously "no," because *Nihongo Nooryoku Shiken* is not designed to measure oral proficiency of any kind nor is it intended for measuring the Japanese proficiency of young children. As pointed out by some of the articles reviewed in this chapter, we also have to take the characteristics of HL proficiency into consideration (CAJLE, 2000; Nakajima, 1988; Nakajima et al., 1994).

Because almost none of the articles reviewed in this chapter explicitly discuss validity, the best we can do is to critically examine each instrument carefully. One way of doing this is to see what theoretical constructs of proficiency the researchers are referring to, and how such constructs are operationalized in each proficiency measurement instrument. Many of the articles refer to the distinction between basic interpersonal communicative skills (BICS) and cognitive academic language proficiency (CALP), and/or the Common Underlying Proficiency, both proposed by Cummins (1979, 1981) (CAJLE, 2000; Hayashi, 2003; Ikuta, 2001; Minami et al., 2002; Nakajima, 1988; Nakajima et al., 1994; Nakajima & Nunes, 2001; Okazaki, 2002). As a matter of fact, Cummins' models are the only theoretical depictions of language proficiency explicitly referred to in the articles reviewed in this chapter.[9] Cummins' models illustrate the different timescales that L2 children need to acquire BICS and CALP and how bilingual children's knowledge of L1 and L2 are interrelated. Cummins (2000) extends the discussion and argues that academic language is a different register of the

---

[8]*Nihongo Nooryoku Shiken* is a widely used paper-and-pencil Japanese proficiency test for adult learners of Japanese. According to Japan Foundation (2004), the reliability estimates for *Nihongo Nooryoku Shiken* were always above .95 (Cronbach alpha) during the period of 1997–2002.

[9]For commonly cited models of language proficiency of adult second/foreign language learners, see Canale (1983), Bachman (1990), and so on.

language that L2 children need to acquire, even after attaining oral fluency. I hope this line of research will help us construct valid child HL proficiency measurement instruments in the future, especially at advanced and near-native levels.

In order to discuss validity of proficiency measurement instruments, we first need to understand what the researchers intend to measure with the instruments. In the following two cases, the authors are trying to measure very specific aspects of language proficiency. Nakajima (2003) measures free *kanji* production by asking Grades 4–7 children to write down as many *kanji*, or Chinese characters, as possible in 10 minutes, and reports the number of *kanji* that were produced as a measure of ability to use *kanji*. However, it is not clear from the article how the tests were scored, especially how imperfectly written *kanji* were treated. The author merely points out that the children needed training in *kanji* writing.[10] Here, what we need to clarify in terms of validity is what we mean by productive knowledge of or ability to use *kanji*. How accurate, for example, do HL learners need to be for declaring that they have *kanji* productive abilities? Moreover, does being able to write *kanji* mean that the children know the meaning as well?[11] This is not a simple question to answer, but it illustrates well the sorts of issues that should be raised when examining validity. In other words, what do we mean by *kanji* proficiency?

Another instrument that measures a very specific aspect of language is the BVAT used in Minami et al. (2002). If one believes that vocabulary knowledge is a good indicator of academic language proficiency, as Cummins (2000) discusses, one can justify focusing on vocabulary knowledge to estimate one's overall academic language proficiency. However, Minami et al. discuss one limitation to using the BVAT saying that the instrument is designed for investigating bilingual proficiency, in which English is the second language, and might not be valid for JHL children, whose primary language is English (Minami et al., 2002). This is a good example of discussing the validity of the instrument within a study, and through this type of discussion by the authors, readers can more easily evaluate the instrument as well as how it was used in the study.

Some studies use only written mode proficiency measurement, such as written grammar tests or writing sample scoring (Ikuta, 2001; Kataoka et al., this volume; Nagasawa, 1995). Kataoka et al. use the Japanese test developed

---

[10]Table 2 in Nakajima (2003) shows the number of incorrect *kanji*. The question here is what the scorer counted as incorrect. Is missing one minor stroke counted as an incorrect answer? Or, as long as we can tell which *kanji* a child tried to write, does it count as correct? According to endnote 7 of the article, the author and the scorer are different in this study.

[11]The author points out the similar question in discussing knowledge of *kanjukugo*, or *kanji* idioms (Nakajima, 2003, p. 13).

by Ono et al. (1989). One of the concerns in measuring HL children's language proficiency is that some of them lack training in the written mode of their HL. When using written tests, the researchers should make it clear that they are not extending the results to oral proficiency and make sure that children are receiving enough writing and reading training. Ikuta's participants were attending public junior high school in Japan, and she was clearly interested in writing proficiency, which she claimed was a part of the academic language proficiency that she discussed in her study. In Kataoka et al's and Nagasawa's cases, the children were attending *Nihonjin gakkoo/ hoshuukoo*,[12] or schools primarily for oversea Japanese children, where the curriculum was based on that of elementary and secondary schools in Japan, thus we can assume that the children had been trained in writing and reading to some extent. However, it should be emphasized that the results from written mode measurements must be interpreted as measures of overall language proficiency of HL children only with extreme caution.

Many studies use multiple proficiency measurement instruments, both in written and spoken modes. For example, Nakajima (1988) included two types of reading tests, one developed for children who speak Japanese as a native language and the other for college-level JFL learners, as well as writing sample rating and oral interviews. When we are interested in our examinees' overall proficiency, it is desirable to measure all four skills, or as many skills as possible. This is especially true when measuring HL proficiency, because many learners have unbalanced proficiency in productive and receptive skills. Also in the case of the three East-Asian languages being discussed in this volume, the difference in orthography often makes it difficult for English-dominant speakers to become highly competent in the written mode of their HL.

Measuring Heritage Language Proficiency

The discussion in this subsection applies to HL learners of any age. Among the articles that I reviewed in this chapter, types of HL learners vary from studies to studies. Although all the participants in those studies fall into the HL learner category their language learning environments and the goals of their Japanese language learning may be quite different from each other. For example, Noro's (1990) two groups of learners were children of

---

[12]*Nihonjin gakkoo* meets everyday and covers all of the academic subjects that are taught in elementary and secondary schools in Japan. *Hoshuukoo* meets only on Saturday, thus sometimes referred to as a Japanese Saturday School, and covers only the gist of main academic subjects such as language art. The children at *hohuukoo* attend local schools on weekdays, usually in English in U.S. Japanese is the medium of instruction both at *Nihonjin gakkoo* and *hoshuukoo*.

Japanese immigrants, who were planning to stay in Canada, and children of Japanese business people, who would eventually go back to Japan. For the former group, English is probably their stronger language and Japanese is more likely their L2, whereas for the latter group, no matter which language they are stronger in, most of them probably want to retain Japanese proficiency that is similar to monolingual Japanese children of their age. One of the questions that arises in measuring bilingual proficiency is, as Valdés and Figueroa (1994) discuss, whether it should be measured using instruments that are developed for native speakers of the target language or for L2 learners of that language. Also, as Valdés (1995) illustrates, many bilingual speakers are stronger in one or more domains of one language and different domains of the other language (p. 315; Figures 6 and 7). For example, bilingual speakers may be stronger in their family language when talking about domestic issues, whereas the same speakers may be stronger in their school language when discussing academic matters. All of the issues just discussed need to be kept in mind when measuring HL proficiency. Further, researchers need to have a clear idea about the types of HL learners to be examined and about the relevance of available measurement instruments for such learner groups. As I discussed earlier, using multiple measurement instruments that tap into different aspects and skills of language proficiency is ideal for improving the validity of HL proficiency measurement.

If HL proficiency has different characteristics from those of L1 and L2, the question that naturally arises is whether we want to develop proficiency measurement instruments that are specifically designed for HL learners. Ideally, we would like to have special instruments for this specific target population, and CAJLE (2000) is a good example for such an instrument. However, knowing that there is a great deal of within group variation among HL learners, a single instrument will probably not serve the entire population. We also have to think about different target language norms for children of different ages.

Leaving such problems aside, what should we do if we decide to develop a new proficiency measurement instrument for HL learners? In order to develop such an instrument, we first need to understand the characteristics of HL proficiency and how HL proficiency is different from L1 and L2 proficiency. For example, it is reported that the spoken language proficiency of HL learners is often overestimated due to high conversation skills, compared with classroom JFL learners (Nakajima, 1988; Nakajima et al., 1994). For instance, Au, Knightly, Jun, and Oh (2002) found that adult learners who were overhearing a target language as they grew up, which is often the case in HL settings, were able to pronounce the target language in native-like manner. These findings imply that we should not credit heritage learners' good conversational skills and/or good pronunciation as good overall proficiency.

So what other aspects of language should we look at to make sure that HL learners really know the language? We need to know their linguistic strengths as well as weaknesses. According to Kondo-Brown (this volume), empirical studies that aim to identify the differences in linguistic skills between college-level HL and non-HL learners are emerging in Japanese and Korean. For example, Kanno and her colleagues conducted a descriptive study, in which they compared grammatical and lexical knowledge of advanced Japanese learners, both heritage and nonheritage, by presenting grammatical and lexical analyses of oral narratives as well as results from a written grammar test (Kanno, Hasegawa, Ikeda, & Ito, 2005; Kanno, Hasegawa, Ikeda, Ito, & Long, forthcoming). Although it is a small-scale study, it presents some important linguistic characteristics of HL proficiency through detailed descriptions and comparisons, and provides some empirical evidence for the working hypotheses of HL proficiency characteristics articulated by Campbell and Rosenthal (2000). All of the interviews, writing samples, and results from the discrete-point grammar tests which were used to measure proficiency in the articles reviewed in this chapter can be great resources for more extensive linguistic analyses with much larger sample sizes. There seems to be a great amount of data available for investigating characteristics of child JHL proficiency.

Adopting Nonheritage Proficiency Measurement Instruments

Given the limited availability of proficiency measurement instruments for HL learners, we often have to utilize non-HL instruments in measuring HL proficiency. One type of promising non-HL instruments that can be used for JHL children is the instruments developed for Japanese-as-a-second language (JSL) children who are attending schools in Japan.[13] Those instruments may work well for HL children who are trying to attain Japanese proficiency that is equivalent to native speakers but whose Japanese proficiency shows some characteristics of L2 learners (Nakajima, 1988; Valdés & Figueroa, 1994).

The Japanese tests developed by Ito (2002) were part of curriculum development for JSL children, and the tests measure all four skills in both oral and written test formats. The reading test includes a multiple-choice grammar subsection, a cloze test in which 21 *hiragana*, or Japanese syllabaries, are left out from three short passages, and a true–false reading comprehension section. The oral and writing tests come with prompts and evaluation sheets. Ito (2002) includes discussion of reliability and validity as well as results from an item analysis, and provides useful ideas for future

---

[13]To my knowledge, there seems to be no instrument that specifically targets naturalistic L2 adult learners of Japanese.

work in developing child JSL proficiency measurement. However, as the author admits, there seems to be a lot more work to be done to improve the tests.

Kawakami (2003) presents a number of ideas for developing proficiency assessment procedures for JSL children in elementary and secondary schools. This project seems to be still a work in progress, including the development of the rating scale. The TOAM, reported in Okazaki (2002), is for measuring academic language proficiency, and it was used in Nakajima and Nunes (2001); however, little information about the instrument is available to the public, according to Kawakami (2003, endnote 5).

For Chinese, Japanese or Korean as a foreign language, Thompson (1997) provides an annotated bibliography of available proficiency measurement instruments, and Carpenter et al. (1995) also summarize some interview procedures developed for other languages. Of course, before adopting any of these instruments, we need to examine the reliability and validity of the instruments and examine their relevance to our own research or teaching contexts.

Measuring Child Language Proficiency

Measuring the proficiency of young children imposes some methodological problems that are usually not major concerns in adult proficiency measurement. For example, the tasks need to be simple enough so that we can claim that failure to complete the tasks is due to language proficiency and not nonlinguistic task difficulty. Also, paper-and-pencil tests are probably not good instruments for young HL children, especially if we are testing children who have not received sufficient reading and writing instruction. Even when limiting ourselves to testing oral proficiency, conducting language proficiency interviews with young children is often challenging. CAJLE (2000) carefully developed interview procedures that can measure language proficiency per se, not something else, such as children's personality or attitude towards unfamiliar adults. The interview attempts to tap both communicative language use and more cognitively demanding explanation and opinion statement. Kondo-Brown (2004) investigated the influence of interviewer support in oral language proficiency interviews with elementary school children and found that children's performances were significantly linked to interviewers' support. Unlike adult learners, who usually try their best in oral proficiency interviews, some children show hesitation in talking with unfamiliar adults and/or engaging in artificial conversation like oral proficiency interviews. In addition to these empirical findings, we intuitively know that the amount of time that young children can concentrate is often considerably shorter than adults and older children. All of these empirical and intuitive concerns are related to the reliability and validity of the proficiency measurement instruments. Children's failure to perform any assessment tasks should be due to lack of language proficiency, not to shyness, hesitation, fatigue, nonlinguistic task difficulty, and so on.

Child language proficiency measurement is not easy. However, there is a good reason to focus on children in the HL learning context, because HL learning often takes place when learners are young. It is important to know how children are developing their HL proficiency in order to nurture their language learning.

One last remark I would like to make to conclude this chapter is that some studies in the current review emphasize the fact that children enjoyed the testing procedures and/or that children gained motivation for HL learning through the proficiency measurement activities (CAJLE, 2000; Nakajima, 2003). In many cases of HL learning, children do not have clear motivation and goals in language learning, although learning the language of their family origin is what many parents want (Kondo-Brown, 2005). We do not want to make such learning experiences boring and tiring by administering exhaustive testing. In developing and administering proficiency measurement instruments for young language learners, making the tasks interesting and encouraging is one of the most important aspects (Hasselgreen, 2005). When children enjoy the tasks, they will not hesitate to demonstrate what they can and cannot do in the language being tested, which I believe will lead to more reliable and valid proficiency measurement.

ACKNOWLEDGMENT

I would like to thank Professor Kimi Kondo-Brown for encouraging me to write a chapter on this topic and supporting me throughout the writing process, and Professor J.D. Brown for his inspiring lectures and books, from which I discovered an interest in language testing. I would also like to thank Douglas Margolis for helping me with editing the manuscript.

APPENDIX A
List of Proficiency Measurement Instruments
(* Denotes an Article About Test Development)

Authors	Proficiency Measurement Instruments (Ex. Tests, Rating Scales)	Skills Being Tested	Reliability of Proficiency Measurement	Availability of Instrument
*CAJLE (2000)	Oral Proficiency Assessment for Bilingual Children (OBC)	Listening, speaking	Not reported	Detailed procedures and materials are included in the manual.
*Carpenter et al. (1995)	Oral interviews developed by the researchers	Listening, speaking	Not reported	Descriptions of the interview procedures can be found in the article.
Chinen (2004)	Self-assessment questionnaire	Listening, speaking, reading, writing	Not reported	English and Japanese versions of the questionnaire are provided as appendices.
Hayashi (2003)	Self-evaluation [English]	Listening, speaking, reading, writing	Not reported	→ O'Malley & Valdez-Pierce (1996)
	Self-evaluation [Japanese] developed by the author	Listening, speaking, Reading, writing	Not reported	No.
	Observation: Bilingual language assessment record	speaking	Not reported	→ Haworth & Joyce (1996)
	Analytic scoring rubric for writing [English]	Writing	Not reported	→ O'Malley & Valdez-Pierce (1996)
	Analytical scoring (similar to the English version?) [Japanese]	Writing	Not reported	No.
Ikuta (2001)	Writing samples	Writing	Not reported	→ Wolfe-Quintero et al. (1998)

APPENDIX A (Continued)

Authors	Proficiency measurement Instruments (Ex. Tests, Rating Scales)	Skills Being Tested	Reliability of Proficiency Measurement	Availability of Instrument
*Ito (2002)	Japanese test for L2 Japanese children	Listening, speaking, reading, writing	Cronbach alpha (writing test only)	A complete set of test items can be found in the article (technical report)
Kataoka et al. (this volume)	Japanese language test	Written grammar, vocabulary, *Kanji* vocabulary	Not reported	→ Ono et al. (1989)
	English vocabulary test	vocabulary	Not reported	→ Ono et al. (1989)
*Kawakami (2003)	Japanese speaking tests for L2 Japanese children	Listening, speaking, reading, writing	Not reported	Sample rating scales can be found in the article
Minami et al. (2002)	Bilingual Verbal Ability Tests (BVAT)	Vocabulary	Not reported	BVAT is commercially available
Nagasawa (1995)	Written Japanese grammar tests	Written grammar	Split-half reliability	No
Nakajima (1988)	L1 Japanese test: Grade 4 reading test	Reading, writing? (not reported)	Not reported	→ Ooyou Kyooiku Kenkyuusho (1981) The original report was not available
	L2 Japanese test: University of Toronto placement test (Levels 1 & 2)	Reading, writing? (not reported)	Not reported	No
	Essay rating	Writing	Not reported	No
	Individual oral interview (20 questions)	Listening, speaking	Not reported	No

(Continued)

APPENDIX 4A (*Continued*)

Authors	Proficiency Measurement Instruments (Ex. Tests, Rating Scales)	Skills Being Tested	Reliability of Proficiency Measurement	Availability of Instrument
*Nakajima et al. (1994)	Oral Proficiency Assessment for Bilingual Children (OBC)	Listening, speaking	Not reported	Descriptions of the interview procedures can be found in the article
Nakajima & Nunes (2001)	Test of Acquisition and Maintenance (TOAM)	Listening, reading, oral vocabulary	Not reported	→ Okazaki (2002)
	Oral Proficiency Assessment for Bilingual Children (OBC)	Listening, speaking	Not reported	→ CAJLE (2000)
Nakajima (2003)	Free-association kanji production test	*Kanji*	Not reported	Descriptions can be found in the article
Noro (1990)	Proficiency tests in Japanese and English	Not reported	Not reported	No
*Okazaki (2002)	Test of Acquisition and Maintenance (TOAM)	Listening, reading	Not reported	No
*Ono et al. (1989)	Japanese language test	Written grammar, vocabulary, Kanji	—	The original report was not available for this review
Oriyama (2001)	Diary entries	Writing	Not reported	A list of analytical procedures is available in the article

REFERENCES

Au, T. K., Knightly, L. M., Jun, S. A., & Oh, J. S. (2002). Overhearing a language during childhood. *Psychological Science, 13*, 238–243.

Bachman, L. (1990). *Fundamental considerations in language testing.* Oxford: Oxford University Press.

Brown, J. D. (2005). *Testing in language programs: A comprehensive guide to English language assessment.* New York: McGraw-Hill.

Canadian Association for Japanese Language Education (CAJLE). (2000). *Kodomono kaiwaryoku no mikata to hyooka: Bairingaru kaiwa test (OBC) no kaihatsu* [Oral proficiency assessment for bilingual children]. Welland, Canada: Soleil.

Campbell, R. N., & Rosenthal, J. W. (2000). Heritage languages. In J. W. Rosenthal (Ed.), *Handbook of undergraduate second language education* (pp. 165–184). Mahwah, NJ: Lawrence Erlbaum Associates.

Canale, M. (1983). From communicative competence to communicative language pedagogy. In J. C. Richard & R. W. Schmidt (Eds.), *Language and communication* (pp. 2–27). London: Longman.

Carpenter, K., Fujii, N., & Kataoka, H. (1995). An oral interview procedure for assessing second language abilities in children. *Language Testing, 12*, 167–181.

Chinen, K. (2004). *Heritage language development: Understanding the roles of ethnic identity, attitudes, motivation, schooling, family support and community factors.* Unpublished doctoral dissertation, Carnegie Mellon University, Pittsburgh, PA.

Cummins, J. (1979). Cognitive/academic language proficiency, linguistic interdependence, the optimum age question and some other matters. *Working Papers on Bilingualism, 19*, 197–205.

Cummins, J. (1981). The role of primary language development in promoting educational success for language minority students. In California State Department of Education (Ed.), *Schooling and language minority students: A theoretical framework* (pp. 3–49). Los Angeles: Evaluation, Dissemination and Assessment Center, California State University.

Cummins, J. (2000). *Language, power, and pedagogy: Bilingual children in the crossfire.* Clevedon, UK: Multilingual Matters.

Hasselgreen, A. (2005). Assessing the language of young learners. *Language Testing, 22*, 337–354.

Haworth, M., & Joyce, J. (1996). A resource for assessing the language skills of bilingual pupils. In T. Clines & N. Frederickson (Eds.), *Curriculum related assessment: Cummins and bilingual children* (pp. 116–145). Bristol, PA: Multilingual Matters.

Hayashi, A. (2003). Japanese English bilingual children in three different educational environments. In J. Cohen, K. McAlister, K. Rolstad & J. MacSwan (Eds.), *Proceedings of the 4th International Symposium on Bilingualism, 4* (pp. 1010–1033). Somerville, MA: Cascadilla Press.

Hayashibe, H. (1999). *Gengo nooryoku no hyooka to tesuto no kaihatsu* [Language proficiency assessment and test development]. In H. Ono (Ed.), *Bairingaru no kenkyuu* [Research on bilingualism] (pp. 29–37). Tokyo: Daigaku Nyuushi Sentaa [College Entrance Examination Center].

Ikuta, Y. (2001). *Burajirujin seito no sakubun ni okeru bun no hukuzatsusa ni tsuite* [On the complexity of sentences in essays written by Brazilian students]. In Japanese Association of Second Language Acquisition (Ed.), *Dai 12 kai Dainigengo Shuutoku Kenkyuukai Zenkokutaikai Yokooshuu* [Proceedings of the 12th National Meeting of Japanese Association of Second Language Acquisition] (pp. 64–69). Tokyo: Japanese Association of Second Language Acquisition.

Ito, S. (2002). *Zainichi gaikokujin jidoo seito no Nihongo nooryoku sokutei hoohoo ni kakawaru kiso kenkyuu oyobi tesuto kaihatsu* [Research and test development on measuring Japanese proficiency of non-Japanese speaking children in Japan]. Grant in aid for Scientific Research, The Ministry of Education, Science Sports and Culture, Japan.

Japan Foundation (*Nihongo Nooryoku Shiken Jisshi Iinkai*). (2004). *Heisei 14 nen-do Nihongo Nooryoku Shiken bunseki hyooka ni kansuru hookokusho* [Test analysis report from the year 2004 administration of the Japanese Language Proficiency Test]. Tokyo: Japan Foundation.

Kanno, K., Hasegawa, T., Ikeda, K., & Ito, Y. (2005). *Shuutoku kankyoo no chigau Nihongo jookyuu gakushuusha no gengochishiki purofairu* [Linguistic profiles of advanced learners of Japanese]. *The Journal of the Canadian Association for Japanese Language Education: Japanese Linguistics and Pedagogy, 7*, 1–22.

Kanno, K., Hasegawa, T., Ikeda, K., Ito, Y., & Long, M. H. (forthcoming). Prior language-learning experience and variation in the linguistic profiles of advanced English-speaking learners of Japanese. In D. Brinton, O. Kagan, & S. Baucks (Eds.), *Heritage language acquisition: A new field emerging*. Mahwah, NJ: Lawrence Erlbaum Associates.

Kawakami, I. (2003). *Nenshoo Nihongo kyooiku ni okeru Nihongo nooryoku sokutei ni kansuru kanten to hoohoo* [Japanese proficiency measurement and teaching Japanese as a second language to young children]. *Waseda Daigaku Nihongo Kyooiku Kenkyuu Kiyoo [Waseda University Japanese as a Second Language], 2*, 1–16.

Kondo-Brown, K. (2003). Heritage language instruction for post-secondary students from immigrant backgrounds. *Heritage Language Journal, 1*. Retrieved May 15, 2005, from http://www.international.ucla.edu/lrc/hlj/volume1.asp

Kondo-Brown, K. (2004). Investigating interviewer–candidate interactions during oral interviews for child L2 learners. *Foreign Language Annals, 37*, 602–615.

Kondo-Brown, K. (2005, May). *Recent work on teaching heritage students in East Asian languages: What have we accomplished so far and what should we do next?* Paper presented at the Heritage Language Instruction Symposium, Los Angeles, CA.

Minami, M., Fukuda, S., & Fujiyama, E. (2002, April). *Goi kakutoku tassei reberu ni okeru daiichi gengo to daini gengo no sookansei: Keisyoo Nihongo no kanten kara no koosatsu* [Correlation between L1 and L2 vocabulary proficiency levels: Discussion from a Japanese heritage language perspective]. [Electronic version]. Paper presented at the Association of Teachers of Japanese Seminar, Washington DC. Retrieved May 15, 2005 from http://www.colorado.edu/ealld/atj/SIG/heritage/fujiyama.html

Muños-Sandoval, A. F., Cummins, J., Alvarado, C. G., & Ruef, M. L. (1998). *Bilingual verbal ability tests: Comprehensive manual*. Itasca, IL: Riverside Publishing.

Nagasawa, F. (1995). *L1, L2, bairingaru no Nihongo bunpoo nooryoku* [Japanese grammar proficiency of L1, L2 and bilinguals]. *Nihongo Kyooiku [Journal of Japanese Language Teaching], 86*, 173–185.

Nakajima, K. (1988). *Nikkei shijyo no Nihongo kyooiku. Nihongo Kyooiku [Journal of Japanese Language Teaching], 66*, 137–150.

Nakajima, K. (2003). *Keishoo Nihongo gakushuusha no kanji shuutoku to Kokugo kyookasho* [The role of Kokugo textbooks in kanji instruction for heritage Japanese learners]. *Oobirin Synajii [Obirin Synergy], 1*, 1–21.

Nakajima, K., & Nunes, R. (2001, March). *Nihongo kakutoku to keishoogo sooshitsu no dainamikusu* [Losing heritage language while learning Japanese: Portuguese-speaking children in Japanese schools]. [Electronic version]. Paper presented at the Association of Teachers of Japanese Seminar, Chicago, IL. Retrieved May 15, 2005 from http://www.colorado.edu/ealld/atj/SIG/heritage/nakajima.html

Nakajima, K., Oketani, H., & Suzuki, M. (1994). *Nenshoosha no tame no kaiwaryoku tesuto kaihatsu* [Development of oral proficiency test for children]. *Nihongo Kyooiku [Journal of Japanese Language Teaching], 83*, 40–58.

Noro, H. (1990). Family and language maintenance: An exploratory study of Japanese language maintenance among children of postwar Japanese immigrants in Toronto. *International Journal of the Sociology of Language, 86*, 57–68.

Ooyou Kyouiku Kenkyuusho [Center for Applied Education]. (1981). *Dokushoryoku shindan kensa* [Reading ability assessment]. Tokyo: Nihon Tosho.

Okazaki, T. (2002). *Gakushuu gengo o doo hakaruka* [How can we measure academic language proficiency?]. In E. Ishii & S. Imai (Eds.), *Tagengo kankyoo ni aru kodomo no gengo nooryoku no hyooka* [Language proficiency measurement for children in multilingual environment] (pp. 45–59). Tokyo: Kokuritsu Kokugo Kenkyuusho [The National Institute for Japanese Language].

O'Malley, J. M., & Valdez-Pierce, L. (1996). *Authentic assessment for English language learners: Practical approaches for teachers.* Reading, MA: Addison-Wesley.

Ono, H., Deguchi, T., Hotta, A., Nozawa, N., Horiuchi, J., Fujiki, M., et al. (1987). *Kaigai kikokushijo nado no Nihongoryoku hyooka shisutemu no kaihatsu ni kansuru kenkyuu* [Evaluation of the Japanese language ability for overseas children]. *Tokushu Kyooiku Kenkyuu Shisetsu Hookoku* [The Research Institute for the Education of Exceptional Children Report], *36,* 3–16.

Ono, H., Shigemasu, K., Hayashibe, H., Okazaki, T., Ichikawa, M. Kinoshita, H., et al. (1989). *Nihongoryoku kensa no kaihatsu* [Development of Japanese proficiency measurement]. Grant-in-Aid for Scientific Research Report, Ministry of Education, Japan.

Oriyama, K. (2001). Japanese as a translanguage: A developing minority language in Japanese-English bilingual children in Australia. *Proceedings of the 2001 Conference of the Australian Linguistic Society.* Retrieved May 15, 2005, from http://linguistics.anu.edu.au/ALS2001/proceedings.html

Thomas, M. (1994). Assessment of L2 proficiency in second language acquisition research. *Language Learning, 44,* 307–336.

Thompson, L. (1997). *Foreign language assessment in grades K–8: An annotated bibliography of assessment instruments.* Washington, DC: Center for Applied Linguistics and Delta Systems.

Tsujimura, N. (1996). *An introduction to Japanese linguistics.* Malden, MA: Blackwell Publishers.

Valdés, G. (1995). The teaching of minority languages as academic subjects: Pedagogical and theoretical challenges. *The Modern Language Journal, 79,* 299–328.

Valdés, G., & Figueroa, R. (1994). *Bilingualism and testing: A special case of bias.* Norwood, NJ: Ablex.

Wolfe-Quintero, K., Inagaki, S., & Kim, H-Y. (1998). *Second language development in writing: Measures of fluency, accuracy, & complexity.* Honolulu: Second Language Teaching & Curriculum Center, University of Hawai`i at Mānoa.

Chapter 5

Heritage and Nonheritage Learners of Korean: Sentence Processing Differences and Their Pedagogical Implications

Hi-Sun Helen Kim
University of Chicago

Due to heritage language (HL) experience and complex sociopsychological issues, HL learners possess distinctive language behaviors and needs that are clearly different from those of non-HL learners (Choi, 1999; H. Kim, 2002; King, 1998; C. Lee, 2000; S. Sohn, 1995). For instance, King (1998) argued that Korean language programs in North America attempt to teach HL and non-HL curricula at once and consequently fail to meet the needs of both populations. As a result, within Korean-as-a-foreign language (KFL) studies, identifying differences between HL and non-HL learners has been an ongoing and critical issue. In efforts to characterize the linguistic and learner profiles of Korean heritage and nonheritage learners, such studies have attempted to find differences in: curricular needs (e.g., S. Sohn, 1995, 1997); groups based on their linguistic and cultural backgrounds (e.g., S. Lee, 2000); interlanguage through error analysis (e.g., H. Kim, 2001; Wang,

1997); the degree of learning difficulty of grammar, such as particles (e.g., E. Kim, 2002), morphosyntactic cues (e.g., O'Grady, Lee, & Choo, 2000), and wh-questions & the pro-drop settings (J. Kim, 2001); and acquisition of sociolinguistic and pragmatic skills (J. Lee, 1995; M. Lee, 1997; Wang, 1995).

Like most HL learners, Korean HL learners have been known to have a head start in their listening comprehension skills and cultural knowledge. Yet, HL learners also exhibit various and significant weaknesses in other areas, such as productive skills and grammar competency, which tend to persist despite years of formal (college-level) instruction. Various error analysis studies have found that of the more frequent and habitual errors by HL learners, many are case particle-related, that is, omission and incorrect use of particles (e.g., E. Kim, 2002; J. Lee, 2000, etc.). Case particle-related errors may be accounted for by the type of language exposure learners have received at home (spoken and intimate style), in which case dropping is common in Korean spoken language. In general, due to their particular language experiences, the errors and difficulties of HL learners are in the productive skills, and hence as H. Kim (2001) points out, there is a severe imbalance between HL learners' low-level productive skills and their high-level, sometimes native-like, listening skills. These generalizations, however, have mostly been descriptive, intuitive, and hypothetical in nature (see Kondo-Brown, this volume). Hence, more empirical research is needed to further probe the interlanguage and linguistic characteristics of Korean HL learners. The present study empirically investigates the differences in language transfer and strategy use of HL and non-HL learners when processing Korean sentences.

LINGUISTIC PROFILES OF HL
AND NON-HL LEARNERS OF KOREAN

In order to identify how HL learners process language differently from non-HL learners, a few empirical studies have compared the syntactic development in Korean between the two types of learners. O'Grady, Lee, and Choo (2001), for example, examined the ability to process morphosyntactic cues to correctly interpret the subject- and object-gap relative clauses. Sixteen HL learners and 20 non-HL learners of second- and fourth-semester KFL students at two American universities were asked to do a picture selection task. Results showed no strong evidence that HL learners had any "headstart" in comparison to non-HL learners. Similar findings were shown in J. Kim (2001), who examined the early interlanguage forms of wh-questions and the pro-drop settings produced by HL and non-HL learners of Korean to compare degree of negative L1 transfer.

J. Kim concludes that HL learners have no advantages over nonheritage learners in acquisition of the parametric values that are different from their L1 (i.e., English) values, when measured by written-production tasks.

However, the results are difficult to generalize due to a particularly small number of participants and the fact that not enough information was given on the varying degrees of bilingualism of the HL learners or other sociopsychological issues. For instance, in J. Kim's study, although background information of the HL and non-HL learners under study was provided for the categories of age, proficiency level, source of informal exposure, months of formal instruction, and country of L2 Korean learning, only five HL learners and four non-HL learners participated. In O'Grady, Lee, & Choo, (2001) HL learners were defined as those who were assigned to "an accelerated second semester course" based on their placement test and interview results. No other background information was provided. A follow-up study with a larger number of participants and a more thorough background analysis might yield different results that shed light on the gap between HL and non-HL learners.

Based on the studies just discussed, the field requires considerably more empirical evidence and control of background variables for any of the generalizations to be validated (Kondo-Brown, 2003). Thus, in Korean HL research studies, there is an urgency to first determine how HL learners should be operationalized by exploring which language background variables can best predict the learner's performances. That is, due to linguistic variations within HL learners, it is essential to identify the subgroups instead of assuming HL learners as a homogeneous group. In an empirical study by Kanno, Hasegawa, Ikeda, Ito, and Long (forthcoming), differences in the learning experiences of the five groups of advanced learners of Japanese were identified: naturalistic learners, classroom learners, and three groups of HL learners with different types of HL exposure. The five groups, including the three HL subgroups, exhibited different profiles, suggesting a need for curricular adjustments for each learner type. Although this study is a small-scale study, it provides some evidence that HL learners also vary in linguistic profile depending on their language experiences outside of class.

Because HL learners of Korean receive the most input from home, parental information seems to be a promising variable to examine. However, as reported in J. Lee (2000), it may be more beneficial to distinguish HL learners based not only on the existence of Korean-speaking parents, but rather on the primary language (English vs. Korean) used and the nature of how they communicate to each other. As Kanno et al. pointed out, prior learning experience (e.g., formal vs. informal instruction) may also be valuable information in identifying subgroups of HL learners. Other language background variables that may be useful indicators are the learners' first language, frequency of language use inside and outside the home, familiarity and exposure of different speech registers, number of visits to HL country, and fluency of productive skills (see Kondo-Brown, this volume, for discussion of some of these variables as predictor variables). Thus, in future studies in KFL and Korean SLA, correlation studies between language background and linguistic performance may be useful in accurately defining HL learners of Korean.

In general, a more defined and detailed exploration of the strengths and weaknesses of HL learners' comprehension and production abilities should be investigated. For instance, the following questions might be relevant: To what extent do HL learners process language like a native speaker and to what extent do they process like an L2 learner? What types of language transfer do HL learners have that differ from those of the non-HL learners? By what means do they comprehend linguistic input? What strategies do they employ when processing a syntactic structure? What are the factors that cause them to be more like an L2 learner as opposed to a native speaker? To what extent does L1 background in early years influence the processing of Korean language? To begin answering these questions, the present study looks into the sentence processing differences between Korean native speakers, HL learners, and non-HL learners in which the L2 groups are determined by the L1 background variable.

L2 PROCESSING OF KOREAN RELATIVE CLAUSES

Due to inherent structural difference and difficulties, several processing studies have employed relative clauses to investigate the strategies and language transfer of English speaking L2 learners of Korean and Japanese (Kanno, 2001; O'Grady, Lee, & Choo, 2003). Using picture selection comprehension tasks, these studies examined learners' abilities to process the morphosyntactic cues (i.e., case particle) critical for accurately interpreting subject-gap versus object-gap relative clause structures. Findings in both studies were similar in that English-speaking learners of Japanese and Korean found subject-gap relative clause significantly easier than direct object-gap relative clauses. From these results, the papers suggest that structural distance is the principal determinant of difficulty in these constructions.

Furthermore, when the researchers looked at the nature of errors, two types of errors were identified. The first type of error (Reversal Error) involved the interpretation of the subject in the relative clause as the direct object and vice versa. From this, one can conclude that L2 learners find difficulty in processing case markers. The second error type (Head Error) involved a misidentification of the noun that serves as head of the relative clause. Hence, the head errors suggest that English-speaking learners are imposing the English word-order strategy in interpreting the Korean sentences. By examining how learners process complex syntax structures such as relative clauses, the two studies just discussed revealed the source of difficulty and language strategies used by English-speaking L2 learners of Korean and Japanese.

By describing the inherent linguistic and pragmatic differences between Korean and English, H. Sohn (2002) suggests that a language that is typologically and genetically distant to the learner's L1 will bring difficulties in processing and interfere in their acquisition. These assumptions are attested to by various research results that provide insights into why English speakers have such difficulty in learning Korean. In error analysis studies, numerous error types were identified, in which the syntactic errors involving case particle, verb inflection, complex embedded structures, and so on were the most frequent and extensive. In these experiments, it is clear that one source of difficulty lies in the learners' reliance on the dominant language strategy used in their L1 (e.g., MacWhinney, 1987; MacWhinney & Bates, 1989; MacWhinney, Bates, & Kliegle, 1984). Thus, the conflict between English's dominant SVO word order cue and the considerable dependency on case marker cues for Korean results in negative transfer.

In this vein, complex structures such as Korean relative clauses are considered as one of the more difficult patterns for English speaking L2 learners to acquire for various reasons. First, because Korean is a head-final and left-branching language, relative clauses (along with all modifier constructions) precede the head noun, whereas in English the noun that determines the referent of the gap always occurs first. Second, to comprehend a relative clause structure in Korean, learners must not only recognize the gap, but also identify its grammatical role within the clause and determine its reference, which requires the learners to rely on case marking cues. Lastly, Korean is a pro-drop language in which gaps occur rather freely and are not restricted to relative clauses. Hence, Korean relative clauses may be an effective target structure for analyzing the processing strategies of L2 learners of Korean.

THE STUDY

A listening comprehension (picture-selection) test was designed to determine whether learners of Korean with different language histories and exposures diverge in processing Korean relative clauses. Thus, the following research questions are addressed:

1.   To what extent do HL learners and non-HL learners use case marker cues when processing Korean subject and object-gap relative clauses?

2. Do HL learners process relative clauses differently from non-HL learners in the following conditions: (a) +/− case markers; (b) +/− animacy cues; and (c) complex construction?
3. What kind of language transfer (e.g., forward, backward) is found in HL and non-HL learners of Korean when processing Korean relative clauses?

METHOD

Participants

The participants ($N = 128$) were enrolled in beginning, intermediate, and advanced levels of Korean language classes offered at Rutgers University, Princeton University, University of Hawai`i at Mānoa, Kapi`olani Community College, and Northwestern University. Six native speakers of Korean also participated as a control group.[1]

Language Background

The learners of Korean who participated in this study were asked to provide information regarding their language background such as their L1 before the age of 5 and the degree of exposure and use of Korean with native speakers. In the language background questionnaire (Appendix A), the participants were asked to report their first language (L1), which was described as the dominant language used with the parents from the ages of 0–5. The summary of the participants' L1 is reported in Table 5.1.

Based on the L1 information, the HL learner participants were classified into one of the three subgroups: (1) those who reported Korean as their L1 (HL KL1), (2) both Korean and English as their L1 (HL BL1), and (3) English as their L1 (HL EL1). For non-HL learners, two subgroups were identified based on the language they reported as their L1. The first subgroup included those whose L1 is English, Chinese, and Russian (NHL SVO) and, because Japanese and Korean share similar basic properties of syntax (e.g., word order, overt case markers), the learners who reported Japanese as their L1 (NHL SOV) were the second subgroup.

To examine whether the transfers and strategies used in sentence processing are dependent on one's language experience, the learners were first

---

[1]Data from 12 participants were excluded for the following reasons: (a) they had no formal instruction, thus were unable to indentify level ($N = 4$); (b) they were beyond 400 level ($N = 3$); or (c) they provided incomplete data ($N = 5$).

TABLE 5.1
First Language Used From Ages 0–5

	N	%
Heritage Learners		
Korean	38	29.7
Both Korean & English	24	18.8
English	26	20.3
TOTAL	88	
Non-heritage Learners		
English	30	23.4
Chinese	1	0.8
Russian	8	0.8
Japanese	40	6.3
TOTAL		100.1*

*The total is 100.1% due to rounding error.

TABLE 5.2
Exposure of Korean Language
and Culture Growing Up

Heritage Language Learners	
Korean as L1 (HL KL1)	4.17
Both Korean & English as L1 (HL BL1)	4.33
English as L1 (HL EL1)	3,46
Non-Heritage Language Learners	
English, Chinese, Russian (NHL SVO)	0.75
Japanese (NHL SOV)	0.0

asked to rate the degree of their exposure to Korean language and culture growing up, where 1 indicated "never," 2 "rarely," 3 "sometimes," 4 "often," 5 "always," and 0 for "not applicable." Table 5.2 summarizes the mean amount of exposure for the five groups. HL KL1 and HL BL1 learners appear to have received a significant amount of exposure, whereas HL EL1 learners received a moderate amount of exposure. As expected, the non-HL learners rarely if ever received any exposure to the language and/or culture.

As HL learners have been fairly well exposed to Korean language and culture, another concern of interest is the type of exposure they have received. Hence, the learners were asked about their exposure to the target country, that is, length of residence or visits to Korea. As shown in Table 5.3,

TABLE 5.3
Exposure to Target Country

| | HL Learners | | | | | | Non-HL Learners | | | |
| | KL1 | | BL1 | | EL1 | | SVO | | SOV | |
	N	%	N	%	N	%	N	%	N	%
Lived in Korea	10	8	3	2	3	2	6	5	0	0
Visited Korea	32	25	21	16	20	16	9	7	4	3

TABLE 5.4
Formal Instruction

| | HL Learners | | | | | | Non-HL Learners | | | |
| | KL1 | | BL1 | | EL1 | | SVO | | SOV | |
	N	%	N	%	N	%	N	%	N	%
In Korea	9	7	5	4	3	2	4	3	0	0
K–12	4		2		2	2	0		0	0
Study Abroad	5		3		0		2		0	0
Research	0		0		0		2		0	0
In the U.S.										
Weekend school)	16	13	14	11	7	5	0	0	0	0

a small number of learners have resided in Korea (17%), of which the HL KL1 learners, (mostly those who were born in Korea) had the longest length of residence (mean length = 3.5 years). Eighty-three percent of the HL learners have visited Korea, whereas 33% of the non-HL learners have visited Korea. The type of visit also differs, where HL learners go to Korea to visit family and relatives, whereas non-HL learners either go for study abroad, research, or travel.

The last type of exposure that was examined for the learners was whether or not they had formal Korean language instruction either in Korea or in the United States prior to taking Korean language classes at a university. A summary report is provided in Table 5.4. Note here that, for the purpose of controlling the instruction variable for the experiment, among HL learners who were born and resided in Korea, those who had entered primary school (age 7) and received formal instruction were excluded from the study. Thus, of the 17 HL learners who studied in Korea (mean length of instruction received = 3.5 months), eight of them had either studied at the Kindergarten level or in the primary school setting for the duration of a summer. The rest of the learners had learned Korean language through study abroad programs offered by Korean universities. In their effort to maintain the HL, the parents of learners often send their children to community language schools, also known as weekend or Saturday schools. These schools are often run by the community churches or temples and are usually taught by members of the community. About 42% of HL learners have attended community schools, for an average of 2.7 years. What is interesting here is that, the data potentially suggest that among HL learners, the effort or personal values of the parent to maintain their children's language and culture may be shown to play an important role in HL learner's interlanguage. This question is not pursued in this study, but future research might take the type and amount of parent influence as a primary independent measure in comparing the subgroups of HL learners.

The questionnaire also investigated the frequency and nature of Korean language communication between learners and native speakers of Korean. Using the five-point scale for rating the frequency of Korean language use, where 1 indicated "never" and 5 "always" (and 0 as "not applicable"), participants were asked to provide an impression of the relative frequency of their language use with native speakers of Korean such as their immediate family and/or relatives. Within those categories, participants further indicated how frequently they speak to native speakers in Korean (output) and how frequently they are spoken to in Korean (input).

A few interesting details emerge if we consider how the HL learners reported that they interact with immediate family members (see Table 5.5). First, the mean rated frequency of Korean language use with siblings differs patently from that with the family members of the older generation (grandparents, parents, relatives). Furthermore, the data show that the mean of the input is always higher than that for the output when communicating with the older generation. This indicates that a two-language

TABLE 5.5
Mean Rated Frequency of Language Use with Family Members

		HL Learners			Non-HL Learners	
		KL1	BL1	EL1	SVO	SOV
Grandparents	Output	2.95	3.29	2.27	0.09	0.00
	Input	3.29	3.79	3.04	0.00	0.00
Mother	Output	3.53	3.42	2.38	0.00	0.00
	Input	4.32	4.13	3.19	0.00	0.00
Father	Output	3.21	2.83	1.50	0.00	0.00
	Input	4.11	3.33	1.81	0.00	0.00
Siblings	Output	1.21	1.13	0.50	0.09	0.00
	Input	1.29	0.88	0.42	0.03	0.00
Relatives	Output	3.00	3.13	2.15	0.16	0.00
	Input	3.18	3.42	2.38	0.16	0.00

communication occurs where HL learners speak or respond in English while their family members speak to them in Korean. Based on this information, the general strengths and weaknesses of the receptive versus productive skills can be predicted.

According to the background questionnaire, HL learners of Korean can be characterized as those who have received significant exposure and input of the language and culture principally from family (e.g., parents), in which the HL was used more receptively than productively. Three qualities that divided the HL learners into subgroups were: the L1 used as a child, degree of language exposure, and the frequency of language use with their parents.

As for the current course level of the participants, with the exception of the Korean language program at Northwestern University, the rest of the programs employ the same Korean language textbook entitled *Integrated Korean* (KLEAR textbook series). In this textbook series, the relative clause is first introduced in the first semester of the beginning level and again at the intermediate level. Therefore, the experiment was conducted during the second semester (Spring 2004) to ensure that participants had been exposed to Korean relative clauses. Table 5.6 shows the distribution of participants by L1 type and by course level.[2]

Instruments

Test items for the four general experimental conditions were constructed in order to investigate the processing differences between HL and non-

TABLE 5.6
Participants by Course Level

Level	Total N	HL KL1	HL BL1	HL EL1	NHL SVO	NHL SOV
Beginning	54	7	8	16	21	3
Intermediate	55	25	8	9	9	5
Advanced	19	7	8	2	2	0

---

[2]There is a high proportion of HL EL1 and NHL SVO learners in the beginning level and of HL KL1 in the intermediate level. Based on this, it is plausible that the significant difference between L1 type groups in the accuracy score comes from the unbalanced distribution of the course levels rather than their L1 variable. A follow-up analysis was done on a more balanced distribution (randomly selected) in which the results of the two-way ANOVA illustrated the L1 type to be significantly different ($F(4, 68) = 11.637$, $p \ll .001$) in terms of their accuracy rate.

TABLE 5.7
Experimental Test Conditions

Test Condition	Subject-Gap RC Object-Gap RC	+/−Case	Animacy (Rev/Non-Rev)	Simple / Complex
A (6)	Subject-gap RC	+ Case	Reversible (AA)	Simple
B (6)	Object-gap RC	+ Case	Reversible (AA)	Simple
C (6)	Subject-gap RC	− Case	Reversible (AA)	Simple
D (3) (3)	Subject-gap RC Object-gap RC	+ Case	Non-Reversible (IA/AI)	Simple
E (3) (3)	Subject-gap RC Object-gap RC	− Case	Non-Reversible (IA/AI)	Simple
F (4)	Subject-gap RC	+ Case	Reversible (AA)	Complex
G (4)	Object-gap RC	+ Case	Reversible (AA)	Complex
H (4)	Subject-gap RC	− Case	Reversible (AA)	Complex

HL learners: (a) subject-gap versus object-gap; (b) +/− case marker, to examine how differently HL learners process relative clauses without case markers; (c) +/− animacy cue, to examine how much animacy discrepancy aids the processing of Korean relative clauses and also to provide -case object-gap relative clauses; and (d) simple versus complex structures, to explore the effect of additional clauses with two conjunctives preceding the relative clause. All lexical words (nouns and verbs) were taken from the first- and second-year Korean language textbooks (*Integrated Korean*). As just discussed, the aim of this condition was to investigate how well learners utilize case marker cues when listening to Korean sentences. As a result, 42 experimental relative clause items (eight conditions) and 42 distracter items (nonrelative clause sentences) were constructed, making a total of 84 test items (see Appendix B for complete list of the experimental items). Table 5.7 is the summary of each of the experimental test conditions.

Procedure

The experiment made use of a picture-selection task to assess comprehension of the Korean relative clauses in the conditions described in the previous section. The procedures were the same as those of O'Grady, Lee, and Choo (2001) and Kanno (2001).

The participants were given a booklet that began with the following written instructions (in English):

Each page of this booklet contains a series of three pictures. As you go to each page, you will hear a tape-recorded voice describing a person/ animal/ thing in one of the three pictures. Your job is to put a circle around the item described in the sentence (Do NOT put the circle around the entire box).

Test sentences (84 test items) were pre-recorded in randomized order by the author and played at the rate of about one every seven seconds. Moreover, the relative clause structure was embedded in a matrix clause to provide syntactic context for the noun phrase containing the relative clause and thus being more a natural input. An example is given in the following structure.

(1) *"namca-lul po-nun yeca, edi isseyo?"*

man-ACC see-RL woman, where exist-POL?

"Where is, the woman who sees the man?"

Figure 5.1.   Sample page from the test booklet.

Figure 5.1 presents a sample page from the test booklet (see Appendix C for a sample picture for the test conditions). If the participant heard the subject-gap relative clause as in (1), the correct answer would be to circle the woman in the upper left panel. However, if the participant understood it incorrectly and circled the woman in the upper right panel, then this would illustrate a Reversal error, which involves the interpretation of the subject in the relative clause as the direct object. This error type indicates that the participant is not using the case marker cues. If the participant circles either of the men in the upper panels, then this can be explained as a Head Error, where the participant has misidentified the noun that serves as head of the relative clause. This would suggest that learners are using their English word order in that they take the head to precede rather than follow the relative clause. Lastly, if the participant circles either the man or the woman in the lower panel (distracter panel), this would indicate that they are not comprehending or recognizing the input as a relative clause structure.

RESULTS

The data from 128 participants were used for the subsequent analysis of two aspects of the data. The first part of the data evaluates the accuracy rates of each of the test conditions and compares the five experimental groups. The second part examines the error types (Head error vs. Reversal error) of the learners.

Overall Accuracy Rates

As shown in the Figure 5.2 and Table 5.8, the native speakers (control group) displayed no difficulty with the test items, responding correctly 96.6% of the time. As for the results of participants by L1 type, HL KL1 learners and NHL SOV learners scored the highest (67.3% and 70.5%, respectively). On the other hand, NHL SVO learners had the lowest accuracy score (26.4%), followed by HL EL1 learners (42.3%), exhibiting a great deal of difficulty in comprehending Korean relative clauses. Overall, it appears that the variability of HL learners as well as non-HL learners is determined strongly by their L1. This pattern is generally observed in each of the test conditions, which are summarized in Table 5.8. Furthermore, the results of a one-way ANOVA showed the five subgroups of HL and non-HL learners to be significantly different ($F = 23.79$ (5, 128), $p = .000$) on the total mean accuracy scores of the experimental items. Figure 5.2 shows a summary of mean accuracy for the experimental items of each L1 type group.

The accuracy rate of each participant was coded and analyzed. The analysis was designed to study the effect and interaction of the following

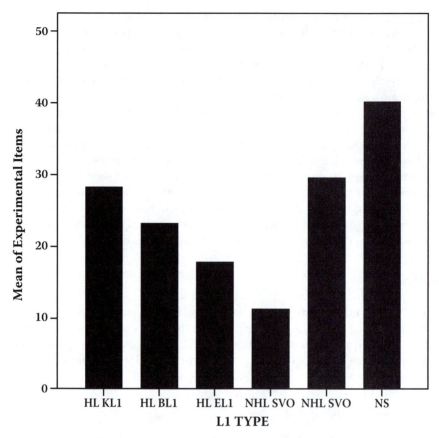

Figure 5.2.   Mean accuracy score of total experimental items.

seven explanatory variables: (a) Individual effect (Id); (b) L1 type: HL KL1, HLBL1, HL EL1, NHL SVO, NHL SOV (L1 Type); (c) Course level: Beginning, Intermediate, Advanced (Level); (d) Relative clause (subject-vs. object -gap (RC gap); (e) +/– Case marker cue (Case); (f) Animacy cue (Animacy); and (g) Relative clause construction: simple versus complex (Complex)

For the accuracy rate analysis, a quasi-binomial logistic model, which is a generalized linear model (GLM) for binomial response cases (e.g., success vs. failure), was applied. The generalized linear model is an extension of a classical linear model that relieves the requirement of equality and constancy of variances. This model extends analyses to predict the mean of variables that are not normally distributed (e.g., binomial distribution) via a "link function," that describes the nonlinear relationship between the

TABLE 5.8
Mean Accuracy Rates of Experimental Items

Conditions[b] / Item Number	HL Learners			Non-HL Learners			
	KL1	BL1	ELI	SVO	SOV	NS	Total
A Sub-gap RC	3.92	3.50	2.31	1.28	3.38	5.67	2.95
+, R, S / 6	(2.27)[a]	(2.41)	(2.09)	(1.61)	(2.13)	(.82)	(2.357)
B Obj-gap RC	3.58	2.21	1.65	.75	5.25	5.67	2.48
+, R, S / 6	(2.07)	(1.87)	(1.50)	(1.02	(.89)	(.52)	(2.15)
C Sub-gap RC	3.00	2.63	2.15	1.09	3.00	5.33	2.42
−, R, S / 6	(2.04)	(2.14)	(2.01)	(1.44)	(1.60)	(.82)	(2.07)
D Sub/Obj-gap	4.89	4.63	3.58	2.31	5.38	5.83	4.04
RC +, NR, S / 6	(1.23)	(1.13)	(1.65)	(1.09)	(.74)	(.44)	(1.66)
E Sub/Obj-gap	5.34	5.00	3.77	2.69	5.75	5.67	4.38
RC −, NR, S / 6	(.94)	(1.25)	(1.82)	(1.06)	(.46)	(.52)	(1.64)
F Sub-gap RC	2.89	1.92	1.77	1.28	1.88	4.00	2.10
+, R, C / 4	(1.35)	(1.50)	(1.53)	(1.22)	(1.13)	(.00)	(1.51)
G Obj-gap RC	2.21	1.25	.96	.53	3.50	4.00	1.55
+, R, C / 4	(1.54)	(1.07)	(1.22)	(.88)	(.53)	(.00)	(1.51)
H Sub-gap RC	2.42	2.12	1.62	1.19	1.50	4.00	1.93
−, R, C / 4	(1.41)	(1.65)	(1.44)	(1.15)	(.76)	(.00)	(1.49)
Total: 42 items	28.26	23.25	17.81	11.12	29.63	40.17	21.86
	(8.83)	(9.12)	(10.11)	(6.29)	(5.90)	(1.47)	(11.32)

[a]Standard deviation in the parenthesis
[b]+/− = +/−Case marker; R=Reversible (e.g., Animate-Animate); NR=Non-Reversible (Inanimate-Animate); S=Simple RC structure; C=Complex RC structure.

dependent variable and the covariates (see McCullagh & Nelder, 1989, for relevant discussion). The quasi-binomial family differs from the binomial family only in that the dispersion parameter is not fixed at one, but can "model" overdispersion (see Appendix D for the coefficient estimates of accuracy rates).

Subject- Versus Object-Gap RC Condition

Although the main effect of the RC-gap condition did not reach significance (estimated log odds ratio = -0.473, $p = 0.071$), it can clearly be seen that (with the exception of the Japanese speakers), both HL and NHL learners performed better on subject relative clauses (mean % = 53.6) than on direct object relatives (mean % = 44.2). This is similar to the results of previous studies, such as O'Grady et. al (2001) and Kanno (2001).

The analysis further revealed significant interactions between the RC gap condition and the L1 type. Figure 5.3 illustrates a comparison of the accuracy rates in processing subject- versus object-gap relative clauses for

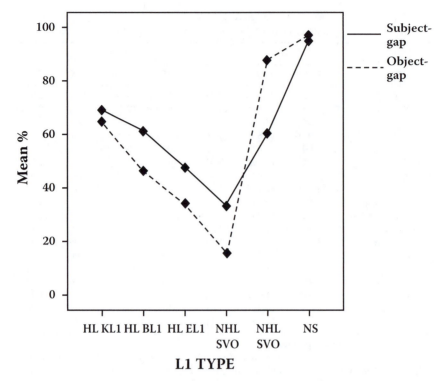

Figure 5.3.   Mean percentage accuracy score of subject- and
object-gap RC by LI type.

each of the L1 type groups. For instance, the interaction of HL KL1 (base
line) x HL BL1 x RC Gap type reached significance (estimated log odds
ratio = -0.895, p = 0.003) suggesting that in processing relative clauses, HL
KL1 learners exhibit the use of strategies that differ from those of other HL
learners and non-HL learners.

As indicated in the Figure 5.3, although all learner groups generally display a similar pattern, NHL SOV learners show a significantly unusual pattern (estimated log odds ratio = 2.237, p = 0.000). This seems to suggest that
NHL SOV learners may experience different processing difficulties with
subject- and object-gap relative clauses than from those of other L1 Type
groups. In particular, the results imply that Japanese-speaking learners have
a strong preference for object-gap relative clauses over subject-gap relative
clauses. However, this conclusion is questionable considering that (a) previous studies have shown that speakers of Japanese indeed find object-gap relative clauses more difficult to process than the subject-gap (e.g., Nakamura,
2003) and (b) in Japanese, the nominative case marker (-*ga*) is phonetically

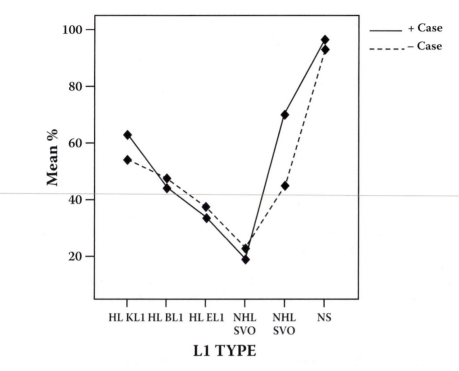

Figure 5.4.   Mean percentage accuracy score of
+ /– case (reversible) RC by L1 type.

identical to the nominative marker (*-ka*) in Korean, whereas the accusative
marker is patently different (*-lul* in Korean and *-o* in Japanese).

+ /– Case Marker Condition.

The main effect of + /– case marker on comprehending relative clauses by
HL and NHL learners was significant (estimated log odds ratio = -0.367,
p = 0.001), which indicates that L2 learners found RC with case markers
(mean % = 43) to be easier than those without (mean % = 41.2), but no
interaction of + /– Case and L1 Type was shown. The analysis also indicated
that all learners found the object-gap RC without case markers to be less difficult than its counterpart (estimated log odds ratio = 1.304, p = 0.000), as
shown in Table 5.9. This can be explained by the fact that all -case object-
gap RC structures were nonreversible (i.e., extra animacy cue), which was
found to be a helpful cue for L2 learners when processing RC sentences.
   According to the mean percentage score of the + case versus - case of the
reversible RC condition (Fig. 5.4), HL KL1 and NHL SOV learners diverge

TABLE 5.9
Mean Percentage of Case Marker
and RC-Gap Conditions

	Subject-Gap	Object-Gap
+ Case	56.5 (31.27)[a]	40.1 (32.45)
– Case	50.7 (28.32)	61.7 (38.81)

[a]Standard deviation in the parentheses.

from the rest of the learners where they performed better with the case markers than without. This outcome indicates that among HL learners, HL KL1 learners exhibit some sensitivity to case markers, whereas the other HL learners (and NHL SVO learners) do not notice or distinguish the two types of sentences, which in turn suggests their lack of reliance on case marker cues. On the other hand, as native speakers of Japanese, NHL SOV learners demonstrate strong reliance on case marker strategy to process Korean RCs.

Animacy Condition

As Figure 5.5 clearly show, the nonreversible relative clauses (Animate–Inanimate/Inanimate–Animate) were easier (mean % = 69) to comprehend than their reversible counterparts (mean % = 42.4) for all learners (estimated log odds ratio = 2.845, $p = 0.000$). This is because the learners have an additional cue to assist them in determining the grammatical relation of the overt NP and of the gap that occurred in each relative clause. Similar results have been reported in Kanno (2001) and Sasaki (1991).

RC-Structure Complex Versus Simple

The main effect of simple versus complex relative clause construction reached significance (estimated log odds ratio = 0.323, $p = 0.008$) with the simple construction being more challenging (mean % = 41.3) than its counterpart, showing that complex construction turned out to facilitate the understanding of the relative clause (mean % = 44.1). Moreover, a significant interaction of object-gap RC and complex RC construction was observed (estimated log odds ratio = -0.516, $p = 0.021$), revealing that, whereas subject-gap complex RCs are easier to process than the simple construction, object-gap complex RCs are found to be rather difficult. This is illustrated in Table 5.10.

In summary, the overall accuracy rates of the experimental items showed that the performance of correctly interpreting relative clauses may be strongly associated with the L1 type for both HL and non-HL learners. HL

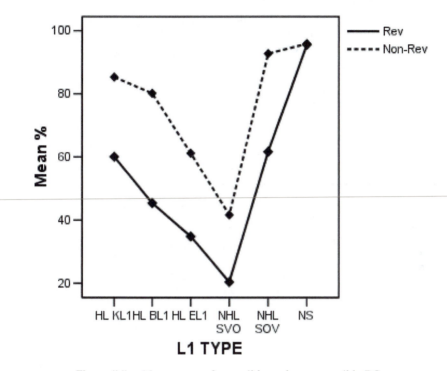

Figure 5.5.   Mean score of reversible and nonreversible RC.

TABLE 5.10
Mean Percentage of RC Structure
and RC-Gap Conditions

	Subject-Gap	Object-Gap
Simple (Reversible	42.5 (34.90)[a]	38.8 (34.75)
Complex (Reversible)	48.1 (34.01)	35.9 (36.28)

[a]Standard deviation in the parentheses.

KL1 learners had the highest accuracy among HL learners, followed by the HL BL1 group and then by HL EL1 learners. Similarly, the two subgroups of non-HL learners were demonstrated to be considerably different in that the NHL SOV learners repeatedly outperformed the NHL SVO learners, who always had the lowest accuracy rate. Generally, this pattern was consistent in all of the conditions, with some variations.

TABLE 5.11
Single Term Deletions from the Model

	df	Deviance	LRT	Pr(Chi)
<none>		4463.0		
L1 Type: Level	14	4493.4	30.4	0.007*

TABLE 5.12
Mean of Error Rates by L1 Type

	HL Learners			Non-HL Learners			
Error Type	KL1	BL1	ELI	SVO	SOV	NS	Total
Total	13.47	18.33	22.73	29.19	12.38	1.50	19.29
	(8.60)[a]	(9.03)	(9.12)	(6.85)	(5.90)	(1.38)	(10.77)
Reversal	6.16	7.96	5.27	4.03	8.13	.33	5.66
	(5.05)	(4.47)	(3.83)	(2.95)	(4.79)	(.82)	(4.46)
Head	6.53	9.38	14.65	18.97	.88	1.00	11.00
	(7.32)	(9.88)	(10.59)	(9.04)	(1.46)	(.63)	(10.34)
Other	.79	1.00	2.81	6.19	3.38	.17	2.63
	(1.34)	(1.25)	(2.47)	(3.50)	(2.20)	(.41)	(3.14)

[a]Standard deviation in the parentheses.

Error Rates

For the error analysis, errors in all the experimental items of each participant were coded in terms of their types: reversal error, head error, or other error. This analysis was designed to compare the nature of the errors of each experimental group in order to examine the language transfer and strategies of the learners. There are three response variables (Reversal, Head, or Other) and two independent variables (L1 Type and Proficiency level). For this portion of the analysis, a multinomial logistic linear model was used to see the effects of L1 Type and Level and the interaction between those two factors. According to the likelihood ratio test (Table 5.11), the interaction (i.e., L1 Type + Level + L1 Type: Level) turned out to be significant with no evidence of overdispersion (see Appendix D for coefficient estimates of the error type).

This study analyzed the type of errors made by the learners to investigate how they differ in error types. As mentioned, both studies by Kanno (2001) and O'Grady et al. (2001) reported two types of errors in the L2 learners: reversals and head errors. To recap, reversal errors involve the interpretation of the subject in the relative clause as the direct object and vice versa, and head errors involve a misidentification of the noun that functions as head of the relative clause. Table 5.12 presents the means of error rate types for each L1 Type group.

TABLE 5.13
Mean Percentage Distribution of Error Type by L1 Type

Error Type	HL Learners			Non-HL Learners	
	KL1	*BL1*	*EL1*	*SVO*	*SOV*
Reversal	45.7%	43.4%	23.2%	13.8%	65.7%
Head	48.5%	51.2%	64.5%	65.0%	7.1%
Other	5.8%	5.5%	12.4%	21.2%	27.3%

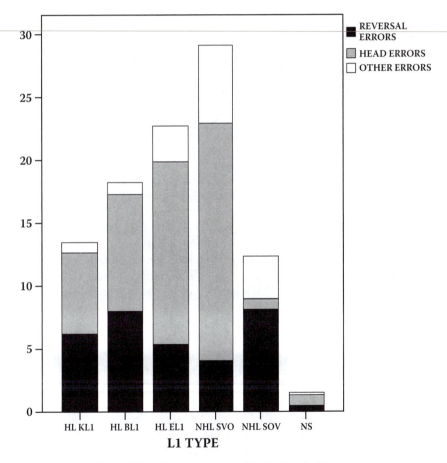

Figure 5.6.   Mean error rate distribution by L1 type.

As illustrated in both Table 5.13 and Figure 5.6, the distribution of error types appeared to be different for each L1 Type group. In general, all learner groups (except the NHL SOV group) displayed more head errors

TABLE 5.14
Estimated Probability of HL Learner Errors

| | HL KL1 | | | HL BL1 | | | HL EL1 | | |
	Rev	Head	Other	Rev	Head	Other	Rev	Head	Other
BEG	0.46	0.46	0.07	0.31	0.64	0.06	0.27	0.59	0.15
INT	0.45	0.49	0.06	0.50	0.43	0.07	0.18	0.72	0.10
ADV	0.51	0.49	0.00	0.51	0.45	0.04	0.22	0.69	0.08

TABLE 5.15
Estimated Probability of Non-HL Learner Errors

| | NHL SVO | | | NHL SOV | | |
	Reversal	Head	Other	Reversal	Head	Other
BEG	0.14	0.63	0.22	0.56	0.10	0.33
INT	0.12	0.68	0.20	0.72	0.05	0.23
ADV	0.15	0.73	0.12	0.85	0.15	0.00

than reversal errors. However, for the HL KL1 and HL BL1 learners, the distribution of the two types of errors were rather equal (e.g., HL KL1 = 45.7% Reversal, 48.5% Head), whereas HL EL1 and (especially) NHL SVO learners had notably more head errors than reversals (e.g., NHL SVO = 65% Head, 13.8% Reversal). The errors of the NHL SOV group were distinctly different from the rest of the groups with the dispersion of only 7.1% being head errors, 65.7% being reversals, and 27.3% being "other" errors. The third error type implies that the learner does not understand the test item input either due to the lack of lexical comprehension or to misunderstanding the relative clause. In this vein, HL learners have relatively fewer "other" errors as compared to non-HL learners, which implies that they can at least recognize the input as a relative clause, which in turn can be explained by their superior command of listening skills and vocabulary.

Tables 5.14 and 5.15 provide the estimated probabilities of each error type by level and L1 type. Looking at the two tables (estimate probability of HL and non-HL learners), the probability of reversal errors and head errors does not necessarily decrease as the course level increases. In other words, reversal and head errors are manifested not only in the low-proficiency group, but also in the advanced group. These results thus indicate that learners find utilization of case markers difficult, which in turn leads to difficulty determining the grammatical relation of the gap to a relative clause. Likewise, with the exception of the NHL SOV learners, learners have a tendency to process relative clauses using English word order strategy, with the head preceding the relative clause. Conversely, Tables 5.14 and 5.15 clearly show that proportion of other errors decreases as the proficiency level increases, suggesting that learners improve over time with respect to general listening comprehension of relative clauses.

In summary, although the accuracy rate revealed relationships with the learners' L1, the error analysis provided further evidence of HL learners and non-HL learners' utilization of various language strategies in processing subject- and object-gap relative clauses. For instance, HL KL1 and HL BL1 displayed equal distributions of both types of errors indicating that they have English word order transfers as well as a rather weak command of case marker cues. As expected, the nature of errors of NHL SVO (English native speakers) suggests that they are imposing the head-initial order of their L1 on the Korean sentences. In contrast to this group, the Japanese-speaking learners exhibited mostly case-marker errors (and other errors), but rarely produced head errors. As for the interaction of proficiency level and error type, no pattern of improvement in case marker use was identified. Moreover, the probability estimate of head errors also suggests that learners in all levels manifested English word order transfers in the processing of Korean relative clauses.

DISCUSSION

The first finding in this study was that information on the parental language of the learner and what L1 learners chose as their own (defined as language used from ages 0–5) best predicted the variability in their language performance, amount and type of language exposure, and the nature and frequency of language use. Five learner groups were identified: three subgroups of HL learners; those who reported either Korean (HL KL1), both Korean and English (HL BL1), or English (HL EL1) to be their L1, and two subgroups of non-HL learners; those who either reported English, Chinese, Russian (NHL SVO), or Japanese (NHL SOV) to be their L1. Out of the three subgroups, HL KL1 learners had the most HL input (and output) followed by the HL BL1 group and then the HL EL1 group. In turn, supporting the expectation for an interaction between the learners' language processing and their language exposure, HL KL1 learners consistently performed better (but not always significantly better) than the two sup-groups in all test conditions of the listening comprehension task.

The two subgroups of NHL learners were shown to be similar in that they had minimal (if not zero) exposure to and Korean culture and language, which is a typical trait of a foreign language learner. However, the experiment showed that the Japanese-speaking learners performed remarkably better than the English-speaking learners in comprehending Korean relative clauses. This can be simply explained by the inherent syntactic resemblance between Japanese and Korean. Thus, it can be concluded that the (listening) comprehension skills of HL learners are affected chiefly by the quality and quantity of HL exposure and use, whereas the native language of non-HL learners is the main variable that interacts with comprehension (and acquisition) of the target language. From the evidence of a strong interaction between language background and the L2 processing of a learner, one can easily see the importance of language background variables in not only the HL learner population but also in the non-HL learners, meaning such variables must therefore be factored into the research design.

Looking at the results of the non-HL learners, learners who are speakers of a head-initial language (e.g., English) clearly differ from the speakers of a head-final language (e.g., Japanese) when processing Korean relative clauses. As just mentioned, evidence from the accuracy scores implied that the relative clause is far more difficult to process for English-speaking learners of Korean than the Japanese-speaking learners. In examining the types of errors, one source of difficulty for NHL SVO learners is the word order discrepancy between English (SVO) and Korean (SOV). Hence, a greater proportion of NHL SVO learners' errors were head errors (65%), which reveals that they are employing an English word order L1 strategy. The opposite was evident in NHL SOV learners with 65.7% of their errors being reversal errors, implying that they had not yet fully acquired the Korean case particles,[3] whereas the general syntactic structure of the relative clause was not the main source of difficulty. In this regard, the question would be, how and to what extent do HL learners vary from the two polar subgroups of non-HL learners?

Based on the language background of HL learners, two outcomes can be predicted: (a) HL learners (especially HL KL1 and BL1) will not have Head errors due to ample exposure to Korean and Korean language input; and (b) HL learners will mostly have Reversal errors because their type of exposure is limited to spoken language, in which case-drops occur. However, unlike either of the NHL learner subgroups, the error analysis indicates that HL KL1 and HL BL1 learners do not exhibit more errors of one type over another, but rather have both error types, revealing that HL learners also employ the English word order strategy. As studies in bilingual processing point out, (e.g., Fernandez, 2004), when HL learners use English strategies in sentence processing that may be due to the language dominance of the bilingual. Thus, English as the dominant language could

---

[3]Note that there were no advanced level Japanese learners of Korean. Thus, it can be presumed that they have not yet acquired the Korean case system.

account for the head errors in HL learners. Although HL learners were expected to use similar processing strategy to those of the Japanese speakers, the results here show that HL learners find both utilization of case marker cues and syntactic structure of a relative clause equally difficult when processing relative clause structures.

Despite these difficulties, how is it that HL learners generally comprehend input considerably better than English-speaking non-HL learners? According to many SLA researchers, this may be so because meaning-based comprehension (i.e., semantic processing) may occur independently of acquisition (i.e., syntactic processing), through the sole use of top-down processing strategies that draw on learners' existent linguistic knowledge and contextual information (Han, 2004, p. 134). Viewed in this light, HL learners may have not fully acquired the syntactic structures of Korean (and thus exhibit English word order transfer) but have sufficient semantic knowledge and contextual skills to comprehend even the complex structures.

From the point of view of instruction, HL learners' natural tendency to focus on content and their inability to notice linguistic features pose problems for their acquisition. According to Long (e.g., 1983, 1997), "a pure focus on meaning has been shown to be inefficient by comparisons that find great advantages for learners who receive formal instruction of various kinds." (Long, 1997, p. 156). He further suggests that such learners do not simply notice, in Schmidt's sense (Schmidt, 1990), items from the input as well as the output. The Noticing Hypothesis proposed by Schmidt (1990, 1993, 1994, 1995) emphasizes the subjective experience of noticing as a necessary and sufficient condition for converting input to intake. Furthermore, in this scheme, the second condition for acquisition to occur is that learners must "notice the gap" between the current state of their developing linguistic system, as realized in their output, and the target language system available as input.

Following this thinking, if one wants to discuss the pedagogical implications for HL learners, one must presume that the HL learners' language is stabilized and not yet fossilized (and thus provides the possibility of being destabilized). Given that, the previous discussion holds strong implications for instruction with the main goal of having HL learners "notice" linguistic features. These implications generally apply to all L2 learners. However, for HL learners, the difference would be that there should be significantly stronger emphasis on the latter condition of noticing, which is for them to notice the input-output discrepancies. In other words, HL learners must notice their own gaps by being able to compare the stabilized form to the correct form of the target language, which in turn focuses on accommodating and restructuring the interlanguage rather than processing input. According to VanPatten (2004), accommodation refers to "either the partial penciling in or complete incorporation of a surface feature (form-meaning connection) of language into the developing system ..." and restructuring refers to "what may happen to the developing system after a form has been accommodated" (p. 33).

Guided by this conception, considering that HL learners have partially acquired the language implicitly, it can be inferred that they lack explicit meta- and rule-based knowledge to figure out why their stabilized language is incorrect. Thus grammar-based instruction, though not adequate in itself, could have a significant contribution to make to at least the noticing (and restructuring) of certain stabilized features of an L2 learner. Of particular relevance to this discussion, Schmidt claims that "intentional learning (explicit learning), including the attempt to form and test conscious hypotheses, is important ... probably for learning some features of natural languages and not others" (Schmidt, 1994, p. 198). In other words, explicit instruction is necessary for at least the acquisition of some features of the target language.

One study relevant to the idea of stabilization and instruction would be the Canadian-French immersion program. According to Krashen, the French immersion program is the "most successful program ever recorded in the professional language-teaching literature" (Krashen, 1984, p. 61). However, many criticisms have been leveled in respect to these learners' grammatical inaccuracies in that their productive skills remained far from being native-like when in fact they have attained levels of receptive skills comparable to native speakers. Thus, Swain (1991) and others (e.g., Salomone, 1992) have conducted classroom observations to investigate student–teacher interactions in the French immersion classrooms. Results of the observations illustrated the limited output of the learners due to the teacher's failure to create opportunities for learners to "notice" and systematically use the forms and functions of the language in meaningful situations. Aside from the limited opportunities to speak in class, when there was output by the learners, the feedback they received was more likely to be content-focused rather than form or language-focused. In other words, teachers were described as providing insufficient and inconsistent negative feedback to the learner's output.

Despite the different language-learning environments (e.g., instructional vs. naturalistic context), one can see the parallels between the teacher–student interactions from the immersion program and the parent–child interactions of HL learners. From the natural exposure that HL learners have received since childhood, we can infer that adequate negative feedback was (not) given in plenty. Hence, in formal language instruction, it may be crucial for teachers to provide HL learners with consistent interaction with negative feedback that draws attention to the form, rather than meaning. This naturally leads to the question of what type of feedback (explicit vs. implicit) would be most efficient for HL learners. According to

Doughty and Williams (1998), combinations or variety of feedback are likely to be most useful. Some proven combinations are "promoting perceptual salience through input flooding (Sharwood-Smith, 1991, 1993), directing learner attention to salient or frequent linguistic features, corrective recasting (Long, 2000), and interaction enhancement" (Doughty & Williams, 1998, p. 243). More importantly, as pointed out by Swain (1991), one chief source of stabilization in learners who have learned implicitly is their lack of engagement in language production. Thus, a vital pedagogical implication for HL learners would be to maximize the combination of the learner's production and efficient negative feedback of the teacher (i.e., interaction) to promote noticing of the discrepancies between their output and the corrective feedback.

Although SLA is input-dependent, VanPatten (2004) also points out that in the case of developing fluency and accuracy (i.e., skill building), output is most likely required. He further points out that based on Pienemann's work on Processability Theory (Pienemann, 1998), "learners may be able to develop an underlying competence without output," but only output would push learners toward building degrees of fluency and accuracy (p. 43). In this vein, based on the quality of the input (e.g., lack of corrective feedback) and (lack of) output by the HL learners, such learners can be defined as those who have "developed an underlying competence without output" and in order to promote accuracy and fluency in their language production, a focus on output with proper and consistent feedback must be incorporated into instruction. That is, in comparison to other NHL learners of Korean, HL learners may be at a different stage of interlanguage development and therefore instruction should be targeted accordingly. Evidently, more research on instructed SLA is necessary to consider what kinds of instruction affect what kinds of processes for the acquisition of which kinds of forms and skills (VanPatten, William, & Rott, 2004).

CONCLUSION

This chapter reported the findings based on empirical data showing that HL learners exhibit processing strategies and language transfer that differed from those of non-HL learners. Furthermore, interesting evidence was revealed through error analysis that showed that HL learners, who have received considerable exposure to the HL, have processing strategies similar to both subgroups of the NHL learners: NHL SVO learners, whose L1 is an head initial language (English), and NHL SOV learners, whose L1 is an head-final language (Japanese). This is not too surprising, considering that HL learners have received significant input in both Korean and English. The more essential issue would be to understand what it means psycholinguistically when strategies of two distinct languages are employed and what pedagogical implications this would have for teaching HL learners. As the discussion of this chapter has shown, many of the questions that were posed for investigation have been answered. However, as always, another body of questions and research motives has surfaced in area of instructed SLA in relation to stabilization and bilingual sentence processing.

APPENDIX A
Language Background Questionnaire

The following survey is part of a research project on the prior Korean language experience and comprehension of learners. Simply circle / check the response that seems most appropriate for your case. Some questions require a brief written response(s). If you need more space, use the last page and mark your answers with the corresponding question number. Thank you for taking part in the survey. Your time and participation are greatly appreciated.

Section II
1. When you were a child, what was your first language(s)? (Check all that apply) (e.g., if your parents spoke to you in Korean before your age of 5, your first language is Korean.)

    ☐ English   ☐ Korean   ☐ Both

    Others (please specify): _____

2. When growing up, I have received exposure of Korean language and culture.

    N/A   1: never 2: rarely 3: sometimes 4: often 5: always

3. Have you ever lived in Korea? (for more than 3 months)

    ☐ Yes   ☐ No

    3-1. If YES,   At what age(s): _____ For how long (total time): _____ yr _____ mo

4. Have you ever studied in Korea?

    ☐ Yes   ☐ No

    4-1. If YES,   List the school level / Program (e.g., K–12, college, summer school, study abroad, etc.):

    For how long: _____yr _____mo

5. Have you ever studied Korean at other formal <u>noncollege</u> institution in the U.S.? (e.g., Saturday Weekend School; high school, etc.)

    ☐ Yes   ☐ No

    5-1. If YES,   List Institution/ Affiliation : _____

    At what age: _____ For how long: _____yr _____mo

6. Have you visited Korea? (for less than 3 months)

    ☐ Yes   ☐ No

    6-1. If YES,   At what age(s): _____   For how long (total time): _____yr _____mo

    Reason(s) of visit: _____

(Continued)

APPENDIX A (*Continued*)

7. How often do you speak Korean with the following people?
   (1: never   2: rarely   3: sometimes   4: often   5: always)

• Friends	N/A	1	2	3	4	5
• Significant other / Spouse	N/A	1	2	3	4	5
• Korean Classmates/ Teacher	N/A	1	2	3	4	5
• Grandparent(s)	N/A	1	2	3	4	5
• Mother	N/A	1	2	3	4	5
• Father	N/A	1	2	3	4	5
• Sibling(s)	N/A	1	2	3	4	5
• Relatives	N/A	1	2	3	4	5
• Others (specify):_____		1	2	3	4	5

8. How often do the following people speak Korean to you?

• Friends	N/A	1	2	3	4	5
• Significant other / Spouse	N/A	1	2	3	4	5
• Korean Classmates/ Teacher	N/A	1	2	3	4	5
• Grandparent(s)	N/A	1	2	3	4	5
• Mother	N/A	1	2	3	4	5
• Father	N/A	1	2	3	4	5
• Sibling(s)	N/A	1	2	3	4	5
• Relatives	N/A	1	2	3	4	5
• Others (specify):_____		1	2	3	4	5

APPENDIX B
Experimental Items

Condition A: Subject-gap RC / + Case / Reversible / Simple

1. 남자를 보는 여자
   'the woman who is looking at the man'
2. 여자를 소개하는 남자
   'the man who is introducing the woman'
3. 남자를 부르는 여자
   'the woman who is calling the man'
4. 여자를 생각하는 남자
   'the man who is thinking about the woman'
5. 남자를 좋아하는 여자
   'the woman who likes the man'
6. 여자를 싫어하는 남자
   'the man who dislikes the woman'

Condition B: Object-gap RC / + Case / Reversible / Simple

1. 남자가 보는 여자
   'the woman who the man is looking at'
2. 여자가 소개하는 남자
   'the man who the woman is introducing'
3. 남자가 부르는 여자
   'the woman who the man is calling'

(*Continued*)

APPENDIX B (*Continued*)

4. 여자가 생각하는 남자
   'the man who the woman is thinking about'
5. 남자가 좋아하는 여자
   'the woman who the man likes'
6. 여자가 싫어하는 남자
   'the man who the woman dislikes'

Condition C: Subject-gap RC / - Case / Reversible / Simple

1. 남자Ø 보는 여자
   'the woman who is looking at the man'
2. 여자Ø 소개하는 남자
   'the man who is introducing the woman'
3. 남자Ø 부르는 여자
   'the woman who is calling the man'
4. 여자 Ø 생각하는 남자
   'the man who is thinking about the woman'
5. 남자 Ø 좋아하는 여자
   'the woman who likes the man'
6. 여자 Ø 싫어하는 남자
   'the man who dislikes the woman'

Condition D: Subject (3) & Object (3) -gap RC / + Case / Non-Reversible / Simple

1. 케이크를 좋아하는 여자
   'the woman who likes cake'
2. 햄버거를 싫어하는 남자
   'the man who dislikes hamburgers'
3. 아이스크림을 생각하는 여자
   'the woman who is thinking about ice-cream'
4. 남자가 부르는 노래
   'the song that the man is singing'
5. 여자가 보는 텔레비전
   'the TV that the woman is watching'
6. 남자가 받는 꽃
   'the flower that the man is receiving'

Condition E: Subject (3) & Object (3) -gap RC / - Case / Non-Reversible / Simple

1. 여자Ø 좋아하는 케이크
   'the cake that the woman likes'
2. 남자 Ø 싫어하는 햄버거
   'the hamburger that the man dislikes'
3. 여자 Ø 생각하는 아이스크림
   'the ice-cream tha the woman is thinking about'
4. 노래 Ø 부르는 남자
   'the man who is singing a song'
5. 텔레비전 Ø 보는 여자
   'the woman who is watching TV'
6. 꽃 Ø 받는 남자
   'the man who is receiving flowers'

(*Continued*)

APPENDIX B (*Continued*)

Condition F: Subject-gap RC / + Case / Reversible / Complex

1. 친구를 소개하고 싶어서 남자를 부르는 여자
   'the woman who is calling the man, because she wants to introduce a friend'
2. 질문을 하고 싶어서 여자를 보는 남자
   'the man who is watching the woman, because he wants to ask a question'
3. 데이트를 하고 싶어서 남자를 생각하는 여자
   'the woman who is thinking about the man, because she wants to date him'
4. 결혼을 하고 싶어서 남자를 좋아하는 여자
   'the woman who likes the man, because she wants to get married'

Condition G: Object-gap RC / + Case / Reversible / Complex

1. 동생을 소개하고 싶어서 남자가 부르는 여자
   'the woman the man is calling, because he wants to introduce a younger sibling'
2. 얘기를 하고 싶어서 여자가 보는 남자
   'the man that the woman is watching, because she wants to talk to him'
3. 전화를 하고 싶어서 남자가 생각하는 여자
   'the woman that the man is thinking about, because he wants to call her'
4. 사랑을 하고 싶어서 여자가 좋아하는 남자
   'the man that the woman likes, because he wants to love'

Condition H: Subject-gap RC / - Case / Reversible / Complex

1. 동생Ø 소개하고 싶어서 여자 Ø 부르는 남자
   'the man who is calling the woman, because he wants to introduce a younger sibling'
2. 질문 Ø하고 싶어서 남자 Ø 보는 여자
   'the woman who is looking at the man, because she wants to ask a question'
3. 전화 Ø하고 싶어서 여자 Ø 생각하는 남자
   'the man who is thinking about the woman, because he wants to call her'
4. 결혼 Ø하고 싶어서 남자 Ø 좋아하는 여자
   'the woman who likes the man because he wants to get married'

APPENDIX C
Sample Test Pictures

Sample 1. Subject versus object-gap RC

Sample 2. Subject versus object-gap

APPENDIX C (*Continued*)

Sample 3. Subject versus object-gap

Sample 4. Non-reversible RC

APPENDIX D
Coefficients Estimates of Accuracy Rates

	Estimate	Std. Error	t value	Pr(>|t|)
Obj-gap	−0.473	0.2618	−1.807	0.071
– Case	−0.367	0.1097	−3.342	0.001
Non-Rev	2.845	0.2787	10.208	0.000
Complex	0.323	0.1216	2.654	0.008
HL BL1: Obj-gap	−0.895	0.2948	−3.035	0.003
HL EL1: Obj-gap	−0.293	0.2821	−1.038	0.299
NHL SVO: Obj-gap	−0.495	0.2893	−1.711	0.087
NHL SOV: Obj-gap	2.237	0.4614	4.849	0.000
Obj-gap: Non-Rev	−2.157	0.2756	−7.827	0.000
Obj-gap: – Case	1.304	0.2686	4.856	0.000
Int level: Obj-gap	0.197	0.2166	0.908	0.364
Adv level: Obj-gap	1.097	0.2966	3.698	0.000
HL BL1: Non-Rev	0.623	0.3632	1.715	0.087
HL EL1: Non-Rev	−0.275	0.3264	−0.843	0.399
NHL SVO: Non-Rev	−0.718	0.3111	−2.307	0.021
NHL SOV: Non-Rev	−0.028	0.6041	−0.046	0.963
Obj-gap: Complex	−0.516	0.2231	−2.315	0.021

(Dispersion parameter for quasi-binomial family taken to be 1.580698)
Null deviance: 4266.9 on 1279 degrees of freedom
Residual deviance: 1839.9 on 1135 degrees of freedom

REFERENCES

Choi, H. (1999). Incorporating identity into language pedagogy: The case of Korean heritage students. *Proceedings of the Third International Conference on Korean Studies* (pp. 403–415). Los Angeles: Academia Koreana of Keimyung University.

Choo, M. (1999). Teaching language style of Korean. In S. Kang (Ed.), *Korean language in America 3* (pp. 77–95). Monterey, CA: American Association of Teachers of Korean.

Doughty, C., & Williams, J. (1998). Pedagogical choices in focus on form. In C. Doughty & J. Williams (Eds.), *Focus on form in classroom second language acquisition* (pp. 197–216). Cambridge: Cambridge University Press.

Fernandez, E. (2004). *Bilingual sentence processing: Relative clause attachment in English and Spanish. Language acquisition and language disorders, 29.* Amsterdam: John Benjamins.

Han, Z. (2004). *Fossilization in adult second language acquisition. Second language acquisition, 5.* Clevedon, UK: Multilingual Matters.

Izumi, S. (2002). Output, input enhancement, and the noticing hypothesis: An experimental study on ESL relativization. *Studies in Second Language Acquisition, 24,* 541–577.

Kanno, K. (2001, February). *Processing strategies by L2 learners.* Paper presented at the American Association for Applied Linguistics (AAAL), St. Louis, Missouri.

Kanno, K., Hasegawa, T., Ikeda, K., Ito, Y., & Long, M. H. (forthcoming). Prior language-learning experience and variation in the linguistic profiles of advanced English-speaking learners of Japanese. In D. Brinton, O. Kagan & S. Bauckus (Eds.), *Heritage language education: A new field emerging.* Mahwah, NJ: Lawrence Erlbaum Associates.

Kim, E. J. (2002). Investigating the acquisition of Korean particles by beginning and intermediate learners. In J. J. Ree (Ed.), *The Korean language in America 7* (pp. 165–176). Tallahassee, FL: The American Association of Teachers of Korean.

Kim, H.-S. H. (2001). Issues of heritage learners in Korean language. In J. J. Ree (Ed.), *The Korean language in America 6* (pp. 257–274). Honolulu: The American Association of Teachers of Korean.

Kim, H.-S. H. (2002). The language backgrounds, motivations, and attitudes of heritage learners in KFL classes at University of Hawai'i at Mānoa. In J. J. Ree (Ed.), *The Korean language in America 7* (pp. 205–221). Tallahassee, FL: The American Association of Teachers of Korean.

Kim, J.-T. (2001). The degree of L1 interference among heritage and non-heritage learners of Korean: Do heritage students have advantages over nonheritage students? In J. J. Ree (Ed.), *The Korean language in America 6* (pp. 285–296). Honolulu: The American Association of Teachers of Korean.

King, R.(1998). Korean as a heritage language (KHL) vs. Korean as a foreign language (KFL) in North America and the former USSR: Ambiguous priorities and insufficient resources. *ACTA Koreana, 1,* 27–40.

Kondo-Brown, K. (2003). Heritage language instruction for post-secondary students from immigrant backgrounds. *Heritage Language Journal, 1.* Retrieved May 15, 2005, from http://www.international.ucla.edu/lrc/hlj/

Krashen, S. (1994). The input hypothesis and its rivals. In N. Ellis (Ed.) *Implicit and explicit learning of languages* (pp. 45–77). New York: Academic Press.

Lee, C.-B. (2000). Two-track curriculum system for university Korean language programs. *Academia Koreana, 3,* 77–86.

Lee, J. (1995). *Hankwuk.e kyeng.e.pep chey.kye.yui pyen.hwa.wa kyeng.e.pep kyo.ywuk.ul wui.han cey.an* [Changes in Korean honorific usage and their pedagocial implications]. In H.-M. Sohn (Ed.), *Korean language in America 1* (pp. 153–165). Honolulu: American Association of Teachers of Korean.

Lee, J. (2000). Error analysis and corrective measures for intermediate Korean. In S. Kang (Ed.), *Korean language in America 4* (pp. 163–179). Monterey, CA: American Association of Teachers of Korean.

Lee, M. (1997). Acquisition of Korean referent honorifics by adult learners of Korean as a second language. In Y.-H. Kim (Ed.), *Korean language in America 2* (pp. 99–110). Honolulu: American Association of Teachers of Korean.

Lee, S. K. (2000). A critical analysis of issues in secondary Korean education: A comparative study—1997 and 2000. In S.-O. S. Sohn (Ed.), *Korean language in America 5* (pp. 29–40). Los Angeles, CA: The American Association of Teachers of Korean.

Long, M. H. (1983). Does second language instruction make a difference? A review of the research. *TESOL Quarterly, 17,* 357–382.

Long, M. H. (1997). Authenticity and learning potential in L2 classroom discourse. In G. M. Jacobs (Ed.), *Language classrooms of tomorrow: Issues and responses* (pp. 148–69). Singapore: SEAMEO Regional Language Center.

Long, M. H. (2000). Recast in SLA: The story so far. In M. Long (Ed.), *Problems in SLA.* Mahwah, NJ: Lawrence Erlbaum Associates.

MacWhinney, B. (1987). The competition model. In B. MacWhinney (Ed.), *Mechanisms of language acquisition* (pp. 249–308). Hillsdale, NJ: Lawrence Erlbaum Associates.

MacWhinney, B., & Bates, E. (Eds.). (1989). *The crosslinguistic study of sentence processing.* New York: Cambridge University.

MacWhinney, B., Bates, E., & Kliegle, R. (1984). Cue validity and sentence interpretation in English, German, and Italian. *Journal of Verbal Learning and Verbal Behavior, 23,* 127–150.

McCullagh, P., & Nelder, A. (1989). *Generalized linear models.* London: Chapman & Hall.

O'Grady, W., Lee, M., & Choo, M. (2000). The acquisition of relative clauses in Korean as a second language. In S.-O. Sohn (Ed.), *Korean language in America 5* (pp. 245–256). Los Angeles, CA: American Association of Teachers of Korean.

O'Grady, W., Lee, M., & Choo, M. (2001). The acquisition of relative clauses by heritage and non-heritage learners of Korean as a second language: A comparative study. *Korean Language Education, 12*(2), 283–294.

O'Grady, W., Lee, M., & Choo, M. (2003). A subject–object asymmetry in the acquisition of relative clauses in Korean as a second language. *Studies in Second Language Acquisition, 25-3,* 433–448.

Pienemann, B. L. (1998). *Language processing and second language development: Processability theory.* Philadelphia: John Benjamins.

Salomone, A. (1992). Student–teacher interactions in selected French Immersion classrooms. In Bernhardt, E. (Ed.) *Life in language immersion classrooms* (pp. 97–109). Clevedon, UK: Multilingual Matters.

Sasaki, Y. (1991). English and Japanese interlanguage comprehension strategies: An analysis based on the competition model. *Applied Psycholinguistics, 12,* 47–73.

Schmidt, R. (1990). The role of consciousness in second language learning. *Applied Linguistics 11,* 129–158.

Schmidt, R. (1993). Awareness and second language acquisition. *Annual Review of Applied Linguistics, 13,* 206–26.

Schmidt, R. (1994). Cognitive unconscious: Of artificial grammars and SLA. In N. Ellis (Ed.), *Implicit and explicit learning of languages* (pp. 65–209). New York: Academic.

Schmidt, R. (1995). Consciousness and foreign language learning: A tutorial on the role of attention and awareness in learning. In R. Schmidt (Ed.) *Attention and awareness in foreign language learning. Technical Report No. 9* (pp. 1–63). Honolulu: University of Hawai`i, Second Language Teaching & Curriculum Center.

Sharwood-Smith, M. (1991). Speaking to many minds: On the relevance of different types of language information for the L2 learner. *Second Language Research, 7,* 165–179.

Sharwood-Smith, M. (1993). Input enhancement in instructed SLA: Theoretical bases. *Studies in Second Language Acquisition, 2,* 165–179.

Sohn, H.-M. (2002, November). *Why is Korean a "Category 4" language?—What should we do about it?* Lecture delivered at the Annual Symposium on East Asian Studies at the State University of New York at Binghamton, New York.

Sohn, S.-O. (1995). The design of curriculum for teaching Korean as a heritage language. In H.-M. Sohn (Ed.), *Korean language in America 1* (pp. 19–35). Honolulu: The American Association of Teachers of Korean.

Sohn, S.-O. (1997). Issues and concerns in teaching multi-level classes: Syllabus design for heritage and non-heritage learners. In Y.-H. Kim (Ed.), *Korean language in America 2* (pp. 139–158). Honolulu: American Association of Teachers of Korean.

Swain, M. (1991). French immersion and its offshoots: Getting two for one. In B. Freed (Ed.), *Foreign language acquisition research and the classroom* (pp. 91–103). Lexington, MA: D. C. Heath.

VanPatten, B. (2004). Input and output in establishing form-meaning connections. In B. VanPatten, J. Williams, & S. Rott (Eds.), *Form-meaning connections in second language acquisition.* (pp. 29–47). Mahwah, NJ: Lawrence Erlbaum Associates.

VanPatten, B., William, J., & Rott, S. (2004). Form-meaning connections in second language acquisition. In B. VanPatten, J. Williams, & S. Rott (Eds.), *Form-meaning connections in second language acquisition.* (pp. 2–26). Mahwah, NJ: Lawrence Erlbaum Associates.

Wang, H.-S. (1995). The impact of family background on the acquisition of Korean honorifics. In H.-M. Sohn (Ed.), *Korean language in America 1* (pp. 197–211). Honolulu: The American Association of Teachers of Korean.

Wang, H.-S. (1997). The effects of topic on lexical errors in writings by intermediate learners of Korean. In Y.-H. Kim (Ed.), *Korean language in America 2* (pp. 39–56). Honolulu: American Association of Teachers of Korean.

A Separate-Track for Advanced Heritage Language Students?: Japanese Intersentential Referencing

Kimi Kondo-Brown
Chie Fukuda
University of Hawai'i at Mānoa

THEORETICAL AND PEDAGOGICAL ISSUES AND THE STATEMENT OF PURPOSE

Heritage Versus Nonheritage Students in Postsecondary Foreign Language Programs

A number of postsecondary foreign language programs in the United States provide separate tracks for heritage language (HL) versus non-HL learners as a pedagogically sound strategy (e.g., Kondo, 1998; McGinnis, 1996; Shen, 2003; Sohn, 1995, 1997). One rationale for this strategy is that HL learners' language profiles and needs are distinctly different from those of non-HL learners (Andrews, 2000; Campbell, 1996; Campbell & Rosenthal, 2000; King, 1998; Mazzocco, 1996; Pino & Pino, 2000). One uninvestigated issue concerning the separate-track policy is that such systems are primarily implemented at the beginning and/or intermediate levels, but not at the advanced level (Kondo-Brown, 2003). This practice is based on the assumption that there is little linguistic difference between HL learners and non-HL learners at the advanced level. However, to our knowledge, such an assumption has little empirical foundation.

Studies that compared the differences in linguistic skills between university HL versus non-HL learners *are* emerging in Japanese and Korean, especially in Korean (see Kondo-Brown, this volume). Among such studies, two with a focus on Japanese reading skills argue that university Japanese heritage language (JHL) learners outperformed non-JHL learners in reading comprehension ability (Kondo-Brown, 2005; Matusnaga, 2003). In Kondo-Brown's (2005) study, 185 English first language (L1) incoming college students of Japanese were divided into four groups based on their degrees of connection to Japanese heritage. They took three Japanese placement tests including a reading comprehension test that consisted of five Japanese texts of beginning to advanced levels. The results indicated that the JHL group with at least one Japanese-speaking parent outperformed the other groups. Matsunaga's (2003) study similarly compared JHL learners' reading comprehension skills on two Japanese texts with different amounts of *kanji* (Chinese characters) to those of their English L1 non-HL counterparts and found that the former outperformed the latter.

Purpose of the Present Study

The present study extends this line of research by focusing on JHL learners and non-JHL learners who had been enrolled in advanced-level college Japanese courses. Both Matusnaga (2003) and Kondo-Brown (2003) were primarily concerned with performance *outcome differences* on reading comprehension tests between JHL learners and non-JHL learners. However, the present study investigates the *processes* involved. More specially, this study investigates how similarly and differently JHL learners and non-JHL learners monitor and recover phonologically empty Japanese pronouns, also known as zero pronouns, in order to establish intersentential reference when reading an advanced level Japanese narrative text for meaning.[1] The present study also extends previous research by taking non-JHL learners' living abroad experience into consideration as an additional variable. The experience of living or studying abroad has been reported as a variable critically influencing second-language proficiency (e.g., DuFon, & Churchill, 2006; Freed, 1998; Rivers, 1998)

---

[1]Researchers sometimes label phonetically empty pronouns differently: "zero anaphor" (Huang, 1984), "null pronoun" (Pérez-Leroux & Glass, 1999), and "null subject/object" (Liceras & Díaz, 1999). In this study, we use the term *zero pronoun* (Hasegawa, 1984; Hinds & Hinds, 1979; Rubin, 1992).

The Japanese language belongs to the category of least referentially informative languages allowing extensive use of zero pronouns (Huang, 1984). For students in advanced-level Japanese language classes who are required to comprehend authentic Japanese texts, the ability to recover zero pronouns is necessary for the efficient and accurate comprehension of Japanese texts (see Noda, 2001; Ogawa, 1991; Ueyama, 1990). However, as Kanno (1997) pointed out, Japanese-as-a-foreign-language textbooks and instruction pay little attention to zero pronouns. Also, according to Polio (1995), L2 teachers may use more lexical pronouns than zero pronouns in instruction in their efforts to help learners keep track of referents. However, Polio argues that such modified input from teachers may prevent learners from developing the ability to identify or use zero pronouns.

Kitajima (2001) recommended referential strategy training for improving intermediate-level learners' reading comprehension of simplified, intermediate-level texts. However, we still do not know how effective such training would be for advanced-level learners of Japanese who are expected to read unsimplified, advanced-level texts, or how effectively the learners would process subject-less and/or object-less sentences that frequently appear in such texts. Also, if there are sizable individual differences in inferencing ability among these learners, do learner variables as heritage background and living-abroad experience factors contribute to such differences?

Furthermore, in order to help the learners identify unstated personal referents in intermediate-level texts, Kitajima (2001) directed learners to look for predicates that usually come at the end of phrases or sentences (e.g., Ø *Asa gohan o tabe nakatta* "Ø didn't eat breakfast"). What if the learner cannot identify a predicate that provides critical information about the referent in question? To what degree, is the inability to identify the predicates in the text related to the efficiency of identifying their referents? In order to provide effective referential strategy training for advanced-level JHL learners and non-JHL learners in reading unsimplified, authentic texts, all of these questions need to be answered.

COMPARING JAPANESE AND ENGLISH ANAPHORA

English Pronominalization Versus Japanese Zero Pronouns

Different languages may adopt different ways of reducing redundancy through anaphora.[2] Some languages such as English mobilize lexical

---

[2]All natural languages allow anaphora as a primary means of redundancy reduction (Flynn, 1987, p. 40). Anaphora is "a process or result of a linguistic unit deriving its interpretation from some previously expressed unit or meaning (the antecedent)" (Crystal, 1997, p. 19). The referent of a given anaphor can be recoverable either from prior discourse, the context, or general knowledge (Williams, 1988, p. 340).

pronouns (i.e., pronouns with phonological content, such as "s/he," "they"), but others such as Japanese utilize zero pronouns in order to substitute for nouns and avoid redundancy (Hasegawa, 1984; Hinds & Hinds, 1979; Rubin, 1992).[3] For example, Hinds and Hinds (1979) explain that there are close parallels between English pronominalization and Japanese ellipsis or the use of zero pronouns. In the examples that follow, instead of repeating a noun, "parents," that can be inferred from the context, English uses lexical pronouns (in the present case, "they"), whereas Japanese uses zero pronouns, indicated by the symbol ∅.[4]

English (lexical pronoun)

My parents died young. When *they* were traveling through historical, ruins in Asia, *they* got into an accident.

Japanese (zero pronoun/ellipsis)

Boku	*no*	*ryooshin*	*wa*	*sorotte*	*wakajini*	*shiteiru.* ∅	*Ajia*	*no*	*meisho*
my	GN	parents	Top	together	died	young	Asia	CN	famous place

kyuuseki	*o*	*junreki*	*shiteita*	*toki,* ∅	*jiko*	*ni*	*atta*	*no*	*da.*
ruin	O	travel	through	when	accident	DT	met	Nom	Cop

"My parents died young. When (they) were traveling through historical ruins in Asia, (they) got into an accident."

In Japanese, ellipsis may also occur when a noun phrase can be specified by a certain syntactic construction (Hinds, 1982). For example, ellipsis may occur in the constructions with: a verbal adjective *-rashii* "to look like," which requires a third-person subject; another verbal adjective *-tai* "to want to," which requires a first-person subject; or a verb *mairu* "to come/go," which requires that the speaker or his/her in-group person is the subject (Hinds, 1982, p. 80). Ellipsis may also occur in constructions with auxiliary verbs such as *-te kuru* (e.g., *denwa o kakete kuru* "(someone) calls the speaker,"

---

[3] According to Hinds and Hinds (1979), under certain circumstances, the speaker may not choose to use zero pronouns even when that choice may result in repeating the same noun phrase (pp. 205–208). For example, Hind and Hinds suggest the speaker may repeat noun phrases if the speaker judges that their absence may confuse the listener/reader. As a related issue, Takami (1987) argues that the use of Japanese pronouns (including zero pronouns) may also be explained pragmatically in terms of "empathy."

[4] The following abbreviations were used in the present study: AG (agentive marker: agent of passive verb); CN (connecting particle); Cop (various forms of copula verb be); DT (dative maker); GN (genitive marker); Nom (nominalizer); O (object marker); QT (quotation maker); S (subject marker); and Top (topic marker).

which require that the subject be a person other than the speaker (Iori, 2003). Thus, Japanese has several linguistic items that specify subjects in the given sentences (Masuoka & Takubo, 1989). In fact, according to Chung (2004), compared to Korean L1 speakers (who speak a pro-drop, head-final language), Japanese L1 speakers may use more zero pronouns because Japanese has more linguistic devices including the *uchi-soto* ("inside–outside") distinction that specify referents.[5]

Pro-Drop and Non-Pro-Drop Parameters

The anaphoric difference between Japanese and English just illustrated may be in part ascribed to differences in the parameter settings. In the Universal Grammar (UG) theory, variation between languages is described in "parameters" (Cook & Newson, 1996, p. 15). A language that allows the lack of a lexical subject like Japanese, Korean, and Chinese is called a "pro-drop language," whereas a language that requires a lexical subject (e.g., English, German, French) is called a "non-pro-drop language" (Cook & Newson, 1996, p. 55). Thus, from the perspective of UG theory, successful second language (L2) learning may require the resetting of parameters (Flynn, 1987). However, it appears to be difficult for English L1 learners of Japanese to reset parameters and detect the referents of Japanese zero pronouns (Rubin, 1992).

Head-Initial and Head-Final Parameters

An additional potential difficulty that English L1 learners of Japanese may face in identifying the referents of Japanese zero pronouns has been discussed in terms of the head-initial versus head-final parameter distinction (e.g., Mazuka, 1991). In head-initial languages like English, the predicate appears at the beginning of the sentence (on the left), whereas in head-final languages like Japanese, the predicate appears at the end of the sentence (on the right). Based on this distinction, Mazuka (1991) argued for a difference between Japanese and English in the processing of "Empty Categories" (ECs), defined as "referentially dependent elements that are phonetically empty, but present syntactically" such as zero pronouns and reflexive pronouns (p. 215). Mazuka also pointed out two problems in processing ECs in Japanese: (a) detecting the presence and location of a zero pronoun, and (b) determining its referent (pp. 221–222). According to Mauka, these problems may occur because, in head-final languages like

---

[5]Japanese people's behavior including language behavior is often described using such dichotomous concepts as *uchi* "inside" versus *soto* "outside" or *omote* "front" versus *ura* "back" (e.g., Lebra, 1976; Maynard, 1997; Sukle, 1994).

Japanese, predicates that express the semantic relationship or thematic role between arguments—such as what is the subject/agent and the object/patient in a sentence—are not available until the end of the sentences (see Cook & Newson, 1996, p. 60).[6] The following examples are adopted from Mazuka et al. (1989, p. 201):

(1) *Yuujin   ga   moochoo   de nyuuin   shite ita.*
    friend   S   appendicitis   due to   was hospitalized

   "(My) friend was hospitalized because of appendicitis."

(2) *Yuujin ga Ø moochoo   de   nyuuin shite ita   toki,   mimai ni kite kureta.*
    friend S   appendicitis due to was hospitalized when   came to visit

   "When (I) was hospitalized with appendicitis, a friend came to visit (me)."

In (1), it is clear that *yuujin* "friend" is the subject of the sentence. However, in (2), readers may wrongly interpret *yuujin* as the subject of the subordinate clause until they reach the main verb containing the benefactory verb *-te kureru* at the very end of the sentence.[7] Because a benefactory verb *-te kureru* requires that the subject be person other than the speaker, at that point, for the first time, it becomes clear to the readers that *yuujin* is actually the subject of the main clause verb, *kite kureta* "came to (for my benefit)." Then, in turn, the readers need to reanalyze the subject of the subordinate clause: it is the speaker, not *yuujin*. Furthermore, according to Mazuka (1991), the fact that the Japanese language does not use relative pronouns in relative clause constructions may make the identification of the referents of zero pronouns even more difficult (p. 218).

Identification Process of the Referent of a Japanese Zero Pronoun

Hinds and Hinds (1979, p. 202) suggest a three-step progression process in the identification of participants in a narrative: (a) the participant is introduced; (b) the participant is referred to with a topicalized noun

---

[6]In this chapter, "agent" means the person who performs an action (e.g., *They* got into an accident). In the two cases in the text used for the present study, the agent also refers to the person who is in the state of being (e.g., *She* had been my grandfather's lover). "Patient" means the person being affected by the act (e.g., I might have seen *her*; see Payne, 1997).

[7]Benefactory verbs indicate auxiliary verbs that express "some action as a favor to a person" (Makino & Tsutsui, 1989, p. 216), such as *-te kureru* "to do something for the speaker/his in-group member" and *-te ageru* "to do something for someone other than the actor."

phrase; and (c) the participant is referred to by ellipsis or a zero pronoun. In the example that follows provided by Hinds and Hinds, a participant, *musume* "daughter," is initially introduced with the subject particle *ga* (in sentence 1). Then, the subject is referred to with the topicalized noun phrase, *musume wa* (in sentence 2). And finally, the subject/daughter as the current, ongoing topic is referred to by a zero pronoun (in sentence 3):

(1) *Mukashi mukashi,   miyako no   daijin   ni   hitori no   musume   ga arimashita.*
    once upon a time capital CN minister DT one   CN daughter S exist

   "Once upon a time, a king had a daughter."

(2) *Musume   wa   chiisai toki   kara,   mawari no hito   ni   "ohimesama, ohimesama"*
    daughter Top young when from around CN people AG princess princess

   to   yobarete   sodatta   soo   desu.
   QT   be called   grew up   hearsay Cop

   "The daughter was called 'princess' by the people around her ever since she was a child."

(3) *Tokoroga, ∅ hitonami   hazurete   kiryoo   ga   warukatta node,   yome ni*
    But   ordinary deviated appearance S was bad   because wife DT

   moraite   ga   nakatta   soo   desu.
   receiver   S   not exist   hearsay Cop

   "But (she) was uglier than anyone, and no one wanted to marry her."
   (Adapted from Hinds & Hinds, 1979, p. 205)

Masuoka and Takubo (1989) seem to agree with the identification process of the referents of Japanese pronouns provided by Hinds and Hinds (1982): "In Japanese, the elements we can infer from the context or those mentioned before tend to be ellipted. Nouns that appeared as a topic continue to be ellipted as long as the topic remains the same." (pp. 151–152).

The Issue of Proficiency Levels in the Acquisition of Zero Pronouns

Polio (1995) compared how Japanese L1 speakers (pro-drop) and English L1 speakers (non-pro-drop) at various proficiency levels are able to use zero pronouns in L2 Chinese (pro-drop). Polio found that regardless of the learners' L1 background, the frequencies of using zero pronouns is associated with L2 proficiency levels: although L2 learners at the low level were not able to use zero pronouns, as the proficiency level increased, the use of zero pronouns became native-like.

In Nakahama's (2003) study, one issue examined was how proficiency levels interacted with the use of noun referential forms (including the use of zero pronouns) to manage topic continuity and discontinuity in a silent film retelling task. The participants were Japanese L1 speakers and Japanese L2 speakers at the intermediate or advanced levels. Nakahama's descriptive analysis suggests that, unlike intermediate-level Japanese L2 students, those at the advanced level could use zero pronouns in native-like manners.

Whereas Polio (1995) and Nakahama (2003) investigated the issue of the proficiency variable concerning the acquisition of zero pronouns utilizing production measures, that is, counting the number of their occurrences, White (1985) investigated the issue by utilizing grammatical judgment tests. White found that Spanish L1 learners (pro-drop) who are more proficient in L2 English (non-pro-drop) reject more null subjects in English grammaticality judgment tests than those who are less proficient.

Methodological Issues

As just discussed, a few studies have examined the acquisition of the pro-drop parameter by L1 speakers of a non-pro-drop language or *vice versa* based on production measures (e.g., Clancy, 1980; Nakahama, 2003; Polio, 1995; Williams, 1988). However, when adopting a productive measure, one methodological issue that needs to be raised is whether the adopted measure is dealing with oral or written discourse. For example, Christensen (2000) argues that "Though the zero anaphora is a productive feature of anaphoric reference in Chinese discourse, its productivity depends on the specific genre of discourse being analyzed" (p. 332). In his study, Chinese L1 speakers (pro-drop) were asked to watch a film and narrate it both orally and in writing, and the analysis of the data indicated that written discourse contained more zero pronouns than spoken discourse.

Another methodological concern raised was the use of grammaticality judgment tests. Some researchers who are concerned with the acquisition of pro-drop or non-pro-drop parameters, including identification ability of the referent of zero pronouns, have adopted grammaticality judgment tests at the intra-sentential level (Lantlof, 1990; Kanno, 1997; White, 1985). However, as Williams (1988) pointed out, the analysis of a sentence in isolation may obscure the referential role of zero pronouns (p. 341). This issue seems particularly critical in dealing with Japanese because, as discussed earlier, the identification process of Japanese zero pronouns often involves intersentential inferencing. To our knowledge, no previous study examined Japanese L2 learners' anaphoric inferencing ability at the intersentential level. Unlike previous studies, the present study will just do that.

Research Questions

Based on the literature review, the present study will investigate the following questions:

Question 1.   Do language learner background variables such as heritage background and living-abroad experience significantly influence Japanese L2 learners' ability to identify zero pronouns when reading an advanced-level Japanese narrative text?

Question 2.   Are Japanese L2 learners' abilities to identify zero pronouns in a given text linked with their ability to identify the related predicates in the text as well as their overall reading comprehension of advanced-level Japanese texts?

Question 3.   Is a tracking system necessary for advanced-level Japanese L2 learners?

METHOD

Participants

The present data were collected as part of a larger research project involving advanced learners of Japanese at the University of Hawai`i at Mānoa (UHM). The participants were 42 English L1 learners enrolled in advanced-level Japanese courses at UHM. The 42 participants all identified English as their strongest/native language. They were recruited through flyers in the university's advanced-level Japanese language classes and on the department bulletin board. All participants were paid for their participation. The participants were first divided into two groups, JHL learners ($n = 12$) and the non-JHL learners ($n = 30$). The 12 JHL learners in this study have at least one Japanese-speaking parent. All but one JHL learner had been first placed in a special advanced-level course for bilingual HL students at UHM. [8] One JHL learner had only taken advanced-level Japanese classes in the regular track.

The 30 non-JHL learners, who had been enrolled in the university's fourth-year Japanese classes, were further divided into two groups depending on whether they had studied and/or worked in Japanese for a considerable time. Fifteen non-JHL learners had lived in Japan for 6 months or longer (12 had lived in Japan for 1 to 6 years, and three for 6–11 months).

---

[8]At UHM, whether incoming HL students are bilingual or not is judged based on the Japanese placement test scores and oral interviews.

TABLE 6.1
Background Information

JHLhawai`i Group		JHL (n = 12)	non-JHLabroad (n = 15)	non (n = 15)
Gender	Male	3	9	11
	Female	9	6	4
Average age		20	27	24
Student status	Undergraduate	12	8	13
	Graduate	0	7	2
Major	Japanese	3	7	11
	Non-Japanese	9	8	4
Average years of instruction		6.0	4.7	7.4

Most had studied Japanese formally in Japan while living there. In the present study, these participants are grouped together as the "non-JHLabroad." The remaining 15 non-JHL learners had never visited Japan (three students) or visited Japan for 1 month or less (12 students). They had studied Japanese formally only in American schools in Hawai`i. In the present study, these participants were called the "non-JHLhawai`i."

Table 6.1 compares the background information of the three groups in terms of gender, average age, class standing, major, and average years of formal Japanese instruction. The table shows: (a) whereas there were more male students in the non-JHL groups, the students in the JHL group were predominantly female; (b) average ages ranged from 20 to 27 with the highest average age for the non-JHLabroad group because more than half of the group were graduate students; (c) the majority of the non-JHLhawai`i group were Japanese majors but other groups had less Japanese majors; and (d) the average years of formal and nonformal instruction in Japanese ranged from 4.7 to 7.4 with the highest average for the non-JHLhawai`i group.

Instruments and Procedures

The present data were obtained through: (a) a background information questionnaires; (b) two reading comprehension tests; and (c) reading and thinking aloud sessions using an unsimplifed, advanced-level narrative text that includes the target zero pronouns. The participants attended the sessions individually at a campus room set aside for the investigation. Throughout the sessions, the second author was present.

Background Questionnaire. The background questionnaire, which was given at the end of the last session, asked each participant to report his/her age, gender, class standing, major, strongest language(s), birthplace, HL

TABLE 6.2
Comparison of Reading Comprehension Test Scores

	Group	JHL (n =12)	Non-JHLabroad (n =15)	Non-JHLhawai`i (n =15)
Reading Comprehension	Mean	14.6	12.3	10.9
Tests (max. =20)	SD	3.2	4.2	3.2

background, current and previous Japanese language instruction, short visits to Japan, and experiences of living in Japan. The questionnaire was also used to confirm the participants' unfamiliarity with the Japanese texts used in the study.

Reading Comprehension Tests. The three groups were compared in terms of overall abilities to comprehend two advanced-level texts. Each text was followed by 10 English multiple-choice questions. One of the texts was a narrative text (a slightly modified version of an excerpt from Japanese fiction), and the other text was an expository text (a Japanese newspaper article). We estimated participant's ability to comprehend advanced-level Japanese texts based on the total scores of the two reading comprehension tests (20 points possible). A Pearson product-moment correlation coefficient between these two sets of test scores was reasonably high ($r = .83$, $p < .001$), and the split-half (adjusted) reliability of the total test scores was satisfactory ($r = .91$).

Table 6.2 compares the means and standard deviations (*SDs*) of the total reading comprehension test scores by groups. As the table shows, the JHL group had the highest mean, and the non-JHLhawai`i group had the lowest.

Reading and Thinking Aloud Sessions. There were 22 target zero pronouns referring to previously mentioned persons in the text. They were the elipted agents (20 items) or patients/the affected (2 items). The following is an example of agent ellipsis. In the Japanese sentence, the agent of the action/predicate, *chuugakkoo e agaru* "enter junior high school," is ellipted.

Ø *chuugakko*   *e*   *agaru mae ni, sobo*   *ga* *shinda.*
Junior high school   to   enter before grandmother S   die
"Before (I) entered junior high school, (my) grandmother died."

In order to investigate the participants' abilities to interpret the target zero pronouns and the connected predicates, they were asked to read aloud each of the 21 sentences from the narrative text.[9] The reading of

---

[9]In the present study, the target Japanese predicates were in the form of (a) a verb with complement (e.g., *jiko ni atta noda* "had an accident") or without (e.g., *omotta* "thought"), or (b) a noun or adjective combined with a copula (e.g., *aka no tannin datta* "was a complete stranger").

each sentence from a card was immediately followed by a verbal reporting task where the participants read aloud the sentence for meaning in English. After the participants finished a card, they returned it to the assistant, and received the next card. This procedure was repeated until they completed all 21 cards, which required about 30 minutes for each participant. The read-and-think-aloud task was taped and then later transcribed.

Using the transcriptions, we judged the participants' abilities to interpret the target zero pronouns and the connected predicates. The target predicates was a single verb (e.g., 思った *omotta* "thought"), a verb with an auxiliary verb (混乱していた *konranshi-te ita* "was confused"), or a combination of a verb and an obligatory complement (the removal of which may result in changing the meanings of the verb in question, e.g., 事故に遭った *jiko ni atta* "got into an accident."). No partial scores were given: one point for a correct identification and zero for an incorrect one. The Cronbach alpha reliability estimates for both sets of scores were fairly high ($\alpha = .90$ for both zero pronoun identification scores [*zero pronoun*] and predicate identification scores [*predicate*]).

RESULTS AND DISCUSSION

Comparison of Correctly Identified Predicates and Zero Pronouns by Group

Table 6.3 provides the descriptive overview of the results. Figure 6.1 compares the means between the groups visually. As the table and figure show, for both *zero pronoun* and *predicate*, the JHL group on average performed better than the remaining two non-JHL groups. For example, on average, 74.3% of zero pronouns were correctly identified by the JHL group, whereas 56.7% and 38.8% of the non-JHLabroad and non-JHLhawai`i groups, respectively, did the same.

In order to examine the magnitude of the observed differences in mean scores between groups, an overall one-way repeated-measures MANOVA

TABLE 6.3
Comparison of Correctly Identified Zero Pronouns and Predicates (in Percentages)

	Number of items	r		JHL (n = 12)	Non-JHLabroad (n = 15)	Non-JHLhawai`i (n = 15)
Zero Pronoun	22	.90	Mean	74.3	56.7	38.8
			SD	19.2	24.4	23.6
Predicate	22	.90	Mean	63.3	49.4	30.6
			SD	17.2	24.8	23.0

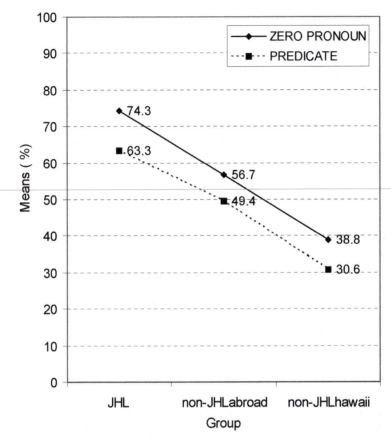

Figure 6.1.   Comparing *zero pronoun* and *predicate*
by group (in percentages).

analysis was conducted with two dependent variables (i.e., *zero pronoun*
and *predicate*) and one independent variable (i.e., grouping with three lev-
els/groups). The overall MANOVA indicated a significant difference
($F = 8.09$, $df = 2$, $p = 0.001$, partial $eta^2 = .29$, *power* = .94). Therefore, an uni-
variate one-way ANOVA was performed for each dependent variable. The
results revealed a significant main effect for both variables: *zero pronoun*
($F = 8.13$, $df = 2$, $p = 0.001$, partial $eta^2 = .29$, *power* = .94) and *predicate* ($F =
7.38$, $df = 2$, $p = 0.002$, partial $eta^2 = .28$, *power* = .92). Post-hoc-comparisons
using Scheffé indicated that the JHL outperformed the non-JHLhawai`i
group on both *zero pronoun* ($p = 0.001$) and *predicate* ($p = 0.002$). No significant difference was found between the JHL and non-JHLabroad groups or
the non-JHLabroad and non-JHLhawai`i groups.

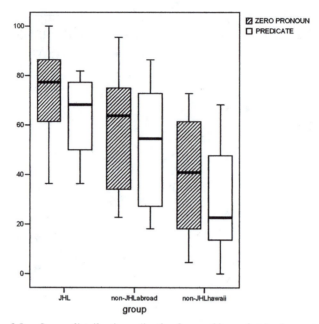

Figure 6.2.   Score distributions (in the form of box plots) of *zero pronoun*
and *predicate* (in percentages).

To explore these results further, score distributions for *zero pronoun* and *predicate* respectively are plotted for each group (see Fig. 6.2). As the box plots clearly show, for *zero pronoun* as well as *predicate*, there seems to be little overlap in score distributions between the JHL and non-JHLhawai`i groups. However, when each of these groups was compared to the non-JHLabroad group, there seem to be considerable overlaps in score distributions between the JHL and non-JHL abroad groups as well as between the non-JHLabroad and non-JHLhawai`i groups. Such overlaps contributed to the fact that the observed mean differences between the JHL and non-JHLabroad groups as well as the non-JHLabroad and non-JHLhawai`i groups turned out to be nonsignificant.

Correlations Between Correctly Identified Zero Pronouns and Reading Comprehension Scores

When the correlation between *zero pronoun* and the reading comprehension test scores was examined, it turned out to be moderate ($r = .71$). This information indicates that, to a considerable degree, the zero pronoun identification scores are ordered much like the overall reading comprehension scores used in the present study.

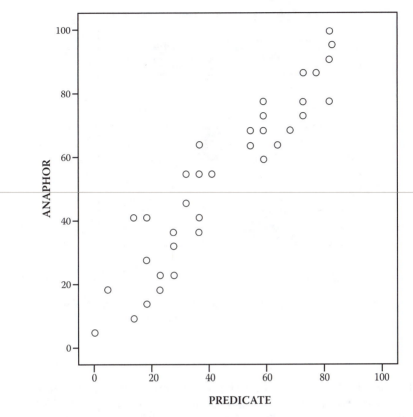

Figure 6.3.   Scatterplot for *zero pronoun* and *predicate* (in percentages).

Correlations Between Correctly Identified Zero Pronouns and Predicates

The correlation between *zero pronoun* and *predicate* proved to be very strong ($r = .94$, $p < 0.001$ estimated by Pearson product-moment correlation coefficient). This indicates that *zero pronoun* had 88% overlapping variance ($r^2 = .94^2 = .88$) with *predicate*, which means that these two sets of scores go together very closely (see the scatter plots of the scores in Fig. 6.3).

In order to further investigate the relationship between *zero pronoun* and *predicate* by group, the frequencies of the following four categories of performance patterns were counted separately for each group: The participant was able to identify (a) both zero pronoun and predicate accurately (*both*); (b) only zero pronoun (*zero pronoun*); (c) only predicate (*predicate*); and (d) neither (*neither*). Appendix A shows examples for these categories.

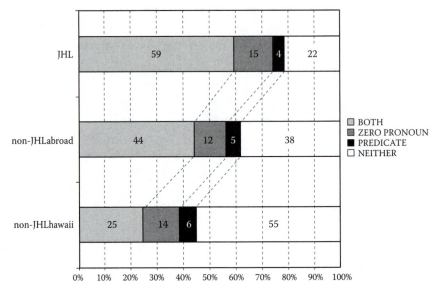

Figure 6.4.   Comparing the frequencies of both, *zero pronoun, predicate,* and
neither by group (in percentages).

Figure 6.4 visually compares each group's frequencies for these four categories (in percentages). For example, there were 156 instances of *both* for
the JHL group, which was 59% of the total number of observed frequencies for this group. As the figure shows, the combined instances of *both* and
neither were the majority or 80% or more for any given group.

The figure shows that the JHL group had the highest percentage of *both*,
and the lowest percentage of *neither*, and that the non-JHLhawai`i group
had exactly the opposite pattern (i.e., the highest percentage of *neither*, and
the lowest percentage of *both*). In other words, the two factors, namely,
learner background and predicate-zero pronoun identification pattern,
seemed to be related. A *chi*-square analysis performed on the data indicated that these two factors were indeed related ($X^2 = 86.54$, $df = 6$,
$p < 0.0001$). The strength of association (calculated by Cramer's V) indicates that the degree of this relationship was .22. In other words, more
successful predicate-and-zero pronoun interpretation is more likely to
occur when the student has heritage or living abroad background.

Thus, the present study appears to confirm both of the hypotheses
set out at the beginning of this study. First, language learner background
variables such as heritage background and living-abroad experience are factors influencing the students' ability to identify zero pronouns in reading an

advanced-level Japanese narrative text for meaning. As just shown, when JHL learners were compared to the non-JHLhawai`i group, the former out-performed the latter in the abilities to identify zero pronouns as well as the related predicates. At the same time, when JHL learners were compared to the non-JHLabroad group, no significant difference resulted because, as Figure 6.2 shows, some of the JHLabroad group seemed to be able to per-form well. Future research should investigate how JHL learners and non-JHL learners' past literacy learning experiences at home and in living-abroad contexts such as the intensity of their exposure to Japanese print materials at home and in the community have contributed to their anaphoric inferencing abilities.

Second, as some linguists would have predicted (e.g., Cook & Newson, 1996; Mazuka, 1991), this study indicated that the learners' ability to detect and identify zero pronouns is closely related to their ability to process the related predicates. That is, when Japanese L2 learners cannot identify zero pronouns, it is very likely that they cannot identify the connected predicates either, and *vice versa*. Third, the learners' ability to identify zero pronouns also proved to be related to their reading comprehension test scores, which seems consistent with previous findings (e.g., Nakahama, 2003; Polio, 1995). Thus, for Japanese L2 learners to be able to process zero pronouns effec-tively, their overall reading ability needs to be sufficient to identify the connected predicates.

CONCLUSION

Both JHL learners and non-JHL learners in advanced-level courses are often expected to be able to read unsimplified, advanced-level Japanese texts not tailored for Japanese L2 readers. This study investigated how these learners monitor and identify zero pronouns while reading such texts, an important reading skill necessary for effective L2 reading (Yoshida, 2001). In the present study, JHL learners who grew up in a bilingual envi-ronment with at least one Japanese-speaking parent were compared to two non-JHL subgroups: (a) the non-JHLabroad group, that is, a group of non-JHL learners who have learned Japanese mainly in American schools, but also studied and/or worked in Japan for 6 months or longer and (b) the non-JHLhawai`i group, that is, a group of those who have studied Japanese exclusively in American schools, and never visited Japan or visited there for 1 month or less.

We found that there were considerable individual differences in the demonstrated abilities to identify zero pronouns among these learners, and that learner background variables such as heritage background and living-abroad background contribute substantially to the observed differences.

More specifically, when the distribution of zero-pronoun identification scores for the JHL group was compared to that for the non-JHLhawai`i group, little overlap between the groups was observed. In other words, JHL learners scored significantly higher than non-JHL learners with little living abroad experience on the zero pronounce identification task. However, the distribution of zero pronoun identification scores for each of the JHL and non-JHLhawai`i groups overlapped considerably with that for the non-JHLabroad group. In other words, after having lived in Japan for a considerable period of time, some of the non-JHL learners' zero pronoun identification abilities seem to have become more like JHL learners, whereas others remained like non-JHL learners with little living-abroad experience.

This study also found that JHL learners' and non-JHL learners' abilities to identify zero pronouns were closely related to their abilities to identify the related predicates as well as their reading comprehension test scores. Although we did not examine the directions of influence between overall reading proficiency, that is, the direction between the ability to identify zero pronouns and the ability to identify the related predicates, it seems that the students' past exposure to Japanese print materials at home or during their time in Japan helped them improve their overall Japanese reading proficiency levels and, therefore, they could identify the related predicates better. Then, in turn, they were able to identify the target pronouns better, which further enhanced their comprehension of the texts used in this study. In order to fully understand how heritage and living-abroad backgrounds contribute to the enhancement of referential processing of zero pronouns, future research should examine the frequency and quality of these students' exposure to Japanese print materials outside classrooms.

As discussed at the beginning of this chapter, many university-level foreign language programs in the United States offer separate tracks for HL and non-HL learners mostly at the beginning and intermediate levels. However, given the sizable individual differences at the advanced level, the establishment of such tracking systems may also be desirable or even necessary to deal with individual differences at that higher level. Separate tracks for advanced learners of Japanese seem to be particularly desirable between JHL learners and non-JHL learners with little living abroad experience. Apparently, the remaining non-JHL learners with long-term living abroad experience should probably be placed in either track depending on their demonstrated proficiency levels. As the present study has shown, Japanese L2 learners seem to be able to process zero pronouns in a given text effectively when their overall Japanese reading abilities are sufficient to identify the connected predicates in the text. Given the considerable individual differences in Japanese reading ability among the present JHL learners and non-JHL learners, a teacher using the same instructional materials for teaching reading skills (including inferencing training) for these different groups of students in the same advanced Japanese class may create a serious mismatch between abilities of some learners and the difficulty of the materials.

ACKNOWLEDGMENT

We thank Dr. John Haig for his valuable comments on this chapter. This research chapter was prepared as part of the funded University of Hawai`i NRCEA (National Resource Center East Asia) Japanese HL instruction project in during 2003–2004. The first author was the principal investigator of the project and the second author was a graduate research assistant. An earlier version of this chapter was presented at the 14th World Congress of Applied Linguistics Conference. July 24–29. 2005. Madison, WI.

Appendix A
Examples of Performance Categories[*]

Performance		*Examples*
Both Predicate and Zero pronoun [*BOTH*]	Prompt	そこで祖父母が僕を育ててくれた。'So, (my) grandparents raised me.'
		→中学校へ上がる前に、祖母が死んだ。'Before (**I**) **entered middle school,** (my) grandmother died.'
	Student (ID#46)	*Sokode sofu ah bo ga boku o sodatete kureta.* So there my grandpa and grandma, my grandparents raised me.
		→*Chuugakkoo e agaru mae ni sobo ga shinda.* And before **I went, entered the middle school**, my grandma had died.
Zero pronoun only [*PRO*]	Prompt	僕の両親はそろって若死にしている。'My parents died young.'
		→アジアの名所旧跡を巡歴していた時、事故に遭ったのだ。 'When (**they**) **were traveling** through historical ruins in Asia, (they) got into an accident.'
	Student (ID#46)	*Boku no ryooshin wa sorotte .. wakajiini shiteiru.* Uhm my parents, ah both of them have died early. They have been dead.
		→*Ajia no meisho kyuu .. seki o nantoka shiteita toki, jiko ni atta no da.* When they were … when **they were in doing something** in Asia's .. office .. *kyuuseki kyuuseki* uhm … they're probably looking at bonds and the history . . .

(Continued)

Appendix A
(Continued)

Performance		Examples
Predicate only [*PRE*]	Prompt	僕の両親はそろって若死にしている。'My parents died young.'
		→アジアの名所旧跡を巡歴していた時、事故に遭ったのだ。 'When (they) were traveling through historical ruins in Asia, **(they) got into an accident.**'
	Student (ID#4)	Boku no ryooshin wa sorotte: wakajini: shiteiru. I don't know the kanji but . . . my parents . . was young and died.
		→ Ajia no: nantoka: o something siteita toki jiko ni: atta no da. So *ajia no: na* that *tokoro.* . somethi:ng looks like *meguru* to come by so when I was traveling around different places in Asia? Just one time, ah, **I got into an accident?**"
Neither [*NEITHER*]	Prompt	先日なんと祖父が他界してしまった。'The other day, to my shock, my grandfather passed away.
		→ 動揺した。'**(I) was shaken.**'
	Student (ID#4)	Senjitsu nanto sofu ga taka ? shite shimatta. Takai? Uhm the other day my grandfather passed way.
		→ *Yuu e? doo:* something *shita.* **I have no idea.**

*The zero pronoun symbol and English translations were not included in the original prompts. Bolded items were the target *zero pronouns* and *predicates*

REFERENCES

Andrews, D. R. (2000). Heritage learners in the Russian classroom: Where linguistics can help. *ADFL Bulletin, 31*, 39–44.

Campbell, R. (1996). New learners and new environments: Challenges and opportunities. In R. C. Lafayette (Ed.), *National standards: A catalyst for reform* (pp. 97–117). Lincolnwood, IL: National Textbook Company.

Campbell, R. N., & Rosenthal, J. W. (2000). Heritage languages. In J. W. Rosenthal (Ed.), *Handbook of undergraduate second language education* (pp. 165–184). Mahwah, NJ: Lawrence Erlbaum Associates.

Christensen, M. (2000). Anaphoric reference in spoken and written Chinese narrative discourse. *Journal of Chinese Linguistics, 28* (2), 303–336.

Chung, H. (2004). *Nihongo to kankokuogo no ninshooshi no shiyoo hindo—taiyaku shiryoo kara mita hindosa to sono yooin* [The frequency in pronominal use in Japanese and Korean—the difference and its factors through the analysis of translation texts]. *Nihongo Kyooiku* [Journal of Japanese Language Teaching], *114*, 30–39.

Clancy, P. (1980). Referential choice in English and Japanese narrative discourse. In W.

Cook, V. J. & Newson, M. (1996). *Chomsky's universal grammar: An introduction* (2nd ed.). Oxford: Blackwell.

Crystal, D. (1997). *A dictionary of linguistics and phonology* (4th ed.). Oxford: Blackwell.

Flynn, S. (1987). *A parameter-setting model of L2 acquisition: Experimental studies in anaphora.* Dordrecht, The Netherlands: D. Reidel Publishing Company.

Freed. B. F. (1998). An overview of issues and research in language learning in a study abroad setting. *Frontiers: The Interdisciplinary Journal of Study Abroad, 4,* 31–60.

DuFon, M., & Churchill, E. (Eds.). (2006). *Language learners in study abroad contexts.* Clevedon, UK: Multilingual Matters.

Hasegawa, N. (1984). On the so-called "zero pronouns" in Japanese. *The Linguistic Review, 4*(3), 289–341.

Hinds, J. (1982). *Ellipsis in Japanese.* Edmonton, Canada: Linguistic Research.

Hinds, J., & Hinds, W. (1979). Participant identification in Japanese narrative discourse. In G. Bedell, E. Kobayashi, & M. Muraki (Eds.), *Explorations in linguistics: Papers in honor of Kazuko Inoue* (pp. 201–212). Tokyo: Kenkyusha.

Huang, C.-T. J. (1984). On the distribution and reference of empty pronouns. *Linguistic Inquiry, 15,* 531–574.

Iori, I. (2003). *Shoryaku* [Ellipsis]. In Iori et al. (Eds.), Y*asashii nihongo no shikumi* [Easy explanation for the Japanese language system] (pp. 44–45). Tokyo: Kuroshio Shuppan.

Kanno, K. (1997). The acquisition of null and overt pronominals in Japanese by English speakers. *Second Language Research, 13,* 265–287.

King, R. (1998). Korean as a heritage language (KHL) vs. Korean as a foreign language (KFL) in North America and the former USSR: Ambiguous priorities and insufficient resources. *Acta Koreana, 1,* 27–40.

Kitajima, R. (2001). The effect of instructional conditions on students' vocabulary retention. *Foreign Language Annals, 34,* 470–482.

Kondo, K. (1998). The paradox of U.S. language policy and Japanese language education in Hawai`i. *International Journal of Bilingual Education and Bilingualism, 1, 47*–64.

Kondo-Brown, K (2003). Heritage language instruction for post-secondary students from immigrant backgrounds. *Heritage Language Journal, 1.* Retrieved December 30, 2003, from http://www. heritagelanguages.org/

Kondo-Brown, K. (2005). Differences in language skills: Heritage language learner subgroups and foreign language learners. *The Modern Language Journal, 89,* 563–581.

Lantlof, J. P. (1990, March). *Reassessing the null-subject parameter in second language acquisition.* Paper presented at the Annual Second Language Research Forum, Eugene, OR.

Lebra, S. T. (1976). *Japanese patterns of behavior.* Honolulu, HI: University of Hawai`i Press.

Liceras, J. M., & Díaz, L. (1999). Topic-drop versus pro-drop: Null subjects and pronominal subjects in the Spanish L2 of Chinese, English, French, German and Japanese speakers. *Second Language Research, 15,* 1–40.

Makino, S., & Tsutsui, M. (1989). *A dictionary of basic Japanese grammar.* Tokyo: Japan Times.

Masuoka, T., & Takubo, Y. (1989). *Kiso nihongo bunpo* [Basic Japanese grammar]. Tokyo: Kuroshio Shuppan.

Matsunaga, S. (2003). Instructional needs of college-level learners of Japanese as a heritage language: Performance-based analyses. *Heritage Language Journal, 1.* Retrieved December 30, 2003, from http://www. heritagelanguages.org/

Maynard, S. K. (1997). *Japanese communication: Language and thought in context.* Honolulu: University of Hawai`i Press.

Mazzocco, E. H. D. (1996). The heritage versus the nonheritage language learner: The five college self-instructional language program's solutions to the problem of separation or unification. *ADFL Bulletin, 28,* 1, 20–23.

Mazuka, R. (1991). Processing of empty categories in Japanese. *Journal of Psycholinguistic research, 20,* 215–232.

Mazuka, R., Itoh, K., Kiritani, S., Niwa, S., Ikejiri, K., & Naitoh, K. (1989). Processing Japanese garden path, center-embedded, and multiple left-embedded sentences: Reading time data from and eye movement study. *Annual Bulletin of the Research Institute of Logopedics and Phoniatrics (University of Tokyo)*, *23*, 187–212.

McGinnis, S. (1996). Teaching Chinese to the Chinese: The development of an assessment and instructional model. In J. E. Liskin-Gasparro (Ed.), *Patterns and policies: The changing demographics of foreign language instruction* (pp. 107–121). Boston, MA: Heinle & Heinle.

Nakahama, Y. (2003). Development of referent management in L2 Japanese: A film retelling task. *Gengo Bunkaron Shuu* [Journal of Language and Culture] *25*, 1, 127–146. Retrieved May 15, 2005 from http://www.lang.nagoya-u.ac.jp/proj/genbunronshu/25–1/nakahama.pdf

Noda. M. (2001). Selection and development of learning materials. In H. Nara & M. Noda (Eds.), *Acts of reading: Exploring connections in pedagogy of Japanese* (pp. 223–244). Honolulu: University of Hawai`i Press.

Ogawa, T. (1991). *Yomi no sutoratejii, purosesu to jyookyuu no dokkai shidoo* [Reading strategy and process instruction for learners of advanced Japanese]. *Nihongo Kyooiku*, *75*, 78–86.

Payne, T. E. (1997). *Describing morphosyntax: A guide for field linguists*. Cambridge: Cambridge University Press.

Pérez-Leroux, A. T., & Glass, W. R. (1999). Null anaphora in Spanish language acquisition: probabilistic versus generative approaches. *Second Language Research*, *15*, 220–249.

Pino, B. G., & Pino, F. (2000). Serving the heritage speaker across a five-year program. *ADFL Bulletin*, *32*, 27–35.

Polio, C. (1995). Acquiring nothing?: The use of zero pronouns by nonnative speakers of Chinese and the implications for the acquisition of nominal reference. *Studies in Second Language Acquisition, 17*, 353–377.

Rivers, W. P. (1998). Is being there enough? The effects of homestay placements on language gain during study abroad. *Foreign Language Annals, 31*, 492–500.

Rubin, J. (1992). *Making sense of Japanese: What the textbooks don't tell you*. Tokyo: Kodansha International.

Shen, H. H. (2003). A comparison of written Chinese achievement among heritage learners in homogeneous and heterogeneous groups. *Foreign Language Annals, 36*, 258–266.

Sohn, S.-O. (1995). The design of curriculum for teaching Korean as a heritage language. In H.-M. Sohn. (Ed.), *The Korean language in America 1: Papers from the first national conference on Korean language education* (pp. 19–35). Honolulu: American Association of Teachers of Korean.

Sohn, S.-O. (1997). Issues and concerns in teaching multi-level classes: Syllabus design for heritage and non-heritage learners. In Y.-H. Kim (Ed.), *Korean language in America 2: Papers from the second national conference on Korean language education* (pp. 139–158). Honolulu: American Association of Teachers of Korea.

Sukle, R. (1994). *Uchi/Soto*: Choices in directive speech acts in Japanese. In J. Bachik & C. Quinn (Eds.), *Situated meaning: Inside and outside in Japanese self, society, and language* (pp. 113–142). Princeton, NJ: Princeton University Press.

Takami, K. (1987). Anaphora in Japanese: Some semantic and pragmatic considerations. *Journal of Pragmatics, 11*, 169–191.

Ueyama, T. (1990). *America no daigaku ni okeru nihongo jyookyuu no mondaiten to teian* [Problems of and suggestions for advanced-level Japanese language courses in American universities]. *Nihongo Kyooiku* [Journal of Japanese Language Teaching], *71*, 56–68.

White, L. (1985). The pro-drop parameter in adult second language acquisition. *Language Learning, 35*, 47–62.

Williams, J. (1988). Zero anaphora in second language acquisition: A comparison among three varieties of English. *Studies in Second Language Acquisition, 10*, 339–370.

Yoshida, M. (2001). *Tekisuto o koeta rikai: Yomi ni okeru suiron katei* [Understanding beyond text: Inference processes in reading]. In S. Kadota & T. Noro (Eds.), *Riidingu no ninchi to mekanizumu* [Cognition and mechanism in reading] (pp. 149–162). Tokyo: Kuroshio Shuppan.

III

Attitude, Motivation, Identity, and Instructional Preference

Heritage Language Learners' Attitudes, Motivations, and Instructional Needs: The Case of Postsecondary Korean Language Learners

Jin Sook Lee
University of California, Santa Barbara

Hae-Young Kim
Duke University

ATTITUDES AND MOTIVATION IN HERITAGE LANGUAGE LEARNING

Postsecondary Korean Heritage Language Learners

According to Brod and Welles (2000), there was a 34% increase in enrollment in Korean language courses between the years 1995 and 1998 making it the third largest growth in foreign language programs during this period.

The sharp increase in enrollment can be attributed to the rise in numbers of college-age Korean Americans as a direct outcome of the Hart-Celler Act of 1965 that abolished discrimination in immigration quotas based on national origin. King (1998) reports that 80–90% of Korean language classrooms are composed of heritage language (HL) learners. Many HL learners are voluntarily finding their way into Korean language classrooms. What is interesting about the Korean American community is that Koreans generally reside and work in highly concentrated ethnic locations, thus providing an optimal environment to foster high language maintenance (Min, 2000). However, despite the highly visible and tightly knit communities of native Korean speakers and the high rate of Korean usage by parents in the home, second generation Korean Americans have been found to have one of the lowest rates of HL proficiency in comparison to other Asian American groups in the United States (Lopez, 1996; Min, 2000). Youths in the Korean American community are losing their ability to communicate with parents and relatives and their means to participate in their ethnic communities (Cho, Cho, & Tse, 1997; Ryu Yang, 2003).

Wiley (2002) states that "universities can play a major role in offering a second chance to individuals while helping the nation rebuild its linguistic resources. By so doing, they can play a major role in reversing the legacy of policies that have engendered language loss" (p. 2). However, the complex range of diversity in terms of the levels of proficiency, motivational orientations, attitudes, and degrees of ethnolinguistic affiliation have made it quite difficult to develop a coherent framework for HL learning and teaching (see Van Deusen Scholl, 2003; Wiley & Valdés, 2001). Without such a framework to drive the development of appropriate curricula, instructional strategies, and teaching materials for HL learners, language programs have not had much choice, but to continue to operate with teaching models created for traditional foreign language learners that have not taken into account psycholinguistic, sociolinguistic, or linguistic particulars of second-generation speakers of immigrant languages (Lynch, 2003; Valdés, 1995, 2000).

In order to develop an appropriate HL curriculum, we first need to understand the characteristics of HL learners in terms of their cognitive and linguistic development, language learning motivations, attitudes, and instructional needs (Campbell & Christian, 2001; Kondo-Brown, 2003; Lynch, 2003; Valdés, 1995). This chapter examines the affective and instructional variables of Korean HL learners to further advance our understanding of the characteristics that are unique to HL learners.

Dimensions of Language Attitudes and Motivation

There has been substantial research conducted on the influence of affective variables on language achievement (Gardner, 1985; Gardner &

Lambert, 1972; Gardner & MacIntyre, 1991; Skehan, 1989; Spolsky, 1989). Among the many affective factors that impact language learning, as Van Lier (1996) states, motivation "is a very important, if not the most important factor in language learning" (p. 98). Motivation has been shown to have a significant impact not only on the rate of second/foreign language learning, but also on the ultimate proficiency attainment (Dörnyei, 1994, 1998; Ely, 1986; Gardner, 1985; Oxford & Shearin, 1996; Scarcella & Oxford, 1992; Tremblay & Gardner, 1995; Williams & Burden, 1997). Studies have also revealed the direct impact of attitudes on learning behaviours and learning outcomes (Cotterall, 1995). However, despite the critical role of attitudes and motivations, little empirical work has been done that investigates the nature and impact of attitudes and motivations among HL learners (Lynch, 2003; Van Deusen-Scholl, 2003).

One of the most influential frameworks, one that has integrated attitudes, motivations, and language learning, is Gardner's (1985) socioeducational model. Gardner proposed that acquiring a second language is different from learning any other subject matter because it involves adopting the patterns and behaviors of the target culture, which naturally leads to a new second language identity. The model interrelates four factors—the social and cultural milieu, individual learner differences (e.g., intelligence, aptitude, anxiety, motivation), the setting in which the learning takes place and the linguistic (e.g., actual language knowledge and skills), and/or nonlinguistic (e.g., attitudes) outcomes. Underlying the model are two different motivational orientations that have been used to describe why learners may be invested in learning a particular language. Integrative motivation refers to the desire to become familiar with or even integrate into the society in which the language is used, whereas instrumental motivation is generally characterized by the desire to obtain something practical or concrete from the study of a second language such as fulfilling requirements for school, applying for a job, getting higher pay, or achieving higher social status. Although integrative motivation was initially believed to have greater influence on the language learning process, research has shown that instrumental motivation can significantly impact the language learning outcomes as well (Au, 1988).

Although Gardner's work inspired much research and discussion on the relationship between motivation and language learning, the socioeducational model also drew criticisms with respect to the construct of motivation. Researchers have noted (a) the narrowness in scope and lack of precision of the construct, (b) the problems of distinguishing between integrative and instrumental orientations, and (c) the lack of consideration for varied language learning contexts (Au, 1998; Brown, 2000; Crookes & Schmidt, 1991; Dörnyei, 1994; Oxford & Shearin, 1994). In response to such criticisms, Tremblay and Gardner (1995) presented a revised, expanded motivational model, incorporating insights from other motivational models such as Clément's social context model of second language learning (Clément, 1980; Clément & Kruidenier, 1985) and an industrial model of goal-setting theory (Lee, Locke, & Latham, 1989). In the revised version, motivation is defined as consisting of "motivational behavior," which includes observable characteristics such as attention, persistence, and effort, as well as "motivational antecedent" which cognitively and affectively influences motivational behavior. Motivational antecedents include goal salience, valence, and self-efficacy. *Goal salience* refers to how specific goals are and how frequently these goals are referred to; *valence* refers to the subjective value that is associated with a particular outcome or, in other words, the desire and attitudes toward the second language task; and *self-efficacy* refers to beliefs about one's capability to reach a certain level of performance including second language use anxiety. These motivational antecedents mediate between language attitudes and motivational behavior; that is, goal salience, valence, and self-efficacy are influenced by language attitudes, and in turn, shape motivational behavior (see Dörnyei [1998] for more detailed discussion).

We adopt Tremblay and Gardner's (1995) framework as a heuristic of our investigation and interpretation of the findings. We focus on (a) the learners' attitude toward HL with respect to ethnolinguistic vitality, (b) HL learners' motivational orientation, (c) attitudes towards language courses, and (d) learners' perceptions of self-efficacy.

METHODOLOGY

Informant Profiles

A total of 111 undergraduate students who were enrolled in a Korean language class at two East coast universities, one private and one public, participated in the study. The survey data were collected from 101 Korean HL learners, of whom 49% were born in the United States and 51% immigrated to the United States before the age of 12. Fifty-one students were enrolled in first-year Korean, 23 in second-year Korean and 27 in third-year Korean classes. The mean age of the group was 20 years old ($SD = 1.67$) and the average length of residence in the United States for their family was 19.7 years. There were 47 males and 54 females in the sample population. All the informants reported they were of Korean ethnicity with the exception of one informant, who stated that his mother was Korean and his father, Filipino. All informants in the survey reported that their parents were native speakers of Korean except for one informant, and also rated parents' Korean language use to be high in the home ($M = 4.35$, $SD = .10$, on a Likert scale from 1 [never] to 5 [always]). Despite parents' dominant use of Korean in the home, the patterns of Korean language use by the informants varied. In general, the informants reported speaking in English to their siblings and using a mixture of English and Korean to their parents. The degree of Korean usage was highly correlated with the level of language learning. The more advanced language learners reported using Korean significantly more than the lower level students with both their family [$F(2,98) = 6.66$, $p < .01$] and Korean ethnic friends [$F(2,90) = 10.68$, $p < .001$].

The interview data were collected from 10 Korean HL students, five males and five females. The informants were either born in the United States or had immigrated to the United States before the age of 3. All but two informants indicated that their first and dominant language was Korean until they entered pre-school in the United States Those eight students were of Korean ethnicity, whereas the other two students were from a mixed Korean ethnic background—their mothers were Korean, and their fathers were of European descent. At the time of the interviews, four students had completed the beginning level class and continued to the intermediate level, five students had completed the intermediate level class and one student graduated from the advanced level class.

Procedure

For the survey, students from Korean language classes were recruited on a voluntary basis with the cooperation of the instructors. A 34-item questionnaire employing both Likert-scale items and open-ended questions was constructed in English to target learners' demographic information such as age, gender, ethnicity, level of study (9 items), self-assessment of Korean proficiency and language use (9 items), expectations, attitudes and motivations toward Korean language learning (10 items), and needs, concerns, and recommendations for Korean learning and teaching (6 items). The questions were adapted from Brecht et al. (1995) and Jorden and Lambert (1991) language surveys and altered for the purposes of this study. The learners completed the 20-minute questionnaire in class toward the end of the school year. The informants' responses were anonymous.

In addition, the informants for the interview were recruited via e-mail by their Korean language instructor. Of the 23 students who were sent the e-mail solicitation, 21 responded, and 20 volunteered to participate in the interview. The 10 interviews reported in this chapter were with informants randomly selected from this larger pool. The informants met with the researcher, who was also their former instructor, to discuss issues about their experiences with their HL, reflections on the language courses, and their views about their future use of Korean.[1] The in-depth interviews were semi-structured to allow informants to bring in new topics as the flow of the conversation progressed (Patton, 1987). The interviews were conducted in English, the dominant and preferred language of the students, and lasted between 40 and 60 minutes. Each interview was audio-recorded with the permission of the students and later transcribed for thematic analysis.

Analysis

The analyses incorporated both quantitative and qualitative analytic procedures in a complementary manner to explicate the patterns identified in the informants' responses. The quantitative data were analyzed using analysis of variance and factor analysis. The independent variables were gender, the level of language instruction, and proficiency levels and the dependent variables were the motivational factor scores, family and peer language use patterns, and attitudes toward the language.

The qualitative data, on the other hand, were coded and analyzed for thematic patterns (Strauss & Corbin, 1990), independent of the quantitative analysis. However, the patterns that emerged in the interview data converged a great deal with those in the survey data. We present the analyses of the two data sets in juxtaposition in the following section to give a fuller account of the HL students' language attitudes and motivational traits. The quotes from the informants are tagged with the data set identification (I: the interview; S: the survey), gender (M: male; F: female) and the informant number. For example, IF 2 means interview informant, female, #2, and SM 72 means survey informant male #72.

RESULTS AND DISCUSSION

Attitudes Towards Heritage Language: Status, Vitality, and Utility

Informants in the survey study were asked to rate the perception of the status of Korean in the United States On a Likert scale from 1 (looked down

---

[1]Because of the personal nature of the topics discussed, familiarity and shared experiences between the interviewee and the interviewer were critical in creating a more comfortable environment. It allowed the interviewer to probe certain issues in greater depth based on the participants' prior knowledge of each other. However, the power relationship and degree of familiarity between the interviewer and the interviewees are likely to have influenced the kinds of responses the informants provided. In order to minimize this latter tendency and avoid any concerns the students may have had about how their responses might affect their grades, we only included former students of the interviewer in the interview data collection.

on) to 5 (highly regarded), Korean HL learners rated the status of Korean to be neither highly regarded nor disregarded ($M = 3.03$; $SD = .07$). When asked why they thought so, the informants mainly commented on the perceived value of Korean by the wider society: 25.7% stated that the popularity of the Korean group is not very high; 20.8% stated that the portrayal of Koreans in the media was negative; 30% said that the United States did not care about any other language besides English; and 23.5% either did not respond or stated that they did not know. The observations of low representation and visibility of the Korean language/culture group in the wider dominant society and its marginal status in mainstream American society were common themes in the responses of the informants. For example, the following quote highlights the lack of wider institutional support for the Korean language and speakers.

> The frustrating thing for me is that there is no way to fit it [Korean] into your education here. It's not encouraged ... Just the way they have the whole curriculum set up, it's hard ... In high school, you don't learn anything about it [Korea and East Asia], in Virginia anyway. (IF10)

Foreign language learners' decisions to learn a language are in general driven by their perceptions of the societal and cultural value and the capital the language may bring for the learners, as illustrated by the dramatic increase of enrollment in Spanish programs resulting from the perception that Spanish has high utility in society because of the critical mass of Spanish speakers in the country (Brod & Welles, 2000). On the other hand, for HL learners of less commonly taught languages, the case seems somewhat different. Lee and Farhat (2003) found that HL learners of the less commonly taught languages tended to perceive the language of study to have lower status than the non-HL learners of the language, yet were still motivated to learn the language. Our data also show that the Korean HL learners assessed the Korean language as having fairly low representation, utility, and status in the United States, which is an indication that instrumental motivation did not carry much weight in their decision to learn Korean. This perception is likely to have stemmed from the linguistic and cultural compositions of the areas where the informants grew up and received their educations. Because the sample population was recruited from East coast universities, where Koreans are isolated minorities in comparison to, for example, Southern California, their perceptions of the utility of Korean may be lower than Korean Americans in Southern California.

In spite of views about the limited utility of Korean in their professional or academic lives, learners indicated feeling responsible for passing down Korean to their children. In the survey data, 73.9% of the informants stated that it was their responsibility to pass the HL down to their children to help their children retain a sense of who they are, 13.1% stated that the importance of their children learning the HL was to gain the benefits of bilingualism and intercultural competence, and 13% felt that it was their children's choice whether to learn Korean or not. The sense of responsibility for HL maintenance prevailed among the interview informants as well. However, their professed desire seemed to be at odds with realistic projection of their future language development and use:

> I wanted to progress, I wish I had taken more classes, but I just didn't have time in my schedule. I want my kids to speak Korean, I don't know where they would learn it from, because I don't speak Korean, not very fluently. (IF 2)

> My biggest concern is my kids, because my parents' Korean is really good, but mine is drop-off. My kids are going to be so much worse than me. I don't know what's going to happen. I am gonna send my kids to [Saturday] Korean school, because I want them to learn Korean. (IM 5)

The informants' current proficiency in the HL was not deemed high enough to provide language models to their children, and their hesitation to commit more time and effort to bring it up to an appropriate level are an eloquent reflection of their perception of the declining vitality of Korean language and culture among Korean-American groups. The reasons behind learners' choices to learn Korean, despite the low regard they held for the status of Korean in the wider sociopolitical context of the United States, is addressed in the next section.

Motivational Orientation: Membership and Identity

To determine the learners' motivational orientation towards HL, the informants were provided with 16 items that described various reasons for language learning such as "I want to learn Korean to get a better job" or "I want to learn Korean to communicate with my family." The informants were asked to rate the degree to which they strongly disagreed (1) to strongly agreed (5) with each statement. A principal components analysis with Varimax rotation of the 16 items identified four motivational constructs: school-related motivations, career-related motivations, personal fulfillment-related motivations, and heritage ties-related motivations (see Table 7.1). The first two components have an instrumental orientation, whereas the last two components have an integrative orientation. An analysis of variance revealed that there were no significant differences in the four motivational constructs across proficiency levels, which indicates that regardless of proficiency level, the motivational orientations at least for the first 3 years of language study appear to remain constant. The mean ratings indicate that the informants identified most strongly with the

TABLE 7.1
Principal Components Analysis (with Varimax Rotation)
Loadings of Motivation Items

	Instrumental		Integrative		
	Factor 1 School-Related ($M = 2.21$)	Factor 2 Career-Related ($M = 3.10$)	Factor 3 Personal Fulfillment ($M = 3.25$)	Factor 4 Heritage Ties ($M = 4.10$)	h^2
I learn Korean to transfer credits to college.	0.83	0.01	0.17	−0.11	0.72
I learn Korean because my friend recommended it.	0.82	0.14	0.06	0.22	0.74
I learn Korean because my advisor recommended it.	0.80	0.10	0.36	0.04	0.78
I learn Korean because of the reputation of the program and instructor.	0.77	0.12	0.12	0.22	0.67
I learn Korean for an easy A.	0.69	0.18	−0.29	0.16	0.61
I learn Korean to fulfill a graduation requirement.	0.63	0.11	0.19	−0.18	0.47
I learn Korean to get a better job.	0.04	0.80	0.20	0.11	0.69
I learn Korean because I plan to work overseas.	0.26	0.80	0.11	0.10	0.75
I learn Korean because of the status of Korean in the world.	0.10	0.73	0.20	0.22	0.63
I learn Korean to use it for my research.	0.38	0.48	0.44	0.10	0.58
I learn Korean to further my global understanding.	0.16	0.33	0.71	0.08	0.65
I learn Korean because I have an interest in Korean literature.	0.18	0.04	0.64	0.13	0.56
I learn Korean because it is fun and challenging.	0.04	0.04	0.63	0.46	0.63
I learn Korean because I have a general interest in languages.	0.11	0.03	0.57	0.51	0.59
I learn Korean because it is the language of my family heritage.	−0.01	0.26	0.05	0.80	0.71
I learn Korean because of my acquaintances with Korean speakers.	0.10	0.21	0.20	0.70	0.58
% of variance explained by each factor	0.23	0.15	0.14	0.12	0.64

Extraction Method: Principal Component Analysis. Rotation Method: Varimax with Kaiser Normalization. Eigenvalue > 1.0

heritage-ties construct and least with school-related motivational reasons. This finding may put to rest the attitudes held by many instructors that HL learners are in class solely "for an easy A." Rather these students come to class to fulfill a real and immediate need to develop the means to communicate and stay connected to their family and ethnic community.

Previous research has shown that integrative orientation is not necessarily superior to instrumental orientation in terms of effects on learning outcome (see review in Au, 1988), and integrative and instrumental orientations are not necessarily mutually exclusive (Brown, 2000). Furthermore, orientations can change over time for the learner (Oxford & Shearin, 1994). However, our data show that, for Korean HL learners, integrative orientation seems to play a more significant role in shaping their desire to learn the language consistently across different proficiency levels. This finding is consistent with Cho et al. (1997), Cho (2000), and Ryu Yang (2003), although Cho et al. (1997) and Cho (2000), whose informant population was recruited from Southern California, one of the largest Korean American communities, also reported that informants expressed a desire to learn Korean to expand career options. This instrumental orientation was lacking in the responses of informants in the current study, who mainly grew up on the East coast where the Korean American communities are not as prominent as in Southern California as well as in Ryu Yang's study, which was conducted in the Midwest. This finding highlights that the perception of ethnolinguistic vitality in the ethnic community plays an important role in shaping the motivational orientation of the students.

Korean language learners' attitudes toward their HL were also assessed through an open-ended question in the survey, which asked them the meaning and value of Korean and its study. Of the 93 informants who responded to this open-ended question, the majority of the informants claimed that the Korean language was the main connector to their roots and their family and an expressor of who they are as a cultural being (Table 7.2).

Connecting with parents and understanding their cultural roots were only some main sources of frustration for HL learners, but also the awakening call for the need to develop proficiency in the HL. One student, who spoke a mixture of Korean and English to his mother, reported frustrations and gaps in his Korean skills when the communication touched on subjects outside of familiar domains:

> I try [to speak Korean] with my mom. It just takes me such a long time. We say small things. But if I try to talk to her about internships or something, it just it doesn't work, because I don't know the words. If I talk about something complicated, highly emotional or stressful, it doesn't work. (IM 3)

TABLE 7.2

Heritage Language Learners' Attitudes Toward the Value of Korean

Categories of Responses	Frequency (N= 93)
Connector to roots and family	44 (47.3%)
Definition of my ethnic identity	23 (24.7%)
Key to communicate or bond with other Koreans	13 (13.9%)
Allows one to be bilingual	8 (8.6%)
Representative of my pride as a Korean	5 (5.5%)

Another student, who spoke Korean to her parents, also reported how she felt that her proficiency did not measure up to discussing complex topics or complicated issues:

> It [Korean]'s very important for me because that's the main way I can communicate with my parents, that's what they are comfortable with, speaking in Korean ... There's something that is hard to explain, and they don't really get it. It's hard for me to explain, and so there's always that frustration. (IF7)

The inability to communicate with parents on sensitive and critical matters lies on two levels: lack of linguistic proficiency and lack of shared cultural expectations and beliefs between parents and children. Given that a main motivator for HL learners is to develop interpersonal communication skills, the curriculum needs to address both linguistic development and the knowledge of cultural expectations, values, and beliefs that are central to communication process. The following quotes exemplify the ways in which the interconnectedness of language and culture plays out in the informants' lives:

> After taking Korean, my relationship with my parents just got so much better. Just because I would read stories in Korean, and I would say, wow, that sounds like what my parents are like. I could understand their upbringing more, their Confucian influences. (IF 4)

> If anything, taking Korean helped me to find myself ... I grew up in a all-white community ... With taking Korean, it was more like I want to take this to find out more about who I am, this is the part of me that's not gonna go away. And so I think it was not only trying to communicate better with my parents and other Koreans, it was more self-discovery, really. (IF 4)

For HL learners, despite the fact that they may perceive their language as not having high social capital, the driving force behind their willingness and desire to learn Korean does not lie in their perceptions of what others may think of their language, but rather in what the language can offer them in terms of personal and cultural capital. The informants in this study conferred personal and symbolic meanings on learning the language, and within personal contexts, they saw great value in the language as a central component to the formation of one's ethnic identity and presence within the cultural social network.

In sum, the sociopsychological need to situate oneself as a member of the ethnic speech community and connect with one's heritage seems to override the perceptions of the extrinsic value of the language. In other words, for HL learners, their attitudes and motivations related to learning the language are affected by different factors such as the need to communicate with family, connect to one's heritage, and develop an ethnic identity.

Self-Efficacy: Perceived Heritage Language Competence and HL Use Anxiety

To attain an assessment of learner perceptions of their language proficiencies, the survey participants were asked to assess their skills in reading, writing, speaking, listening, and cultural skills on a Likert scale from 1 (no proficiency) to 5 (native-like proficiency). One-way analysis of variance (ANOVA) showed that there were significant differences in self-assessed proficiencies separately for first-, second-, and third-year students, which was expected (see Table 7.3). However, what is interesting is the pattern of differences in the perceived development of different language skills.

A post-hoc Tukey's HSD pairwise multiple comparison was conducted to examine which groups significantly differed in their perceptions of language skills. In terms of speaking skills and cultural knowledge, first-year learners assessed their proficiency to be significantly different from the second- and third-year learners indicating that the perception of growth in

TABLE 7.3
ANOVA and Means of Self-Assessment of Korean Proficiency

	1st Year Korean (n = 51)	2nd Year Korean (n = 27)	3rd Year Korean (n = 23)
Reading $F(2, 98) = 7.2 1**$	2.78 (.96)	2.74 (.90)	3.61 (.89)
Listening $F(2, 98) = 4.46*$	3.37 (.97)	3.59 (.69)	4.04 (.82)
Writing $F(2, 98) = 16.50**$	2.15 (.86)	2.44 (.64)	3.3 (.82)
Speaking $F(2, 98) = 7.77**$	2.92 (.99)	3.55 (.57)	3.73 (1.1)
Cultural $F(2, 98) = 5.36**$	2.43 (.9)	3.07 (1.0)	3.04 (1.02)

$*p < .01, **p < .001$

TABLE 7.4
Rank Order of Degree of Difficulty of Language Performance Task:
1 (Easiest) to 7 (Most Difficult)

Performance-based Language Tasks (N = 98)	Mean (SD)
Making the sounds of the language	2.56 (1.78)
Writing the characters of the language	3.63 (1.87)
Reading	3.83 (1.86)
Listening comprehension	3.92 (1.67)
Applying appropriate cultural knowledge	3.98 (1.96)
Conversing in the language	4.01 (1.99)
Writing sentences in the language	5.07 (1.77)

speaking skills and cultural familiarity happens between the first- and second-year rather than between the second and third year ($p < .001$). As for reading, listening, and writing skills, the findings show that in the third year, students perceived a significant development of their listening, reading, and writing skills ($p < .001$). Thus, the perception of growth of speaking skills and cultural knowledge seems to precede the perceived development of reading, listening, and writing skills for HL learners. Given such perceptions, more orally based tasks situated in cultural experiences and practices may be effective especially in the beginning stages of formalized language instruction to provide a context in which language learners could build their confidence in their linguistic skills as they gain the time to develop and practice their literacy skills.

Informants were also asked to rank in order the degree of difficulty in the various language skills, the learners rated writing sentences to be the most difficult followed by conversational skills, cultural knowledge, and listening skills (see Table 7.4).

An ANOVA analysis showed that there were no significant differences across the language levels in regard to their perceptions of the difficulties in language learning. In general, HL learners are assumed to be fairly proficient in their oral and listening skills, but weak in their reading and writing skills. However, the results of the learners' self-assessments of their language skills show that the learners rated listening comprehension to be slightly more difficult than reading. One possible explanation for this finding is that reading was probably interpreted as decoding skills, because once the Korean alphabet is learned, decoding the sounds of this phonetic language is easy, whereas the ratings for listening comprehension may have reflected the pressures HL learners often experience in being expected to understand the result of the speaker's expectation of HL learners to be able to understand conversations at a normal rate of speech. This may make it more difficult for HLs to develop their listening comprehension skills because the input may be beyond their comprehension level (Krashen, 1981).

Furthermore, the language HL learners are exposed to in class may not reflect the home language used in familiar contexts. In fact, HL students' oral proficiency is likely to be restricted to informal registers of speech that lack in range of vocabulary and discourse devices, as shown in research of other HL learner groups (Valdés & Geoffrion-Vinci, 1998). It is not surprising that even at the advanced levels, learners were not assessing themselves to be near-native like, which is consistent with their expression of frustration at not being able to meet the expectations placed on them as HL speakers.

Several theorists have focused on anxiety as a critical affective variable in second language acquisition (Gardner, 1985; Krashen, 1981; MacIntyre, 1995). MacIntyre and Gardner (1991) reviewed evidence suggesting that language-learning anxiety results from initial second language learning experiences, which may inhibit acquisition. Gardner, Trembly, and Masgoret (1997) found that anxiety was related to both language achievement and motivation as part of a larger construct that included self-confidence and perceived ability. When informants were asked about their concerns and worries in learning their HL, 48 (67.2%) informants stated the fear of "not being able to live up to the expectations of other Korean speakers" or "not having the proper grammar to sound educated." Furthermore, 20 (26.3%) said that they had no concerns, and four (5.3%) stated that they were worried about their tests and grades.

Heritage language learners stated that they felt the pressure of expectations that teachers and other classmates place on them as HL learners. For example, one student from the survey reported: "People expect me to already be at a certain level because I am Korean" (SF12) and another student commented that he was afraid of "failing to fulfill what is expected of me [as an HL learner]" (SM72). Students from a heritage background appear to be faced with internal and external pressures to live up to the expectations that they should sound like a native Korean speaker. The interview data also revealed the burden that the learners imposed on themselves as HL speakers as well as unease and self-consciousness in speaking the language, particularly with native or more "native-like" peers or juniors.

> It was little difficult, a little frustrating. 'Cuz speaking with my little cousins, I feel very elementary 'cuz they obviously speak better than I do. So when I am trying to talk to them, I feel kind of funny. (IF 2)

> There's a comfort issue, I kind of feel uncomfortable speaking Korean with people who are a lot better than me, when they are my peers. But then I think that there's, it's just more convenient to use English. (IM 6)

Heritage language learners, who lacked confidence about their proficiency but felt pressured to speak like a native speaker, shy away from opportunities to speak Korean and opt to use English. Then, the HL learner's reliance on English to protect one's face limits opportunities to use Korean to practice and gain more confidence and competence in Korean. According to Tremblay and Gardner's (1995) model, self-efficacy influences motivational behavior, and thus low self-efficacy leads to low rates of effort and persistence. Because self-efficacy is in a way the function of how pleasant the contact with speakers of the language is as well as their own expectations of their performance in the contact, HL learners need more sheltered contact with the native speakers as well as increased activities, tasks, and assignments that provide ample opportunities to interact with other HL speakers in the peer group in a safe, non-face-threatening way. It should be recognized that the HL learners exhibit anxiety about their language skills and nervousness about their performance when it comes down to actual use of the language, because the HL plays a central symbolic role for the HL learners. They tend to take lack of proficiency in the HL as personal weaknesses or even failure. Thus the learners need to be informed about the nature of language acquisition and attrition, which are not personal or cultural attributes but are use-based processes.

Perspectives on Heritage Language Instruction: Needs and Satisfaction

When the informants were asked about the educational and institutional contexts of Korean classes, 87% of the students wanted to see the inclusion of Korean language instruction as a part of the world languages framework in the earlier grades; 34% stated that they wanted Korean to be offered in elementary school grades, 19% in the middle schools, 37% in high school, and 10% felt that it was appropriate to offer it at college. The HL learners thus concurred on the importance of including Korean as a part of the regular curriculum, indicating a need for systematicity and academic formalization in HL instruction, as shown in the following quote.

> I had always wanted to take Korean within the methodical, academic approach, with the professor and other students, because I hadn't had that. I never had had that. (IM 6)

The offering of Korean language courses at the college level lends prestige and standing to the language as an academic subject, which weekend community Korean language schools have been unable to do (Lee, 2002; Tse, 2001). Learners appear to value the institutionalized opportunities to learn the language because they give the study of Korean more societal and educational legitimacy.

TABLE 7.5
Heritage Learner Strategies to Improve Language Proficiency

Strategies for Learning Korean	Frequency (N = 80)
Go to Korea	19 (21%)
Enroll in more classes	19 (21%)
Actively practice with other speakers	26 (28%)
Participate in cultural activities	4 (4.3%)
More interaction with Korean media	5 (5.4%)
Invest in learning materials	5 (5.4%)
Develop better attitude toward language	2 (2.2%)

TABLE 7.6
Factors Related to Improving Korean Language Education:
1 (Not Important)–5 (Very Important)

Factors	Ratings (N = 99)
Appropriately trained bilingual teachers	4.73 (.07)
Opportunities to learn language before college age	4.44 (.08)
Materials relevant to the lives of Korean Americans	4.42 (.08)
Opportunities to use language outside of class	4.40 (.08)
Native speakers as teachers	4.19 (.10)
Study abroad opportunities	3.82 (.11)
Increase class hours	3.33 (.11)

In order to solicit ideas about ways to improve Korean language curricula for students, we asked the learners what strategies they used to develop their language skills (see Table 7.5). The three top responses alluded to the need to be able to use the Korean language outside of the classroom in more authentic settings in conjunction with the need for continued formal language instruction support.

The informants were also asked to rate in order of importance the factors needed to improve Korean language education (see Table 7.6). The learners rated the quality of teachers, goal- relevant materials and curricula for Korean American learners, and increased opportunities to learn and use the Korean language to be among the most critical factors in improving Korean language instruction.

The survey informants suggested that teachers need to be aware of the range of psychological and social needs that these language learners bring to class instead of trying to make the HL learners conform to existing models of foreign language learning so they will fit into the curriculum and instructional techniques already in place. For example, the learners expressed great interest in learning more about themselves as Korean Americans. Oral histories and case studies of Korean American immigrants may prove to be a rich and authentic opportunity not only to learn and practice the language, but also to engage in a process of self-discovery through the stories and past histories of other Korean Americans. Relevance seems to be a key factor in directing what learners wanted in the language curriculum.

Interview data also showed that the HL curriculum should incorporate explicit social and cultural content in order to respond to learners' view of the language as a marker of identity and language learning as a way to establish ties with their heritage culture. In reviewing their language classes, the informants spoke enthusiastically about materials and instruction that directly dealt with aspects of Korean history and cultural practices and products, from folk literature to cooking recipes to modern literature.

> There were the readings ... pertaining to cultural elements, like *pansori*[2] and things like that. I've enjoyed [them] because it not only helped me to enhance my language skills but also they also gave me cultural awareness too. (IF 9)

> I really enjoyed more readings on different cultural aspects ... And the cooking section was my favorite, because I always cook with my mom, so it's my favorite. And then I like reading, I like even when you introduced us to modern literature, even poetry. (IM 3)

The informants not only enjoyed reading about and discussing those topics, but also reported better understanding of their parents' cultural norms and values (see IF 4 quoted earlier) and improved self-esteem as a Korean-American:

> It helped me feel more comfortable, with Korean culture and language, because I was pretty uncomfortable with it before, just because I was so acclimated to white people, not to Asian people at all. (IM1).

However, embracing one's minority culture might be based on a problematic, essentialist notion of the culture (e.g., a culture consists of a unique, timeless, and unchangeable set of artifacts, practices, and values), as illustrated in one informant's statement about his view of Korean culture:

> Something very important in my life is Korean culture, me being Korean, Korean culture including food, language, and traditions ... I feel like, being Korean, the overriding theme is closeness in the family, stemming from Confucian ideals. (IM 5)

---

[2]*Pansori* is a traditional Korean fold literacy/performance genre, in which a storyteller, accompanied by a drummer, gives a dramatic rendition of a narrative extolling the virtuous protagonist's suffering and eventual triumph and redemption.

Language courses, which are usually limited to "the anecdotal transmission of cultural facts" or the Three F's: food, fads, and folklore (Kramsch, 2003), can inculcate or reinforce the essentialist idea about culture. To avoid inadvertent contributions to oversimplification, reification, and essentialization of culture, a language curriculum needs to be based on appropriate research in order to guide students to gain broader and more nuanced understandings of the culture and society. The teacher's willingness and commitment to learning additional information with students, in fact, has the effect of increasing teacher motivation and enthusiasm (Stoller & Grabe, 1997). Also, the language teacher can consult or cooperate with specialists in relevant disciplinary areas such as history, anthropology, and cultural studies, which is quite customary in content-based approach (Snow, Met, & Genesee, 1989). Ideally, to fully develop the HL students' interest in language and culture, language instruction should take place in the context of a comprehensive academic program offering courses in culture, history, and literature, for example.

In combination with structured language lessons, learners also wanted more opportunities to use the language. The informants in the survey suggested that, with access to Korean-American communities and businesses and with the use of the Internet, they would like more authentic interactions with native speakers of the language through community-based language learning programs such as internships. Indeed, as Fishman (2001) observed, formal study of language alone will probably not help the maintenance of the language among second generation speakers. Valdés (1995) maintains that "the classroom is limited in what it can accomplish against the assimilative pressure of the wider society" (p. 310). The challenge for the teacher lies in establishing some kind of bridge between the classroom and an active speech community. The teacher can encourage and promote learners' participation in speech communities and interaction with a range of speakers as well as augmenting their interest and confidence in partaking in such endeavors. One feasible way would be to establish a community-based language-learning program such as internships (Douglas, 2003). Also, potential peer-group networking is worth considering. Peer influence is observed to be "central to the development of positive attitudes toward and interest in the heritage language" (Tse, 2001, p. 698). If the students form a peer group where HL plays an important role, the likelihood of regular use of the language will increase.

With regard to instructional approaches and the focus of language instruction, many interview informants ranked literacy skill development as a priority because of their lack of confidence in their literacy skills. These students reported a great sense of accomplishment in learning to read and write in Korean, which ranged from acquiring basic literacy to becoming a better speller to reading and writing more.

I say I just had a great sense of satisfaction that I could read Korean, understand Korean numbers, that I can write Korean ¼ It's more like a pride thing, I feel really happy in that way ... (IM 1)

I was really bad at writing words. I wrote it how I thought it sounded, and it was completely wrong. And so it helped me a lot just with my spelling and reading. I tried to speak more with my parents, and I always go back and show off that I could read newspaper now. (IF2)

Ryu Yang (2003) also found that HL students wanted to learn more grammar, reading, and writing skills, whereas the non-HL students were more interested in improving their oral communication. Several informants in the interview commented on the usefulness of explicit instruction in grammar and vocabulary.

[In] the [intermediate] classes, I learned a lot of grammar, and I thought that was good ... Maybe not with the speaking, but with the writing, it really helped. And then with later [advanced] classes, I didn't learn so much grammar. It was a lot of just history and things like that. But I liked the [intermediate] classes better. (IF 7)

I like having vocabulary quizzes. It made you learn it. I felt like I learned most vocabulary first 2 years ... The ones I want to remember, I remember and I try to use them ... I would hear the word that I remember from my list, and I would be like, oh, I know the word, and I tried to retain. I wish there was more vocabulary [lists and quizzes] in the advanced class. (IF 2)

Students called for a more structured approach, consisting of careful control of vocabulary and grammar at a manageable level and systematic treatment of grammar from less to more complex rules.

For HL learners, explicit grammar instruction offers them the explanations for things that may come intuitively to them or things that may not yet be that familiar to them. Effective linguistic explanations not only give the learner a greater sense of control over the HL learning, but also facilitate language development itself (Doughty & Williams, 1998). What should be taken as an issue from the students' demand for more structure, however, is not whether the curricula should incorporate more grammar instruction in HL programs, but how to articulate and present the goals of the class, whether the focus is on communicative skills, thematic content, or tasks, so that the students have a sense of controlling and monitoring their own learning.

However, it is not the case that HL learners did not see the need to improve their oral skills. Some students in our interviews stated that improvement of their oral skills was just as necessary and crucial. In fact, they regretted the lack of opportunities in class to improve their oral fluency and bring it up to a more comfortable level:

> I think it [Korean class]'s improved my Korean, particularly my writing, writing part of it, but I kind of wished that I developed my verbal skill a little bit more. I still don't really consider myself fluent, not even semi-fluent, because I have to think what I have to say in English first, and I sort of translate that out. (IM 6)

> Ultimately I want to become truly bilingual, I don't know, at this point, it's still pretty lofty goal, but I want to be able to read and write. I want to be able to speak Korean in the same way I speak English and be as comfortable with it. (IM 8)

It should not be overlooked that even if HL learners may sound fluent, their oral proficiency has gaps in linguistic knowledge in terms of lexicon, discourse organization, and speech registers. Moreover, HL learners experience difficulty comprehending and producing speech in real time as the topics become less familiar and information becomes more complex. HL learners' proficiency and familiarity with the language are generally bound within the confines of daily functions in the home, which is why they experience such difficulty communicating with parents on more complex heart-to-heart issues and lack the competence to use the language for professional purposes.

Another critical question in foreign language education is how the combination of HL and non-HL groups in one class affects each other (see also Weger-Guntharp, this volume). We asked students about their views on having HL and non-HL students in the same class. From the HL students' perspective, 57 (59.4%) said that HL and non-HL learners should be in the same classroom and 39 (40.6%) said the two groups should be separated. In order to understand the reasons behind why the learners thought so, we asked them what the advantages and disadvantages would be for having both groups of learners in the same class (see Table 7.7). The foremost advantage for HL learners was perceived to be the opportunity for HL learners to gain academic recognition for their linguistic and cultural knowledge. One student explained that the presence of non-HL learners in the class instills more pride in the language because it demonstrates that Korean has value even for non-HL learners because they want to learn it (SF 94). They also commented that non-HL learners can benefit by having peer language models, who can act as linguistic and cultural brokers for them. The main disadvantages were identified to be unfairness in grading policies and instructional content–pacing issues.

The learners' perspectives on whether HL and non-HL learners should be in the same class or not shed an interesting light on the growing trend

TABLE 7.7

Advantages and Disadvantages of Having Heritage and
Non-Heritage Learners in the Same Class

Advantages		*Disadvantages*	
Increases motivation for both heritage and non-heritage learners	9 (11.5%)	Too difficult and intimidating for non-heritage language learners	18 (24%)
Heritage learners can display their knowledge, show off	11 (14.1%)	Unfair grading	28 (37.3%)
Heritage learners can serve as models and act as brokers	35 (44.9%)	Pace will not satisfy either group	21 (28%)
Diversity in class	15 (19.2%)	None	8 (10.7%)
None	8 (10.2%)		

of separating HL and non-HL tracks. First of all, there seem to be benefits to instructing both HL and non-HL learners in the same class that should be taken advantage of. Second, most two-track systems only offer separate classes at the elementary and intermediate levels, assuming that once HL and non-HL students complete the special tracks, they can take the language class together at the advanced level, even if "such an assumption has no empirical foundation" to date (Kondo-Brown, 2003, p. 6). Contrary to the common practice, it might be more viable to have a mixed class of HL and non-HL students at the lower proficiency levels, whereas the differentiation of goals and focus depending on learner experiences might be even more important at higher proficiency levels. With the HL students' perspectives providing a vision, creative curricula for beginning and intermediate levels can be developed that employ the unique characteristics and strengths of both groups such as the validation of the value of the HL for the HL learners by the presence of non-HL learners in class and exposure to authentic peer language users for the non- HL learners through HL learners' participation. To do so, instructors would need to develop creative measures in assessment procedures and standards as well as work out a plan to meet the needs of both HL and non-HL learners in terms of pacing and instructional focus. The most fundamental needs and expectations that the Korean HL students bring to language classes, thus, reach beyond the walls of the language classroom out to realms of educational programs and institutions at large.

IMPLICATIONS FOR HERITAGE
LANGUAGE CURRICULUM AND PEDAGOGY

In our investigation and analysis of Korean HL learners, we found that (a) learners' attitudes toward the status or utility of Korean in the wider sociopolitical context of the United States were not favorable, but, in light of their personal contexts, they saw the learning of Korean to be the main signifier of their ethnic identity; (b) motivations to learn Korean were clearly integrative, closely tied with affirmation of their ethnic identity and need to keep connected with their family and ethnic community, which remained constant across proficiency levels; (c) learners desired more formalized and innovative approaches to increase conversational fluency and cultural literacy; and (d) their motivation was significantly affected by low self-efficacy due to the sociopsychological burden the learners felt to acquire native-like proficiency in the language because it is the language that represents their identity to others. For these learners, the HL does not simply perform the function of ordinary communication, but it also functions as a symbolic marker of ethnicity for them.

These findings provide fertile grounds for discussing new directions for HL curriculum development. In the results and discussion section just discussed, we touched on a few curricular and pedagogic issues as they arose. Here, we attempt to address them by proposing an encompassing framework of curriculum development based on content-based instruction. Content-based instruction integrates academic content with language-teaching objectives (Wesche & Skehan, 2002), and curricular decisions are content-driven rather than task or language-driven (Stoller & Grabe, 1997). Content in this approach represents "material that is cognitively engaging and demanding for the learner" (Snow, 1998, p. 259). Content-based instruction has been implemented at different levels of education, elementary to postsecondary, and in a variety settings and forms, from immersion programs to sheltered subject classes to second/foreign language courses (Stoller & Grabe, 1997; see Snow, 1998 for a review). Although we still lack direct empirical evidence of its total effects, the rationale for content-based instruction are drawn from an extensive body of research from multiple fields including second language acquisition and educational and cognitive psychology (Grabe & Soller, 1997).

Given HL learners' integrative orientation toward the language and their desire to connect with their heritage culture, culture would be a natural focus or organizing principle for such curriculum. Culture can be instructed effectively through content-based instruction (Hilles & Lynch, 1997). A caveat is that the concept of culture itself is so broad, complex, and even contentious that one needs to be cognizant of what construct one operates under and what aspect of culture is covered. According to Hammerly's (1982) classification, culture can be broken down into behavioral (i.e., the knowledge that enables a person to navigate daily life), informational (i.e., the kinds of information a society values), and achievement (i.e., the hallmarks of civilization) levels. More specifically, behavioral culture pertains to aspects of culture that can be "invisible" and "have a moral status" (Hilles & Lynch, 1997), that is, norms that are almost unconsciously held by the speaker and applied to judge other people's language performance. Behavioral culture is what is often the focus of instruction in cross-cultural awareness training and has also been adopted as an organizing principle of language curriculum (Walker, 2005). Achievement culture, the culture with a capital C, includes high art and literature and has been the territory of scholarly discourse. Informational culture, on the other hand, pertains to shared knowledge of history, geography, political, and economic affairs, educational systems, entertainment, and so on. Behavioral and informational cultures are largely the mechanisms that govern the ways in which communication takes place. However, behavioral culture is much more difficult to explicitly teach through rules and formula because the norms and variable communicative styles that speakers follow are implicit. This type of knowledge is most effectively acquired through experience participating in the culture and interacting with native speakers rather than through formal language instruction. However, explicit training in developing skills to become observers and ethnographers of the culture and language use are needed to acquire the knowledge base associated with behavioral culture. In addition, HL learners need to develop a knowledge base in informational culture so they can access and acquire membership in the language group. Thus, given the importance of cultural knowledge in language learning, informational cultural content may be the most feasible and relevant level of culture for inclusion in content-based instruction for HL learners in terms of classroom content.

Implementing content-based instruction focused on informational culture can start with selection of themes that are conceptually important and relevant to the students, texts that are interesting, accessible, and appropriate, and topics that explore more specific aspects of the theme (Stoller & Grabe, 1997). Theoretically, there is an infinite number of themes to engage students in learning about the Korean society and culture: dating and marriage, educational practices, urban developments, pre-modern Confucius Korea, the cold war, industrialization, democratization movements, and the list can easily continue. However, the selection of themes will be constrained by available content resources relevant to the HL learner's interests and appropriate for their linguistic level. Once the selection of themes, texts, and topics is made and sequenced, "the specification of core objectives for each theme unit in terms of language, content, and strategy learning" is in order (Stoller & Grabe, 1997, p. 92). Clear learning objectives within the framework of content-based instruction will satisfy such learners' desires for a sense of control and hence, increase self-efficacy. The next step in the formulation of the learning objectives is to design tasks for the thematic unit that will "develop the students' language learning, facilitate the learning of content, and model strategies for language and content learning" (Stoller & Grabe, 1997, p. 92).

The language component of the learning objectives and tasks should be derived not only from the texts or content resources selected, but also from analysis of HL learner's language needs. The content resources will determine the language that is necessary to understand and learn the particular content ("content-obligatory" language), whereas the learner's language proficiency should identify the language that is lacking for informed discussion in general ("content-compatible" language; see Snow et al., 1989). Acquiring advanced literacy involves progressing from context-embedded to context-reduced language use, where linguistic information takes on more burden than contextual information. Thus, context-reduced register has its own linguistic, textual, and discourse characteristics (Martin, 2002) and is distinct from the register of everyday, face-to-face interaction. HL learners generally lack exposure to such formal registers (Valdés & Geoffrion-Vinci, 1998). Although the HL learners we investigated did not indicate any interest in pursuing academic study in Korean, they hoped to carry out educated conversations in Korean. For these learners, "content-obligatory" language will not be that important beyond the immediate need to understand the text; however, "content-compatible" language that is required for expression of any complex thoughts will be a worthwhile investment.

Many teaching units developed as in-house materials can lend themselves to thematic units with more elaboration and further development. More research on the interlanguage of HL learners will further define the language learning objectives and design of language learning tasks. Although much more work needs to be done to fully develop content-based instruction for HL education, we believe that this is a promising direction to take.

REFERENCES

Au, S. Y. (1988). A critical appraisal of Gardner's social-psychological theory of second-language (L2) learning. *Language Learning, 38,* 75–100.

Brecht, R., Caemmerer, J., & Walton, R. (1995). *Russian in the United States: A case study of American's language needs and capacities.* [National Foreign Language Center Monograph Series.] Washington, DC: Johns Hopkins University.

Brod, R., & Wells, E. (2000). Foreign language enrollments in United States institutions of higher education. *ADFL Bulletin, 31,* 22–29.

Brown, H. D. (2000). *Principles of language learning and teaching* (4th ed.). Englewood Cliffs NJ: Prentice-Hall.

Campbell, R., & Christian, D. (2001). Heritage language education: Needed research. In J. Peyton, D. Ranard, & S. Mcginnis (Eds), *Heritage languages in America: Preserving a national resource* (pp. 255–266). Washington , DC: Center for Applied Linguistics and Delta Systems.

Cho, G. (2000). The role of heritage language in social interactions and relationships: Reflection from a language minority group. *Bilingual Research Journal, 24,* 333–348.

Cho, G., Cho, K. S., & Tse, L. (1997). Why ethnic minorities need to develop their heritage language: The case of Korean-Americans. *Language, Culture and Curriculum, 10,* 106–112.

Clément, R. (1980). Ethnicity, contact and communicative competence in a second language. In H. Hiles, W. P. Robinson, & P. Smith (Eds.), *Language: Social psychological perspectives* (pp. 147–154). Oxford, UK: Pergamon.

Clément, R., & Kruidenier, B.G. (1985). Aptitude, attitude, and motivation in second language proficiency: A test of Clément's model. *Journal of Language and Social Psychology, 4,* 21–37.

Cotterall, S. (1995). Readiness for autonomy: Investigating learner beliefs. *System, 23*(2), 195–205.

Crookes, G., & Schmidt, R. W. (1991). Motivation: Reopening the research agenda. *Language Learning, 41,* 469–512.

Dörnyei, Z. (1994). Motivation and motivating in the foreign language classroom. *The Modern Language Journal, 78,* 273–284.

Dörnyei, Z. (1998). Survey article: Motivation in second and foreign language learning. *Language Teaching, 31,* 117–135.

Doughty, C., & Williams, J. (Eds.). (1998). *Focus on form in classroom second language acquisition.* New York: Cambridge University.

Douglas, M. O. (2003, April). *Assessing Japanese heritage language learners' needs from community service learning.* Paper presented at NCOLCTL annual conference. LA, California.

Ely, C. (1986). Language learning motivation: A descriptive and causal analysis. *Modern Language Journal, 70,* 28–35

Feuerverger, G. (1991.) University students' perceptions of heritage language learning and ethnic identity maintenance. *Canadian Modern Language Review, 47,* 660–677.

Fishman, J. (Ed.). (2001). *Can threatened languages be saved? Reversing language shift revisited: A 21st century perspective.* Clevedon, UK: Multilingual Matters.

Gardner, R. C. (1985). *Social psychology and language learning: The role of attitudes and motivation.* London: Edward Arnold.

Gardner, R. C., & Lambert, W. E. (1972). *Attitudes and motivation in second language learning.* Rowley, MA: Newbury House.

Gardner, R. C., & MacIntyre, P. D. (1991). An instrumental motivation in language study: Who says it isn't effective? *Studies in Second Language Acquisition, 13,* 266–272.

Gardner, R. C., Tremblay, P., & Masgoret, A. (1997). Towards a full model of second language learning: an empirical investigation. *Modern Language Journal, 81,* 344–362.

Grabe, W., & Stoller, F. (1997). Content-based instruction: Research foundations. In M. A. Snow & D. M. Brinton (Eds.), *The content-based classroom:Perspectives on integrating language and content* (pp. 5–21). New York: Longman.

Hammerly, H. (1982). *Synthesis in second language learning.* Blaine, WA: Second Language Publication.

Hilles, S., & Lynch, D. (1997). Culture as content. In M. A. Snow & D. M. Brinton (Eds.), *The content-based classroom: Perspectives on integrating language and content* (pp. 371–376). New York: Longman.

Hinton, L. (1999). Trading tongues: Loss of heritage languages in the United States. *English Today, 60*, 22–30.

Jorden, E., & Lambert, R. (1991). *Japanese language instruction in the United States: Resources, practice and investment strategy.* [National Foreign Language Center Monograph Series.] Washington, DC: Johns Hopkins University.

King, R. (1998) Korean as a heritage language (KHL) vs. Korean as a foreign language (KFL) in North America and the Former USSR: Ambiguous priorities and insufficient resources. *Acta Koreana, 1,* 27–40.

Kondo-Brown, K. (2003). Heritage language instruction for postsecondary students from immigrant backgrounds. *Heritage Language Journal, 1.* Retrieved October, 2004 from ftp: http://www.heritagelanguages.org/

Kramsch, C. (2003). Why should language teachers teach culture? *Language, Culture and Curriculum, 9,* 99–107.

Krashen, S. (1981). *Second language acquisition and second language learning.* Oxford: Pergamon.

Lee, J. S. (2002). The Korean language in America: The role of cultural identity and heritage language. *Language, Culture, and Curriculum, 15*(2), 117–133.

Lee, J. S., & Farhat, L. (2003, April). *Understanding the goals, motivations, attitudes, and needs of LCTL learners.* Paper presented at the National Council of Less Commonly Taught Languages, Los Angeles, California.

Lee, T. W., Locke, E. A., & Latham, G. P. (1989). Goal setting theory and job performance. In A. Pervin (Ed.), *Goal concepts in personality and social psychology* (pp. 291–326). Hillsdale, NJ: Lawrence Erlbaum Associates.

Lopez, D. (1996). Language: Diversity and assimilation. In R. Waldinger & M. Bozorgmehr (Eds.), *Ethnic Los Angeles* (pp. 139–163). New York, NY: Russell Sage Foundation.

Lynch, A. (2003). The relationship between second and heritage language acquisition: Notes on research and theory building. *Heritage Language Journal, 1.* Retrieved October, 2004 from ftp: http://www.heritagelanguages.org/

MacIntyre, P. D. (1995). How does anxiety affect second language learning? A reply to Sparks and Ganshow. *The Modern Language Journal, 79,* 90–99.

Martin, J. R. (2002). Writing history: Construing time and value in discourses of the past. In M. J. Schleppegrell & M. C. Colombi (Eds.), *Developing advanced literacy in first and second languages* (pp. 87–118). Mahwah, NJ: Lawrence Erlbaum Associates.

Min, P. G. (2000). Korean Americans' language use. In S. McKay & S. Wong (Eds.), *New immigrants in the United States.* (pp. 306–332). New York: Cambridge University.

Oxford, R. L., & Shearin, J. (1994). Language learning motivation: Expanding the theoretical framework. *The Modern Language Journal, 78,* 12–28.

Oxford, R. L., & Shearin, J. (1996). Language learning motivation in a new key. In R. L. Oxford (Ed.), *Language learning motivation: Pathways to the new century* (pp. 121–144). Honolulu: Second Language Teaching & Curriculum Center, University of Hawai`i.

Patton, M. Q. (1987). *How to use qualitative methods in evaluation.* Newbury Park, CA: Sage.

Ryu Yang, J. (2003). Motivational orientation and selected learner variables of East Asian language learners in the United States. *Foreign Language Annals, 36*(1), 44–56.

Scarcella, R. C., & Oxford, R. L. (1992). *The tapestry of language learning: The individual in the communicative classroom.* Boston: Heinle & Heinle.

Skehan, P. (1989). *Individual differences in second language learning.* London: Edward Arnold.

Snow, M. A. (1998). Trends and issues in content-based instruction. *Annual Review of Applied Linguistics, 18,* 243–267.

Snow, M. A., Met. M., & Genesee, F. (1989). A conceptual framework for the integration of language and content in second/foreign language instruction. *TESOL Quarterly, 23*(2), 201–218.

Spolsky, B. (1989). *Conditions for second language learning.* Oxford: Oxford University.

Stoller, F., & Grabe, W. (1997). A six-T's approach to content-based instruction. In M. A. Snow & D. M. Brinton (Eds.), *The content-based classroom: Perspectives on integrating language and content* (pp. 78–94). New York: Longman.

Strauss, A., & Corbin, J. (1990). *Basics of qualitative research: Grounded theory procedures and techniques.*, Newbury Park, CA: Sage.

Tremblay, P. F., & Gardner, R. C. (1995). Expanding the motivation construct in language learning. *The Modern Language Journal, 79,* 505–518.

Tse, L. (1998). Ethnic identity formation and its implications for heritage language development. In S. Krahsen, L. Tse, & J. McQuillan (Eds.), *Heritage language development* (pp. 15–27). Culver City, CA: Language Education Associates.

Tse, L. (2000). The effects of ethnic identity formation on bilingual maintenance and development: An analysis of Asian American narratives. *International Journal of Bilingual Education and Bilingualism, 3,* 185–200.

Tse, L. (2001). Resisting and reversing language shift: Heritage-language resilience among U.S. native biliterates. *Harvard Educational Review, 71*(4), 676–706.

Van Deusen-Scholl, N. (2003). Toward a definition of heritage language: Sociopolitical and pedagogical considerations. *Journal of Language, Identity, and Education, 2*(3), 211–230.

Van Lier, L. (1996). *Interaction in the language curriculum: Awareness, autonomy, and authenticity.* London: Longman.

Valdés, G. (1995). The teaching of minority languages as academic subjects: Pedagogical and theoretical challenges. *The Modern Language Journal, 79*(3), 299–328.

Valdés, G. (2001). Heritage language students: Profiles and possibilities. In J. Peyton, D. Ranard, & S. McGinnis (Eds.), *Heritage languages in America: Preserving a national resource.* (pp. 37–78). Washington, DC: Center for Applied Linguistics and Delta Systems.

Valdés, G., & Geoffrion-Vinci, M. (1998). Chicano Spanish: The problem of the "underdeveloped" code in bilingual repertoires. *The Modern Language Journal, 82,* 473–501.

Walker, G. (2005). *Advanced Chinese skills for the American in China.* Invited symposium presentation, Georgetown University Roundtable.

Wesche, M. B., & Skehan, P. (2002). Communicative, task-based, and content-based language instruction. In R. B. Kaplan (Ed.), *The Oxford handbook of applied linguistics* (pp. 207–228). New York: Oxford University.

Wiley, T., & Valdés, G. (2000). Heritage language instruction in the United States: A time for renewal. *Bilingual Research Journal, 24*(4), i–v.

Wiley, T. (2002, June). *Overcoming the legacy of language policies that engender language shift: An important role for the universities.* Paper presented at the University of California Consortium Heritage Language Institute at UCLA.

Williams, M., & Burden, R. L. (1997). *Psychology for language teachers: A social constructivist approach.* Cambridge: Cambridge University.

Chapter 8

Developing a "Compromise Curriculum" for Korean Heritage and Nonheritage Learners

William H. Yu
University of Hawai`i at Mānoa

BACKGROUND

Genesis of the Study

Recently, numerous scholars in KFL (Korean as a foreign language) have discussed the challenges and complications of having both heritage learners (hereafter HLs) and nonheritage learners (hereafter NHLs) in the same classroom (e.g., H. Kim, 2001; King, 1998; C. Lee, 1999; Ree, 1998; Ryu-Yang, 2002, 2003; Shin & Kim, 2000; S. Sohn, 1995, 1997; Stromberg, 1997; You, 2001). The problems that arise have been described as the NHLs not being able to keep up with the pace of the course and feeling intimidated by HLs, whereas HLs feel that the course is progressing too slowly and often become too bored and unmotivated to learn. Their teachers are confronted with a predicament where satisfying one group will cause dissatisfaction for the other, or in the words of Joseph Heller, a "Catch-22." Some recommend that every KFL program in the United States offer a two-track curriculum similar to that of University of California at Los Angeles (UCLA) and Columbia University, where HLs and NHLs students are divided into two courses (Kondo-Brown, this volume). A few issues, however, have been raised concerning such a recommendation. First, HLs and NHLs are normally provided with separate tracks only at the elementary/intermediate levels based on the assumption that, in 1 or 2 years, the linguistic abilities of HLs and NHLs are equal (Kondo-Brown, 2003). Second, support for the positive effects of two-track systems appears to be based primarily on personal observations; put another way, little formal evaluation has been done of the value of two-track systems for university HLs and NHLs (Kondo-Brown, this volume). Third, the administrators often consider KFL programs to be one of their lowest priorities due to political and financial issues caused by the low enrollment of NHLs (S. Sohn, 1995).

As a means of possibly resolving the many issues just mentioned, I propose developing a curriculum that will not only satisfy both HLs and NHLs needs in the same classroom but also appease those that question the merits of a two-track curriculum. Further, the curriculum, "A Compromise Curriculum," will not create any new financial burdens on administrators.

Previous Studies

The consensus of administrators, educators, and researchers in the field of Second Language Acquisition (SLA) is that needs analysis or needs assessment (hereafter NA) should be the first step in the development of any curriculum. Nevertheless, the amount of literature and study on NA is limited because it is relatively new in language-teaching circles. As for past studies, the majority are found in the ESL (English as a second language) and ESP (English for special purpose) literatures (Berwick, 1989; Brindley, 1989; Munby, 1981; Ostler, 1980; Savignon, 1997; Tarone & Yule, 1989). The few conducted in other fields of SLA include Von der Handt's (1983) identification of needs for teaching German to migrant workers; Reber and Geeslin's (1998) examination of needs of Spanish HLs for a course at the University of Arizona and Arizona State University; Gosalvez's (1999) comparative needs analysis of educators and HLs of Tagalog at the University of California at Berkeley; Saito's (1995) assessment of Japanese language needs perceived by students, business faculty, and business professionals; and Lee and Kim's (2000) small-scale NA to develop materials in third- and fourth-level Korean courses at the University of Hawai`i at Mānoa (hereafter UHM) applying the systematic approach to program development advocated by Brown (1995).

Although the aforementioned papers are excellent sources of information for planning and conducting a NA, previous studies comparing the different repertoire of needs for HLs and NHLs are practically non-existent, with the exception to two recent papers. The first is Kagan and Dillion's (2001) study that begins by comparing the characteristics of Russian HLs and NHLs:

> Heritage students lack the full spectrum of competencies because of their contact with a limited community of speakers, their incomplete or absence of education in Russian, and dominance of English in their formal education. Foreign language learners (nonheritage) typically have no contact with the real life language community outside the classroom. (Kagan & Dillon, 2001, p. 509)

Thereafter, the pedagogical needs of both groups were compared in terms of teaching domains that include pronunciation, vocabulary, grammar, reading, writing, speaking, listening, and culture. Based on the questionnaires and translation tasks of 41 HLs and NHLs of Russian at UCLA, Kagan and Dillon suggested that nonheritage language instruction should be directed towards a micro-approach or a gradual progression in all language skills, whereas language instruction for HL should adopt a macro-approach or teaching language using a full range of fairly complex texts focusing on content. Furthermore, in identifying similar needs, Kagan and Dillon noted that both HLs and NHLs must be taught learning strategies that they may incorporate throughout their language education. In conclusion, Kagan and Dillon stressed the clear need for Russian language textbooks and ancillary materials designed to meet the unique needs of HLs as well as to recognize them as legitimate students in a Russian language class.

The second NA, conducted by S. Sohn (1997), mainly reports on a case study of a new Korean heritage course offered at UCLA. She does, however, include a short analysis of a survey conducted on the different needs of HLs and NHLs. Her findings based on 135 UCLA students (90 HLs and 45 NHLs) enrolled in elementary Korean in the winter of 1997 indicate that HLs perceive the need to improve reading skills first, followed by writing, speaking, and listening, whereas NHLs express the need to improve speaking skills foremost, followed by listening, reading, and writing (S. Sohn, 1997, p. 141). It is also important to mention that S. Sohn (1997) also suggests, as Kagan and Dillon (2001) also did, that the lack of instructional materials designed for HLs increases the difficulty of teaching such learners.

Problems in the Mixed Classroom

The recent growth of interest in HLs has lead to a reassessment of foreign language curriculum at colleges and universities throughout the United

States. The underlying reason for such growth of interest is mainly that there has been a dramatic increase in enrollments in previously less commonly taught languages, such as Chinese, Japanese, Tagalog, Hindi, Vietnamese, and, of course, Korean (Van Deusen-Scholl, 1999). That is, in these foreign language classes, there is an increasing number of HLs who grew up in households where these languages were spoken and who were therefore more heavily exposed to the language and culture than NHLs.

As briefly mentioned in the introduction, the general clash between HLs and NHLs is perceived as being that HLs are unable to abide the slow-paced nature of the courses and that the NHLs feel the exact opposite. More specifically, as S. Sohn (1995) puts it, from a NHL's perspective, even elementary Korean is a laborious and time intensive course that demands enormous amounts of time spent memorizing hundreds of vocabulary items and grammatical patterns. Furthermore, NHLs often forget majority of the words, even after memorizing them due to insufficient opportunity to actually drill and practice them in class. S. Sohn (1995) also states that "The lack of opportunity for oral proficiency is partly due to the majority of students who are from the heritage background and thus already have a certain level of competence in the language" (p. 23). Frustrated and angered by what they feel is unfair treatment from educators and intimidation from HLs, many NHLs have voiced complaints. For example, Stromberg (1997), an African American student in a mixed KFL classroom states, "I was frustrated by what I perceived as a lack of interest in teaching non-Koreans to speak the language" (p. 160). She continues by alleging that HLs often tended to monopolize the class time and teased NHLs for inadequate proficiency. The unhealthy environment directly (or indirectly) caused by the HLs has resulted in many NHLs dropping out of KFL classes (Ree, 1998).

In contrast, HLs are frustrated because NHLs slow down the pace of the course and because their institutions lack courses or sections that attend to their unique needs (King, 1998). The issue of NHLs slowing the pace is addressed in the next section of this chapter. With respect to attending to the unique needs of HLs, one of two major factors prohibiting the development of new courses in the past was the lack of materials and ancillary materials for HLs as King (1998) pointed out, "Virtually all textbooks used at the university level were written with the assumption that the target audience was native speakers of English with no prior exposure to Korean language or culture" (p. 30). King's view that new textbooks must be developed is shared by other KFL scholars (e.g., C. Lee, 1999; Y. Park, 1997; Ree, 1998; S. Sohn, 1995; You, 2001). As a consequence of this overwhelming consensus among KFL scholars, a textbook series known as the Korean Language Education and Research Center (KLEAR) Textbooks in Korean Languages was launched in 2000. The KLEAR textbooks are presently being written with explicit grammatical explanations and various task-based activities that enhance learners' communicative competence. In essence, KLEAR text-books are endeavoring to meet the needs of both HLs and NHLs. The pro-jected 21-volume series seems to have resolved one of the most critical issues in KFL–the need for adequate textbooks.

The second factor prohibiting the development of new courses is the inability to locate qualified teachers and foster their professional develop-ment due to low priority for funds (C. Lee, 1999). For example, S. Sohn (1995) suggests that the lack of support from the administration at the col-lege level is due to the status of Korean teachers, who are often employed only as lecturers or nontenured members despite their qualifications. Similarly, You (2001) states that KFL programs are considered one of the lowest priorities by the administration. Hence, securing adequate funds is a constant issue, one that will exist for many years to come. However, for two institutions, we can see a glimpse of what the future may bring. In 2002, under the National Foreign Language initiative, the National Security Education Program selected and allocated UHM and UCLA funds with the goal of producing students with "professional" proficiency in Korean. This "flagship program" offers HLs the advanced content-based courses they so desperately need along with a possible future in federal employment (D. Lee, 2001). Hence, for at least these two institutions, the needs of both HLs and NHLs may have been addressed.

Suggested Solutions

Despite some skepticism, the advantage of two-track curriculums have been widely celebrated (e.g., C. Lee, 1999; Ree, 1998; Ryu-Yang, 2002, 2003; Shin & Kim, 2000; S. Sohn, 1995, 1997; Stromberg, 1997; You, 2001). For exam-ple, S. Sohn (1997) acknowledges that (a) both types of students were pro-vided optimal opportunity to improve their special needs, (b) a dramatic increase in retention rate occurred, (c) there were remarkable improve-ments in proficiency for NHLs, and (d) there was a substantial increase in enrollment by both groups (pp. 149–150).

Despite its reported high success, most Korean programs cannot afford to entertain the idea of a two-track curriculum, and thus, alternative solu-tions have been proposed, such as those provided by Ree (1998) and You (2001). Ree (1998) suggests a "resource-sharing" approach, that is, a class where HLs and NHLs are individually paired for listening and speaking practice. He asserts that the implementation of such methods will provide both types of students sufficient opportunities to practice their interper-sonal skills as well as eliminate the boredom felt by HLs and the intimida-tion felt by NHLs (Ree, 1998). In a similar view, You (2001) suggests a class where students are separated into small groups based on their interests.

Other innovative suggestions for solving the challenges of teaching HLs and NHLs together in one class include computer-assisted language learning programs (Hope International University, 2001; S. Park, 2001; Park-Cho & Carey, 2001). For example, according to Choi and Koh (2001), the "interactive online exercises" implemented into the Korean program at the State University of New York at Buffalo created an environment that was more focused, individualized, easily available, and less threatening for students who needed extra support and encouragement. The basis for such a positive remark derives from the fact that learners are provided (a) opportunities to revisit their areas of weakness in the language, (b) the freedom to review and redo exercises, and (c) the ability to control their own pace without being conscious of others (Choi & Koh, 2001, pp. 134–135).

Purpose and Research Questions

In hopes of providing a solution for KFL programs struggling with the challenges of having Korean HLs and NHLs in one class, the purpose of this study is to take the first needs analysis (NA) step in the development of "A Compromise Curriculum." To this end, the NA will address the following research questions while adopting a "democratic philosophy" (Stufflebeam, McCormick, Brinkerhoff, & Nelson, 1985) for identifying the learners subjective needs:

1. Which themes do HLs and NHLs feel are most important and how are the two groups' perceived needs different or similar?
2. What component of their current class would they like to see changed or maintained?
3. What comparisons can be made based on their stated ranking of the four integrated skills?
4. Based on the results, what preliminary suggestions can be made in designing "A Compromise Curriculum"?

METHOD

Participants

The participants in the study were 43 students enrolled in Korean 101 (first semester) and 201 (third semester) at Kapi'olani Community College (KCC) and the University of Hawai`i at Mānoa (UHM). The return rates of the responses were:

KCC 101 = 9/11 (81.8%)
KCC 201 = 11/14 (78.6%)

UHM 101 = 11/15 (73.3%)
UHM 201 = 12/14 (85.7%)
Total = 43/54 (79.6%)

A total of 18 (42%) students declared themselves as being ethnically Korean, one (2%) as being approximately three-quarters Korean, seven (16%) as being half Korean, two (5%) as being one-quarter Korean, and 15 (35%) as being non-Koreans. Of the 43 respondents, 24 (55.8%) were categorized as HLs and 19 (44.2%) as NHLs based on whether they answered "yes" or "no" to the first question of the survey, which asked them if they had at least one native-speaking parent living with them.

Table 8.1 illustrates that a majority of HLs (59%) learned Korean exclusively or in combination with English as a first language. Moreover, 71% of the HLs maintained or practiced using Korean by speaking at home whereas 80% of their parents only spoke Korean or combination of Korean/English when speaking to them. This is a manifestation of why HLs have such a significant advantage over NHLs in KFL classrooms.

To further describe the participants, five (11.6%) identified themselves as freshmen, 21 (48.8%) as sophomores, 10 (23.3%) as juniors, three (7.0%) as seniors, and four (9.3%) as graduate students. Their stated majors included seven (16.3%) in Business/Travel Industry Management, 15 (34.9%) in Arts

TABLE 8.1
Language Use at Home

Group		Heritage learners (n = 24)	Non-heritage learners (n = 19)
First language you learned	English	38%	58%
	Korean	42%	5%[a]
	English & Korean	17%	0%
	Korean & others	0%	0%
	Others	4%	37%
Languages you speak at home	English	25%	68%
	Korean	0%	0%
	English & Korean	67%	0%
	Korean & others	4%	0%
	Others	4%	32%
Languages your parents or	English	8%	68%
relatives speak to you	Korean	17%	0%
	English & Korean	63%	0%
	Korean & others	8%	0%
	Others	0%	32%

[a]The nonheritage learner who indicated her first language to be Korean was adopted by Korean parents as an infant.

and Sciences, three (7.0%) in Engineering, and 18 (41.8%) in the Undecided/Others category. And lastly, the majority of students (53%) in the study did not want to study Korean beyond the 2-year foreign language requirement. Only 5 (12%) students stated that they would finish the 300 level and 11 (26%) students indicated they would finish the 400 level.

Instruments

The NA and the proposed curriculum were designed to be consistent with the national movement to redirect foreign language curricula towards a proficiency or performance-based approach (see National Standards in Foreign Language Education Project, 1996). The questions in the study were adapted from the Needs Analysis Subcommittee of the Performance-Based Testing Committee of the Japanese section in the East Asian Languages and Literatures Department at UHM. The committee designed the questions by adopting the classification of domains into three categories—area, theme, and task—from Norris, Brown, Hudson, and Yoshioka (1998). These questions were first modified and used by Iwai, Kondo, Lim, Ray, Shimizu, and Brown (1999) in their NA of Japanese language students and teachers at UHM. The final version of the Iwai et al. (1999) questionnaire was adapted in this study, that is, with some changes deemed necessary for KFL learners (see Appendix A for the list of subjective needs analysis questions [questions #13–50], the section II of the questionnaire).

The first part of the questionnaire consisted of 12 multiple-choice questions requesting students' background information and the second part consisted of 38 Likert-scale questions central to the study. The 38 central Likert-scale questions were classified into four categories (area): (a) academic situations, (b) occupational situations, (c) social/domestic situations, and (d) tour-related situations. Each of the four areas consisted of approximately 10 questions that described the type of activities normally reflected in such situations (theme). Moreover, within each theme, examples of tasks were included in parentheses (task).

The third part of the questionnaire included three open-ended questions that diagnose learners' personal desires and expectations in the language classroom. More specifically, it further examined the components of their current class they might wish to see changed or maintained. The three open-ended questions were as follows:

1. What activities do you wish could be included in your class?
2. Do you feel that you would learn more efficiently if the class catered to your needs and not what your teacher feels you need? Why or why not?
3. Do you wish the teacher would spend more or less time on the textbook? Why or why not?

According to Brindley (1984), such questions as those just mentioned are a critical part of understanding learners' subjective needs. Lastly, the students were asked to rank the four skills (writing, listening, speaking, and reading) in the order that they feel they need the most improvement.

Procedures

The questionnaires were distributed and collected in November, 2001. After collecting the questionnaires, the data were analyzed giving the answers to the Likert scale questions the following values: A = 5 (strongly agree), B = 4 (agree), C = 3 (no opinion), D = 2 (disagree), and E = 1 (strongly disagree). Due to the relatively small sample size in this study, only descriptive statistics (including means, minimum values, maximum values, and standard deviations) were used.

The three open-ended questions were coded based on similarities, differences, and saliency. And finally, the ranking of the four integrated skills was calculated by using a simple point system. For example, the language skill that participants indicated as requiring the most improvement corresponded to 1 point and the skill that required the least improvement corresponded to 4 points. After assigning each language skill a value using a point system of 1 thru 4, the skill with the least total was considered the skill most needed.

RESULTS AND DISCUSSION

Comparing Subjective Needs Between Heritage and Nonheritage Learners

This section addresses the first and the most important question of the study—"Which themes do HLs and NHLs feel are most important in learning Korean and how are the two groups' perceived needs different or similar?" Applying a mean cut-point of 4.58 or above, a total of 14 questions were selected as the "most agreed to items for HL" (see Table 8.2).[1]

Of the 14 items or themes, seven were themes and tasks in the area of tour-related situations, six in social/domestic, one in academic, and none were occupational. The most interesting result here is that the first four items in the dataset are all in the area of social/domestic situations. (The following is a list of the top four themes in order from the highest to the lowest mean.)

---

[1]The designated cut-point seemed ideal for this discussion because there was a noticeable gap (.16) between 4.58 and the next lower mean for NHL.

TABLE 8.2
Most Agreed to Items (Mean $\geq$ 4.58) for the Heritage Learners ($n=14$)

Question #	Mean	SD	Min	Max	A	B	C	D	E
*Q36	4.96	0.20	4	5	96%	4%	0%	0%	0%
*Q33	4.88	0.45	3	5	92%	4%	4%	0%	0%
*Q39	4.80	0.42	4	5	79%	21%	0%	0%	0%
Q35	4.75	0.44	4	5	75%	25%	0%	0%	0%
*Q47	4.75	0.53	3	5	79%	17%	4%	0%	0%
Q13	4.67	0.57	3	5	71%	25%	4%	0%	0%
Q34	4.67	0.64	3	5	75%	17%	8%	0%	0%
Q44	4.67	0.48	4	5	67%	33%	0%	0%	0%
Q45	4.67	0.48	4	5	67%	33%	0%	0%	0%
Q32	4.63	0.58	3	5	67%	29%	4%	0%	0%
Q42	4.63	0.58	3	5	67%	29%	4%	0%	0%
Q46	4.63	0.58	3	5	67%	29%	4%	0%	0%
Q41	4.58	0.72	3	5	71%	17%	13%	0%	0%
Q43	4.58	0.58	3	5	63%	33%	4%	0%	0%

*Indicates those most agreed to by each specific group.

Q36.   Use appropriate speech level towards the addressee.
Q33.   Interact more efficiently with spouse, parents, or relatives.
Q39.   Be able to interact with your children and teach them Korean in the future.
Q35.   Learn more about Korean culture.

Further, every HL "strongly agreed" to Item Q36 except for one student who simply "agreed." The seven tour-related themes in these results varied from eating at restaurants to dealing with emergency situations in Korea. The only theme included from the academic area was "Deal with in-class routines."

The results, especially the first two items, are not surprising as they corresponded to findings from previous investigations. For example, Jo (2001) found that HLs face tremendous difficulty using appropriate speech levels and honorifics. Moreover, Lee and Kim (this volume) and Cho et al. (1997) discovered that the main reason for learning Korean for HLs is to communicate with their parents and relatives. Perhaps the surprising element in the present results is the high mean of the third theme (Q39). Even though (I suspect) most of the students do not have children, they are already thinking about their children's education and realize the value of heritage language maintenance.

With respect to NHLs, 13 items were above the 4.58 cut-point. Of the 13 items, seven were in tour-related situations, three in social/domestic, three

TABLE 8.3
Most Agreed to Items (Mean ≥ 4.58) for the Nonheritage Learners ($n=13$)

Question #	Mean	SD	Min	Max	A	B	C	D	E
Q32	4.79	0.54	3	5	84%	11%	5%	0%	0%
Q34	4.79	0.42	4	5	79%	21%	0%	0%	0%
Q43	4.79	0.56	3	5	84%	11%	5%	0%	0%
Q46	4.79	0.56	3	5	84%	11%	5%	0%	0%
Q13	4.74	0.45	4	5	74%	26%	0%	0%	0%
*Q20	4.68	0.48	4	5	68%	32%	0%	0%	0%
Q35	4.68	0.48	4	5	68%	32%	0%	0%	0%
Q44	4.68	0.58	3	5	74%	21%	5%	0%	0%
Q45	4.68	0.58	3	5	74%	21%	5%	0%	0%
*Q21	4.63	0.60	3	5	68%	26%	5%	0%	0%
Q42	4.63	0.60	3	5	68%	26%	5%	0%	0%
Q41	4.58	0.69	3	5	68%	21%	11%	0%	0%
*Q49	4.58	0.69	3	5	68%	21%	11%	0%	0%

*Indicates those most agreed to by each specific group.

in academic, and none were occupational. Notice that in these particular results (see Table 8.3), the first four items all have the exact same Mean of 4.79. Of the first four, as listed in the following, two are social/domestic situations and two are tour-related.

Q32. Understand Korean for entertainment.
Q34. Socialize with Korean friends.
Q43. Speak with strangers in Korea.
Q46. Eat at a restaurant in Korea.

In comparing the findings of both groups of learners, these results illustrate that Korean HLs and NHLs agreed equally about 7 out of 10 themes in tour-related situations as their primary motives for learning Korean. For both datasets, six of the seven themes were identical (the exceptions were Items Q47 for HLs and Q49 for NHLs that were specific to each group). More specifically, HL seem to believe that the ability to deal with emergency situations in Korea to be more valuable than using the subway/train. (Other items specific to each group are discussed further later.) The following is a list of the six tour-related themes (in no particular order) that were included in the results for both groups.

Q41. Get around at an airport in Korea.
Q42. Shop for gifts in Korea.
Q43. Speak with strangers in Korea.
Q44. Go sightseeing in Korea.
Q45. Stay at a hotel in Korea.
Q46. Eat at a restaurant in Korea.

Needless to say, there were two items (Q48 & Q50) from the tour-related area excluded from the results. To explain this finding, notice that the six just-mentioned items can be considered as being a necessity in traveling to Korea, whereas the two unlisted items ("Talk to law enforcement in Korea" and "Rent a car in Korea") are not.

The items marked with asterisks were those most agreed to by each specific group, namely, Q20, Q21, Q33, Q36, Q39, Q47, and Q49. The last two have already been discussed. However, the remaining five were as follows:

Q20. Use a Korean language dictionary skillfully to meet reading needs.
Q21. Use computer-related skills in Korean.
Q33. Interact more efficiently with spouse, parents, or relatives.
Q36. Use the appropriate speech level towards the addressee.
Q39. Be able to interact with your children and teach them Korean in the future.

Items Q20 and Q21, most agreed to items specific to NHLs, are themes in the area of academic situations. An argument can be made for Q20 as HLs sometimes begin their formal education already familiar with dictionary use. As for Item Q21, for some unexplainable reason, HLs do not feel the need for combining computer skills and Korean language. NHLs in the study, however, strongly agreed that such skills should be incorporated into class. This is further supported in the qualitative section of the study where NHLs clearly stated that computer-oriented activities should be incorporated into class. One possible explanation for these findings is that perhaps the NHLs in this particular study have more computer-related goals than the HLs.

With respect to the last three questions, the most agreed-to items specific to HLs, NHLs rightfully disregarded Items Q33 and Q39 because they are irrelevant in their lives unless they have been adopted by Korean parents or have the prospect of marrying a Korean person. As for Q36, due to their Western backgrounds, NHLs tend to underestimate the importance of using proper speech level (Byon, 2000).

Focusing on just the first two themes in each group, both HLs and NHLs cited social/domestic situation themes as the two most important elements for learning Korean. But despite this commonality, it is crucial to observe that the themes (items) and task samples each group selected were not identical. Specifically, the HLs viewed "Use appropriate speech level towards the addressee" and "Interact more efficiently with spouse, parents, or relatives" as the two most important themes. In contrast, the NHLs cited (along with two tour-related themes) "Understand Korean for entertainment" and "Socialize with Korean friends" as being the most important. The rationale for HLs' needing the aforementioned items has already been presented, but what about the two items most agreed on by NHLs? It is safe to argue that

NHLs' first priorities for learning Korean can be traced back to where they live. Hawai`i has one of the largest Korean communities in the United States along with Chicago, Los Angeles, New York City, and Washington DC. Hence having Korean friends and wanting to communicate with them in their language is not a rarity (Lee, J., Choi, Lee, M., Song, & O'Grady, 2000). Further, in Hawai`i, Korean TV programs are extremely popular among non-Koreans, and, largely due to this non-Korean popularity, they are broadcast daily with subtitles. The popularity of Korean dramas or "K-dramas" is demonstrated by the over 200 members of K-drama fan club in Hawai`i, which only began with 20 members, and tour companies offering 12 days K-drama tour packages that costs $3,000 (Toth, 2005). Nationally, exports of South Korean programs have risen 70% to $71.4 million, and Korean programs can now be seen nationally on the cable channel AZN Television on a daily basis (Hua, 2005).

To further compare the two groups, Table 8.4 shows the highest difference in means between HLs and NHLs applying a cut-point of approximately 1.00 or more. Based on the results here, the following five themes appear to have the most difference:

Q30.   Provide medical advice.
Q28.   Provide legal advice.
Q27.   Provide financial advice.
Q33.   Interact more efficiently with spouse, parents, or relatives.
Q39.   Be able to interact with your children and teach them Korean in the future.

First, Items Q33 and Q39 will be skipped here because I have already presented the rationale for why HLs and NHLs do not agree on these. As for Items Q30, Q28, and Q27, they are all in the area of occupational situations. A logical explanation for the findings is that the NHLs in this study may perceive "professional" proficiency as an unattainable level in a 4-year university program. This is supported by the fact that in order for an NHL

TABLE 8.4

Items with the Largest Mean Differences between the Heritage and Nonheritage Learner Groups (Mean Difference is Approximately 1.00 or More).

Question #	Heritage	Nonheritage	Difference
Q30	3.88	2.66	1.22
Q28	3.92	2.82	1.10
Q27	3.93	2.87	1.06
Q33	4.89	3.90	0.99
Q39	4.79	3.84	0.95

to achieve "professional" or Interagency Language Roundtable's (ILR) Level 3 proficiency, it would take between 2,400–2760 hours of instruction or 20 years in a normal KFL program (D. Lee, 2001). Conversely, HLs may see "professional" proficiency as an attainable level. The National Security Education Program and National Foreign Language Center seem to agree given that HLs are considered the most promising candidate for national security agencies (D. Lee, 2001). The basis for such consideration is the fact that HLs are the fastest and also the cheapest to train, "The cost in instructional time and dollars required to bring them (HLs) to professional levels of competence is significantly less than the cost for individuals without a home language experience" (Brecht & Ingold, 1998, p. 2).

Maintaining or Changing the Current Syllabus

The third part of the questionnaire included three open-ended questions that pertain to the current syllabus. The first of the three questions asked, "What activities do you wish could be included in your class?" A majority of HLs (20) and NHLs (16) felt that videos/TV shows, role-playing, and traditional aspects of Korea should be incorporated as part of the course syllabus. For example, one HL and NHL stated the following:

> Watching videos on Korean culture and Korean soap operas to explain or understand the Korean family structure. (HL)

> Seeing actual Koreans speak to each other then a description of what was said in detail. Playing traditional Korean games. Learning traditional Korean songs, passing out the music on sheets and a description of what the song means. Learning Korean traditional dances. Learning about what is popular in Korean now. Learning what Korean people do. If Korean native speakers came into talk individually to students and we would have to think of stuff to say. (NHL)

The second question asked, "Do you feel that you would learn more efficiently if the class catered to your needs and not what your teacher feels you need? Why or why not?" The students' opinions on this matter were divided both in the HL and NHL groups: twelve (60%) HLs and seven (41%) NHLs preferred class to be conducted according to their teacher's perceived needs of them. For instance:

> No, teacher knows best! (HL)

> Being a first time student in Korean, I'm not too sure what my needs are, so pretty much what the teacher has provided me has been sufficient. If not, there are hours available if I need any help. (NHL)

The most students who wanted their teacher to assess their needs were very unsure about what they needed to learn and often employed the cliché of "Teacher knows best!" Their apprehensiveness may largely be attributed to the fact that the students in this study were from the lower levels, hence they have yet to attain the confidence to state their needs. In the future, it would be very interesting to investigate how the upper level students feel and compare their findings with those given here from the lower levels.

In contrast, seven HLs and eight NHLs believed that they would learn more efficiently if the teacher catered to their needs. For example:

> Yes, I do. Learning something that you personally need will allow you to be more productive. (HL)

> Yes, because sometimes in class the teacher goes over things I already know and it takes up a lot of time. (NHL)

Three students (one HL and two NHLs) in the study stated that a compromise must be reached to incorporate both students' and teachers' perceived needs. Following are two such advocates of compromise:

> I believe it should be half and half although catering the class on my needs would help a lot, the instructor has more experience in the language than I do so, listening to what the teacher feels is right helps also. (HL)

> I think overall you really need to look at the class make-up. Right now, there is a overall high percentage of people who are Korean and some part Korean, but there are the minority who aren't and if the teacher gives needs the class needs than I think it might be difficult for those without any background in Korea. On the other hand, I'm not saying that the teacher should cater to one student or the minority, but I feel that there needs to be some overall balance for all the students in the class. Again, this really depends on the class make-up and the needs as a whole for that class. (NHL)

Finally, the third question asked, "Do you wished the teacher would spend more or less time on the textbook? Why or why not?" Only three HLs and five NHLs stated that their KFL teacher should spend more time on textbook material. For instance:

> Maybe a little more time on the textbooks. I usually don't understand the vocabulary cause we're just expected to look over it & I don't know how to pronounce a lot of the words from just reading the book. (NHL)

Conversely, 11 HLs and seven NHLs held opposing views as the following example shows:

> Textbooks are boring and so fake. I wish we could do more speaking practice. (HL) The remaining 16 students appeared to be generally satisfied

with their teacher's method of distributing class time between various activities and textbook materials.

The Four Integrated Skills

When asked which of the four language skills they felt needed the most improvement, the HLs felt the need to improve their writing skills first, followed by reading, speaking, and listening, in that order. In contrast, the NHLs felt the need to improve their listening skills foremost, followed by speaking, writing, and reading. These findings resemble those of S. Sohn (1997) and other previous studies (e.g., Jo, 2001; H. Kim, 2001; C. Lee, 1999; S. Sohn, 1995, 1997), all of which attributed the poor spelling skills of HLs to writing the oral version of Korean and to lack of formal practice. As for NHLs, they appear to need to improve their listening skills foremost because they simply lack exposure to the language outside the classroom. HLs have the advantage of frequently encountering Korean at home or in the community as majority of their parents speak to them in Korean or in a combination of Korean and English (see Table 8.1), whereas NHLs do not have this luxury.

CONCLUSION

Summary

The comparative study of the instructional needs of HLs and NHLs in Korean 101 and 201 at the UHM and KCC can be summarized as follows:

1. Both groups strongly agreed that the same tour-related situations are critical themes that need to be addressed in a KFL classroom.
2. Although there were more tour-related situations above the 4.58 cut-point than social/domestic situations, HLs felt a stronger need to learn the latter, whereas NHLs cited both areas to be equally important.
3. The themes and task samples HLs and NHLs agreed on in the social/domestic area were not the same. Themes specific to HLs' needs consist of improving pragmatic skills to communicate with family and the community; whereas NHLs' needs appeared to derive from living in a highly concentrated Korean community.
4. HLs viewed "professional" proficiency as an attainable level, whereas NHLs did not.
5. No major difference was identified between HLs and NHLs in terms of how class should be maintained or changed.
6. HLs felt the need to improve their writing skills foremost compared to NHLs who felt the need to improve listening skills first.

A "Compromise Curriculum"

This study examined the needs perceived by Korean HLs and NHLs in KFL classrooms. The overall results suggest that Korean HLs and NHLs, although different in their characteristics, identify a significant number of similar needs. They both place a high priority on improving the same language skills for traveling to Korea. They also placed great emphasis on themes and tasks in social/domestic situations. The differences between the two groups of learners are modest, in that they exist within each classified domain. In other words, despite the fact that both HLs and NHLs agreed on the importance of social/domestic situations, the type of language skills they selected were not the same. And lastly, HLs are able to see themselves using Korean in their future occupations, whereas NHLs do not see it as an attainable goal.

One possible solution is to implement a two-track curriculum, but there is little empirical research that supports such a division (Kondo-Brown, 2003). For most institutions having a dual-track is a moot point because funds are not available. But we cannot ignore the problems that exist in mixed KFL classrooms. Therefore, in hopes of resolving the many problems that have surfaced in this study, I offer a solution: the "Compromise Curriculum," which meets the needs of both HLs' and NHLs' needs simultaneously in one classroom.

Naturally, teachers will need to make judgments based on the particular group of learners in a given class, but for this particular group, the "Compromise Curriculum" will adopt a macro-approach by teaching language using a full range of fairly complex texts focusing on content for HLs and a micro-approach or a gradual progression in all language skills for NHLs as suggested by Kagan and Dillon (2001). The language skills of focus for HLs will be writing/reading and listening/speaking for NHLs based on findings in this and previous studies (e.g., Cho et al., 1997; S. Sohn, 1997). This can be achieved by implementing extensive writing tasks for HLs starting with the reintroduction to the alphabet, syllable structures, complex vowels, sound change rules, word formation rules, and new lexical items as suggested by S. Sohn (1997). Free voluntary reading (McQuillan, 1996) should also be adopted as it will improve reading skills as well as provide HLs opportunities to deepen their interests and identify with other members of the heritage language-speaking community.

For NHLs, teachers must provide extensive exposure to input or "comprehensible input" because their only opportunity for listening practice is in the classroom. The benefits of "comprehensible input" advocated by Krashen (1982) have been heavily documented in various SLA papers (see, e.g., Omaggio-Hadley, 2001). Other forms of input such as authentic audible input via video/TV programs and "natural conversations" (Iwai, 1998) would also be beneficial for NHLs who are weak in the listening and speaking aspects of the language (this will also simultaneously fulfill their need to learn Korean for entertainment purposes). According to Iwai (1998), natural conversations provide learners information on sociopragmatic knowledge shared by native speakers. The input received could then be transferred as output during a "resource sharing" (a NHL paired with a HL who initiates the interaction and also encourages the nonheritage learner's verbal output) as suggested by Ree (1998), or by interacting in small groups according to their interests and needs as suggested by You (2001). And finally, creative role-plays on traveling to Korea, speaking with friends and family members using appropriate speech levels and honorifics must be included in the curriculum. According to (Swain & Lapkin, 1995), activities such as these encourage second language production and have been acknowledged to trigger the cognitive processes involved in language acquisition.

And most importantly, the content of the curriculum must be heavily loaded with tour-related and social/domestic situations. Further, computer labs should be assigned at least once a week (especially for NHLs) in order for students to acquire cultural information through the internet, to complete online exercises, and to practice Korean language typing skills (H. Sohn, 2000). Homework assignments, however, should be different for the two groups of learners. For example, HLs should be assigned extensive writing tasks such as daily journals and reading assignments, whereas NHLs should be assigned communicative tasks and extensive listening tasks in the form of "natural conversations." The application of such a "Compromise Curriculum" may prove extremely useful for both groups of learners. Indeed, KFL programs across the United States may want to seriously consider conducting a NA of their students on the first day of class and creating a syllabus based on the findings instead of relying on a fixed curriculum year after year; as Brown (1995) states, "curriculum is viewed as a process that can change and adapt to new conditions, whether those conditions be new types of students, changes in language theory, new political exigencies within the institutions, or something else" (p. 24).

Limitations and Future Study

There are some limitations to this study. First, despite the fact that a number important issues have been raised here, a larger sample size in the future would result in more powerful results and would allow the possibility of conducting inferential statistics. Second, postsurvey interviews were not conducted; consequently, judgments on how seriously the participants considered each question could not be made. And lastly, the separation of the learners into two groups was only based on the broadest definition of what it means to be an HL, rather than on an extensive evaluation of their actual heritage language background.

Future investigations should consider a larger performance-based NA by combining KFL students in the two of the largest Korean communities in the United States: Hawai'i and California. A performance-based NA should also be conducted for students in upper division courses (Korean 301 – 402) to investigate the degree to which their needs are different than those of lower division students. It would also be ideal to conduct personal interviews with the students in order to understand their frustrations with the current KFL curriculum. Furthermore, NA should be conducted for teachers and administrators and the findings should be compared with those of students in accordance with the principles of a systematic approach to curriculum development (Brown, 1995). And finally, future development of materials aimed at HLs should include teachers and scholars with a heritage language background because; "It is only the Korean-Americans who understand the needs of Korean-American students" (King, 1998, p. 31).

APPENDIX A
Korean Language Student Needs Questionnaire (Section II)

Section II: Subjective Needs

Please read each statement and indicate the extent to which you agree or disagree on the left: A = Strongly agree, B = Agree, C = No Opinion, D = Disagree, E = Strongly Disagree

At the end of my Korean language studies, I want to be able to perform the following in Korean:

_____ 13) Deal with in-class routines (e.g., asking questions, following directions, participating in discussion)

_____ 14) Engage in classroom discussions on current events and social issues (e.g., debating on government spending)

_____ 15) Give in-class presentations/demonstrations (e.g., explaining origins of Korean proverbs)

_____ 16) Consult with instructors (e.g., discussing class-related materials individually, providing valid excuse for absence)

_____ 17) Engage in a formal conversation with a Korean advisor (e.g., asking advice on courses to enroll in the future)

_____ 18) Fill out a scholarship application writing/written in Korean (e.g., background information, present study)

_____ 19) Read and write commonly used Chinese characters[*]

---

[*]Although the Korean alphabet (Hangul) is ubiquitous in Korea, all the major newspaper agencies still consistently use Chinese characters.

(Continued)

APPENDIX A (*Continued*)

_____ 20) Use a Korean language dictionary skillfully to meet reading needs (e.g., memorizing the Korean alphabet)

_____ 21) Use computer related skills in Korean (e.g., typing skills, using e-mail, Korean Web sites)

_____ 22) Help Korean customers at a hotel (e.g., checking in, making reservations, scheduling, giving directions, resolving complaints)

_____ 23) Assist Korean customers in a retail store (e.g., making suggestions, handling money, providing refunds, giving directions)

_____ 24) Guide Korean tourists around Hawai'i (e.g., explaining unique sites, introduce culture, suggest enjoyable spots)

_____ 25) Serve Korean customers in a restaurant (e.g., taking orders, explaining dishes, resolving complaints, confirm their satisfaction)

_____ 26) Translate formal and informal documents (e.g., lawsuits, medical report, letters, newspaper article)

_____ 27) Provide financial advice (e.g., explaining financial terms, suggesting stocks and bonds, assisting in an account)

_____ 28) Provide legal advice (e.g., explaining legal terms, translating lawsuits, suggesting options)

_____ 29) Teach Korean in primary and secondary institutions (e.g., define vocabulary, explain grammatical rules, interact with students)

_____ 30) Provide medical advice (e.g., explaining sickness, provide prescription for drugs, describing symptoms)

_____ 31) Check-in customers at airport (e.g., confirm party members, check-in luggage)

_____ 32) Understand Korean for entertainment (e.g., watch Korean TV programs/videos, sing karaoke, read comic books, and magazines)

_____ 33) Interact more efficiently with spouse, parents, or relatives (e.g., telephone conversations, write letters, interact at family functions)

_____ 34) Socialize with Korean friends (e.g., telephone conversations, plan parties or trips, talk about personal problems)

_____ 35) Learn more about Korean culture (e.g., through books, interaction with native Koreans)

_____ 36) Use the appropriate speech level towards the addressee (e.g., deferential level to grandparents, intimate level to friends)

_____ 37) Attend formal occasions such as weddings, funerals, graduation (e.g., giving money, writing a card, delivering a speech)

_____ 38) Participate in traditional cultural celebrations (e.g., play traditional games at New Year's Day, sing folksongs, understand folklores)

_____ 39) Be able to interact with your children and teach them Korean in the future (e.g., fundamental words and sentences, culture, tradition)

(*Continued*)

APPENDIX A (*Continued*)

_____ 40) Host guests from Korea (e.g., greeting, describing sites, serving food)

_____ 41) Get around at an airport in Korea (e.g., deal with luggage problems, answer questions from custom agent)

_____ 42) Shop for gifts in Korea (e.g., asking questions about a specific gift)

_____ 43) Speak with strangers in Korea (e.g., asking for directions)

_____ 44) Go sightseeing in Korea (e.g., gathering information for a trip, learning about the cultural and historical significance of a site)

_____ 45) Stay at a hotel in Korea (e.g., making reservations, checking in, resolving problems)

_____ 46) Eat at a restaurant in Korea (e.g., ordering food)

_____ 47) Deal with emergency situations in Korea (e.g., calling 911, seeing a doctor at a hospital)

_____ 48) Talk to law enforcement in Korea (e.g., explaining the crime that occurred)

_____ 49) Use the subway/train in Korea (e.g., purchase tickets, read maps, ask for information)

_____ 50) Rent a car in Korea (e.g., learning about options, insurance, what to do if an accident occurs)

REFERENCES

Berwick, R. (1989). Needs assessment in language programming: From theory to practice. In R. K. Johnson (Ed.), *The second language curriculum* (pp. 48–62). Cambridge: Cambridge University.

Brecht, R., & Ingold, C. (1998). Tapping a national resource: Heritage languages in the United States. *CAL Digest*. Retrieved August 26, 2005, from http://www.cal.org/resources/digest/0202brecht.html

Brindley, G. (1984). *Needs analysis and objective setting in the Adult Migrant Education Program.* Sydney, Australia: Adult Migrant Education Service.

Brindley, G. (1989). The role of needs analysis in adult ESL program design. In R. K. Johnson (Ed.), *The second language curriculum* (pp. 63–78). Cambridge: Cambridge University.

Brown, J. D. (1995). *The elements of language curriculum: A systematic approach to program development.* Boston, MA: Heinle & Heinle.

Byon, A. (2000). Teaching Korean honorifics. In S. Sohn (Ed.), *Korean language in America, 5* (pp. 275–289). Honolulu, HI: American Association of Teachers of Korean.

Cho, G., Cho, K.-S., & Tse, L. (1997). Why ethnic minorities want to develop their heritage language: The case of Korean-Americans. *Language, Culture and Curriculum, 10*, 106–112.

Choi, H., & Koh, S. (2001). Interactive online exercises: Retention of non-heritage learners in a mixed class. In J. Ree (Ed.), *Korean language in America, 6* (pp. 129–140). Honolulu: American Association of Teachers of Korean.

Gosalvez, I. (1999). Towards developing a curriculum for heritage students of Tagalog. *Language Teaching at Berekeley, 14*(2), 12.

Hope International University. (2001). Using HyperStudio for teaching Korean. In J. Ree (Ed.), *Korean language in America, 6* (pp. 141–149). Honolulu: American Association of Teachers of Korean.

Hua, V. (2005, August 28). In a lather over south Korean soap operas: Exported TV dramas captivating huge audience around Asia and beyond. *San Francisco Chronicle*, p. A1.

Hurh, W. (1993). The 1.5 generation: A cornerstone of the Korean-American ethnic community. In Ho. Kwon & S. Kim (Eds.), *The emerging generation of Korean-Americans* (pp. 47–79). Korea: Kyung Hee University.

Iwai, T. (1998, September). *Natural conversation as a model for language instruction.* Paper presented at the Second Language Research Forum; Honolulu, HI.

Iwai, T., Kondo, K., Lim, D., Ray, G., Shimizu, H., & Brown, J. D. (1999). *Japanese language needs analysis 1998–1999. NFLRC network #13.* Honolulu: Second Language Teaching & Curriculum Center, University of Hawai`i. Retrieved August 26, 2005, from http://nflrc.hawai`i.edu/Net Works/NW13/NW13.pdf

Jo, H.-Y. (2001). Heritage langue learning and ethnic identity: Korean Americans' struggle with language authorities. *Language, Culture, and Curriculum, 14,* 26–41.

Kagan, O., & Dillon K. (2001). A new perspective on teaching Russian: Focus on the heritage learner. *Slavic and East European Journal, 45,* 507–518.

Kim, H.-S. (2001). Issues of heritage learners in Korean language classes. In J. Ree (Ed.), *Korean language in America, 6* (pp. 257–273). Honolulu, HI: American Association of Teachers of Korean.

King, R. (1998). Korean as a heritage language (KHL) vs. Korean as a foreign language (KFL) in North America and the former USSR: Ambiguous priorities and insufficient resources. *ACTA Koreana, 1,* 27–40.

Kondo-Brown, K. (2003). Heritage language instruction for post-secondary students from immigrant backgrounds. *Heritage Language Journal, 1.* Retrieved December 1, 2003, from http://www.heritagelanguages.org/

Krashen, S. (1982). *Principles and practice in second language acquisition.* New York: Pergamon.

Lee, C.-B. (1999). Two-track curriculum system for university Korean language programs. In S. Kang (Ed.), *Korean language in America, 3* (pp. 3–11). Honolulu: American Association of Teachers of Korean.

Lee, D. (2001). The role heritage learners in recent trends in foreign language teaching in the U.S. In J. Ree (Ed.) *Korean language in America, 6* (pp. 202–211). Honolulu: American Association of Teachers of Korean.

Lee, J., Cho, S., Lee, M., Song, M., & O'Grady, W. (2000). *Studies on Korean in community schools.* Hawai`i: University of Hawai`i.

Lee, Y., & Kim, Y. (2000). Needs assessment, goals and objective setting, and materials development for the third and fourth-level Korean course at the University of Hawai`i at Mānoa: A systematic approach to program development. In S. Kang (Ed.), *Korean language in America, 4* (pp. 12–49). Honolulu, HI: American Association of Teachers of Korean.

Munby, J. (1978). *Communicative syllabus design.* Cambridge: Cambridge University.

National Standards in Foreign Language Education Project (NSFLEP). (1996). *Standards for foreign language learning: Preparing for the 21century.* Lawrence, KS: Allen Press.

Norris, J. M., Brown, J. D., Hudson, T., & Yoshikoa, J. (1998). *Designing second language performance assessments.* Honolulu: Second Language Teaching and Curriculum Center, University of Hawai`i.

Omaggio-Hadley, A. (2001). *Teaching language in context.* Boston, MA: Heinle & Heinle.

Ostler, S. (1980). A survey of academic needs for advanced ESL. *TESOL Quarterly, 14,* 489–502.

Park, S. (2001). Exploring the possibilities of WBLT for operational testing purposes: Web-based Korean as a foreign language test. In J. Ree (Ed.), *Korean language in America, 6* (pp. 101–110). Honolulu: American Association of Teachers of Korean.

Park-Cho, S., & Carey, S. (2001). Increasing Korean oral fluency using an electronic bulletin board and Wimba-based voiced chat. In J. Ree (Ed.), *Korean language in America, 6* (pp. 115–128). Honolulu: American Association of Teachers of Korean.

Park, Y. (1997). Teaching authentic conversation: How to incorporate discourse into teaching. In Y. H. Kim (Ed.), *Korean language in America, 2* (pp. 27–37). Honolulu: American Association of Teachers of Korean.

Reber, T., & Geeslin, K. (1998). An investigation of student opinions and educational experiences in Spanish for the heritage speakers at Arizona State University and the University of Arizona. *Texas Papers in Foreign Language Education, 3*(2), 33–50.

Ree, J. (1998). Korean as a second language: How should it be taught. *ACTA Koreana, 1*, 85–100.

Ryu-Yang, J. S. R. (2002, August). *Motivational and de-motivational factors of Korean language learners at an American university:* A case study. Paper presented at the Conference and Professional Development Workshop of the American Association of Teachers of Korean. Orlando, FL.

Ryu-Yang, J. S. R. (2003). Motivational orientations and selected learner variables of East Asian language learners in the United States. *Foreign Language Annals, 36*, 44–56.

Saito, Y. (1995). Assessing perceived needs for Japanese language training in U.S. business education: Perspective from students, business faculty, and business professionals. *Foreign Language Annals, 28*(1), 104–115.

Savignon, S. J. (1997). *Communicative competence theory and classroom practice: Texts and contexts in second language learning.* New York: McGraw-Hill.

Shin, S., & Kim, S. (2000). The introduction of context-based language teaching to college-level Korean program for heritage learners. In S. Sohn (Ed.), *Korean language in America, 5* (pp. 167–179). Honolulu: American Association of Teachers of Korean.

Sohn, H. (1995). Issues in KFL textbook development. In H. Sohn & D. J. Lee (Eds.), *A new frontier in Korean as a foreign language* (pp. 197–205). Honolulu: Korean Language Education and Research Center.

Sohn, H. (2000). Curricular goals and content standards for K–16 Korean language learning. In S. Sohn (Ed.), *Korean Language in America, 5* (pp. 3–16). Honolulu, HI: American Association of Teachers of Korean.

Sohn, S. (1995). The design of curriculum for teaching Korean as a heritage language. In H. Sohn (Ed.), *Korean Language in America, 1* (pp. 19–35). Honolulu: American Association of Teachers of Korean.

Sohn, S. (1997). Issues and concerns in teaching multi-level classes: Syllabus design for heritage and non-heritage learners. In Y. H. Kim (Ed.), *Korean Language in America, 2* (pp. 138–158). Honolulu: American Association of Teachers of Korean.

Stromberg, C. (1997). Breaking the mold: A non-heritage learner's experience in a multi-level Korean class. In Y. H. Kim (Ed.), *Korean Language in America, 2* (pp. 159–165). Honolulu: American Association of Teachers of Korean.

Stufflebeam, D., McCormick, C., Brinkerhoff, R., & Nelson, C. (1985). *Conducting educational needs assessments.* Boston: Kluwer-Nijhoff.

Swain, M., & Lapkin, S. (1995). Problems in output and the cognitive processes they generate: A step towards second language learning. *Applied Linguistics, 16*(3), 371–391.

Tarone, E., & Yule, G. (1989). *Focus on the language learner: Approaches to identifying and meeting the needs of second language learners.* Oxford: Oxford University.

Toth, C. (2005, October 28). *K-crazed.* Honolulu Advertiser, p. D1.

Van Deusen-Scholl, N. (1999). The Yale conference on heritage languages. *Language Teaching at Berkeley, 14*(2), 9–11.

Von der Handt, G. (1983). Needs identification and curricula with particular reference to German for migrant workers. In R. Richterich (Ed.), *Case studies in identifying language needs* (pp. 24–38). Oxford: Pergamon.

You, C. (2001). Heritage vs. non-heritage issues revisited. In J. Ree (Ed.), *Korean language in America, 6* (pp. 257–273). Honolulu: American Association of Teachers of Korean.

Chapter 9

The Affective Needs of Limited Proficiency Heritage Language Learners: Perspectives from a Chinese Foreign Language Classroom[*]

Heather Dawn Weger-Guntharp
Georgetown University

Marginalized in the discussion of heritage language (HL) learners is the category of learners who are in traditional foreign language classes and who identify the HL as key to their development of self-identity while having limited exposure to the heritage language in the home environment. Although their presence is acknowledged in the literature (e.g., Cho, Cho, & Tse, 1997; Kondo, 1997; Kondo-Brown, 2001), only recently has this category of

---

[*]This chapter is a substantially revised version of a paper titled "Voices from the margin: Developing a profile of Chinese Heritage language learners in the FL classroom," *Heritage Language Journal* (2006) and appears here with permission.

learners begun to gain interest in HL research that calls for a more flexible understanding of who the heritage learner is in recognition of the complexity of individual backgrounds that results in a variety of proficiencies in and exposure to the HL (Wu, 2002). This chapter argues for the need to develop pedagogical strategies that help instructors plan courses that are attended by both traditional foreign language (FL) students and HL students who have variegated HL competence (from those who claimed either Cantonese or Mandarin as their native language to those who reported minimal exposure to Chinese through such social interactions as extended family gatherings). In this chapter, I first briefly summarize two key motivation theories particularly relevant for the heterogeneous language classroom. Then I outline an HL learner profile by focusing on one group of Chinese language learners, which includes a subsection of eight HL learners of varying competencies and home language exposures; I also examine the HL learner profile from the perspective of the instructors. Finally, I present pedagogical strategies designed specifically for the context of heterogeneous language classrooms.

APPLICATIONS OF MOTIVATION
THEORIES TO THE HL CONTEXT

Motivation is one individual difference that researchers have turned to for explanations of variation in second language attainment (for a review, see Dörnyei, 2003); yet few studies outside of the Spanish language context have looked specifically at the intersection of motivational issues and HL learners in heterogeneous language classes (notable exceptions are Kondo, 1999; Kondo-Brown, 2001; and Wen, 1997). The present study extends earlier motivation research by applying two distinct motivation approaches to examining the complexity of what it means to be a learner of one's familial language and its impact on language classroom dynamics. These two contrasting approaches stem from Dörnyei (2000, 2002) and Norton Peirce (1995). Dörnyei's process-oriented model has three phases and distinguishes itself from earlier motivational theories by incorporating a temporal dimension that emphasizes the dynamic nature of motivation. Of particular relevance to classroom dynamics is the second phase of the model, the actional phase, which is concerned with sustaining motivation so that goals/tasks are carried out. Factors influencing the success or failure of this phase include the teacher–student relationship, student–student group dynamics, the classroom environment as cooperative or competitive, and self-regulation (Dörnyei, 2002, p. 141).

Similar to Dörnyei (2000, 2002), Norton Peirce (1995) seeks a means of conceptualizing motivation that challenges the static formulations that are commonly associated with earlier motivation models such as those discussed in Deci and Ryan (1985) and Gardner and Lambert (1959, 1972). Norton Peirce maintains that *investment* is a more useful term as it "conceives of the language learner as having a complex social identity and multiple desires" (1995, pp. 17–18) rather than being fixed and static. Additionally, she argues that investment is more appropriate for explaining patterns of target language (TL) use, as it better captures the relevance of economic metaphors, as learners of a second language "do so with the understanding that they will acquire a wider range of symbolic and material resources" (Norton Peirce, 1995, p. 17).

Both perspectives, though differing in their points of emphasis, recognize that learners' imagined future uses of the second language (L2) affect their choices of engagement in the SLA process. Dörnyei (2000, 2002) refers to *anticipated outcomes*, whereas Norton Peirce (1995) notes that "learners will expect or hope to have a good return on their investment—a return that will give them access to hitherto unattainable resources" (p. 17). Both theories also recognize that the relationship between the learner and other speakers plays a significant role in the language learning process. Norton Peirce (1995) develops this theme by exploring the inequity of power relations that may exist between the L2 learner and native speaker of the TL, which may result in the learner choosing to remain silent rather than speak. Dörnyei (2000, 2002) is concerned with developing this theme by examining how motivation is co-constructed among the members of a dyad or group in a classroom setting. It is, however, their differing foci, most likely attributable to the divergent language contexts in which the theories arose, that make them complementary in the context of HL learners. Basing her work in an immigrant second language context, Norton Peirce (1995) is concerned with the social context of learning and her findings emphasize the relationship between language learning and the learner's social identity, making her approach particularly relevant for understanding HL learners. In contrast, Dörnyei's (2000, 2002) model was developed in a largely FL context. Consequently, his model focuses on how motivational orientations play out in the classroom, an emphasis that can be usefully employed in the context of this study where traditional FL students and HL learners share the same classroom.

RESEARCH QUESTIONS

With the goal of gaining insight into the complexities of the language classroom shared by FL and HL learners, this study explores what it means to be a HL learner who is enrolled in a course predominately attended by FL students. The HL learners that participated in this study have variegated HL competence as well as a variety of types of exposure to the HL in their homes. The university program in which they study does have a separate course for HL learners, but these students either did not have sufficient skills to be placed in that course or did not enroll in the course for a variety of other reasons such as conflicting schedules. The focus of this study is on these students specifically because many have very limited exposure to Chinese and they are easily overlooked by administrators and researchers alike when issues of how best to serve the needs of all HL learners are raised. The central questions guiding this research project were the following: which aspects of identity are salient for HL learners who attend classes with traditional FL students, especially when a separate HL course exists? Whose perspectives do these HL learners perceive as impacting their classroom identity? What are their attitudes toward learning Chinese? And how do faculty teaching in an institution where HL learners are directed towards a separate track of classes perceive the HL students who land in the FL classroom?

METHOD

Setting

This study was conducted at a private U.S. university in a major east coast city. The Chinese Department from which the participants in the study were recruited has a two-tier system for first-year Chinese-language students: a predominately *heritage* track and a *regular* track. Proficiency placement exams are not mandatory in the program. That is, anyone can enroll in the regular track beginner's course (including self-selected HL learners). In contrast, for those who wish to enroll in the accelerated heritage track course, the instructor of the course conducts an obligatory, informal, one-on-one interview. Based on the oral interview and questions about the students' previous training in Chinese characters, the instructor decides who may enroll in the heritage track course. Because this study was designed to investigate differences between HL learners and non-HL learners within a single classroom setting, the participants were drawn from across the four classes of the regular track, which has both traditional FL learners and also Chinese heritage language learners (CHLLs). All classes met 4 days a week and were accompanied by a drill session. In total, there were 6 to 7 hours of class time per week (variation depended on the length of the drill session, which was determined by the professor).

Instruments and Procedures

Data from students for this study were collected in Fall, 2003 using a variety of instruments, including: a biographical data questionnaire; a short answer survey (see Appendix A); and informal, open-ended interviews, which were taped and transcribed (see Appendix B). Faculty members were interviewed after the course had ended.

Analytic induction was used to analyze the transcripts of the student interviews, the biographical data, and short-answer survey responses. Common themes regarding learners' perceptions of themselves in the classroom and their attitudes toward learning Chinese were extracted from across the interviews and grouped together to allow for synthesized analysis. Similarly, common themes from the faculty interviews were also grouped together to allow for cross-group comparisons.

In the discussion that follows, all quotations from students are identified by participant number. Quotations from the biographical data are identified as "BD"; quotations from the short-answer survey are identified as "SA" and include the date; quotations from the interviews are identified as "I" and include their session number (I#) (see Appendix B).

Participants

Twenty-five unpaid volunteers participated in the study. Of these, eight students were identified as CHLLs, which for the purposes of this study are defined as individuals who have one or more parents who speak Chinese as their first language and who self-identified themselves as taking Chinese classes in part because of their ethnic heritage. The study included both male and female participants with ages ranging from 18–22. All students were undergraduates. However, their academic fields varied greatly, including students who were undeclared in their major, Chinese majors, School of Foreign Service majors, biology majors, and one exchange student from Japan (Participant 15). Moreover, although the majority had an L1 of English, a variety of other L1s were represented. Detailed demographic data for the 25 participants is provided in Appendix C.

Four faculty members also participated in semi-structured interviews to offer their perspectives on teaching heritage students. Three of the faculty members taught the regular courses, designed for traditional FL learners; one faculty member taught the heritage course, which was predominately attended by heritage students. These interviews were held in the faculty members' offices and lasted approximately 30 minutes during which time detailed notes on their responses to guided questions were made.

HL Learners' Background Profiles

As is evident in Table 9.1, the students' backgrounds are diverse and their contact with Chinese varies greatly. Six of the eight CHLL students claim English as their first language, and three note that only one parent was

TABLE 9.1
Language Background Profiles and Reported Use of Chinese

Participant ID number	Reported First Language	Country of Birth	Reported Language Background of Parents	Exposure to Chinese Outside of Home Prior to College	Reported Use of Chinese at Home[a]
5	English	U.S.	Father speaks Cantonese. He grew up in Canton and Hong Kong. Mother speaks a little Mandarin.	None	Low exposure
6	English	Taiwan (moved to U.S. at age 3)	Mother speaks Mandarin. She is from Taiwan. Father speaks no Chinese.	One month Chinese course in the summer before starting college.	Low exposure
28	English	U.S.	Parents speak both Cantonese and Mandarin. They grew up in a Chinese community in Indonesia where Cantonese was spoken at home and Mandarin was spoken in school. They also speak a dialect of Indonesian.	Chinese church between the ages of 10–15. English translations of sermons were distributed.	Low exposure
18	English	U.S.	Father speaks Cantonese. He is from Hong Kong. Mother speaks a little of the dialect of ZhongShan.	Chinese school during first and second grade. Lived in Hong Kong and Sinapore during childhood but limited interaction in Chinese.[b]	Mid exposure
24	English	U.S.	Parents speak Mandarin. They are from Singapore.	Chinese school from ages 5–9.	Mid exposure
27	English	U.S.	Parents speak Mandarin. They are from Taiwan.	Chinese school from ages 12–15.	Mid exposure

(Continued)

TABLE 9.1 (*Continued*)

Participant ID number	Reported First Language	Country of Birth	Reported Language Background of Parents	Exposure to Chinese Outside of Home Prior to College	Reported Use of Chinese at Home[a]
11	Mandarin	Saudi Arabia (moved to Canada at age 2 and the U.S. at age 6)	Parents speak Mandarin. They are from Taiwan.	Chinese school from ages 4–5.	High exposure
26	Cantonese	U.S. (began speaking English in U.S. public school system at age 5)	Parents speak Cantonese. They are from Guang Dong, China.	Chinese school from ages 3–13.	High exposure

[a]Key to Responses: Low exposure=Mostly hear Chinese at large family gatherings; do not speak Chinese at home; Mid exposure=Sometimes hear Chinese at home; sometimes speak Chinese at home; High exposure=Hear Chinese at home; speak Chinese or "Chinglish" at home.
[b]Due to her father's employment, this student spent 12 years in a combination of Hong Kong and Singapore, but she reported that they lived in English speaking communities and that she had only limited exposure to Chinese—primarily through service encounters like eating out and using public transportation. School was conducted in English and English was the primarily language spoken at home.

fluent in any variety of Chinese. Half have exposure to Cantonese, which is not the focus of the language classes in the language program where they are studying. For three of the students (5, 6, and 28), interaction in Chinese was reported as non-existent or, at best, extremely limited. Students 18, 24, and 27 reported slightly higher instances of Chinese exposure (in the home or via other means). Only two of the students reported confident use of Chinese, both asserting that they were bilinguals during the course of the study.

The students also varied in their reported self-confidence in using Chinese. Table 9.2 summarizes their opinions on their speaking and reading skills, although the reported confidence does not necessarily align with their exposure to the language. For example, one of the low-exposure students reports high confidence in reading and another reports high confidence for speaking during class. Lastly, Table 9.3 reflects the CHLLs' responses to the statement "Learning Chinese is important to me in order to be able to get to know the life of Chinese speaking people

TABLE 9.2

CHLLs' Reported Confidence Levels in Various Skills by Their Reported
Use of the Target Language at Home

	High Exposure		Mid Exposure			Low Exposure		
Participant Number	11	26	18	24	27	5	6	28
Confidence speaking during class	High	High	Mid	Low	Mid	Low	Low	High
Confidence speaking Chinese in general	High	High	Mid	Low	High	Mid	Low	Mid
Confidence reading Chinese	High	Mid	Low	High	Mid	Mid	High	Mid

[a]Exposure Group Defined: Low exposure = Mostly hear Chinese at large family gatherings; do not speak Chinese at home; Mid exposure = Sometimes hear Chinese at home; sometimes speak Chinese at home; High exposure = Hear Chinese at home; speak Chinese or "Chinglish" at home.

TABLE 9.3

Chinese Heritage Language Learners' Responses to the Prompt,
"Learning Chinese Is Important to Me in Order to Be Able to Get to Know
the Life of Chinese Speaking People Better" by Exposure Group ($N=8$)

	High Exposure		Mid Exposure			Low Exposure		
Participant Number	11	26	18	24	27	5	6	28
Strongly Disagree								
Disagree	X							
Somewhat Disagree				X				
Somewhat Agree		X	X		X			
Agree								
Strongly Agree						X	X	X

[a]Exposure group defined: Low exposure=Mostly hear Chinese at large family gatherings; do not speak Chinese at home; Mid exposure=Sometimes hear Chinese at home; sometimes speak Chinese at home; High exposure = Hear Chinese at home; speak Chinese or "Chinglish" at home.

better." Interestingly, it is the lowest exposure group that consistently reported strong agreement with the statement, which reinforces the contention that HL learners, even those with low proficiencies, have a high sense of motivation, a high level of investment, in pursuing Chinese language learning as a means of connecting with a part of their ethnic identity. This orientation towards the language class is one distinction that sets these students apart from the traditional FL students with whom they share a class.

RESULTS AND DISCUSSION

Profile of the Learner from the Learner's Perspective

Analysis of the interview data, short-answer survey, and biographical data suggests that the heritage status of the learner plays a key role in the construction of their classroom identity. The following discussion explores the classroom profile of CHLLs, which consists of three main aspects that repeatedly surfaced in the data: perception of self, perception of peers, and perception of teachers.

Perception of Self. Exploring one's heritage status was a major reason cited by all of the CHLLs to study Chinese. For example:

> I was born in Taiwan and lived there until I was about three. I could speak Chinese, but when I came to the US, I forgot all of it. When I went back to Taiwan many years later, it was upsetting not being able to communicate with my family over there. I wanted to learn Chinese as a reassertion of my cultural identity and so I can communicate with my Mom's side of the family in the future. (#6, BD)

> I want to be able to speak Chinese fluently as part of my heritage. (#18, BD)

> Because I am Chinese, I think it is only right for me to be able to not only speak [Chinese], but to be able to read and write [in Chinese] as well. I do want to go back to my family in Taiwan one day and communicate with them. (#11, BD)

This orientation is consistent with the preactional phase of Dörnyei's (2000, 2002) process-oriented motivation model, which identifies learner attitudes towards the TL and its speakers as a primary component of the learner's initial decision process. Moreover, these learners parallel the sentiment of other heritage learner groups who actively pursue their HL as a means of connecting with their social identity. For example, in studying the language behaviors of the Saraguros, a minority community in Ecuador, King (2000) found that HL learning provided for many community members "an emotional link to the past" (p. 172). Although the two learner groups differ in that the Saraguros speak a language indigenous to their country, whereas the HL learners of this study are learning what is a foreign language in the United States, it is telling that both identify their ethnic language as a link to their cultural identity. Such an identification was also found in Feuerverger (1991), a study of HL learners from a variety of language backgrounds and their perceptions of their HL and their ethnic identity.

In addition, all eight CHLLs also perceived their heritage as a resource to be tapped for economic and/or academic reasons.

[I am taking Chinese] to complete the language requirement. I am also Chinese and would like to learn a Chinese language. (#5, BD)

[My] motivations include Chinese heritage, existing foundation for Chinese, and anticipation in working abroad (possible international business double major). (#26, BD)

Aside from the obvious motivation to learn for personal reasons, I'd like to be proficient in 3 languages by the time I graduate. Chinese, Arabic, and/or undecided third. This way I can apply for a job in federal law enforcement, and hopefully proficiency in languages such as Chinese and Arabic will help. (#27, BD)

I've been meaning to learn Chinese for a long time in order to understand my family background. ... I really wanted to learn a language anyways, especially since I'll be working soon and could use another [language] on my resume. So I decided it was now time to learn Chinese. (#28, BD)

For these learners, enhancing their Chinese proficiency is seen as a key to future business success, and/or Chinese classes are seen by those who possess some working proficiency in Chinese as an expedient way of fulfilling university language requirements or are seen by those lacking proficiency as a way to begin exploring one's ethnic language heritage while simultaneously meeting university requirements. These goals not only relate to Dörnyei's (2000, 2002) preactional phase, but also support Norton Peirce's (1995) contention that learners engage in language learning as a means of acquiring greater access to symbolic or material resources.

In having economic and academic goals for language learning, the profiles of the CHLLs and the non-CHLLs are the same, but in their choice of which language will help in meeting these goals, the learners' profiles differ. The CHLLs draw on their backgrounds in Chinese language use, their symbolic familial support system, or their desires of regaining a neglected piece of their identity. In contrast, non-CHLLs often allude to the novelty of learning Chinese in comparison to other languages they have learned (or could be learning), "I think it's more fun to be able to say, 'I can speak Chinese,' than, 'I can speak Spanish,' because it's so different" (#21, I1).

Another component of Norton Peirce's (1995) theory relevant to this context is that a learner's social identity is "diverse, contradictory, and dynamic; multiple rather than unitary, decentered rather than centered" (p. 15). In Interview Session 3, three HL learners with high use of Chinese in their immediate families discussed why they had taken the regular track of Chinese, the class intended for students with no Chinese background, rather than the heritage Chinese class, the more advanced course targeted primarily towards HL learners.

#27: [I knew the regular Chinese course] would be a lot easier, 'cause like a lot of this stuff, I don't want to say like I just kind of like slack off, but it's just like, more manageable than just jumping into the more advanced. ... I think I might be able to survive in the other class,

#26: //yeah//

#27: //but this// one, it's like coming in, like this is college blah, blah. You want to do well, and so you might as well help yourself out.

#26: Yeah, same thing. I didn't want to overload myself the first time I got to college and the thing was, I really didn't want to [unintelligible]. I think ... if I'd gone straight to like [the heritage track course] I'd be dead.

#24: First of all [the heritage track course] didn't really fit into my schedule and I didn't know about it. But had I had the choice I probably would have taken this course anyway. It's definitely, like you start off in the very, very beginning and get the base, and that's what I need. That's what it's good for.

#27: It's good for us.

HWG: So you get a good base, and that's important to you?

#27: That, and like the placement tests were at like eight in the morning. (I3)

Although all had echoed the sentiments of Participant 26 (BD), who noted that motivations for studying Chinese included understanding his Chinese heritage, their classroom choices also reflected a desire to balance their HL goals with their larger educational identity as university students of multiple classroom communities. In fact, seven of the eight CHLL students were happy with this level of Chinese; only Participant 11 (I7) wished at times that she had taken the more advanced heritage course because it offered more conversational practice. This profile is similar to that found by Potowski (2002), in which the cited reasons for not taking the available language class for HL learners included scheduling conflicts and the students' belief that it would be easier to earn a better grade in the FL class.

Perception of Peers. Once the decision to enroll in a class has been made, the multiplicity of the learner's classroom identity develops as the perception of self interacts with the perception of those sharing the class-room social space—namely, peers and teachers. During the interview sessions, students were asked about their opinion on doing pair-work or group work. Most students, whether HL or FL, said they liked to work with other students, primarily because it afforded them a greater chance to practice speaking, even though reported instances of group work in their actual Chinese classes were almost non-existent. On the other hand, several non-CHLL students (Participants 13 and 21 in I1; Participant 8 in I5; Participants 9 and 20 in I6) noted that the greatest advantage to minimizing group work was to allow for more interactions with a native speaker teacher who could correct pronunciation and tone.

This theme also was evident in the analysis of the short answer surveys. When asked if the student had a preference of partners to work with during pair or group work, the CHLLs were identified by many non-CHLLs as being desirable partners:

> I also like practicing with one kid who knew Chinese from speaking it with his parents, because he knows a lot of times when things are wrong because of the way they sound, and not because of some grammar rule we memorized. I know I'm reinforcing things the right way when I practice with him. (#13, SA, 10/27/03)

On the other hand, some non-CHLL students noted their discomfort at having partners with mismatched levels of competency, and in some cases, this was directed specifically at CHLLs:

> I don't mind when I have to work with students at my level, but working with students who are Chinese or who have taken Chinese before can be frustrating. (#20, SA, 10/27/03)

In that such a perception would likely affect learner motivation for activities involving group or pair interaction, it is relevant to Dörnyei's (2000, 2002) emphasis on the co-constructed nature of classroom activities (see also Ehrman & Dörnyei, 1998).

Additionally, such an attitude of unease on the part of the non-CHLL might be explained by Norton Peirce's (1995) assertion that the willingness of learners to speak in the TL is in relation to the distribution of power between the learner and the native speaker. Thus those with Chinese HL backgrounds may be viewed as having an advantage over the traditional FL student, regardless of the actual language skills of the CHLL.

Perception of Teachers.   Three themes emerged from the data regarding the CHLLs' perceptions of how their teachers interact with them. They felt that instructors tended to restrict their use of their full language knowledge in the classroom, that instructors often held different expectations towards the CHLLs during class, and/or that their status as a CHLL created opportunities for them to interact informally with teachers outside of class. For example, CHLL Participant 11 (I7) said she limits her use of outside vocabulary because of teacher disapproval[1]: "I definitely do [limit the vocabulary I use during class]. ... My professor actually gets really mad when we use vocab that's not in the lesson" (#11, I7). And when talking about trying to answer test questions using language skills not covered in class lessons, two CHLLs commented as follows:

#26:   [The teacher] probably wouldn't accept it anyway, because he wants what he wants.

#27:   Yeah, it's like, that's how you're always thinking, like in terms about what you are learning right now in class.

(I3)

Perhaps some instructors feel it inappropriate to sanction the use of the CHLLs' knowledge in a class where traditional FL learners and HL learners are mixed. This may be one of the reasons why researchers such as Draper and Hicks (2000) and Gutiérrez (1997) encourage the separation of HL learners from traditional FL students. This standard, however, is problematic in a context where the HL learners themselves have varying levels of knowledge of the TL or in environments where separate classes cannot be sustained due to limited resources.

Another way in which CHLLs' abilities are restricted is in the tension between home and classroom privileged dialect. Mandarin is the valued mode of oral communication in the classrooms in this study. However, for half of the CHLLs of this study, Cantonese is the language of at least one of their parents and is the source of their background knowledge in Chinese. Participant 26 identified Cantonese as his native language; and during the interview session, he mentioned his years spent studying at Cantonese school, "So I didn't learn anything there, just like Cantonese, which is not useful here" (I3). Participant 18 said of her unwillingness to use vocabulary, "I don't want to say [a word] and it's wrong, and then plus

---

[1]Not all participants discussed limiting their vocabulary use because they felt the professor would disapprove. For example, Participant 24 (I3) said she limits her vocabulary use out of a sense of fairness to her fellow classmates: "I think [I limit my vocabulary in class] partly because of, you know, the other people. Especially in my class, there are a lot of people who haven't been exposed to Chinese. And it'd be nice if they understood what was going on." (#24, I3)

it's in Cantonese, so then everyone's like 'What?'" (I5). And Participant 5 commented, "My parents wanted me to take Chinese, because I am Chinese, except almost no one speaks Mandarin in my family, so it's pretty pointless [to take classes here]" (I9). Similarly, for at least one participant, there is a classroom conflict in the writing systems taught. With family ties to mainland China and aspirations to be a published writer in both English and Chinese, Participant 11 complained, "In China it's all simplified characters now. My professor solely teaches us traditional characters, so I won't really be able to read anything [there]" (I7).

The second salient theme on teachers' perspectives is their differential expectations of the CHLLs. While talking about her weekly drill practice, Participant 11 (I7) commented, "I think [my recitation teacher] expects a lot from me. ... When I get a test back and she's like, ... 'You could do better than that,' while, you know, I'm still doing better than the rest of the class. Yeah, you know, that's kind of expected." And a third distinguishing feature of the CHLLs with regards to their teachers is their opportunity for additional interaction with the teacher outside of class: "If I'm walking after class, [my professor] is always asking me these questions. I know what he's saying and I can answer them, but I know he wouldn't be asking anybody else" (#27, I3). Thus, from the student's perspective, on one hand teachers may try to limit the input by CHLLs in the classroom while simultaneously raising their performance expectations.

Given that instructors hold a position of power in relation to their students, especially via the traditional vehicle of grades, how they are perceived by their students is an important consideration for the enactment of one's classroom identity, especially when the learners view language classes as an opportunity for connecting with a heretofore underdeveloped aspect of their ethnic identity. Again, Norton Peirce's (1995) paradigm of investment and its corresponding insights into power relations and language behavior are useful. When applied to this instance of HL learner and native speaking instructor, the classroom behaviors sanctioned and rejected by the teacher, whether "real" or "imagined," impact the choices the HL learner makes in the classroom. Thus the instructor is perceived as a resource or an inhibitor in the development and expression of the HL learners' ethnic identities. Similarly, this speaks to Dörnyei's (2000, 2002) model and its concern for the co-constructed nature of motivation. Although perceptions of peers were just discussed, the instructors also interacted with the individual HL learners; thus they impacted the behaviors that were displayed in the language classroom. In the section that follows, the perspectives of faculty who work with HL learners will be explored in relation to the themes raised in this chapter.

Profile of the Learner from the Teachers' Perspective

As just discussed, both Dörnyei's (2000, 2002) model and Norton Peirce's (1995) theory foreground the significance of the role of "other" in the enactment of language behavior. For Dörnyei, this is reflected in the concept of motivation as co-constructed; for Norton Peirce, it is evident in the themes of investment and power relations. Thus it is beneficial to examine the views held by educators towards their HL students. In this section, themes that emerged during interviews with faculty who work with heritage students either in heritage track or regular track (and primarily FL) courses are discussed and compared with the comments just mentioned.

One theme that emerged from the interviews concerned the presence of HL learners in the regular track beginner's course. When asked about the experience of teaching HL learners in such classes, two of the regular track course instructors initially asserted that HL students had their own course. This attitude may be explained as faculty assuming that those students whose proficiencies are insufficient for entry into the heritage track should not (or can not) be treated any differently than traditional FL students. It could also be that when two-tier systems are in place, even in institutions that do not require a mandatory placement exam, HL students in the traditional FL class are perceived as the odd exception and thus are not foregrounded in the faculty's awareness. In either instance, the result is a lack of understanding that low proficiency HL students bring any special needs or abilities to the classroom.

On the other hand, two instructors were quick to point out that students of mixed proficiency levels do land in the beginning classes of the regular track, with the most notable differences being the use of tones and pronunciation. One professor attributed this variation in abilities to general background experience with Chinese or other Asian languages, and one also specifically noted the presence of HL learners in the FL classroom. (In the course of the interviews, all professors did acknowledge that occasionally HL learners took the regular track beginner's class.)

Two instructors explicitly noted vocabulary disparities, in addition to tone and pronunciation differences, among their non-CHLLs and their CHLLs. For example, one instructor noted that in comparison to CHLLs, traditional FL students were more likely to directly translate inappropriately an idiomatic English expression into Chinese—such as using *hot* to describe an attractive female classmate, a meaning that does not directly map onto any of the terms in Chinese that are commonly glossed in English as meaning *hot*. Also related to vocabulary use was a conflict between students' reports and those of many of the instructors concerning restriction on vocabulary use. As just discussed, half of the CHLL participants noted that they generally felt limited in their freedom to use vocabulary not explicitly presented in the textbook; in contrast, three instructors commented that they encouraged the use of new or relevant vocabulary, especially during student presentations. This difference of opinion might be the result of a simple lack of communication between teacher and student with regards to welcomed classroom practices, or it might be that the explicitly stated practices and the implicitly understood atmosphere of the classroom clash.

Two other salient themes emerged from the interviews with the instructors. First, although instructors in this program did not notice differences in student preferences for partners during pair work (either because pair work occurred infrequently or because students' partners were rotated), two instructors from the regular track courses noted that having CHLLs in the class was beneficial for their peers because of the instructor's perception that the CHLL could sometimes explain a grammatical concept or cultural reference more clearly to his traditional FL counterparts than the instructor herself could. Finally, a common concern of these faculty was the balancing act of challenging the more experienced learners while simultaneously meeting the needs of the true beginner—a concern that most instructors face regardless of the course content, but one that takes on added complexity in the context of learners' family heritage and the presence of multiple dialects (see Kondo-Brown, this volume).

The actional phase of Dörnyei's (2000, 2002) process oriented model highlights the impact that instructors can have on students' motivation for carrying out language tasks. Thus an understanding of faculty perspectives is important for understanding the environment of the heterogenous FL classroom. And, in this section, just such an analysis has allowed us to see that one unique circumstance that some HL students, especially those with limited proficiency, may encounter is their relative invisibility in the FL classroom context. Additionally, their language abilities and affective needs may not be fully apparent to their instructors and/or there may be a mismatch in what each individual expects from the other in terms of performance and knowledge. As just argued, instructors are in obvious positions of power relative to their students. Consequently, the environments they promote in their classrooms will have an impact on the path that HL learners take as they explore connections to their ethnic identity.

PEDAGOGICAL IMPLICATIONS

This study has described the social identity brought by a diverse group of CHLLs to the language classroom setting by contrasting comments of CHLLs and non-CHLLs and by examining the reflections of classroom instructors. The study has also investigated how these contrasting identities affect motivation for language learning and classroom orientations. One notable pedagogical implication concerns the dynamics of pair and group work, an important topic due to pair/group work's increased presence in language classrooms in the United States (Brown, 2001). As seen in the perceptions of students in this study, peer interactions among non-CHLLs and CHLLs are not always welcomed. For experienced teachers, negotiating among students' preferences and personalities is not novel, nor confined to an HL/non-HL dichotomy. However, awareness of the variance in perceptions is important for keeping in check the assumptions that might be made about students and what roles they are comfortable with during classes.

More notable is that the CHLL participants in this study reflect a remarkable degree of divergence in the amount and quality of contact they have had with Chinese prior to starting the beginner's class, yet they all self-identified as learners of Chinese for ethnic identity reasons. Awareness among faculty that even classrooms dominated by traditional FL students have such CHLL students with varying degrees of ability is an important step for pedagogical planning. Although sensitivity towards the language skills of HL learners and the need to develop HL specific materials has been the focus of many researchers (for example, Kagan & Dillon, 2001, 2004; Roca & Colombi, 2003; Valdés, 1995, 2000, 2001), the pedagogical suggestions are generally targeted toward helping HL learners reach advanced levels of proficiencies in the TL (Kagan & Dillon, 2004; Valdés & Geoffrion-Vinci, 1998; see also Roca, 1992 for general teaching strategies for many levels). The needs of low-proficiency HL learners who often find themselves in a class with true beginning FLLs should also be addressed.

One means of learning about the diversity of one's class is to employ diagnostic testing at the beginning of a course. Similar to the recommendation of using placement testing as a means of meeting the needs of HL learners (Draper & Hicks, 2000; Kagan & Dillon, 2004) at the program design level, at the micro-level of classroom instruction, a diagnostic test elicits information on the breadth of the students' linguistic abilities, especially if it includes open-ended questions aimed at identifying HL learners by asking about the learners' language exposure, dialect knowledge, and motivations for taking the course. This is a concrete strategy useful in both beginning and higher level courses that allows instructors to raise their metaknowledge of the particular dynamics of that classroom. It is all too easy for classroom teachers to ignore the background knowledge of HL learners and others with prior knowledge of Chinese if all classroom learners are not tested diagnostically in the beginning to reveal the extent of their knowledge, and many teachers may find themselves in the trap of believing that HL learners do not exist in the classroom if, in theory, there is a heritage track in which supposedly all HL learners are enrolled.

For students similar to those in this study, that is, students in heterogeneous classes at the beginning level for whom the FL class is perceived as an opportunity for reconnecting with their heritage, one instructional goal outlined by Valdés (2000) that is useful in planning classroom instruction is "language maintenance."[2] Valdés notes that the less frequently used pedagogies for obtaining this goal include "consciousness-raising around issues of identity and language" and "reading of texts focusing on issues of race, class, gender and other socio-political topics" (p. 390). Even textbooks that present stereotypical caricatures of life in China can be made into critical reflection pieces, for both the CHLL and the non-CHLL, by a dedicated instructor. Additionally, the selection of supplemental classroom materials should be sensitive to the need to encourage HL learners in their development of (or rediscovery of) their identity. This might also extend to encouraging students in their selections of particular topics for class presentations or writing assignments.

It is also important for instructors to create avenues through which students can display their HL knowledge. Such outlets are means of validating and embracing learners' abilities and incorporating them into the classroom environment rather than ignoring them or dismissing them as inappropriate. This may aid in student retention in that a more welcoming environment may be projected. At the most basic level of instruction, students could be encouraged to use the vocabulary that they do have, even if it is not the explicit focus of a textbook lesson. In the case of regional dialect differences, this might also involve the mapping of known lexical terms to the lexical items taught from the textbook and would require the instructor to be explicit about the notion of register. (For more information on register see Kondo-Brown, 2003, and Valdés, 2000.)

Individual journaling and dialogue journaling are two other means by which students can express their knowledge. Though not new suggestions (see Roca, 1992, which suggests these methods for the teaching of Spanish to HL learners), these two strategies offer the following advantages: An individual journal can provide the student with a means of personal reflection on daily activities, whereas the dialogue journal offers a means of communication with the instructor. When used at the basic levels, before writing skills (especially complicated by the different orthographic systems

---

[2]In this context where the language itself is not endangered in the global sense, but rather is lost at the familiar or individual level, the term *language reclamation* (as used by Dorian, 1999, p. 39) or *language (re)discovery* might be a more appropriate nomenclature.

for American learners of Chinese) have developed sufficiently, code-switching among English, Chinese characters, and Pinyin could be employed. Another possibility is to use oral journaling through cassette tapes, phone messaging, or digital media that can be emailed or uploaded to a shared teacher/learner Web site or virtual classroom management center, for example, to Blackboard (http://www.blackboard.com/) or WebCT (http://www.webct.com/). For learners caught in the cracks (that is, those not linguistically advanced enough to go into a course specifically for HL learners, but more advanced than others in their FL course), technology based systems, such as one hosted by LangNet, can be useful in providing extra, individualized lessons. Recommended by both McGinnis (2001) and Schwartz (2001), LangNet provides online resources to self-directed learners and language instructors at academic institutions who subscribe to the system (http://www.langnet.org/index.php). LangNet includes a searchable collection of Chinese language materials (traditional and simplified) that could be used to supplement instruction for HL learners.

CONCLUSION

As Valdés (2001) notes, "Most teachers have not been trained to work with students who already speak or understand the target language or who have a strong connection with it" (pp. 66–67). This could be equally true of institutions that can only support a single-tier system as well as those with two-tier systems. The pedagogical suggestions just outlined provide a starting point as they are practical measures that can be used in the day-to-day operations of heterogeneous language classes. They are based on the assumptions that (a) knowing the abilities and goals of the students helps instructors to plan effective lessons, establish the realities of the classroom environment, and be aware of the classroom atmosphere in terms of student preferences; (b) it is a responsibility of the instructor to find avenues that allow students to use their existing language knowledge and link that current knowledge to new forms of meaning; and (c) all students should be challenged to stretch their language abilities.

   Although linguistic needs are of obvious significance for language classrooms, the affective needs of learners with ethnic connections to the language should also be addressed. As this study has shown, limited (or "no") proficiency heritage students are in the language classrooms and do approach the learning experience with different needs and expectations than HL learners with high proficiency. As educators, our goals should include efforts to create an atmosphere where all heritage students can foster a sense of investment in the language learning experience and should include measures to validate all HL learners' efforts to reconnect with their ethnic background through language.

ACKNOWLEDGMENTS

I would like to thank Professor Kendall King for her guidance and patience during the writing of this chapter. I would also like to thank Professors Heidi Byrnes and Paula Winke for their feedback and encouragement. All errors that remain are my own.

APPENDIX A
On-line Short-Answer Survey

1. What types of classroom activities do you like doing the most? (& Why?)

2. What types of classroom activities do you like doing the least? (& Why?)

3. What types of homework do you like doing the most? (& Why?)

4. What types of homework do you like doing the least? (& Why?)

5. Do you ever work in pairs or groups with other students during class?

6. Do you like to work with other students during class? Why or why not?

7. If you do not work in pairs or groups during class, would you like to do this? Why?

8. Are there certain students you prefer to work with? If yes, what characteristics do those students have?

APPENDIX B
Student Interview Session Demographics

Session Number	Date	Participant Number	CHLL or Non-CHLL	Video-taped or Audio-taped	Length	Interviewer
I1	8 Nov. 03	13	Non-CHLL	Video-taped	19 min.	HWG[a]
		15	Non-CHLL			
		21	Non-CHLL			
I2	9 Nov. 03	16	Non-CHLL	Video-taped	18 min.	HWG
I3	10 Nov. 03	7	Non-CHLL	Video-taped	21 min.	HWG
		10				
		23	Non-CHLL			
		24	Non-CHLL			
		26	CHLL			
		27	CHLL			
			CHLL			
I4	11 Nov. 03	6	CHLL	Video-taped	16 min.	HWG
I5	12 Nov. 03	8	Non-CHLL	Video-taped	24 min.	HWG
		18				
		19	CHLL			
		28	Non-CHLL			
			CHLL			
I6	12 Nov. 03	2	Non-CHLL	Video-taped	15 min.	PW[b]
		9	Non-CHLL			
		12	Non-CHLL			
		20	Non-CHLL			
I7	16 Nov. 03	1	Non-CHLL	Video-taped	23 min.	HWG
		11				
		17	CHLL			
			Non-CHLL			
I8	17 Nov. 03	4	Non-CHLL	Audio-taped	9 min.	PW
		25				
			Non-CHLL			
I9	19 Nov. 03	05	CHLL	Audio-taped	13 min.	PW

[a]The author.
[b]Secondary researcher.

APPENDIX C
Participant Demographics

Participant Number	Heritage Learner	Sex	Age	Academic Concentration	Native Language
1	No	Female	19	International Affairs	Korean
2	No	Male	18	School of Foreign Service	Russian
4	No	Male	19	School of Foreign Service	English
5	Yes	Female	20	Biology	English
6	Yes	Female	18	Undeclared	English
7	No	Female	18	School of Business	English
8	No	Male	19	Undeclared	English
9	No	Male	18	School of Foreign Service / International Affairs	English
10	No	Female	19	School of Foreign Service	Japanese
11	Yes	Female	18	School of Foreign Service	Chinese
12	No	Male	19	School of Foreign Service	English
13	No	Female	18	School of Foreign Service International Political Economy	English
15	No	Female	20	Exchange Student	Japanese
16	No	Male	18	Chinese	English
17	No	Female	19	School of Business	Korean
18	Yes	Female	18	School of Foreign Service	English
19	No	Female	18	Chinese	Finnish
20	No	Female	18	School of Foreign Service	English
21	No	Female	18	School of Foreign Service	English
23	No	Male	19	School of Foreign Service	English
24	Yes	Female	18	School of Foreign Service	English
25	No	Female	18	School of Foreign Service	English
26	Yes	Male	18	School of Business / Undeclared	Cantonese
27	Yes	Male	18	Undeclared	English
28	Yes	Female	22	School of Foreign Service	English

REFERENCES

Brown, H. D. (2001). *Teaching by principles: An interactive approach to language pedagogy* (2nd ed.). White Plains, NY: Addison Wesley Longman.

Cho, G., Cho, K.-S., & Tse, L. (1997). Why ethnic minorities want to develop their heritage language: The case of Korean-Americans. *Language, Culture and Curriculum, 10,* 106–112.

Deci, L., & Ryan, M. (1985). *Intrinsic motivation and self-determination in human behavior.* New York: Plenum.

Dorian, N. C. (1999). Linguistic and ethnographic fieldwork. In J. A. Fishman (Ed.), *Handbook of language and ethnic identity* (pp. 254–25–41). Oxford: Oxford University.

Dörnyei, Z. (2000). Motivation in action: Towards a process-oriented conceptualisation of student motivation. *British Journal of Educational Psychology, 70,* 519–538.

Dörnyei, Z. (2002). The motivational basis of language learning tasks. In P. Robinson (Ed.), *Individual differences and instructed language learning* (pp. 137–158). Amsterdam/Philadelphia: John Benjamins.

Dörnyei, Z. (2003). Attitudes, orientations, and motivations in language learning: Advances in theory, research, and applications. In Z. Dörnyei (Ed.), *Attitudes, orientations, and motivations in language learning* (pp. 3–32). Malden, MA: Blackwell.

Draper, J. B., & Hicks, J. H. (2000). Where we've been; What we've learned. In J. B. Webb & B. L. Miller (Eds.), *Teaching heritage language learners: Voices from the classroom* (pp. 15–35). Yonkers, NY: ACTFL.

Ehrman, M. E., & Dörnyei, Z. (1998). *Interpersonal dynamics in second language education.* London: Sage.

Feuerverger, G. (1991). University students' perceptions of heritage language learning and ethnic identity maintenance. *Canadian Modern Language Review, 47*(4), 660–677.

Gardner, R. C., & Lambert, W. E. (1959). Motivational variables in second language acquisition. *Canadian Journal of Psychology, 13,* 266–272.

Gardner, R. C., & Lambert, W. E. (1972). *Attitudes and motivation in second-language learning.* Rowley, MA: Newbury House.

Gutiérrez, J. R. (1997). Teaching Spanish as a heritage language: A case for language awareness. *ADFL Bulletin, 29*(1), 33–36.

Kagan, O., & Dillon, K. (2001). A new perspective on teaching Russian: Focus on the heritage learner. *Slavic and East European Journal, 45*(3), 507–518.

Kagan, O., & Dillon, K. (2004). Heritage speakers' potential for high-level language proficiency. In H. Byrnes & H. H. Maxim (Eds.), *Advanced foreign language learning: A challenge to college programs* (pp. 99–112). Boston, MA: Heinle & Heinle.

King, K. A. (2000). Language ideologies and heritage language education. *International Journal of Bilingual Education and Bilingualism, 3*(2), 167–184.

Kondo, K. (1997). Social-psychological factors affecting language maintenance: Interviews with Shin Nisei University students. *Linguistics and Education, 9,* 369–408.

Kondo, K. (1999). Motivating bilingual and semibilingual university students of Japanese: An analysis of language learning persistency and intensity among students from immigrant backgrounds. *Foreign Language Annals, 32,* 77–88.

Kondo-Brown, K. (2001). Bilingual heritage students' language contact and motivation. In Z. Dörnyei & R. Schmidt (Eds.), *Motivation and second language acquisition* (Technical Report #23; pp. 433–459). Honolulu: University of Hawaii, Second Language Teaching and Curriculum Center.

Kondo-Brown, K. (2003). Heritage language instruction for post-secondary students from immigrant backgrounds. *Heritage Language Journal, 1*(1). Retrieved May 10, 2005, from http://www.international.ucla.edu/lrc/hlj/article.asp?parentid=3600

McGinnis, S. (2001). Refreshing the mainstream: Heritage language education in the United States. In R. Z. Lavine (Ed.), *Beyond the boundaries: Changing contexts in language learning* (pp. 45–59). New York: McGraw Hill.

Norton Peirce, B. (1995). Social identity, investment and language learning. *TESOL Quarterly, 29,* 9–31.

Potowski, K. (2002). Experiences of Spanish heritage speakers in university foreign language courses and implications for teacher training. *ADFL Bulletin, 33*(3), 35–42.

Roca, A. (1992). Spanish for U.S. Hispanic bilinguals in higher education. *ERIC Digest.* Washington, DC: ERIC Clearinghouse on Languages and Linguistics.

Roca, A., & Colombi, C. (Eds.). (2003). *Mi lengua: Spanish as a heritage language in the US, research and practice.* Washington, DC: Georgetown University.

Schwartz, A. M. (2001). Preparing teachers to work with heritage learners. In J. K. Peyton, D. A. Ranard, & S. McGinnis (Eds.), *Heritage languages in America: Preserving a national resource* (pp. 229–252). McHenry, IL/Washington, DC: Delta Systems and Center for Applied Linguistics.

Valdés, G. (1995). The teaching of minority languages as academic subjects: Pedagogical and theoretical challenges. *Modern Language Journal, 79,* 299–328.

Valdés, G. (2000). The teaching of heritage languages: An introduction for Slavic-teaching professionals. In O. Kagan & B. Rifkin (Eds.), *The learning and teaching of Slavic languages and cultures* (pp. 375–403). Bloomington, IN: Slavica.

Valdés, G. (2001). Heritage language students: Profiles and possibilities. In J. K. Peyton, D. A. Ranard, & S. McGinnis (Eds.), *Heritage languages in America: Preserving a national resource* pp. 37–77). McHenry, IL/Washington, DC: Delta Systems and Center for Applied Linguistics.

Valdés, G., & Geoffrion-Vinci, M. (1998). Chicano Spanish: The problem of the "underdeveloped" code in bilingual repertories. *Modern Language Journal, 82,* 473–501.

Weger-Guntharp, H. D. (2006). Voices from the margin: Developing a profile of Chinese heritage language learners in the FL classroom, *Heritage Language Journal.* Retrieved November 1, 2006, from http://www.international.ucla.edu/languages/heritagelanguages/journal/article.asp?parentid=53016.

Wen, X. (1997). Motivation and language learning with students of Chinese. *Foreign Language Annals, 30,* 235–251.

Wu, S. (2002). Integrating learner-centered and technology strategies for heritage students. In W. Li & C. Lee (Eds.), *Proceedings of the Southeast Conference on Chinese Language Teaching* (pp. 90–95). Duke University and University of North Carolina at Chapel Hill.

PART

IV

Curriculum Design, Materials Development, and Assessment Procedures

Chapter 10

Curriculum Design for Young Learners of Japanese as a Heritage Language

Masako O. Douglas
California State University, Long Beach

Heritage language (HL) schools, especially for less commonly taught languages, have played a primary role in the maintenance and development of the heritage languages of young learners (e.g., Chao, 1997; Douglas, 2003; He, 2001; Shibata, 2000; Siegel, 2004; Wang, 2003). Typically, HL schools have been funded by individual ethnic communities or religious organizations and their education has been outside the formal school system in the United States. Despite the important role of HL schools, they commonly experience insufficient funding, inadequacy of teaching methodology, lack of instructional materials, and lack of well-qualified teachers (Brook, 1988; Gambihir, 2001; Sasaki, 2001; Schwarts, 2001; Valdés, 2001; Webb, 2000). In fact, several studies have been unable to find any positive correlation between the length of attendance to community-based HL schools and the students' demonstrated proficiency levels (e.g., Oketani, 1997; Sohn & Merill, in press). Curriculum development for HL schools is one area in which existing studies do address the immediate needs of such students (see

Kondo-Brown, this volume). However, in general, the existing literature on curriculum design for HL schools based on pedagogical theories and theories of language acquisition is relatively small.

This chapter presents a model for curriculum design, specifically for Japanese heritage language (JHL) schools. However the model may serve the same purpose for other HL schools that are in learning situations similar to these JHL schools. This chapter consists of four sections on the following topics: (a) an overview of young JHL learners in the United States regarding their educational environment and language profiles, (b) theories and approaches for curriculum design, (c) curriculum design and material development, and (d) a summary. Douglas (2005) attempts to construct a theoretical framework for curriculum design. This chapter, utilizing that framework, places its focus on the actual processes of curriculum design.

OVERVIEW OF YOUNG JAPANESE HERITAGE LANGUAGE LEARNERS IN THE UNITED STATES

Educational Environment

There are two types of schools in the United States involved in young JHL learner education. One is JHL schools, which were established by immigrant parents before World War II in order to maintain the Japanese language and culture of the next generation. The other is *hoshuukoo*, which were established in the 1970s and 1980s to educate children whose parents planned to return to Japan after a few years of stay in the United States. Historically speaking, JHL schools served their purpose for the Nisei[1] (second generation) of immigrants before World War II, and *hoshuukoo* for the Shin-Nisei (new second generation) of new immigrants who came to the United States in the 1970s and 1980s. These two types of schools, however, have distinct instructional goals. The original educational goal of the JHL schools was teaching reading and writing with lesser focus on oral skills (Brook, 1988), and the current goal is exclusively to teach language per se, emphasizing drill and practice of isolated language skills (Sasaki, 2001), or basic literacy skills only (Usui, 1996). *Hoshuukoo*, with a few exceptions, adhere to the curriculum developed by the Japanese government for elementary schools in Japan and teach academic content in separate subject areas such as language arts, math, social studies, and science (see also Kataoka, Koshiyama, & Shibata, this volume, for further discussion of *hoshuukoo*).

When the developmental needs in the linguistic, cognitive, social, and affective domains of young JHL learners are considered, the instructional

---

[1]The phrase *Shin-Nisei* in this chapter includes those who were born in the United States and those who were born in Japan and came to the United States before they started formal education.

goals and methodology of these two types of schools are inadequate (Douglas, Kataoka, & Kishimoto, 2003). Young JHL learners develop, with a wide range of proficiency levels, basic communication skills at home. However, the language ability necessary to discuss significant matters and academic language proficiency are not developed by simply interacting daily with their family members and friends. In her study on language maintenance among Nisei, Brook (1988) states that "as the Nisei progressed in school and English vocabulary grew and their interests broadened, Japanese vocabulary did not expand at anywhere near the same pace, which consequently diminished the opportunity for the Nisei to develop a high level of oral language ability" (p. 60). Nakajima's (1998) study on Shin-Nisei argues that focusing on teaching language per se does not support the learners in developing age-appropriate cognitive academic language proficiency. Although the *hoshuukoo* teach academic subject matter, the curriculum content is not always relevant to the life of the children who grow up in the United States (Nakajima, 1989, 2002). Furthermore, covering 1 week's worth of curriculum content in 1 day forces learners into rote memorization. Consequently, children lose interest in and motivation for going to these schools (Kondo, 1998).

In addition to the mismatch between the learner's needs and the curriculum, which leads to loss of interest in learning, the children's motivation for studying at a weekend school in addition to their other work at regular schools is very weak (Brook, 1988; Nakajima, 1998). The students do not see learning heritage languages at weekend schools as a legitimate school subject (Feuerverger, 1989). As Curdt-Christiansen (2002) writes, "if the experience of minority language education in childhood is a dismal affair, if a heritage language school is perceived as a boring and unattractive place to be, the heritage language is unlikely to be maintained or valued" (p. 36).

Developmental Profile

Douglas (2005) argues that it is important to consider heterogeneity of development in two domains in JHL education for young learners: (a) language proficiency and (b) cognitive, social and emotional skills. The degree of access to the Japanese language for JHL children varies widely, depending on their language experiences with their parents and siblings at home, friends, and others in the community, or with native speakers in Japan. For example, Douglas, Kataoka, and Kishimoto (2003) find that 46% of children at JHL schools come from bilingual homes, where both Japanese and English are spoken. Children at *hoshuukoo*, on the other hand, are from monolingual homes, where parents speak to each other in Japanese (88%). The wide difference in language environments results in varying degrees of language acquisition in oral and literacy skills (Nakajima, 1998), which poses a challenge in JHL pedagogy (see also Kondo-Brown, this volume).

In addition to the issues of heterogeneity of language development, JHL pedagogy for young learners needs to consider issues of developmental differences in cognitive, social, and emotional domains as well. This is a primary difference between JHL pedagogy for college students and that for young learners. Researchers on early childhood and elementary school education emphasize the importance of considering young learners' unique and idiosyncratic experiences and backgrounds, which lead to heterogeneous cognitive, social, and emotional development, and advocate designing developmentally appropriate practice with heterogeneous approaches (Hart, Burts, & Charlesworth, 1997; Katz & Chard, 1997; Stone, 1996)

THEORIES AND APPROACHES FOR CURRICULUM DESIGN

Drawing from the existing literature of theories and approaches for language education and early childhood and elementary education, Douglas (2005) discusses the following three topics: (a) integrated instruction, (b) developmentally appropriate practice, and (c) assessment. This section summarizes the discussion.

Integrated Instruction

The word "integration" is used in two ways: integration of content and language, and integrated curriculum, that is, integration of subject areas. The approach of integrating content and language has become fairly developed in the field of teaching foreign or second languages (for teaching young learners, see Spanos, 1989; for adult learners, see Brinton, Snow, & Wesche, 1989; Stryker & Leaver, 1997). This approach aims for the simultaneous learning of a language and school subject areas taught in that language. Met (1999, p. 144) describes six models for this approach based on the degree of content and language integration: total immersion, partial immersion, sheltered courses, adjunct courses, theme-based instruction, and language classes with frequent use of content for language practice.

The models particularly relevant to young JHL education are those that involve second language education for students of limited English proficiency (LEP) and immersion models. The traditional curriculum at JHL schools is based on a language-driven model, which focuses on discrete language skills. With this approach, as Nakajima (1998) points out, the child's bilingual range in academic content areas stays extremely limited.

A number of studies report positive effects for integrated instruction on students' academic language learning (García, 1991; Hampton & Rodriguez, 2001; Kessler & Quinn, 1987; Thomas & Collier, 1995). The common attributes of effective programs from these studies are: a high level of communication, language education through cognitively complex content, utilization of problem solving and discovery learning in highly interactive classroom activities, and an inquiry-based hands-on approach. Other studies found that the quality and nature of academic language that students use will vary depending on the academic tasks involved. Thus the studies suggest that instruction needs to provide students with various academic tasks and ample opportunities to strengthen their underdeveloped functional use of academic language (Liang, 2002; Solomon & Rhodes, 1995).

The immersion approach as a content-driven approach provides valuable information and strategies for young JHL learner education. From evaluation research on a variety of immersion programs, there are at least three elements of general relevance for language instruction (ERIC Digest, 1995): (a) instructional approaches that integrate content and language are likely to be more effective than approaches in which language is taught in isolation; (b) an activity-centered approach that creates opportunities for extended student discourse is likely to be beneficial for second language learning; and (c) language objectives should be systematically targeted along with academic objectives in order to maximize language learning. Snow (1990) based on her survey responses from 58 experienced teachers in immersion programs summarizes the following core instructional strategies, which are most frequently utilized: body language, building redundancy and repetition, and vocabulary development.

For selection of curriculum content, weak motivation to study JHL at weekend schools needs to be considered. Unlike immersion programs and those programs with heritage language instruction integrated into the regular school day (as described in Feuerverger, 1989), JHL students see learning JHL as an extra burden in addition to regular school homework (Brook, 1988, p. 105), or they do not see the heritage language as a legitimate school subject (Feuerverger, 1989). Teaching Japanese language in isolation at JHL schools or curriculum content at *hoshuukoo*, which is irrelevant to regular school curriculum, may in part contribute to this perception. In order to make learning JHL meaningful and relevant for the students, while considering limited instructional time, curriculum content needs to be related to that of the regular school curriculum by selecting important and interesting content. Use of curriculum content in this way, defined as a "content-related" approach by Curtain and Dahlberg (2004), reinforces learning reciprocally at the regular school and the JHL school.

Integrated curriculum in early childhood and elementary education is a series of theme-based and cross-disciplined curriculum that integrates all areas of development across physical, emotional, social, and cognitive domains. Krogh (1997) states that an integrated curriculum provides meaningfulness to children's learning by combining various curricula areas into a unified whole. Research and theory support the fact that young children learn best through a curriculum that is integrated (Seefeld, 1997).

Design of an integrated curriculum starts with selecting areas of children's interest related to a theme. In addition, the model of JHL curriculum design proposed in this chapter considers children's background knowledge as a base line, and the content relevancy of the curriculum to that of their regular school. Once a theme is selected, instructional goals that match with the children's development across multiple disciplines are set up, and the design proceeds to the selection of instructional approaches and activities that further lead to the implementation of developmentally appropriate practice.

Developmentally Appropriate Practice

Developmentally appropriate practice is defined as educational practice that takes into account individual differences in the children's development in age, individual growth patterns, and cultural orientations (Krogh, 1997). Kats and Chard (1997) emphasize that an appropriate curriculum first strengthens children's procedural knowledge and then introduces them to abstract representations that are directly related to the procedural knowledge. From their research synthesis on developmentally appropriate practice, Hart, Burts, and Charlesworth (1997) conclude that the weight of evidence appears to favor developmentally appropriate practice, especially in the affective domain because it will lead to less stress related behaviors, less distractibility, more prosocial and conforming behavior, and higher motivation for learning.

Douglas (2005), synthesizing research on developmentally appropriate practice presents the following six approaches: (a) learner-centered approach, (b) multiage instruction, (c) standards-based approach, (d) inquiry-based approach, (e) hands-on and activity-based approach, and (f) interactive approach. The first three approaches are relevant to curriculum decisions as a whole, and they guide the teachers' decisions in what to teach in what sequence. The remaining approaches are related to designing instructional activities, that is, how to teach.

Learner-Centered Approach. In contrast to the teacher-centered instruction with a uniformly prescribed curriculum with prescribed learning objectives, a learner-centered curriculum starts with heterogeneity in child's development. Starting curriculum design with assessing child's interest and background knowledge for instructional goals and objectives, as discussed previously, is an example of a learner-centered approach. Learner-centeredness requires utilizing instructional activities that facilitate active rather than passive interaction among children, and ample opportunities for children to initiate and be engaged (Katz & Chard, 1997).

Multiage Instructional Approach. Multiage classes consist of children from different ages, commonly across a range of 3 or more years. Children in the multiage classes stay with the same teacher(s) for several years. The distinctive characteristics of the multiage instruction are that there is no single grade-segregated curriculum, and a child's development is assessed by his or her development rather than on the basis of time. Grouping children by age or by single grades fails to consider the heterogeneity of children's development, and thus does not provide developmentally appropriate practice. Although the degree of effectiveness varies, the weight of evidence in the studies that control variables well appears to favor the approach in terms of the students' academic achievement and the affective domain, indicating more prosocial behaviors, better attendance, and less stress-related behaviors (Gutiérrez & Slavin, 1992; Kelly-Vance, Caster, & Ruane, 2000; Lloyd, 1999; Nye, Caine, Saharias, Tollett, & Fulton, 1995).

Standards-Based Approach.   Because curricula of multiage instruction are not grade-segregated, curriculum designers need to construct continuous progress indicators based on children's development in the linguistic, cognitive, social, and affective domains. The continuum of continuous progress enables teachers to provide children with instruction suited to their level. Giacone (2000) emphasizes the importance of the integration of language learning standards and language arts standards, which present all the following elements in an integral way: communication skills, thinking processes that include higher level thinking, work habits and attitudes such as collaboration and cooperation, and awareness of diverse cultures. Hart, Burts, and Charlesworth (1997) also establish the connection between developmentally appropriate practice and standards for young learners. Note, however, that there are not adequate empirical data on heritage language acquisition by both young and adult learners. We therefore need a great deal of research in this area to establish language standards for JHL, and consequently, we might need to adjust the language standards that are used in this chapter.

Inquiry-Based Approach.   This approach fosters higher order thinking skills, which are scientific process skills, such as formulating and testing hypothesis, explanations, inferring, and reflecting. The approach consists of the following five phases (Joyce & Weil, 1986, p. 61):

- Phase one: Confrontation with the problem (puzzling situation).
- Phase two: Data gathering-verification
- Phase three: Data gathering-experimentation
- Phase four: Formulating an explanation
- Phase five: Analysis of the inquiry process (reflection to improve the inquiry process)

Studies have supported the effectiveness of this approach in developing higher order thinking skills and understanding of science (see Joyce & Weil, 1986, for a research synthesis), as well as development of science inquiry and second language (Hampton & Rodriguez, 2001; Kessler & Quinn, 1987).

Hands-On and Activity-Based Approach. Kessler and Quinn (1987) emphasize the importance of the distinction between this approach and a textbook-oriented approach. They argue that overdependence on textbooks in preference to hands-on investigation seriously constraints the opportunities to understand the content, which can become comprehensible by interaction with others through hands-on activities. Cummins (1992), proposing his theoretical framework of conversational and academic language proficiency, argues that language minority student's failure in developing high levels of L2 academic skills is due to their initial instruction, which has emphasized "context-reduced" communication. Textbook-based instruction is an example of such context-reduced communication. Cummins further writes, "the more context-embedded the initial L2 input, the more comprehensible it is likely to be, and paradoxically, the more successful in ultimately developing L2 skills in context-reduced situations" (Cummins, 1992, p. 21). Krogh (1997) states that "children learn to reason more logically and understand their learning more fully, *as long as concrete objects are present in reality or in their thoughts*" (emphasis added). Providing compelling evidence, Donaldson (1978, in Cummins, 1992) affirms that children are able to manifest much higher levels of cognitive performance when the task is presented in a concrete context.

Interactive Approach. Recent research commonly indicates that interaction among learners, or between a teacher and learners is an essential factor for both the language acquisition (first and second languages) and cognitive development of young learners (for research synthesis see Garcia, 1991; Katz & Chard, 1997; Kinsey, 2001; Thomas & Collier, 1995). Based on a thorough analysis of research findings, the Center for Research on Education, Diversity and Excellence includes interaction as one of the five principles in the Standards for Effective Teaching and Learning, and proposes to utilize instructional conversation in classroom teaching, which allows sensitive contextualization, and precise and stimulating cognitive challenges (Echevarria, 1998).

Assessment

The following elements of ideal assessment, originally developed by Goodlad and Anderson (1963, 1987) and adapted by Gutiérrez and Slavin (1992, p. 337) for the assessment of multiage instruction, are quite applicable as principles for constructing assessment instruments in young JHL learner education.

- Children are evaluated in terms of their past achievements and their own potential, not by comparison to group norms. Expectations differ for different children.
- Evaluation by teacher and/or child is done for diagnostic purposes and results in the formulation of new education objectives.

- Evaluation must be continuous and comprehensive to fulfill its diagnostic purpose.
- A child strives mainly to improve his or her performance and develop potential rather than to compete with others.
- Teachers accept and respond to the fact that growth patterns will be irregular and will occur in different areas at different times.
- Individual pupil progress forms are used to record the learning tasks completed, deficiencies that need new assignments to permit mastery, and all other data that will show the child's progress in relation to past achievements and potential or that will help the teacher in suggesting possible future learning experiences for the individual.
- Evaluation and reporting will consider all five areas of the child's development: aesthetic, physical, intellectual, emotional, and social.

In the past, the focus of assessment has shifted from evaluating children's factual knowledge only to performance-based assessments that measure what they can do with the acquired knowledge and to what extent and how they can perform various procedures. Short (1993) proposes an assessment matrix to be used for LEP children, which consists of eight skills: problem solving, content-area skills, concept comprehension, language use, communication skills, individual behavior, group behavior, and attitude. As measures to assess these skills, Short proposes various alternative instruments with a brief description of advantages and disadvantages of each measure: skill and concept check lists; reading and writing inventories; anecdotal records; teacher observations; student self evaluations; portfolios, task-based performances; written essays, reports; oral reports; and student interviews.

In addition to academic language proficiency and content mastery, assessment instruments for young heritage learners need to measure basic communication skills. The varied JHL environments of children affect the degree of the development of the basic communication skills. Oral Proficiency Assessment for Bilingual Children (OBC) developed by Canadian Association for Japanese Language Education (2000) proposes three dimensions for assessment, which consist of basic structural knowledge with accuracy as its component, interpersonal skills with contextual support, and cognitive language ability without contextual support, which requires high cognitive ability such as ability to narrate in a discourse level. The cognitive language ability includes ability to explain and discuss academic subjects as well as story telling (see Hasegawa, this volume, for this and other proficiency instruments for child JHL learners).

CURRICULUM DESIGN AND MATERIAL DEVELOPMENT

This section presents a process of curriculum design for JHL learners in grades K-8, integrating the theories and approaches discussed in the previous section. Considering the heterogeneous nature of child development in cognitive, affective, and social domains, as well as the heterogeneous language proficiency of young JHL learners, a multiage approach is utilized in this design. K-8 JHL learners are placed in different levels, according to the stages of child cognitive and language development, as discussed in the previous section. One level consists of two or three different age groups. A number of the levels in a program may vary based on many factors such as the range of learners' language proficiency levels and the number of enrollments for example. The model discussed in this chapter has three levels (grades K–1, 2–4, and 5–8). However there is no clear-cut line between the levels, and depending on the child's performance level, he or she may be placed one level higher or one level lower. The process of curriculum design discussed in this section applies to all different levels of a JHL program.

The process of curriculum development is shown in Figure 10.1. There are five steps, each briefly described here along with the relevant theories and approaches just discussed.

Step 1

Instruction starts from what the learners are interested in, know, and can do in relation to what needs to be taught (i.e., it is a learner-centered approach). The first stage is particularly important in a JHL curriculum. Unlike FL learning, in which the learners' language development is more or less uniform from simple to complex, JHL children come to school with varied bilingual ranges. With certain limitations, some are only good at listening, some others are capable of communication on familiar topics, and others can read and write in addition to their oral skills (Nakajima, 1998, pp. 9–10). Content knowledge is also varied among children. As the first step, a learner profile needs to be constructed and recorded as a reference for selecting curriculum content, and to measure the language development of each child during the course.

In the beginning of the academic year, the Oral Proficiency Assessment for Bilingual Children (OBC), which was discussed in the previous section, is conducted to assess children's Japanese language ability in structural knowledge, interpersonal skills, and extended discourse. In order to assess children's content knowledge and academic language ability to express the given content knowledge, the teacher works with the children to collaboratively construct an idea web. Utilization of an idea web is commonly advocated in early childhood education (Bingham, Dorta, McClaskey, & O'Keef, 1995; Chard, 1998) and in foreign language education (Curtain & Dahlberg, 2004; Graves, 2000). As for the usefulness of the web, Curtin and Dahlberg (2004) state that a web "allows the planner to extend the theme in many directions and to flesh out the topic with meaningful categories and subcategories" (p. 148).

There is an example of the idea web in Figure 10.2, which was made by Level 2 (grades 2–4) students. I translated the idea web originally generated in

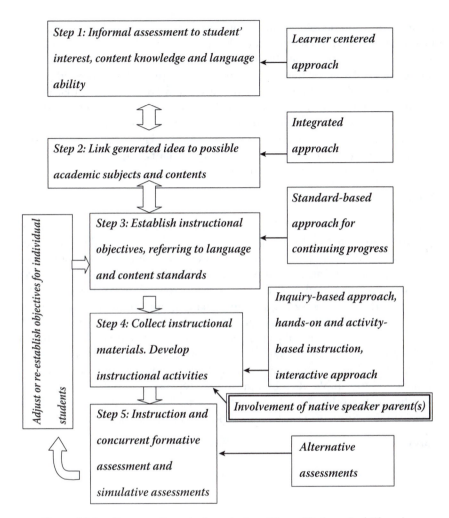

Figure 10.1.   Process of curriculum design. (From "Pedagogical Theories
and Approaches to Teach Young Learners of Japanese as a Heritage
Language" by Masako O. Douglas (2005). *Heritage Language Journal, II*(2).
Reprinted with permission.)

Japanese into English for the readers' convenience. In the case, the teacher
chooses the concept of "cycle" as the theme, then writes the word on the blackboard and asks children to each tell the class any ideas that come to mind
about the word. All those words circled by a thick line are what the children
generated in their responses, which are a starting point for the curriculum
design: "Seeds become trees and flowers, and they make seeds," "Rain becomes
water, and it goes up to the sky and becomes clouds, and it rains," "Animal's
droppings are food for vegetables, and vegetables are animals' food," "Trees

make oxygen and people take it in, and people make carbon dioxide and trees take it in" (note that children used English for the chemical terminology). These utterances show that children understand the concept of "cycle" in various contexts. However they need to develop the procedural knowledge necessary for explaining the changing processes in a cycle in detail, that is how clouds and rain are formed, how animal feces becomes food for vegetables, for example. In addition they need to develop the extended discourse ability for coherent and detailed explanations and age appropriate vocabulary that is specific to different subject areas, such as nutrition, plants, *sanso*, and *nisankatanso*, instead of food, trees, oxygen, and carbon dioxide.

Step 2

Starting from the children's knowledge, potential topics (shown in boxes in Fig. 10.2) are generated in different academic subject areas. There are four topics for earth science: how clouds and rain are formed, weather and temperature, acid rain, and measurement of pH; three topics for life science: nutrition and digestion, observe how plants grow, photosynthesis, and the human body; and one topic for math: making graphs of daily temperatures. In the figure, not as many topics are generated in math and language (JHL) as in science. These two subject areas are viewed in this design as integrated in the other subject areas. Math skills are developed when students compute the data that they collect in science study, and make tables and graphs for presentation, for example. Reading, writing, and speaking in JHL accompany all activities in the other subject areas, be it arts, literature, music, science, or social studies. Students use JHL as a tool for learning these subject areas.

Step 3

From the topics generated in Figure 10.2, "observe how plants grow," "food chain," and "how clouds and rain are formed" are chosen, for example, as target topics for Levels 1, 2, and 3, respectively. In order to establish learning objectives, subject matter standards and language learning standards are referred to. For subject matter standards, the Science Content Standards for California Public Schools (California State Board of Education,1998) were used here. They present a set of standards for Kindergarten to Grade 12.

Each topic for these three levels has standards for life science or earth science. In the topic for Level 1, by observing how plants grow and by comparing the growth in different sites, students will compare and sort common objects by one physical attribute (e.g., color, shape, texture, size, weight; Kindergarten, Standard 4-d).[2] When the students in Level 2 learn about food chain, they know producers and consumers are related in food

---

[2]The Science Standards (Kindergarten) for "Life Science" and "Investigation and Experimentation" are listed in Appendix A with the ones used in the present project marked with asterisks.

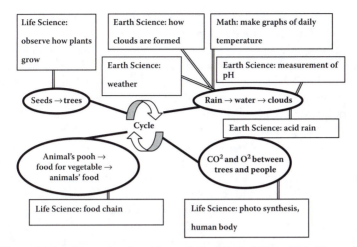

Figure 10.2.   Example of an idea web for "Cycle." Note. This idea web originally generated in Japanese has been translated into English for the readers' convenience. (From "Pedagogical Theories and Approaches to Teach Young Learners of Japanese as a Heritage Language" by Masako O. Douglas (2005), *Heritage Language Journal, II*(2). Reprinted with permission.)

chains and food webs and may compete with each other for resources in an ecosystem (Grade Four, Standard 2-b). In Level 3, students will engage in an experiment to generate clouds and rain in order to learn the water cycle, as well as how water vapor in the air moves from one place to another and can form for or clouds, which are tiny droplets of water or ice, and can in turn fall to Earth as rain, hail, sleet, or snow (Grade Five, Standard 3-c).

For language arts standards, the Learning Standards for Native Language Arts (LSNLA) are referred to here. The LSNLA were developed in 2004 by the New York State Education Department in collaboration with University of the State of New York and Office of Bilingual Education (OBE) for their limited English proficient students. The LSNLA aim at developing the child's home language arts other than English, which consequently leads, according to the OBE, to acquisition of English language arts. Although the LSNLA do not use the term "heritage language," they can serve as standards for heritage language arts by their very nature. The LSNLA combine K–1, 2–4, and 5–8 to make three levels.

The general goals of the standards for oral language skills in the LSNLA include the development of basic language ability, including correct pronunciation, in Level 1 (Grades K–1); development of accuracy in language forms, as well as age and culturally appropriate language use in Level 2 (Grades 2–4); and development of the awareness of the audience and purpose in Level 3 (Grades 5–8). When development of literacy skills is considered, the LSNLA categorization, which distinguishes between an early literacy stage and later stages, is useful for designing a JHL curriculum. For example, the standards for the Level 1 address the development of pre-literacy to early literacy skills such as distinguishing between print and pictures, matching sounds and letters, recognizing words, decoding skills, and word level production. In Level 2, the LSNLA aim at higher level literacy skills such as effective use of decoding strategies, increases in reading fluency, recognition and discrimination among a variety of informational texts, writing in a logical order, and using basic strategies such as self-monitoring and correction. In Level 3, the LSNLA focus on literacy skills at the discourse level. In terms of language forms in each level of the LSNLA, they progress from word to sentence level, and then to the connected discourse level. Note that the development of language ability addressed in lower levels might need to be included in the standards for higher levels in a JHL curriculum due to the heterogeneity in language proficiency among young JHL learners.

Each level of LSNLA consists of the following four standards for the four skills (listening, speaking, reading and writing): Standard 1 focuses on obtaining and presenting information, Standard 2 on literary works, Standard 3 on critical analysis and evaluation, and Standard 4 on social interaction. Particularly relevant to the science topics in this chapter is Standard 1. With a progress through the levels, language forms and cognitive skills that students learn for gathering information in scientific inquiry increase in complexity. The performance indicators for Standard 1 in Level 1 are listed in Appendix B with the ones used in the present project marked with asterisks.

By integrating the Science Standards and the LSNLA, learning objectives can be established for Level 1 on the given topic, as listed in the following section. Instructional activities are introduced orally first to demonstrate new topics and their contents, and then proceed to literacy activities. The following objectives, therefore, include both oral and written language skills.

Level 1: (grades K–1)[3]
Topic: How plants grow (plant cycle)
Students will able to:

1. Follow directions on how to care for plants
2. Demonstrate how to care for plants
3. Follow directions on how to measure length
4. Use a scale and measure the length of the plants
5. Identify parts of plants in illustrations
6. Classify plants by patterns of the leaves and flowers, comparing similarities and differences in shapes
7. Observe and record the growth with illustrations, words and numbers for a month

---

[3]Grouping the grades here follows LSNLA. Performance requirements for language skills, however, need adjustment especially for literacy skills. As discussed previously, there is a great difference in language ability at the early literacy stage and the stage that follows.

8. Identify words on the growth records of the plants
9. Describe the growth with illustrations and words, or sentences for more proficient students
10. Describe the conditions that lead to success or failure of plant growth, compare the difference, and explain why they are different, using illustrations and words, or sentences for more proficient students
11. Present and share their observation results on how plants grow over time with illustrations and words, or sentences for more proficient students
12. Interpret growth charts of the plants
13. Interpret information about plants presented in written materials (e.g., books, magazines, and Internet materials)
14. Use appropriate vocabulary, Chinese characters, and structures
15. Maintain their writing works in portfolio with teacher assistance

Step 4

When objectives are established, instructional activities can be designed, and then materials can be developed or collected. In order to make learning content comprehensible, thus meaningful for students, a hands-on approach that provides students with concrete learning experiences is utilized when a new topic is introduced. In addition, an inquiry-based approach that fosters higher order thinking skills, as discussed in the previous section, plays a primary role in this curriculum. Instructional activities are designed to facilitate interaction between the teacher and students, and among the students while they discuss their hypothesis, procedures of experiments, observation results, and findings. Outlines of the activities for Level 1 are provided in the following text, together with instructional objectives indicated in brackets. The activities are implemented in two subsequent lessons, that enable students to familiarize themselves with a new topic and engage in the same activities as in the first lesson, and to review the content and work independently in the second lesson. For JHL schools that offer instruction once per week for 3 hours a day, this cycle of instruction aims at ensuring that students progress from understanding the content with help from others to being able to learn by themselves, or being able to apply the content to the other situations. The second phase provides teachers with an opportunity to assess the student's learning.

Level: 1 (grades K–1)
Topic: How plants grow (plant cycle)
Day 1: Introduction of a new topic

1. The teacher distributes seeds without telling students that they are seeds, and asks them to discuss in groups what they think they are (inquiry-based approach, phase one: puzzling situation).

2. The teacher tells the students that they will plant the seeds of mysterious plants. The students discuss what they think the mysterious plants are: how tall they will grow, what they will look like, what the leaves will look like, whether or not they will have flowers, and what colors and shapes of the flowers will be (inquiry-based approach, phase one: puzzling situation). The teacher will informally assesses students' content knowledge and language ability and supply content specific vocabulary while discussing these with students.

3. The teacher shows how to plant seeds and water them, verbally explaining each step with a gesture. Students retell the steps with teacher's help (see discussion of Total Physical Response Storytelling (TPRS) in Step 5). [1]

4. The teacher shows the steps silently and the students retell the steps by themselves. [1]

5. In pairs, one student shows the gestures and the other one retells the steps. [1]

6. Students plant seeds in pots, which are placed either in sunny spots or shade. [2]

7. Showing pictures, the teacher will introduce plant related vocabulary: seed, root, leave, bud, stalk, and flowers, for example (see Appendix C, Fig. C1). Students in pairs work on a card game (Appendix C, Fig. C2). With pictures of plant parts spread on a table, one student names one of the parts, and the other student must find it. Switch the roles and repeat the game. The pairs of students compare the number of the cards they have gotten right, and record that number on the game score sheet in their portfolios. Students write the names of the plant parts on a handout. [5, 15]

8. The teacher will ask students to show, if they know, how to count plants and flowers (i.e., classifiers "-hon/-pon/-bon" for plants and flowers, and "-mai" for leaves.) Students engage in a "Bun-bun game" that is adapted from a Japanese TV show. In a circle, the first student names an object (e.g., pencil) and the second student counts it with a classifier *ippon* (one pencil). Then the second student names an object (e.g., leaf) and the third one counts it with a classifier *ichimai* (one leaf). Those who give wrong classifiers are out of the game and the last one who stays in the game becomes the winner. The result is recorded on the game score sheet in their portfolio. Students work on their handout to count flowers and write numbers with classifiers. [14, 15]

9. The teacher shows a scale to the students and asks what it is and when it is used. Then the teacher talks out loud about how to measure length using a scale, and how to record it in the table in their handout. The metric and U.S. systems of measurement are introduced here. (The TPRS technique is used here again. The Japanese *structure "monosashi de ~no nagasa o hakarimasu"* [I will measure the length of ~ with a scale] and

"*~no nagasa wa ~senchi desu*" [the length of ~ is ~ cm] are also practiced here.) [3]

10. In pairs, the students practice measuring different objects, talking out loud to each other, and recording the lengths they get (see Appendix C, Fig. C3). [4]

11. The students present the results of their measurements to the whole class. [11]

12. The teacher introduces a song that is related to plants (e.g., "*Chuurippu*" [tulip]).

13. The teacher reads out loud a picture storybook that is related to plants and has repeated patterns (e.g., "*Ookina kabu*" [A Great Turnip], "*Ojiisan no tsuru tsuru kobocha*" [Grandpa's pumpkin with tendril]). The students construct a story by watching the pictures in the book with or without teacher assistance. [13]

Homework assignment:

- Students complete worksheets: Measurement of length of objects at home and record the lengths, as well as language related exercises for vocabulary and structures (see Appendix C, Fig. C5).
- Students read a book of their choice, which is related to plants, and record the number of the pages in their "*hon no chokinbako*" (a piggy bank for book reading). The book is brought to school every week. [13]

JHL curriculum requires parents who are native speakers of Japanese to assist their children in learning Japanese. Considering the extremely limited instructional time at JHL schools, parental involvement is indispensable (Li, 2005; Nakajima, 1998; Wang, 2003). The content coverage at school and instructions for parents about how to assist their children while they work on homework are provided on the first page of the homework handout (see Appendix C, Fig. C5).

Day 2: Continuation of the topic

1. The students read the books of their choice independently. The teacher assesses the student's reading skills individually by Reading Miscue Inventory (see Step 5, assessment). [13]

2. The students review the vocabulary for plant parts and classifiers by playing the same card game as the one they did on the first day, and review how to measure length. [4, 14]

3. The students observe their plants and record any changes in the number and length of the buds, as well as their shapes and colors in illustration (Appendix C, Fig. C4). Teacher informally assesses their vocabulary knowledge and skill in measuring length. [6, 14]

4. The teacher provides vocabulary for students' drawings of the plants orally and writes on the blackboard. The students copy the vocabulary into their notebooks. [14]

5. The students discuss in groups their observations, compare the growth of their plants, discuss why the growth is different among the plants, and provide possible explanations (inquiry approach, phase one: puzzling situation). They present the content of their discussions to the class. [10, 11]

6. The students in pairs describe to each other their cards with illustrations of the plant that are slightly different in length and numbers with the goal of discovering the differences.[4] The teacher introduces Chinese characters for recognition. The students practice in pairs how to pronounce them using flash cards first; then all children are divided into two groups and they compete for how many cards each group can collect. [14]

7. The last session of the second day is allocated for individualized learning. The students select one of the activities among the following: make flash cards of plant parts, picture cards and word cards separately to be used at competition, making flash cards of Chinese characters, playing games using the cards, measuring the length of objects that they have not measured and recording it on a sheet in their portfolio. [15]

Home assignment:

- Students continue their pleasure reading
- Students complete a worksheet: Chinese characters, vocabulary (shapes and colors), measurement [14]

This unit continues until the plants grow big enough for the students to identify the mysterious plants by referring to books and comparing shapes of their plants with those in the books (inquiry-based approach, phases two, four, and five). [6, 9, 11]

The instructional activities just listed for each level are divided into the following three blocks for each day:

Day 1

- First block: introduction of an inquiry
- Second block: conducting an experiment, observing and recording the results, and presenting the results to the whole class

---

[4]The idea to use an information gap activity in a content-related way was adapted from Gibbons (2002).

- Third block: reading and writing up the experiment, and language related activities (structures and vocabulary, and Chinese characters)

Day 2

- First block: individual reading and assessment of reading skills, and an independent experiment as a review, and assessment of the skills necessary for conducting the first-day experiment, or a continuation of the content of the first day
- Second block: reading and writing that includes a report of the experiment with graphs, and language related activities
- Third block: individualized learning (students choose one to two activities from the list.)

Step 4 has shown examples of the instructional activities for Level 1, which integrate subject areas and language. This approach is widely supported as just discussed. Gibbons (2002), however, argues that language instruction needs to be systematically integrated into the curriculum topics by careful and explicit planning, and the development of the students' language abilities should be assessed on daily base. This issue is discussed in Step 5.

Step 5

Step 5 first presents some approaches for implementing instructional activities designed in Step 4 then discusses assessment issues. As listed in the learning objectives in Step 4, producing logically coherent texts both in oral and written language is one common, yet difficult, goal to achieve. Similar to many other kinds of development in learning, production skills develop along a continuum from assisted learning with help from adults or more capable peers to independent learning without any assistance, also known as the Zone of Proximal Development in Vygotskian terms (Cole, 1998). Students first need to expose themselves to good examples of the language they want to use. Adapting an approach called Total Physical Response Storytelling (TPRS; created by Blaine Ray as described in Curtain & Dahlberg, 2004) to the inquiry-based approach in this chapter, teachers can provide good language samples while students listen at first without responding, have their students follow the examples quietly with gestures, and then have the students produce utterances like those in the samples. The Language Experience Approach (LEA) is another way to assist students in productive skills with a focus on writing. The students say what they want to out loud, and the teacher writes what students are saying on the blackboard to demonstrate how to transfer oral language to written language in terms of orthography, including Chinese characters in the case of JHL education. Although the original principle is that the teacher writes exactly what the students say without any correction, variation is possible, in which the teacher provides correct forms while interacting with students. Gibbons (2002) encourages students to talk to each other while they engage in the activities. She states that it is "this kind of talk that allows learners to explore and clarify concepts or to try out a line of thought, through questioning, hypothesizing, making logical deductions, and responding to others' ideas" (p. 14).

Assessment in the curriculum proposed in this chapter is viewed as integral to pedagogy. As discussed in the previous section, assessment is a source of information about students' needs in both learning academic content and the associated language, which changes over the process of learning. Thus assessment is formative, ongoing in day-to-day teaching and learning activities, and individualized in its nature. It always starts with examining what the students already know and what they have learned in the course. Learning of the content knowledge is assessed informally while students engage in activities as well as by a paper-and-pencil assessment at the end of the topic being studied. In the assessment at the end of the lesson, the students' interest in the topic (i.e., affective domain) is also assessed for revision, if necessary, of subsequent teaching and learning activities (see Appendix D for a sample assessment for Level 1). In this type of assessment, students are allowed to answer the questions in whichever language they feel most comfortable in order to assess their content mastery, rather than their language mastery.

Similarly, in order to assess oral language development, assessment is conducted whenever possible while students are engaging in authentic meaning-making activities, be they discussing experimental procedures with a teacher or with their peers, sharing their findings, or engaging in information gap activities, to name a few. Table 10.1 shows some planned instructional activities used to assess mastery for Level 1 in Step 4 and language forms that are required to carry them out.[5]

The results of assessing the content domain and language domain are recorded in several different ways, as discussed in Short (1993): checklist or inventory; anecdotal record; teacher observation; student self-evaluation; portfolios; performance manipulatives (such as math formulas); written essays, reports; oral reports; and student interviews. One thing common to all these types of assessments is the Vygotskian view of child development, namely progress in the Zone of Proximal Development. Table 10.2 shows a sample assessment form for the learning activities in Level 1 (i.e., those listed in Table 10.1).

Development of reading ability consists of three stages (Bialystok, 2001): emergent literacy, early reading, and fluent reading. *Emergent literacy* is a pre-reading stage, in which young readers develop the concept of reading: how to turn the pages and proceed through a book, the pleasure of being

---

[5]This procedure is adapted from the Language Inventory shown in Gibbons (2002, p. 124).

TABLE 10.1
Learning Activities and Language Forms for Level 1 (Grades K–1)

Learning Activities	Language
Use a scale and measure length of plants	Vocabulary: numeric systems including decimals for older students, inch and centimeter, scale. Structures: "~de~o hakarimasu" (I measured ~ by ~), " ~no nagasa wa ~senchi desu" (the length of ~ is~)
Identify parts of plants	Vocabulary: names of the parts of plants
Describe the growth of the plants	Structures: "(data), ~wa ~senchi ni narimashita" (~has become ~cm) "~wa ~senchi nobimashita" (~ grew~cm)
Compare the conditions for the growing plants	Structures: "~to ~o kuraberuto, ~no hoo ga ookikunarimashita" (Compared ~ and ~, ~became bigger) "nazeka to iu to ~" (The reason is~)

TABLE 10.2
A Sample Form of the Assessment Record

Learning Activities	Assessment Tools	Progress Indicators			Note
		Getting better	Can do with assistance	Can do independently	
Use a scale and measure length of plants	Content-area skills				
Identify parts of Plants	Language use				
Describe the growth of plants	Communication skills				
Compare conditions for the plants to grow	Communication skills				

Note. The types of the assessment tools listed here are adapted from Short (1993).

read, and interest in reading. In the *early reading* stage, readers acquire the lower level reading skills such as word recognition, orthographic processing, phonemic or phonological coding, morphemic or morphological coding, working memory activation, and sentence parsing (Grabe, 1999). According to Grabe, readers at the *fluent reading* stage can utilize higher level processing skills such as discourse structuring, inference in genre difference, and effective use of various reading strategies.

Children in grades K–8 are somewhere at early reading and full reading stages. In order to assess decoding skills (i.e., lower level skills), *miscue analysis* is used, which shows how readers use various systems of language and a variety of strategies to construct meaning while they read aloud uninterrupted texts (Goodman, Watson, & Burke, 1987). To use this assessment, the original Reading Miscue Inventory (RMI) developed for English was modified for reading in Japanese by adding codes for unusual segmentation of the words and particle miscues, which are counted as indicators of underdevelopment of grammar knowledge (Douglas, 2003). In addition to miscue analysis, retelling of the story, and student's preference of the story are assessed. Text difficulty is also gauged. A sample form to record students' performances is shown in Table 10.3.

To assess reading ability at the fluent reading stage, the following skills (depending on the text types) from Curtain and Dahlberg (2004, p. 86) can be assessed:

- Identifying the main idea and important details
- Predicting outcomes/anticipating events
- Identifying story sequence
- Summarizing and paraphrasing
- Discriminating between fact and opinion
- Recognizing cause and effect
- Recognizing important feelings and motivations of characters
- Identifying the conflict

The results of the reading assessment should be placed in students' portfolios.

TABLE 10.3
Coding for Japanese Reading Miscue Inventory

Student's name:	Date:	Story:
Miscue Codes		*Sample Miscues*
C (correction)		
AC (abandoning a correct form)		
UC (unsuccessful correction)		
$ (unintelligible)		
' (intonation)		
/ (unusual boundary)		
O (omission)		
S (substitution)		
A (additional information to the text)		
P (particle miscues)		
Retelling	Main ideas are included	Main ideas are not included
Story preference	Liked	Disliked
Difficulty of the story	Difficulty so-so	Easy

Writing is assessed using the following seven categories (Gibbons, 2002, p. 73):

- General comments: Is the overall meaning clear? Are the main ideas developed?
- Text type: What kind of text is this? Is this appropriate for the writer's purpose?
- Overall organization: Is the overall structural organization appropriate to the test type?
- Cohesion: Are the ideas linked with the appropriate connectives?
- Vocabulary: Is appropriate vocabulary used?
- Sentence grammar: Is this correct use of tense and conjugation, correct use of word order?
- Spelling: Is this accurate?

The weight assigned to each of the seven categories, however, will shift during the process of learning to write. In the early stages of writing, for example, assessment focuses on text types and overall organization, while looking at whether students can include main and supporting ideas in the appropriate order based on the text types. Through progress in writing toward the final drafts, assessment includes smaller units of language such as structure, vocabulary, and spelling. The records from these assessments are kept in students' portfolios together with their work.

Adjustment or Reestablishment of Objectives

When assessment results are analyzed and a mismatch between the student's needs and the curriculum objectives is found, or when the need to expand the instructional activities arises, instructional objectives should be adjusted, reestablished, or repeated by returning to Step 3 and by proceeding to Steps 4 and 5 as shown in Figure 10.1. The entire process of the curriculum design is repeated when new topics are introduced.

SUMMARY

Based on the theories and approaches applied to young JHL learner education, this chapter has presented a step-by-step process of curriculum design. The goals of the training are to develop extended discourse ability and academic language skills in JHL. Serious challenges for curriculum design are presented by the children's heterogeneous development in language proficiency, academic knowledge, and cognitive skills, all of which may require employing multiage and multilevel teaching. Curriculum needs to be as flexible as possible in planning and teaching strategies to accommodate varied needs of JHL young learners in these domains. In order to make learning meaningful for and relevant to students, the proposed curriculum employs a learner-centered approach and integration with academic subject areas. As Thomas and Collier (1995) argue, the content of the selected topics from various subject areas should be cognitively complex so it can be effective not only for language development, but also for the development of higher order cognitive skills and for increasing academic procedural and factual knowledge.

To make learning continuous, the curriculum integrates content standards and language arts standards. For implementation of learning activities, the proposed curriculum design utilizes an inquiry-based approach with hands-on activities, which enable students to comprehend cognitively complex ideas by concrete presentation. In addition, hands-on activities contribute to increasing children's motivation to learn Japanese at weekend schools. Some parents of the children who used to go to traditional JHL schools anecdotally mentioned that their children had become willing to go to school after they had changed their schools to the one that was implementing an inquiry-based approach with hands-on activities in their curriculum.

Based on these principles, this chapter has presented a process of curriculum design for Level 1 (grades K–1) with instructional objectives, some sample activities, and assessment tools. Assessment of students' learning is formative in its nature and should be conducted on a daily basis by using various types of assessment tools on various occasions, but guided by the same notion that the development of learning proceeds in the Zone of Proximal Development.

The proposed model of curriculum design is constructed particularly for weekend JHL schools. However, this model may serve the purposes of other HL schools, which are in similar situations as the JHL schools in terms of students' limited motivation to learn HL languages on weekend, and a lack of funding and human resources to develop appropriate curricula.

AUTHOR NOTE

Based on Douglas (2005), which presents a theoretical framework for curriculum design for young heritage learners of Japanese, this chapter focuses on application of those theories and demonstrates the process of curriculum design. Thus the two papers compliment each other and form a complete set of discussion about designing curriculum for young learners of Japanese as a heritage language. For the convenience of readers, this chapter provides a summary of the theories and approaches that are discussed in Douglas (2005). For detailed information, readers are referred to the original article.

ACKNOWLEDGMENT

I would like to express my sincere gratitude to Dr. Kimi Kondo-Brown and Dr. James Dean Brown, the editors of this book, for their thorough review and valuable feedback on my chapter and for their assistance at every stage of the publication process. I am fortunate that my manuscript is part of this book under their editorship. Any shortcomings or remaining errors are my sole responsibility.

APPENDIX A

Standards for "Life Sciences" and "Investigation and Experimentation"
(Kindergarten) taken from *The Science Content Standards for California Public Schools,
Kindergarten through Grade Twelve* (Asterisks are added for those used in the present project)

Life Sciences (California State Board of Education, 1998, p. 1)

2. Different types of plants and animals inhabit the Earth. As a basis for understanding this concept:
   a. *Students know* how to observe and describe similarities and differences in the appearance and behavior of plants and animals (e.g., seed-bearing plants, birds, fish, insects).
   b. *Students know* stories sometimes give plants and animals attributes they do not really have.
   c. *Students know* how to identify major structures of common plants and animals (e.g., stems, leaves, arms, wings, legs).

Investigation and Experimentation (California State Board of Education, 1998, p. 2)

4. Scientific progress is made by asking meaningful questions and conducting careful investigations. As a basis for understanding this concept and addressing the content in the other three strands, students should develop their own questions and perform investigations. Students will:
   a. *Observe common objects by using the five senses.
   b. *Describe the properties of common objects.
   c. Describe the relative position of objects by using one reference (e.g., above or below)
   d. *Compare and sort common objects by one physical attribute (e.g., color, shape, texture, size, weight).
   e. *Communicate observations orally and through drawings.

From *The Science Content Standards for California Public Schools, Kindergarten through Grade Twelve. California Department of Education* (California State Board of Education, 1998). Reprinted, by permission, California department of Education, CDE Press, 1430 N Street, Suite 3207, Sacramento, CA 95814.

APPENDIX B
Performance Indicators from Standard 1 in Learning
Standards for Native Language Arts
(Asterisks are added for those used in the present project)

Level 1 (grades K–1) (p. 21)

Listen in order to:
- Acquire information from native language nonfiction texts
- *Identify words and sentences in the home language on a chart
- *Follow directions involving a few steps
- Identify and respond to environmental sounds that provide information: for example, school bell or fire alarm
- *Identify similarities and differences in information about people, places, and events in the first language.

Speak in order to:
- Dictate information in the primary language
- *Report information briefly to peers and family adults
- Connect information from personal experiences to information from native language nonfiction texts
- *Retell more than one piece of information in sequence
- *Share observations from classroom, home, or community
- Ask questions in the first language to clarify topics, directions, and/or classroom routines
- *Respond verbally to questions and/or directions
- *Use appropriate visual aids to illustrate a word or concept when speaking in the native language to convey information.

Read in order to:
- Locate and use classroom and library media center resources, with assistance, to acquire information in the first language
- *Begin to collect data, facts, and ideas from informational texts with repetitive language and simple illustrations
- *Interpret information represented in pictures, illustrations, and simple charts and webs
- Recognize and interpret familiar signs and symbols from the environment: for example, labels on classroom furniture, equipments labels, and STOP signs
- Distinguish between native language texts with stories from those with information
- Draw on prior experience and cultural traditions to understand new data, facts, and ideas
- Use a picture dictionary as a resource for vocabulary in the primary language
- Select native language books, with teacher assistance, to meet informational needs.

Write in order to:
- Copy words, phrases, and sentences from primary language books, magazines, signs, charts, and own dictation
- Put own name on pictures, drawings, paintings, and written products
- Write data, facts, and ideas gathered from personal experience in the first language
- Use graphics (e.g. posters) to communicate information from personal experience
- Maintain, with teacher assistance, a portfolio of informational writings and drawings in the home language.

Taken from University of State of New York. (2004). *Teaching of language arts for limited English proficient/English language learners: Learning standards for native language arts.* New York: University of State of New York, p. 21.

APPENDIX C
Sample Instructional Materials for Level 1

Figure C1. Plant parts (Illustration of a sunflower in Figure C1: From
Rikabou no Kansatsu Jikken Kuizu (Gakken, 2000). Retrieved June, 2005,
from http://kids.gakken.co.jp/kagaku/rika/33-2.htm. Reprinted with
permission from Rikabou no Kansatsu Jikken Kuizu. Illustration of peanuts
in Figure C1: From Yonen no Kagaku (Gakken, 2002, p. 39). Reprinted with
permission from Gakken 4-nen no Kagaku 10 (2002, p. 39).

Figure C2.   Plant parts for flash cards and a card game. Thirteen pictures
of flowers, seeds, leaves, buds, and roots in Figures C2 and C5: From
Kyooikuyoo Gazoo Sozaishuu Saito, by Dokuritsu Gyoosei Hoojin Joohoo
Shori Suishin Kikoo. Retrieved June, 2005, from
http://www2.edu.ipa.go.jp/gz/. Reproduced by permission from
Dokuritsu Gyoosei Hoojin Joohoo Shori Suishin Kikoo
[Information-Technology Promotion Agency].

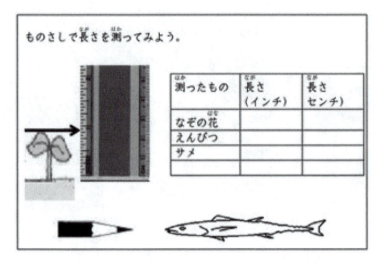

Figure C3.   Measurement.

ﾂ なぞの花   名前 _____

かだんのなぞの花が大きくなっています。長さを測って書いてください。葉
の数も数えて書いてください。絵も描いてください。

_____月_____日_____曜日_____時

長さ_____インチ、_____センチ

葉の数：_____まい
          ➢ 絵を描いてください

Figure C4.   Observation record.

✏ 宿題 名前＿＿＿＿＿＿ ＿月＿＿日 ＿曜日

1．あれれ。おなじなかまじゃないのがまじっていますよ。どれでしょう。
さがして0をつけてください。それから、どんななかまかを＿＿＿＿の上に書いてください。

a ＿＿＿＿＿＿ なかま＿＿＿＿＿＿＿＿

b. ＿＿＿＿＿＿ なかま＿＿＿＿＿＿＿＿

2．花を数えてください。

花は＿＿＿＿＿＿本あります。

3．家で,ものさしで長さを測りましょう。そして、例のように書いてください。

測ったもの	長さ(インチ)	長さ(センチ)
例 えんぴつ	6インチ	15.4センチ

例、ものさしで、えんぴつの長さを測りました。6インチでした。

ものさしで、えんぴつの長さを測りました。15.4センチでした。

＿＿＿＿＿で、＿＿＿＿＿の長さを測りました。＿＿＿＿＿でした。

＿＿＿＿＿で、＿＿＿＿＿の長さを測りました。＿＿＿＿＿でした。

===============保護者の方へ===============

今月は庭園に植えた「なぞの花」を観察します。今日は植物の成長、葉・花・芽などの名前、長さの測り方、同じグループとそうでないものというカテゴリーの勉強をしました。宿題は声をだして問題と答えを読むようご指導ください。

Figure C5. Homework sheet. This homework sheet lists sample tasks with a reduced number of the exercises due to space limitations.

APPENDIX D
Sample Assessment for Level 1

名前＿＿＿＿＿＿＿＿＿＿＿＿＿＿＿＿＿ ＿＿＿＿月＿＿＿＿＿＿ 日

まとめ

1. なぞの花を見て、ものさしで長さを測ってください。

インチ	センチ

2. ☐ なぞの花の絵を描いて、

どれが花で、どれが葉で、

どれが茎か書いてください。

2. 葉の数を数えて＿＿＿＿＿の上に書いてください。 ＿＿＿＿＿＿＿＿
＿＿

4. なぞの花は、どんなふうに大きくなりましたか。（日本語か英語で

書いてください）

なぞの花の勉強はどうでしたか。一つ選んで○をしてください。

1．とてもおもしろかった。　　2．おもしろかった。

3．まあまあおもしろかった。　　4．あまりおもしろくなかった。

REFERENCES

Bialystok, E. (2000). *Bilingualism in development: Language, literacy, and cognition.* Cambridge: Cambridge University.

Bingham, A. A., Dorta, P., McClaskey, M., & O'Keef, J. (1995). *Exploring the multiage classroom.* York, ME: Stenhouse.

Brinton, D. M., Snow, M. A., & Wesche, M. B. (1989). *Content-based second language instruction.* Boston, MA: Heinle & Heinle.

Brook, K. L. (1988). *Language maintenance in the Japanese American community in the Los Angeles area.* Unpublished master's thesis, California State University, Long Beach, Long Beach, California.

California State Board of Education. (1998). *Science content standards for California public schools.* Retrieved September, 2005 from http://www.cde.ca.gov/re/pn/fd/

Canadian Association for Japanese Language Education. (2000). *Oral proficiency assessment for bilingual children.* Toronto: Soleil.

Chao, T. H. (1997). Chinese heritage community language schools in the United States. *ERIC Clearinghouse on Languages and Linguistics Digest.* [ERIC Digest No. ED409744]. Retrieved March, 2004, from http://www.cal.org/resources/digest/chao0001.html

Chard, S. C. (1998). *The project approach: Making curriculum come alive.* New York: Scholastic.

Cole, M., John-Steiner, V., Scribner, S., & Sourberman, E. (1978). *L. S. Vygotsky: Mind and society: The development of higher psychological processes.* Cambridge, MA: Harvard University Press.

Cummins, J. (1992). Language proficiency, bilingualism, and academic achievement. In P. A. Richard-Amato & M. A. Snow (Eds.), *The multicultural classroom: Readings for content-area teachers* (pp. 16–26). New York: Longman.

Curdt-Christiansen X. (2002, October). Heritage languages: Using Canadian experiences. *Language Magazine,* 33–36.

Curtain, H., & Dahlberg, C. A. (2004). *Languages and children: Making the match.* New York: Pearson.

Dokuritsu Gyoosei Hoojin Joohoo Shori Suishin Kikoo. (2004). *Kyooikuyoo Gazoo Sozaishuu Saito.* Retrieved June, 2005, from http://www2.edu.ipa.go.jp/gz/.

Douglas, M. O. (2003, May). *Assessing Japanese heritage learners' needs from community service learning.* Paper presented at the meeting of the Six National Council of Less Commonly Taught Languages. Los Angeles, California.

Douglas, M. O. (2005). Pedagogical theories and approaches to teach young learners of Japanese as a heritage language. *Heritage Language Journal, 3.* Retrieved March 2006, from ftp: http://www.heritagelanguages.org/

Douglas, M., Kataoka, H., & Kishimoto, T. (2003). *Keishoogokoo to nihongo hoshuukoo niokeru gakushuusha no gengohaikei choosa* [Study on language background of the young learners of Japanese as a heritage language at heritage schools and hoshuukoo]. *Kokusai Kyooiku Hyooron, 1,* 1–13.

Echevarria, J. (1998). *Teaching language minority students in elementary schools* (Research Brief #1). Center for Research on Education, Diversity & Excellence. Retrieved February, 2004, from http://www.cal.org/crede/pubs/ResBrief1.htm

ERIC Digest. (1995). Integrating language and content: Lessons from immersion. *ERIC Clearinghouse on Languages and Linguistics.* [ERIC Digest No.ED390284]. Washington, DC. Retrieved June, 2005, from http://www.ericdigests.org/1996–3/immersion.htm

euerverger, G. (1989). Ethnographic vitality of Italo-Canadian students in integrated and non-integrated heritage language programs in Toronto. *Canadian Modern Language Review, 46,* 50–72.

Gakken (2000). *Rikaboo no kansatsu jikken kuizu.* Retrieved June, 2005, from http://kids. gakken.co.jp/kagaku/rika/33–2.htm.

Gambihir, S. (2001). Truly less commonly taught languages and heritage language learners in the United States. In J. K. Peyton, D. A. Ranard, & S. McGinnis (Eds.), *Heritage languages in*

America: Preserving a national resource (pp. 207–228). McHenry, IL: Center for Applied Linguistics and Delta Systems.

Garcia, E. E. (1991). *The education of linguistically and culturally diverse students: Effective instructional practices* (Report EPR 1). National Center for Research on Cultural Diversity and Second Language Learning. Office of Educational Research and Improvement. Retrieved June, 2005, from http://www.ncela.gwu.edu/pubs/ncrcdsll/epr1/

Giacone, M. C. (2000). Standards and the teaching of heritage languages. In J. B. Webb & B. L. Miller (Eds.), *Teaching heritage language learners: Voices from the classroom* (pp. 99–110). Yonkers, NY: American Council on the Teaching of Foreign Languages.

Gibbons, P. (2002). *Scaffolding language, scaffolding learning: Teaching second language learners in the mainstream classroom.* Portsmouth, NH: Heinemann.

Goodman, Y. M., Watson, D. J., & Burke, C. (1987). *Reading miscue inventory: Alternative procedures.* New York: Richard C. Owen.

Grabe, W. (1999). Developments in reading research and their implications for computer-adaptive reading assessment. *Studies in Language Testing, 10,* 11–48.

Graves, K. (2000). *Designing language courses.* Boston, MA: Heinle & Heinle.

Gutierrez, R., & Slavin, R. (1992). Achievement effects of the nongraded elementary school: A best evidence synthesis. *Review of Educational Research, 62*(4), 333–376.

Hampton, E., & Rodriguez, R. (2001). Inquiry science in bilingual classroom. *Bilingual Research Journal, 25,* 417–434.

Hart, C., Burts, D. C., & Charlesworth, R. (Eds.). (1997). *Integrated curriculum and developmentally appropriate practice: Birth to age eight.* New York: State University of New York.

He, A. W. (2001). The language of ambiguity: Practices in Chinese heritage language classes. *Discourse Studies, 3,* 75–96.

Joyce, B., & Weil, M. (1986). *Models of teaching* (3rd ed.). Englewood, NJ: Prentice Hall.

Katz, L. G., & Chard, S. C. (1997). *Engaging children's minds: The project approach.* Norwood, NJ: Ablex.

Kelly-Vance, L., Caster, A., & Ruane, A. (1997). Nongraded versus graded elementary schools: An analysis of achievement and social skills. *Alberta Journal of Educational Research, XLVI*(4), 372–390.

Kessler, C., & Quinn, M. E. (1987). ESL and science learning. In J. A. Crandall (Ed.), *ESL through content-area instruction: Mathematics, science, social studies* (pp. 55–88). Englewood Cliffs, NJ: Prentice Hall.

Kinsey, S. J. (2001). *Multiage grouping and academic achievement.* Champaign, IL: ERIC Clearinghouse on Elementary and Early Childhood Education [ERIC Digest No. ED448935]. Retrieved June, 2005, from http://www.ericdigests.org/2001–3/grouping.htm

Kondo, K. (1998). The paradox of US language policy and Japanese language education in Hawaii. *International Journal of Bilingual Education and Bilingualism, 1,* 47–64.

Krogh, S. L. (1997). How children develop and why it matters: The foundation for the developmentally appropriate integrated early childhood curriculum. In C. Hart, D. C. Burts, & R. Charlesworth (Eds.), *Integrated curriculum and developmentally appropriate practice: Birth to age eight* (pp. 29–50). New York: State University of New York.

Li, M. (2005). The role of parents in Chinese heritage language schools. *Bilingual Research Journal, 29.* Retrieved March, 2006, from http://brj.asu.edu/content/vol29_no1/abstracts.html

Liang, X., & Mohan, B. (2003). Dilemmas of cooperative learning and academic proficiency in two languages. *Journal of English for Academic Purposes, 2,* 35–51.

Lloyd, L. (1999). Multiage classes and high ability students. *Review of Educational Research, 69,* 187–212.

Met, M. (1999). Making connections. In J. K. Phillips (Ed.), *Foreign language standards: Linking research, theories, and practices* (pp. 137–164). Lincolnwood, IL: National Textbook Company.

Nakajima, K. (1989). *Kokugo kyookasho wa hitsuyooka: Nikkeijin shijo no rei* [Do we need Kokugo textbook?: In case of children of Japanese descent]. *Gekkan Nihongo, 8,* 28–29.

Nakajima, K. (1998). *Bairingaru kyooiku no hoohoo* [Methods of bilingual education]. Tokyo: Aruku.

Nakajima, K. (2002, March). *Keishoo nihongo gakushuusha no kanji shuutoku to kokugo kyookasho* [Acquisition of kanji by learners of Japanese as a heritage language and Kokugo text book]. Paper presented at the Association of Japanese Teachers Seminar. Washington, DC.

Nye, B., Cain, V. A., Saharias, J. B., Tollett, D. A., & Fulton, B. D. (1995, April). *Are multi-age/nongraded programs providing students with a quality education? Some answers from the school success study.* Paper presented at the fourth Annual National Create the Quality Schools Conference. Oklahoma City, OK.

Oketani, H. (1997a). Additive bilinguals: The case of post-war second-generation Japanese Canadian youths. *Bilingual Research Journal, 21,* 15–35.

Peyton, J. K., Ranard, D. A., & McGinnis, S. (Eds.). (2001). *Heritage languages in America.* McHenry, IL: Center for Applied Linguistics and Delta Systems.

Sasaki, M. (2001, March). *Japanese as a heritage language classes in Hawaii and Brazil: Their differences and similarities.* Paper presented at the annual meeting of the Association of Teachers of Japanese Seminar. Chicago, IL. Retrieved May, 2005, from http://www.japaneseteaching.org/ATJseminar/2001/sasaki.html

Schwartz, A. M. (2001). Preparing teachers to work with heritage language learners. In J. K. Payton, D. A. Ranard, & S. McGinnis (Eds.), *Heritage languages in America* (pp. 229–254). McHenry, IL: Center for Applied Linguistics and Delta Systems.

Seefeldt, C. (1997). Social studies in the developmentally appropriate integrated curriculum. In C. Hurt, D. C. Burts, & R. Charlesworth (Eds.), *Integrated curriculum and developmentally appropriate practice: Birth to age eight* (pp. 171–200). New York: State University of New York.

Short, D. (1993). Assessing integrated language and content instruction. *TESOL Quarterly, 27*(4), 627–656.

Shibata, S. (2000). Opening a Japanese Saturday school in a small town in the United States: Community collaboration to teach Japanese as a heritage language. *Bilingual Research Journal, 24*(4) [Online journal]. Retrieved December, 2000, from http://brj.asu.edu/

Siegel, S. Y. (2004). A case study of one Japanese heritage language program in Arizona. *Bilingual Research Journal, 28,* 123–134.

Snow, M. (1990). Instructional methodology in immersion foreign language education. In M. Amado, H. F. Padilla, & C. M. Valadez (Eds.), *Foreign language education: Issues and strategies* (pp. 156–171). Newbury Park, CA: Sage.

Sohn, S., & Merrill, C. (in press). The Korean/English dual language program in the Los Angles unified school district. In D. Brinton & O. Kagan (Eds.), *Heritage language acquisition: A new field emerging.* Mahwah, NJ: Lawrence Erlbaum Associates.

Solomon, J., & Rhodes, N. (1995). *Conceptualizing academic language.* (Report No. PR15). Washington, DC: National Center for Research on Cultural Diversity and Second Language Learning.

Spanos, G. (1989). On the integration of language and content instruction. *Annual Review of Applied Linguistics, 10,* 227–240.

Stone, S. J. (1996). *Creating multiage classroom.* Glenview, IL: Good Year Book.

Stryker, S. B., & Leaver, B. L. (1997). *Content-based instruction in foreign language education.* Washington, DC: Georgetown University.

Thomas, W. P., & Collier, V. P. (1995). *Language minority student achievement and program effectiveness: Research summary of study in progress* (California Association of Bilingual Education Newsletter 17.5). Covina, CA: California Association of Bilingual Education.

University of State of New York. (2004). *Teaching of language arts for limited English proficient/English language learners: Learning standards for native language arts.* Albany, NY: University of State of New York. Retrieved June, 2005, from http://www.emsc.nysed.gov/ciai/biling/resource/NLA/CH0intro.pdf

Usui, Y. (1996). *An ethnographic perspective on language shift, maintenance, and revitalization: Japanese in Hawaii.* Unpublished masters thesis University of Hawaii at M_noa, Honolulu, HI.

Valdés, G. (2001). Heritage language students: Profiles and possibilities. In J. K. Peyton, D. A. Ranard, & S. McGinnis (Eds.), *Heritage languages in America* (pp. 37–77). McHenry, IL: Center for Applied Linguistics and Delta Systems.

Wang, M. (2003). An ethnographic study of Chinese heritage language education and technological innovations. *Journal of National Council of Less Commonly Taught Languages, 1,* 69–94.

Webb, J. B. (2000). Introduction. In J. B. Webb & B. Miller (Eds.), *Teaching heritage language learners: Voices from the classroom* (pp. 3–13). Yonkers, NY: American Council on the Teaching of Foreign Languages.

Webb, J. B., & Miller, B. L. (Eds.). (2000). *Teaching heritage language learners: Voices from the classroom.* Yonkers, NY: American Council on the Teaching of Foreign Languages.

Yonen no Kagaku. (2002). *Piinattsu mame chishiki* [About Peanuts]. Tokyo: Gakken.

Chapter 11

Robust Learning for Chinese Heritage Learners: Motivation, Linguistics and Technology

Sue-mei Wu
Carnegie Mellon University

The phrase "Chinese Heritage Learners (CHL)" generally refers to students who have had exposure to Chinese outside the formal educational system, typically in their home or community (Wu, 2002).[1] At Carnegie Mellon University (CMU), CHL make up approximately one quarter of the students at the elementary level, one third of the students at the intermediate level, and two thirds of the students at the advanced level. Because of their diverse prior experiences with Chinese and the fact that their needs differ from those of Chinese True Beginners (CTB hereafter), CHL provide us with both an opportunity and a challenge. CMU has been working to develop and revise courses, teaching materials, and pedagogical approaches to meet the special

---

[1]Sometimes the term *False Beginners* or *Advanced Beginners* is used to describe the category of students described in this chapter as "Chinese Heritage Learners."

needs of our CHL. The Chinese program at CMU began with five students in a trial Elementary Chinese course in Fall, 1992. Since then, enrollment in Chinese courses has been growing steadily, and CMU now offers a full range of courses from Elementary Chinese to Advanced Chinese and Classical Chinese. Since 2005, CMU has offered a Chinese major. As CMU expanded the Chinese program, separate course tracks were offered for CHL and CTB (beginning in 2001), a practice that has been positively reported at other institutions (e.g., McGinnis, 1996; see also Kondo-Brown, this volume). The first CHL course started with one section of 10 students. As of Fall, 2005, there are two sections and around 30 students enrolled in the CHL course, which represents roughly a quarter of the total Elementary Chinese learners (there are six sections for CTB, with about 100–120 students enrolled).

This chapter examines the motivation and linguistic needs of the CHL, and then discusses how to blend a learner-centered approach, technology, and the 5Cs principles of the National Standards for Foreign Language Education—Communication, Cultures, Comparisons, Connections and Communities—in the pursuit of robust learning for CHL. The chapter draws heavily on my experiences as a CMU Chinese faculty member designing a curriculum and developing a textbook to provide effective and efficient Chinese instruction for CHL, doing research on CHL, discussing CHL instruction with language professionals, as well as multiple efforts to collect data from students to shed light on their specific goals for Chinese language study and feedback on our courses.

IDENTIFYING LEARNING NEEDS AND OBJECTIVES FOR CHINESE HERITAGE LEARNERS

Beginning with our investigation of the possibility of offering separate tracks for CHL and CTB, we have endeavored to better understand the needs of our CHL, and have collected data from several different sources. On the first day of class each semester, every student completes a questionnaire about the student's background and goals for the course. During the semester, each student also has several individual conferences with the instructor. One of the functions of these meetings is to ask students for feedback on whether the course is meeting their needs, and, if not, how it could be improved. Finally, at the end of the semester students fill out course evaluation forms, which give them an opportunity to express ways in which the course did or did not meet their needs.[2] In addition to these

---

[2]We conduct two Faculty Course Evaluations (FCE) at the end of each semester. One consists of a Department of Modern Languages survey, and the other is the CMU University FCE. Both are conducted anonymously, and the results are returned to the instructors after final

ongoing sources of information, the Chinese program at CMU also conducted a survey of all the students in our Chinese language program in 2003 in order to assess their backgrounds and needs. The observations in this section of the chapter are based on these sources of information, as well as personal interactions with students during my teaching career.

As Chinese learners, CHL and CTB share many similarities. However, it is instructive to focus on their differences here. Several differences are observed between CHL and CTB, and these differences go beyond the simple observation that CHL have more advanced Chinese language skills because of their prior exposure to the language. There are differences between CHL and CTB in their motivations, distribution of language skills, comfort level with language unknowns, approach to learning grammar, pronunciation difficulties, and cultural awareness. In this section, these differences are discussed in greater detail.

Different Motivations and Goals

In recent years, Chinese language instruction has been one of the fastest growing fields in foreign language education in the United States. According to a 2002 survey of foreign language enrollments in U.S. institutions of higher education, conducted by the Modern Language Association (MLA), Chinese, at 34,153 students enrolled nationwide, was in 2002 the seventh most commonly studied language in American colleges and universities, increasing 20% since the last MLA survey in 1998.[3]

A likely explanation for this trend is that students recognize that Chinese is becoming an important language on the world stage. China has recently emerged as a key player in the new global economy and become a member of the World Trade Organization (WTO). When asked to rank foreign languages in terms of their importance to international business, executives of the 1,000 largest U.S. companies ranked Chinese in first place (400 votes). Other major languages received less than half as many votes.[4] China has also become a popular destination for tourists, and the

---

course grades have been submitted. The following are some of the major items on the departmental survey: What was your purpose in taking this course? Was the workload appropriate? Did the course meet your goals? What did you like most and least about this course? How has this course increased or not increased your interest in the fields of language, language learning, or literary and cultural studies? Which features would you retain and which would you change? Overall quality of the course and overall quality of the instructor's teaching?

[3]Information is retrieved from http://clta.osu.edu/flyer/enrollment_stats.htm. The statistics were compiled on 18 February 2005 by Dr. Scott McGinnis, Academic Advisor for the Defense Language Institute, Washington Office.

[4]According to *Family Education Today*, September, 1998, Chinese received 400 votes, Spanish 170 votes, French 150 votes, Japanese 145 votes, and German 100 votes.

selection of Beijing, China as the host city for the 2008 Olympic Games should strengthen this trend. As reported by Chi (2005), another reflection of the increasing influence of Chinese is that College Board Advanced Placement courses in Chinese will be offered in 2006 and the Advanced Placement exam in Chinese will be held for the first time in May of 2007.

At CMU we have experienced the explosion in demand for Chinese language instruction firsthand, both for CHL and CTB. In addition to the career motivations just mentioned, which apply to both CHL and CTB, there are other motivations to study Chinese. For example, CHL and CTB are frequently motivated to study Chinese because of personal interests, such as Chinese martial arts or a Chinese friend. CHL may also be motivated to learn Chinese to make a connection with their heritage (see Weger-Guntharp, this volume). They wish to be able to communicate better with their parents, grandparents, or other relatives, and be more literate within their Chinese communities. Many CHL are also interested in learning more about Chinese traditions, literature, and legends. As pointed out by McGinnis (2005), the Chinese heritage language community has taken the lead in facilitating the preservation, promotion, and proliferation of Chinese language and culture in the past few years. Moreover, the U.S. government has recently begun to recognize immigrant and heritage languages as a national resource because heritage learners can meet the professional needs the country demands. Chinese is among the languages singled out for promotion. In summary, three general categories of motivations for Chinese study that typically apply to CHL have been identified: (a) long-term career goals, (b) seeking their heritage, and (c) personal interests.

Goals for learning Chinese may also differ between CHL and CTB. Learning the Chinese writing system provides a challenging task for both. According to the 2003 survey of our CMU Chinese students, literacy improvement, that is, being able to read and write better, ranks as the most important goal for CHL. Thus, it is crucial to provide CHL with ample opportunity to practice reading and writing. Although CHL ranked literacy improvement as their top goal, the vast majority of CHL wished to improve all four language skills (speaking, listening, reading, and writing). On the 2003 survey, CHL also expressed a desire to learn to read both simplified and traditional character forms because they recognize the benefits that knowing both forms can provide to their careers and personal lives. For CTB, on the other hand, although balanced development of the four skills is seen as ideal, speaking and listening usually rank as the most immediate goals they would like to achieve in their Chinese learning.

Chinese Heritage Learners Have More Uneven Distribution of Language Skills

Although they may naturally develop small differences in relative skills in the four language skill areas (speaking, listening, reading, and writing), CTB in general develop these skills together from the basic level as they progress through a language learning program. In contrast, Chinese programs frequently encounter CHL with a markedly uneven distribution among the skill areas. At the extremes are CHL who speak Mandarin fluently but are unable to read and write, or CHL who can read and write Chinese well but speak a dialect other than Mandarin. The CHL are a heterogeneous group, and besides these extremes, there are several other common language skill patterns that they exhibit based on where they have lived and studied and what languages are spoken in their homes and communities (see Weger-Guntharp, this volume). Some CHL came to the United States from mainland China or Taiwan when they were children. Some were born in the United States, but speak Chinese or Cantonese in their home. Others are from Cantonese-speaking areas such as Hong Kong. Some have had prior formal Chinese educational experiences, such as attending school for a few years before immigrating to the United States, attending Sunday Chinese school, or being taught at home by their parents or relatives. CHL language skills are extremely varied (Wu, 2002).

Chinese Heritage Learners Are More Comfortable With Language Unknowns

Another major difference between CHL and CTB is how they deal with the challenge of encountering language they do not fully understand. In courses designed for CTB, instructors know that, for most of the students, the course is their first exposure to Chinese, and for some of them, their first exposure to learning any foreign language. Consequently, as instructors create a Chinese environment in the classroom, they are usually careful to limit their language use to grammatical forms and vocabulary already studied by the students. If CTB encounter too much that they do not understand they may become frustrated. CHL, on the other hand, are experienced in dealing with multiple languages. They have usually been exposed to Chinese as spoken by native speakers and are accustomed to encountering language that they do not fully understand. So, whereas CTB may be frustrated by instructors who use language that is too advanced and that they haven't studied yet, CHL may be frustrated if they perceive that instructors are purposely choosing simpler language to conduct the class. They usually expect more "authentic" and "advanced" spoken expressions to be used in the classroom.

Differences in Their Approach to Grammar

Chinese heritage learners are frequently able to use intermediate-level grammar points and expressions during the very first few days of class, whereas CTB presumably are not. For example, during the first day of class, CHL are often able to use constructions such as the *ba* (把) construction, the directional complement (趨向補語), resultative complement 結果補語 *le* (了) indicating completed action, and the *shi ... de* (是...的) construction (see Table 11.1, for further explanations and examples for these grammar points). During the course of classroom activities in a class designed for CHL, the instructor may ask the students to open their textbooks with the sentence "*qing ba shu dakai*" (請把書打開 "Please open your books."). The instructor assumes that the use of the *ba* (把) construction is likely in the CHL's previous exposure to Chinese. However, in a course designed for CTB, the instructor would typically say "*qing dakai shu*" (請打開書 "Please open your books.") to avoid the *ba* (把) construction and make the sentence simpler.[5] The *ba* (把), *le* (了) and the directional and resultative complements are usually not introduced until the second semester of Elementary Chinese or later for CTB. Similarly, on the first day of class it is common for CHL to be able to talk about themselves and share their previous Chinese study background in Chinese. (Table 11.2 shows examples of typical heritage background questions for CHL.) Many of them are able to use the *shi ... de* (是...的) construction to talk about "when, where, and how" in their reports, whereas in the CTB classroom the *shi ... de* (是...的) construction is usually introduced later. Table 11.3 lists several grammatical constructions that CHL can typically use, as well as where they are introduced to CTB in two beginning Chinese textbooks.

Although CHL often can already use many intermediate-level grammatical structures, grammar points should be introduced clearly and systematically for both CHL and CTB students (Wu, 2005). CTB generally use the grammar presentation as a prescription for their own practice and use of the language, whereas CHL tend to use the grammar presentation as a means of organizing, confirming, and validating the language they already use. Although CHL can already use many grammatical structures in their oral communication, they generally don't know how and why these structures are used as they are. Thus, a systematic presentation of Chinese grammar for CHL is necessary and beneficial in the curriculum. Moreover, CHL may show dialectal influences in their Mandarin. For example, students with a Taiwanese dialectal background might use the *you (meiyou)* 有(沒有) *VP* expression, which

---

[5]For example, in the classroom expressions phase in our new textbooks, we use Example 1 for CTB and Example 2 for CHL: (1) 請打開書 ("Please open your book"); (2) 請把書打開 ("Please open your book"). Examples 1 and 2 are both imperative sentences meaning "Please open your book." However, Example 2 is more common among native speakers because the (把) construction is preferred in imperative sentences (commands).

Table 11.1

Grammatical Forms Commonly Mastered by CHL and Where
They Occur in a Curriculum for CTB

Explanations and examples for the *ba* construction, the directional complement, resultative complement, *le* indicating completed action, and the *shi...de* construction

- The (把) construction is known as a "disposal" construction. In other words, the (把) construction usually indicates that the object is disposed of, dealt with, or affected by the subject. For example, in the sentence *wo ba nawanfan chile* (我把那碗飯吃了) (I ate that bowl of rice.) the (把) indicates that due to the subject, "I," the bowl of rice has been eaten (disposed of).

- The directional complement 趨向補語 (DC) is a construction formed when a motion verb, such as *hui* (回 to return) is followed by a verb indicating direction, such as *lai* (來 to come) or *qu* 去 (to go) to give direction of a motion to the action. For example, in *huilai* 回來 (to return) the motion is towards the speaker, while in *huiqu* 回去 (to return), the motion is away from the speaker.

- The resultative complement 結果補語 indicates the result, extent or goal of an action. It is formed by attaching an adjective or a verb directly to another verb. For example, 打 (to hit) and 破 (broken) are attached to form 打破 (hit-broken).

- The 是...的 construction is used when an event has already occurred and we want to emphasize when, where, or how the event took place. For example,

A: 你是在哪兒學中文的? (Where did you learn Chinese?)

B: 我是在中國學中文的。(It was in China that I studied Chinese.)

The 是...的 construction may also be used without a time, place, or manner expression to emphasize what appears between 是 and 的. For example, sentence (1) below emphasizes that the subject studies Chinese literature, while sentence (2) is a simple statement.

(1)   我是學中國文學的。(It is Chinese Literature that I study.)

(2)   我學中國文學。(I study Chinese literature.).

- 了 is an aspect particle which is usually placed after a verb or at the end of a sentence to indicate the completion of an action. For example, 我吃了晚飯。and 我吃晚飯了 (I ate dinner already.)

---

is one of the typical markers of the Mandarin spoken in Taiwan.[6] Such dialectal influences and regional differences should be pointed out and explained to students because they come from many different areas of the Chinese speaking world. Indeed, having CHL from different dialect backgrounds in

---

[6]For example, consider the sentence "I ate dinner already." In standard Mandarin, 了 would probably be used to indicate the completion of the action of eating, and the Chinese sentence would be 我吃晚飯了。 However, in Taiwan Mandarin, it is common to express the fact that an action has been completed by adding 有 ("to have") before the main verb. So in Taiwan Mandarin, the sentence would be 我有吃晚飯。.

Table 11.2
Typical Heritage Background Questions for Chinese Heritage Students

---

The following dialogues are typical examples from the placement test or first day of class for CHL, when the instructor uses Chinese to ask about the students' heritage and background. These examples below illustrate how the 是...的 construction is commonly used by CHL in providing information about themselves:

(A: Instructor; B: CHL)

A: 你是什麼時候來美國的? (When was it that you came to the United States?)

B: 我是四歲的時候來美國的。 (It was when I was four years old that I came to the United States.)

A: 你爸爸媽媽是從哪兒來的? (Where was it that your parents came from?)

B: 我爸爸媽媽是從北京來的。 (It was Beijing that my parents came from.)

A: 你是怎麼學中文的? (How did you learn Chinese?)

B: 我是跟媽媽學中文的 [or 我是跟奶奶學的。 or 我是在中文學校學的。] (It was from my mom that I learned Chinese. [or It was from my Grandma that I learned Chinese. or It was from Chinese school that I learned Chinese.])

---

the class provides a good backdrop against which to introduce grammar differences among regional dialects. CHL usually find this an interesting topic, especially when they can discuss the differences with classmates from other dialect backgrounds. Such discussion also can help motivate students to be more aware of and interested in grammar.

Differences in Pronunciation Challenges

Differences are also found between CTB and CHL in the elements of standard Mandarin pronunciation that give them the most difficulty. Whereas CTB in the United States are usually speakers of English, the CHL are a more heterogeneous group. We encounter CHL whose Mandarin pronunciation is influenced by several different dialect backgrounds. CHL who speak Taiwanese, Shanghainese, or Cantonese, or who learned Mandarin from Mandarin speakers who speak these dialects, typically have an accent that features less retroflex (Ramsey, 1987, pp. 43–44), less differentiation of front nasal and back nasal finals, and very little vocabulary with the suffix -er (兒) (Ramsey, 1987, pp. 63–64). On the other hand, CHL from Northern China typically have a stronger retroflex, make a clear distinction between the front and back nasal finals, and have heavier use of the suffix "-er (兒)" (see Table 11.4, for explanations and examples of variations in Chinese pronunciation).

Pronunciation effects from the first language are also common for CTB. For example, CTB generally have trouble with the tone change of third tone

TABLE 11.3
Grammatical Forms Commonly Mastered by CHL and Where
They Occur in a Curriculum for CTB

Grammar Points: CHL can use orally and aurally during the first few days	Textbook for CTB [a]Chinese Link: Zhongwen Tiandi 中文天地	Textbook for CTB [b]Practical Chinese Reader
1. action completion le (了) (e.g., 我看了一本書 'I read one book.')	appears in Lesson 17 (late in 1st sem of Elem)	appears in Lesson 27 (late in 2nd sem of Elem)
2. *Ba* construction (把) (e.g., 我把我女朋友 帶來了 'I brought over my girl friend.')	appears in Lesson 20 (late in 2nd sem of Elem)	appears in Lesson 46 (late 2nd sem of Inter)
3. directional complement (e.g., 他從樓上跑下來 'He is running down from upstairs.')	appears in Lesson 20 (late in 2nd sem of Elem)	appears in Lesson 41 (late 2nd sem of Inter)
4. resultative complement (e.g., 我把鏡子打破了。 I broke the mirror.)	appears Lesson 1 of the 2nd year (early 1st sem of Inter)	appears in Lesson 38 (late 1st sem of Inter)
5. *shi....de* (是...的) (e.g., 我是坐公車來的 'It was by bus that I came over')	appears in Lesson 6 (middle 1st sem of Elem)	appears in Lesson 16 (2nd sem of Elem)

(sem = semester; Elem = Elementary Chinese; Inter = Intermediate Chinese)
[a]Wu, Sue-mei et al. (2005). Chinese Link: Zhongwen Tiandi. 中文天地 (Elementary Chinese). Upper Saddle River, NJ: Prentice Hal.
[b]Bejing Language Institute. (1988). Practical Chinese Reader. Boston: Cheng & Tsui Company.

and the half third tone, and Korean speakers have trouble with the fourth tone.[7] For CTB, the change of tones of *yi* (一) and *bu* (不) are also a challenge.[8] However, these tones and tone changes usually provide less trouble for CHL due to their experience in Chinese speaking environments.

---

[7]The level of pitch and the contour of a full third tone is 214 (1: low pitch; 2: mid-low; 3: middle; 4: mid-high; and 5: high pitch), first falling then rising. The special tone rule for third tone is that when it occurs alone, it is pronounced as full third tone. However, when two third tones co-occur, the first third tone will be pronounced as second tone. And when third tone is followed by first, second, fourth tone and most neutral tones, the third tone is pronounced as half third tone. Half third tone means the rising part of the tone is curtailed, resulting in a half finished third tone (i.e., the tone contour changes from 214 to 21).

[8]The conditional tone changes for *yi* (一) and *bu* 不 are summarized as follows: When yi 一 occurs alone, it is pronounced as first tone. When it is followed by fourth tone, it is pronounced as second tone. When it is followed by other tones, it pronounced as fourth tone. Similarly, 不 when it stands alone or is followed by first, second, or third tone, it is pronounced as fourth tone. However, when 不 is followed by a fourth tone, it is pronounced as second tone.

Table 11.4

Explanations and Examples of Variations in Chinese Pronunciation

The following are some explanations and examples of variations in Chinese pronunciation:

- The retroflex group of initials (zh ch sh r) in Mandarin Chinese are pronounced by curling the tip of the tongue to touch the hard palate, leaving a narrow opening between the tongue and roof of the mouth to allow some air to flow through. The following table shows the contrast between standard Mandarin pronunciation, common in the North of China, and pronunciation with less retroflex, as is common in the South of China.

Comparative Pronunciation of Retroflex Initials in Northern and Southern Mandarin

English / Chinese	Center / 中 initial with zh-	eat / 吃 initial with ch-	master / 師 initial with sh-	people / 人 initial with r-
Northern Mandarin (stronger retroflex)	[zhong]	[chi]	[shi]	[r]
Southern Mandarin (less retroflex)	less retroflex, sounds close to [zong]	less retroflex, sounds close to [ci]	less retroflex, sounds close to [si]	[r] with less retroflex

- In Mandarin, finals ending with "n" are called front nasals, and finals ending with 'ng' [ŋ] are called back nasals. In standard Mandarin a clear distinction is made between front and back nasal. The distinction is unclear or missing in Southern regions of China. For example, 生病 [shengbing], which has two back nasal finals, would frequently be pronounced as [shenbin] by people from the Southern regions of China.

- In Mandarin Chinese, the retroflex final -er (-兒) is attached to another final to form a retroflex final. The retroflex final -er sound occurs more frequently in the Northern part of China. See the following examples:

English	Flower	boy	play	branch	matter	stool
Northern Mandarin (commonly used with -er 兒)	花兒	男孩兒	玩兒	樹枝兒	事兒	板凳兒
Southern Mandarin (commonly used without -er)	花	男孩	玩	樹枝	事	板凳

Another important difference between CHL and CTB in relation to pronunciation is that CTB are encountering a new language and usually have no preconceived notions about correct pronunciation. Although most CTB experience some interference from their native language, they are motivated to work with the instructor to overcome their problem areas and achieve standard Mandarin pronunciation. CHL, on the other hand, may be more attached to their particular Mandarin accent. They have usually had more time to practice it, so it has become reinforced. Moreover, they may hear family members and friends using that accent and so feel that it sounds more natural than standard Mandarin pronunciation. They may fear that friends and family will find it strange if they begin speaking with a standard Mandarin accent.

Thus for both CHL and CTB, a brief introduction to Chinese dialects and their influences on Mandarin pronunciation should be provided to explain the reality of regional differences among Mandarin speakers. For CHL, it is desirable to explain the different features in their dialects and Mandarin and encourage them to respect their heritage dialect, yet point out to them the reality of regional differences and the importance of also learning standard Mandarin pronunciation.

The most commonly taught phonetic transliteration system for the U.S. college level is Pinyin. Studying Pinyin helps students pay attention to their Mandarin pronunciation, look up new words, type Chinese on a computer, and so on. Pinyin exercises should be consistently emphasized and practiced throughout the curriculum for both CHL and CTB (see Zhang & Davis, this volume).

Culture Awareness Versus Culture Acquisition

Cultural information should be integrated into the language curriculum in order to help students use the target language in an appropriate manner within the target culture. Providing information on Chinese culture and traditions in the CHL class will help reinforce students' awareness of their heritage. CHL are generally very interested in sharing their Chinese culture experiences and learning more about Chinese culture and traditions. On the other hand, in a class for CTB, what is presented in class is usually the students' first exposure to Chinese culture and traditions. They usually find it fresh, interesting, and sometimes "amazing." They are motivated to learn more about it and experience it firsthand.

Summary

Several of the special characteristics of CHL have just been discussed. It is important to keep these characteristics in mind when developing general goals for a curriculum that will meet the needs of CHL. For example, CHL have more heterogeneous language backgrounds and skills than CTB. For this reason, the curriculum should be designed to provide flexibility so that CHL can practice and improve their skills where they have relative weaknesses. CHL also place a strong emphasis on improving literacy skills. Thus, it is important to provide them with plenty of opportunities to practice reading and writing. Finally, CHL are familiar with Chinese culture and comfortable with language unknowns. They usually have significant language-learning resources in the form of Chinese speaking family members and communities with which they are motivated to make a connection. Thus, they should be challenged, and they should be given assignments that require them to connect with their family or community and share that connection in the classroom. These goals—flexibility, improving literacy skills, providing challenge, and building connections with a Chinese community—have guided the development of our CHL curriculum at CMU.

DEVELOPING ROBUST LEARNING OPPORTUNITIES FOR CHINESE HERITAGE LEARNERS

Adopted Pedagogical Approaches

Recognizing the motivational and linguistic differences between CHL and CTB, it is a challenge to design and develop a curriculum that can meet the needs of these two categories of learners. This section will present three pedagogical approaches that can be used to develop a program supporting robust learning for CHL: a learner-centered approach, the 5 Cs, and the use of technology.

Learner-Centered Approach

A learner-centered approach (Campbell & Kryszewska, 1992; Deller, 1989; Nunan, 1988; Tudor, 1997) is one that focuses on the capabilities and goals of the individual students (Wu, 1998; 2002; Wu & Haney, 2005). Instructors act as facilitators, guiding students and helping them to reach their language goals. The relationship between the instructor and students is one of teamwork, working together to reach common goals. Learners are active recipients of knowledge and often take a decision-making role in the learning process as they decide what to learn, how, and at what pace. Learners can also provide resources to the classroom environment by sharing elements of their background and experience, which is particularly relevant to the CHL classroom. Because students come from different backgrounds and have different goals, a learner-centered approach also aims to be adaptable, so that each student can learn what is most important to them. Because the heritage learners at CMU are a very diverse group of students, the learner-centered approach requires us to provide the flexibility necessary to meet their needs. This, in turn, helps to keep the students interested and motivated.

The 5 Cs

The 5 Cs principles are part of the National Standards for Foreign Language Learning developed by a coalition of national language organizations in the United States to guide language learning in the 21st century (*ACTFL,* 1999). The 5 Cs—*Communication, Cultures, Connections, Comparisons,* and *Communities*—represent five goal areas that encompass all the various reasons for studying a foreign language. As such, they are an excellent reference for designing and creating foreign language teaching materials. Indeed, these principles have been adopted by two new Chinese textbook series for the elementary to intermediate levels, called *Chinese Link: Zhongwen Tiandi* 中文天地 (for CTB; see Wu, S. et al., 2007; Wu, S. et al., 2005) and Zhongguo Yuan 中國緣: *Keeping Our Heritage* (for CHL; see Yu, Wu, & Zhao, 2005), which were designed and created by a group of CMU Chinese instructors. *Communication,* the heart of language learning, is the ability to communicate in languages other than English. To develop communicative competence in a foreign language, knowledge of vocabulary and syntactic patterns alone are insufficient; students should also develop knowledge and understanding of other *Cultures* (Wu, 2004). *Connections* are the ties to other disciplines and bodies of knowledge that are enabled by foreign language study. Through *Comparisons* and contrasts between languages and cultures students can become more aware of their own language and culture and more tolerant of the cultural differences inherent in diverse sociocultural contexts. Finally, these elements together enable students to participate in multilingual *Communities.*

Although the 5 Cs framework was developed with traditional foreign language students in mind, it is nevertheless an excellent guide for heritage language learner curricula as well. Communication is a primary goal for all language learners, whether they are true beginners or heritage learners, and heritage language learners can benefit from connections to other bodies of knowledge as much as true beginners. CHL are frequently highly motivated to learn more about Chinese culture and to make connections with their Chinese family or community. They are also in a unique position to make comparisons between languages and cultures, because they already have experience in more than one of each. Thus, we have adopted the 5 Cs as a guideline for developing our CHL curricula. It is reflected in our adoption of the communicative approach to language teaching (Canale & Swain, 1980), our focus on comparisons of cultural differences and regional differences in Chinese language, as well as several assignments that require students to make a connection to their Chinese family or community.

Use of Technology

Traditional classroom instruction has been the dominant paradigm for language learning because it facilitates two-way interactions between the instructor and students as well as instructor-managed student-to-student interactions. This emphasis on face-to-face communication, as well as the technical difficulty of simulating it, has caused many to dismiss online language learning as impractical. However, online language learning tools used as a supplement or complement to classroom instruction can provide many benefits to instructors and language learners (see also Zhang & Davis, this volume), among them the following:

- Multimedia: Online language learning tools can integrate text, audio, and video together into one package more efficiently than can classroom instruction. This allows for presentation of supporting cultural materials, as well as authentic examples of language use within a specific cultural context. For example, classroom study of greetings is usually accompanied by role-play with instructors and fellow students. In the online materials, study of greetings can be conveniently accompanied by video segments of native Chinese speakers greeting each other in varied social situations, providing realistic models for students to imitate.
- Interactive: Interactivity can be provided by giving individual feedback immediately after a student has finished an exercise. The student can also be provided with audio or video models to imitate and can practice imitating one or both sides of a particular interaction.
- Repeatable: Whereas classroom time is limited, online presentations and exercises can be repeated as many times as the student wishes. In addition, by using random pulls from pools of exercise questions, online exercises can be structured so that each instance of an exercise is unique. This provides challenge for the students and prevents boredom.
- Easily monitored: Whereas an instructor may spend long hours grading paper-based assignments, many online exercises can be graded automatically by the computer. Furthermore, the scores can be written to a database or sent to an instructor automatically via e-mail. The instructor can also monitor exercise use statistics to see how often students use the exercises and for how long they use them.
- Accessible: Online exercises can be accessed at any time of day from any computer that is connected to the Internet.
- Convenient: Through the browser interface, the student can access everything needed for the exercise. He or she need not go to a lab for tapes or videos, carry around paper exercises, and so on. In addition, time spent printing, distributing, and collecting paper-based exercises can be reduced or eliminated.
- Customized: Online materials can be tailored to an individual's specific needs in many ways that could not be done with traditional classroom exercises. For example, an individual online learner may choose which modules and exercises to pursue, whereas an individual in a classroom

must follow essentially the same curriculum as the other students. In addition, online exercises can store information on a particular student's progress, strengths, and weaknesses, and use that information to tailor the content and presentation of future exercises.

- Entertaining: Many of today's students are technologically proficient and enjoy using technology. Online exercises and activities may be interesting and entertaining for such students because of the multimedia content, the ability to control the experience, and the use of technology.

These advantages of online modules fit well with our goals for the CHL curriculum. First, one of the primary goals of CHL is to improve the students' literacy skills. Reading and writing exercises are easily adaptable to online presentation. Moreover, because computers are very good at dealing with text, many reading comprehension and character learning exercises can be graded automatically by the computer, providing immediate feedback to the student. Their repeatable nature allows students who are very motivated to improve their literacy to perform exercises over and over again for extra practice. This is particularly effective with online exercises that are dynamically generated so that each instance of the exercise is unique. Having the computer generate exercises and provide feedback is very important to literacy development because these are generally very time-consuming activities for instructors. Thus, in traditional classroom and paper-based exercises students' opportunities to get more practice may be limited by the resource of instructor time.

Online exercises also help provide some of the flexibility and adaptability that is important in dealing with the homogeneous nature of CHL. Online exercises can be customized to the individual student's needs by automatically adapting level of difficulty to the student's skill level. The repeatable nature of online exercises also means that students can perform the exercise as much as they need to in order to master the necessary skills.

Finally, online exercises can take advantage of online communities such as bulletin boards and chat rooms to further improve CHL literacy and help students make connections to the Chinese community.

BLENDING THESE APPROACHES FOR PROMOTING ROBUST LEARNING

This section provides a description of how these approaches may be blended into a Chinese curriculum to better meet the needs of CHL. Separate course tracks for CHL and CTB, textbook materials tailored to CHL, and the use of technology to provide online reading and writing modules are discussed.

Separate Course Offerings

It is not uncommon to see a beginning Chinese course with CTB and CHL mixed together in the same classroom (Christensen & Wu, 1993), even though Chinese instructors usually believe that these two groups present different needs and challenges and should be divided into separate courses (see Kondo-Brown, this volume). Empirical research has suggested that CHL learn better when they learn in a group of their peers, rather than a group of mixed CHL and CTB (Shen, 2003). Of course the availability of courses specifically designed for CHL depends on the availability of resources as well as demographics. Some institutions are lucky to be able to offer courses specifically catering to CHL, but many institutions lack resources and support for providing separate classes, and thus mix the CTB and CHL together in the beginning courses. In these cases, the curriculum is usually designed for the CTB. CHL who take beginning Chinese courses designed for CTB often feel that the pace is too slow and that the level of challenge is insufficient (see Weger-Guntharp, this volume). Our CMU course feedback forms also indicate that CHL feel that in mixed classes there are not enough reading and writing exercises to meet their needs. Such courses may be less attractive and motivating for the CHL.

As discussed earlier, since Fall, 2001 CMU has offered separate tracks for CTB and CHL (at the elementary and intermediate levels). Typically, approximately one quarter of the students at the elementary level and one third of the students at the intermediate level are in the heritage learner track.

The heritage track courses require faculty approval to register for the course. Each placement consists of an oral/aural interview with a faculty member followed by reading and writing exercises. The questions are based on our elementary- and intermediate-level test questions. Placement testing is generally conducted beginning in the pre-registration time for the next semester and continuing through the drop/add period. We also identify heritage learners in the regular Elementary Chinese sections who may be better suited to the heritage course.

The CHL at CMU can generally be divided into four main groups (Wu, 2002). Table 11.5 shows these groups and lists the course they are typically placed into. Please note that this table shows only the four main classifications of CHL at CMU. The table is not meant to be an exhaustive listing of categories of CHL There also can be much variability within each classification.

Textbook for Chinese Heritage Learners

Providing separate courses for CHL and CTB is a positive first step, but there are still other challenges in designing a curriculum that meets the needs of CHL One is that there is a lack of textbooks and other teaching

TABLE 11.5
Common Categories of CHL at CMU (Adapted from Wu, 2002, p. 90)

Background	Oral/Aural Skills	Reading/ Writing Skills	Typical Placement
U.S. born. Cantonese spoken at home	Minimal	Minimal	Elementary Chinese for CTB
Native Cantonese speakers from Hong Kong	Intermediate	Fluent	Advanced spoken Chinese
Mandarin spoken at home. Little or no formal education in Chinese	Basic to intermediate	Minimal	Elementary Chinese for CHL
Mandarin spoken at home. Some formal education in Chinese	Intermediate	Ranging from basic to intermediate	Regular intermediate Chinese

materials designed specifically for CHL. Because of this, Chinese language programs usually use textbooks designed for CTB in their CHL courses and then develop their own supplementary materials in an attempt to address the shortcomings of the CTB materials. The effort required to adapt materials and provide supplementary materials can be very time-consuming.

The few available textbooks designed for CHL usually focus on reading and writing skills. Their content is usually based on Chinese stories, mythology, and traditions. The vocabulary and expressions that occur in these types of content are useful for helping CHL learn to read and write, but they are usually not very useful in helping CHL improve their oral communication skills. Moreover, the grammar points usually lack systematic treatment. Although improving reading and writing skills is an important goal for many CHL, a textbook designed for CHL should help develop their communicative competence in all of the four basic skills of listening, speaking, reading, and writing the Chinese language, as well as their awareness of Chinese culture. Reading and writing should be relatively emphasized, but developing all four skills is important. Our survey of Chinese students at CMU indicated that although the most important goal for CHL was improving their literacy skills, they also wished to improve in the other language skills as well. In addition, it is important to realize that although CHL usually begin their study with significant speaking and listening skills, they have usually not reached so advanced a level that they cannot benefit from systematic training in speaking and listening. The textbook should also provide systematic presentation of the commonly used grammar points, take a functional view of language, be content-based, and have task-rich activities that facilitate communicative language learning. (Note: The functional view contrasts with the structural view of language, which is traditionally associated with the Grammar-Translation method of language learning.)

Because of the lack of suitable materials for CHL, I am working with several Chinese instructors at CMU to develop a new textbook called *Zhongguo Yuan* 中國緣: *Keeping Our Heritage* that is specifically designed for CHL. *Zhongguo Yuan* 中國緣: *Keeping Our Heritage* attempts to provide a practical, learner-centered, and enjoyable language and culture learning experience for beginning to intermediate CHL, as well as an efficient and comprehensive teaching resource for instructors. The topics start from tasks in everyday life and gradually move to more complicated issues in the context of social occasions. The linguistic elements are also systematically introduced, progressing from simple language students need in their everyday life to more sophisticated language phenomena that are required in order for them to function in various social environments.

Activities and Exercises

In the courses designed for CHL, we acknowledge that the students have prior knowledge, not just of Chinese language, but also Chinese culture. Because of this, the instructors feel comfortable giving CHL challenging assignments and expecting them to perform at a high level. The following are descriptions of some of the types of activities and assignments that may be used to challenge CHL.

As discussed earlier, many CHL are motivated to learn Chinese in order to communicate with family members and relatives, and to connect to part of their heritage. In addition, CHL, who have varied first-hand experiences with Chinese culture, often find explorations of Chinese culture especially interesting. Because of these motivations, several activities that require students to make connections with Chinese communities and Chinese culture are utilized. Following readings on some aspect of Chinese culture, students are sometimes required to interview native speakers and discuss the topic of the reading. For example, if the reading is about a particular Chinese holiday, students might ask the native speaker their impressions of the holiday, how they celebrate it, and so on. Many use this opportunity to interview their grandparents or relatives in China or Taiwan. Students are also given the opportunity to reflect on their Chinese experience and to share it with their classmates. The students are asked to write short essays on topics related to their Chinese experience, such as their family, friends, experiences studying Chinese, and so on. As with the culture readings, some of these short essays require students to conduct an interview with a native speaker. Language learning is, after all, about communication, and it makes the course more effective if the learners are given activities where they can enjoy communicating with each other, with family members, or with other members of the Chinese community.

Another activity that may be used to increase literacy is to require the students to keep a Chinese journal in which they record at least three entries each week. This activity helps students learn to write about topics that are important or interesting to them.

Because of the large amount of writing done by CHL, the Chinese program provides native Chinese writing assistants with whom the students can make appointments for extra help or targeted help. Students can also use this time to ask the writing assistants for help expressing ideas in their journals. The instructors also conduct several individual interviews with each student throughout the semester during which students have an opportunity to ask questions about their writing assignments.

CHL are encouraged to be able to read both simplified and traditional characters, and readings are provided in both forms. However, for writing assignments the student can choose to write in either simplified or traditional characters according to their preference.

Because CHL come from different dialect groups, their Mandarin pronunciation is usually influenced by their dialect. The acquisition of standard pronunciation is stressed, and pronunciation exercises are consistently emphasized throughout the entire text and classroom activities. Although standard Mandarin pronunciation is emphasized, we make an effort to point out regional differences in pronunciation and usage.

Other components that we incorporate for CHL at the early stages include an introduction to how to use a dictionary to look up unknown characters; information about the special characteristics of Chinese such as tones, importance of word order, pictographic characters, and the language's history and development; and basic information on the Chinese writing system such as the common components, radicals, and the structure of Chinese characters.

Technology

Course Web Sites and Management. Since Fall, 2000, most of Chinese courses at CMU have their own course Web sites (Wu, 2001). The course Web sites include course information, sound files for the materials, online listening, reading, and vocabulary exercises, online sign-up sheets for speaking and writing assistant activities, event photos, and information on the Chinese minor and study abroad. We have also implemented the course management system "Blackboard" into Chinese courses for sending e-mails, posting announcements, discussion boards, homework and project submission, online grading, and so on.

Online Exercises.   At CMU, we have attempted to take advantage of new technologies and implement them in the heritage curriculum. In particular, aspects of technology that help us to apply the learner-centered approach by giving more individualized corrections and attention to the learners are favored. We have developed several online modules that take advantage of technology in order to incorporate the 5 Cs principles with a learner-centered, customizable approach to fit the needs of individual students. These modules help learners develop their communicative competence in Chinese language, improve their understanding of Chinese culture, compare aspects of different cultures, and connect to other sources of knowledge through participation in multilingual communities. For details about the modules, please see Wu (2001, 2002, 2004; Wu & Haney, 2005; see also Table 11.6 for URLs of the modules).

These online interactive reading and writing modules are designed with the goal of developing language and cultural literacy skills in CHL who have basic to intermediate oral/aural skills in Chinese, but with minimal reading and writing skills. Content includes original essays, photos, and audio and video segments. The content is presented according to a logical pedagogical strategy and supplemented by exercises that are interactive, personalized, and innovative. The language content is keyed to the 800 most commonly used characters, and the foundation grammatical patterns usually taught through intermediate Chinese. From a pedagogical standpoint, this focus ensures that the modules contain a full set of the building blocks that students will need in order to learn Chinese well. In addition to its pedagogical function, the indexing of the exercises to the commonly used characters and grammatical patterns will enable us to collect detailed data to be used to research the learning patterns and literacy skills of our heritage students. This is an advantage of computer-based exercises that has yet to be utilized to its full potential; instructors can keep track of when students use the exercises, which vocabulary items and sentence patterns give them trouble, the rate of their improvement, and other similar data. These data can, in turn, be used to help us design more effective learning experiences.

INSTRUCTIONAL SAMPLE

An instructional sample is provided in the following section to further demonstrate how motivation, linguistics, and technology may be blended to provide opportunities for robust learning for CHL. As an illustration, consider a chapter about going to a Chinese restaurant to eat. This chapter is typically completed in 1 week. Class meets 4 days a week for 50 minutes each day. The instructor acts as a facilitator to help students in the class activities.

Table 11.6

URLs of Online Modules for the Chinese Program at Carnegie Mellon University

Since Fall 2000, I have received several grants to support the development of online modules for our Chinese program. Their URLs are listed below:

The Chinese Wedding Banquet: An Online Module for Teaching Chinese Language, Culture and Social Engagement.
http://ml.hss.cmu.edu/courses/suemei/banquet/banquet.html

Language and Culture Literacy Development for the Heritage Learners: An Online Interactive Reading and Writing Modules.
http://ml.hss.cmu.edu/courses/suemei/Moon/

Internet café: Online Modules for Advanced Chinese Learners
http://ml.hss.cmu.edu/courses/suemei/china/cafe/cafe.html

A Changing China: Online Modules for Chinese Language and Culture Acquisition.
http://ml.hss.cmu.edu/courses/suemei/china/index.html

Online Chinese Exercise Modules.
http://ml.hss.cmu.edu/courses/suemei/examples2.htm

At the beginning of the chapter, the instructor discusses with students the goals of the chapter, which are to introduce various Chinese dishes, help students learn how to order at a restaurant, and introduce the importance of food in Chinese culture.

Next, the class proceeds to some "warm-up" activities. The instructor first raises students' interest and motivation by showing them some visual aids, such as Chinese cookbooks or photos of Chinese dishes, accompanied by some questions. The questions begin with simple personal experiences, such as what dishes students have tried in their homes, who can cook, which restaurants are good, and favorite Chinese foods. These questions and activities then proceed to more social and cultural connections and comparisons such as the differences between the Western and Chinese (or Asian) food culture, Chinese foods associated with certain festivals, and so on. During these discussions, the instructor also writes on the board some of the new vocabulary that will be introduced in the chapter or other interesting vocabulary items that occur naturally in the discussion.

After the warm-up activities, core vocabulary items that appear in the main text of the chapter are introduced. Other supplementary vocabulary items are also introduced, such as common Chinese dishes for example. Traditional and simplified character forms are presented. Students take turns pronouncing the items and using the items to make sentences. This checks their preparation as well as their familiarity with the proper usage of the items. The instructor repeats the sentence each student produces to make sure all the students understand it. This also helps draw students' attention in class. Students feel they all have made a contribution to the class activities.

Following the introduction of core and supplementary vocabulary items, important sentence patterns from the main text are introduced and practiced. The sentence patterns are practiced by pairs of students in a dialogue format. This activity helps students to be familiar with the phrases before they jump into the main text. It helps provide a systematic and gradual transition from smaller units, such as vocabulary items, to phrases and sentences before encountering the situation dialogue.

The main text is a dialogue between two Chinese people eating out at a Chinese restaurant. They discuss what they would like to eat and then order their dishes from the server. The instructor asks students to read the dialogue aloud and checks comprehension with questions. Sometimes the instructor asks students to raise a few questions and assigns others to answer them in order to provide an alternative to instructor–student interaction. Then the students are assigned to groups to perform the dialogue. Some perform the dialogue, and others perform it with slight changes, such as in the dishes ordered, and so on. After this the instructor will lead a reading of the main text again to reinforce good pronunciation and intonation.

Core grammar points from the chapter are explained with ample examples. In-class exercises such as character exercises, grammar exercises and communicative activities are conducted next. For characters, the instructor emphasizes the radical and the character's formation so that students can analyze the characters as well as build up their vocabulary capacity. As for the communicative activities, some authentic Chinese menus from Chinese restaurants near campus are distributed. Students are then guided to act out eating in a Chinese restaurant, ordering take out, consulting with friends for advice on where to take your Chinese friend to dinner, and so on. Homework assignments include listening, character practice, grammar exercises, and situational translation. Students are also asked to write an essay about inviting friends to eat at a restaurant.

As a secondary reading, a short essay introducing the Chinese food culture is provided for cultural knowledge, awareness, comparison, and discussion.

During this chapter students are also asked to utilize an online cultural literacy module, the mid-Autumn festival module (http://ml.hss.cmu. edu/courses/suemei/Moon/). Students do the reading and writing exercises in the module. They also use the "How to make moon cakes" page as an example of Chinese food culture and tradition and how to write recipes. After studying that page, students are required to write an essay and do a presentation on a recipe.

The mid-Autumn festival module begins with an introductory essay followed by the main essay, which is designed to provide students with a self-learning activity. Selected vocabulary items in the essay are hyper-linked to glosses of their pronunciation and meaning, so that students can do close reading without taking time to look up characters in the dictionary. The essay is supplemented by related pictures and has links to sound files of native speakers reading the essay. Because CHL typically have fairly good oral and aural skills, they can use this resource to help understand the reading. A secondary function of the sound files is designed to reinforce standard Mandarin pronunciation.

Interactive and personalized reading comprehension, grammar, and vocabulary exercises are provided so that students can review and test their mastery of the language skills highlighted in the readings. The correct answers and some feedback are provided immediately to the students after they complete the exercises. The results of the exercise are submitted to the instructor automatically via e-mail.

This mid-Autumn festival module provides students with a concentrated learning experience on Chinese food and its role in Chinese traditions and festivals. Because CHL have usually been exposed to the Mid-Autumn festival, have tasted moon cakes (the traditional food of the mid-Autumn festival), and have heard the legends behind the festival, the module provides a good way to connect their heritage experience with reading, presentation, and comprehension. The module provides a variety of writing tasks. For example, students are asked to keep a journal about the Chinese mid-Autumn festival and summarize the readings or write a short reaction essay. Written assignments are entered in a form on the Web site and collected in a database. From there, they can be e-mailed to the instructor. They will also be used to analyze how the language skills of the CHL are progressing.

An online bulletin board system is provided so that students can discuss and share their opinions and experiences on the Mid-Autumn festival, eating moon cakes, and Chinese food culture.

ASSESSMENT MATERIALS AND PROCEDURES

A multifaceted approach to the assessment of CHL is most effective. It provides an understanding of the student's overall progress in learning the language, rather than simply their performance on a few tests. The following are the components that are used to assess CHL performance.

- *Attendance*. Class attendance and participation are very important in a language course. Students are required to attend all scheduled classes and take an active part in classroom activities. Attendance and performance are recorded every day.

- *Character quizzes*: In order to help the CHL gradually advance their literacy skills, character quizzes are given. The main format for character quizzes is that the instructor dictates phrases and sentences and the students write them out. The phrases and sentences consist of previously studied vocabulary items mixed with 8 to 10 new characters or vocabulary items. They are held in almost every class session. This helps encourage students to develop the habit of learning and reviewing characters daily. Another format for the character quiz requires students to analyze a character by providing the character's pronunciation and meaning, radical and its meaning, total number of strokes, and stroke order (demonstrated by writing the character progressively).
- *Assignments*: Homework is assigned each week for each lesson. A homework assignment for each lesson is included in the main textbook. A typical assignment is three to four pages long, including space for students to write their responses. Homework activities are divided among listening, reading comprehension, grammar exercises, and essay writing. Reading and writing exercises make up a significant portion of the assignments. There are also regular journal writings assigned (usually three entries per week).
- *Culture Research & Presentation*: Students do research on an aspect of Chinese culture of their choosing and then present the results of their research to the class. As part of the research, students are required to conduct an interview with a native Chinese speaker about the topic. Before the presentation, students prepare an outline of their presentation in Chinese, as well as a list of new vocabulary items they will use in their presentation. These are distributed to their classmates prior to the presentation.
- *Interviews:* At least one individual student–instructor interview is conducted before mid-semester, and another before the final. Each student usually has 25–30 minutes. The interview usually includes an achievement test (50%, 8–10 minutes), proficiency test (50%, 8–10 minutes) and time for feedback (8–10 minutes). The achievement test assesses students' comprehension of the textbook. Students are asked to write out a summary for the assigned reading, and then report their summary followed by some question-answer activities with the instructor. The proficiency test also consists of reading, summarizing, and question and answer, but the text is a new short essay on a familiar topic. Students are given 2 minutes to read the essay, after which they are asked to summarize and then answer questions from the instructor. During the feedback portion of the interview, the instructor gives students feedback on their performance during the interview and in the course, and asks students for feedback on the course.

- *Tests:* Tests are administered approximately every 2 weeks. The tests emphasize character writing and recognition, grammar exercises, reading comprehension, and short essay writing. It takes students about an hour to complete the test in class.
- *Final exam:* The final exam is divided into two parts, an in-class written test and an oral presentation. The written test is similar to the lesson tests, but is longer and more comprehensive.

The oral presentation requires students to write a long essay and present it in class. The essay passes through several draft cycles, with feedback from instructors or native writing assistants at each stage. In the essay, students need to incorporate at least 10 grammar points that they have studied. The essays are 400–600 characters in length. Students also need to prepare new character lists and handouts for the audience, as well as several thought questions (based on their essay) that they can ask the audience. After the presentation of the essay, the presenter acts as a discussion leader for a question and answer session with the audience, including the instructor.

In addition to this multifaceted approach to assessing student performance, students are provided information about and encouraged to take standardized tests, such as the *Hanyu Shuiping Kaoshi* (HSK) 漢語水平考試, a standardized Chinese proficiency test developed by the HSK Center of Beijing Language and Culture University. The purpose of the HSK is to assess the Chinese proficiency of non-native speakers of Mandarin Chinese. Foreign students who wish to attend university or graduate school in China must score above a certain threshold score on the HSK in order to be admitted. Test results are also frequently requested as part of job applications for positions in China.

CONCLUSION

This chapter has touched on some aspects of blending technology, motivation, and linguistics to create robust learning for CHL, with a focus on the Elementary level of CHL. It has demonstrated that, due to the special features of CHL, the incorporation of these three aspects should provide an effective, innovative, and interesting learning environment for the CHL. The incorporation of the online module and exercises demonstrates our attempt to take advantage of technology to help deliver the CHL curriculum more effectively, efficiently, and enjoyably.

There are surely many more areas to investigate in future studies and research on CHL, including linguistic differences, learning strategies, cognitive learning of CHL, e-learning for CHL, comparison with other languages, and so on. I look forward to the work and contributions of other language professionals and researchers in these areas. It is hoped that this chapter will provide and invite at least a few points for criticism and discussion from other language professionals.

REFERENCES

American Council on the Teaching of Foreign Languages (ACTFL). (1999). *Standards for foreign language learning in the 21st century including Chinese, Classical Languages, French, German, Italian, Japanese, Portuguese, Russian, and Spanish.* Lawrence, KS: Allen.

Campbell, C., & Kryszewska, H. (1992). *Learner-based teaching.* Oxford: Oxford University.

Canale, M., & Swain, M. (1980). Theoretical bases of communicative approaches to second language teaching and testing. *Applied Linguistics, 1*(1), 1–47.

Chi, R. T.-L. (2005). *Tuidong meiguo AP zhongwen kecheng yu zhongxue zhongwen jiaoyu suo mianlin de tiaozhan* [The challenges facing the promotion of the Chinese AP curriculum and high school Chinese education]. In S. Teng (Ed.), *Proceedings of the Conference on Operational Strategies and Pedagogy for Chinese Language Programs in the 21ˢᵗ Century: An International Symposium* (pp. 325–328). Taipei: Mandarin Training Center, National Taiwan Normal University.

Christensen, M., & Wu, X. (1993). An individualized approach for teaching false beginners. *JCLTA, 28*(2), 91–100.

Deller, S. (1989). *Lessons from the learner.* London: Longman.

McGinnis, S. (1996). Teaching Chinese to the Chinese: The development of an assessment and instructional model. In J. E. Liskin-Gasparro (Ed.), *Patterns and policies: The changing demographics of foreign language instruction.* (pp. 107–121). Boston, MA: Heinle and Heinle.

McGinnis, S. (2005). From mirror to compass: Chinese as a heritage language education in the United States. *Reflecting on the future of Chinese language pedagogy: Honoring the 40-year distinguished career of Professor George Chih-ch'ao Chao.* Taipei: Shihta Book.

Nunan, D. (1988). *Learner-centered curriculum design.* Cambridge: Cambridge University.

Ramsey, R. S. (1987). *The languages of China.* Princeton, NJ: Princeton University.

Shen, H. H. (2003). A Comparison of written Chinese achievement among heritage learners in homogeneous and heterogeneous groups. *Foreign Language Annals, 36*(2), 258–266.

Tudor, I. (1997). *Learner-centeredness as language education.* Cambridge: Cambridge University.

Webb, J. B., & Miller, B. L. (Eds.). (2000). *Teaching heritage language learners: Voices from the classroom.* Yonkers, NY: American Council on the Teaching of Foreign Languages (ACTFL).

Wu, S. (1998). Designing a Chinese newspaper reading course. *Journal of the Chinese Language Teachers Association, 33*(3), 25–38.

Wu, S. (2001). The design and application of Chinese course Web sites and online exercises. In S. Hsin (Ed.), *Proceedings of the International Conference on Internet Chinese Education* (ICICE 2001; pp. 20–24). Taipei: Global Chinese Language and Culture Center Online.

Wu, S. (2002). Integrating learner-centered and technology strategies for heritage students. In the W. Li & C. Lee (Eds.), *Proceedings of the Southeast Conference on Chinese Language Teaching* (SCCLT; pp. 90–95). Chapel Hill, NC: University of North Carolina.

Wu, S. (2004). Integrating webpages into a language and culture curriculum: Issues, techniques, and examples. In D. Xu & P. Zhang (Eds.), *Proceedings of the Third International Conference and Workshops on Technology and Chinese Language Teaching* (TCTC-3; pp. 24–30). New York: Columbia University.

Wu, S. (2005). Teaching the disposal construction in the context of pedagogical grammar and content-based instruction. In S. Teng (Ed.), *Proceedings of the Conference on the Operational*

Strategies and Pedagogy for Chinese Language Programs in the 21ˢᵗ Century: An international symposium (pp. 374–378). Taipei: Mandarin Training Center, National Taiwan Normal University.

Wu, S., & Haney, M. (2005). Robust Chinese e-learning: Integrating the 5Cs principles with content and technology. In S. Hsin (Ed.), *Proceedings of the 4th International Conference on Internet Chinese Education* (ICICE 2005; pp. 541–548). Taipei: Overseas Chinese Affairs Commission (OCAC).

Wu, S., Yu, Y., Zhang, Y., & Tian, W. (2005). *Chinese Link: Zhongwen Tiandi* 中文天地 *(Elementary Chinese)*. Upper Saddle River, NJ: Prentice Hall.

Wu, S., Yu, Y., & Zhang, Y. (2007). *Chinese Link: Zhongwen Tiandi* 中文天地 *(Intermediate Chinese)*. Upper Saddle River, NJ: Prentice Hall.

Yu, Y., Wu, S., & Zhao, R. (2005). *Zhongguo Yuan* 中國緣: *Keeping Our Heritage*. Unpublished manuscript.

Chapter 12

Online Chat for Heritage Learners of Chinese

De Zhang
Niki Davis
Iowa State University

This chapter provides a description of an action-oriented case study of the ways synchronous chat may be valuable to heritage learners of Chinese. It begins by reviewing research on the teaching of foreign or second languages to heritage language (HL) learners and the introduction of technology to facilitate learning. An introduction to the Chinese language sound and writing systems is provided because it is necessary for readers to understand how the Chinese language is written using computers. Similarly, the theoretical underpinning for the pedagogic design is briefly introduced and linked to the literature.

Heritage language acquisition and the education of HL learners are emerging as increasingly important fields, especially at the college level (Kondo-Brown, 2003). From the perspective of the language educators in the United States, HLs are associated with an endangered indigenous or immigrant language. An HL learner "is raised in a home where a non-English language is spoken" and "speaks or merely understands the language" and "is to some degree bilingual in the language and in English" (Valdés, 2001, p. 1). A substantial number of Chinese language learners at all levels are HL students from families where one Chinese language/dialect is spoken (Moore, Walton & Lambert, 1992). With the increasing number of Chinese immigrant families, examining how to educate HL learners effectively has been considered a priority issue and a new challenge in the field of Chinese as a foreign language (CFL) (Schrier & Everson, 2000; Wang, 1996).

Currently, studies on educating HL learners using technology integration in the classroom are hard to find. Literature on the use of technology in Chinese language curriculum is not rich. In the field of CFL in the United States, grammar translation and audio-lingualism have been widely used for some time (Chi, 1996). The field of teaching Chinese as a foreign language has experienced severe challenges, all of which are very common in the whole foreign language education area, especially in the context of higher education in the United States: a very weak tradition of language pedagogy research, out-of-date teaching approaches, and instructors are not always up to date on current practices (Chi, 1996; Chu, 1996). By studying integrating technology in the Chinese language classroom and by completing research on the impact of the technology in the classroom, we aim to present solutions to the existing problems and bring some pedagogical innovations to the field.

INTRODUCTION TO THE CHINESE LANGUAGE SOUND AND WRITING SYSTEMS

The Chinese language has been considered very difficult to learn by native speakers of other languages, especially European languages, mainly because of its complicated language writing systems and numerous dialects. Chinese language teachers are believed to face a challenge more complex than those facing teachers of any other foreign language in the American educational system (Moore, Walton, & Lambert, 1992).

Pinyin is the Chinese sound/phonetics system. Pinyin symbols are Romanized letters, but they do not necessarily have the same pronunciations as the Romanized letters. Therefore, in learning the Chinese language, the learners appear to deal with two separate language systems: the sound system and the writing system. Learning to write Chinese characters by hand, stroke by stroke, is very time consuming and difficult for learners because the correct order and number of the strokes in each Chinese character must be mastered. The difficulty in learning to handwrite Chinese characters has been reported as the greatest hindrance to all Chinese second/foreign-language learners, including HL learners (Xu & Jen, 2005).

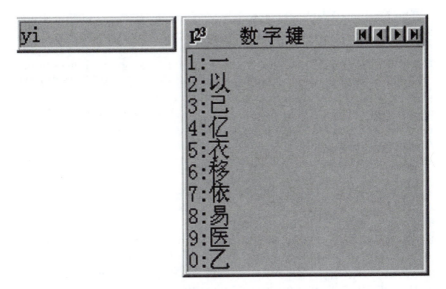

Figure 12.1. The list of characters that appears when the letters "y" and "i" are typed using the Pinyin input method.

The Pinyin Input Method has been developed to input Chinese characters into a personal computer. The Pinyin Input Method involves inputting the Pinyin symbols of the characters on a regular computer keyboard, after which the user selects a character from a menu generated by the Pinyin symbols, that is, the sound system of the character. The following example demonstrates how the Pinyin input system works to reproduce a Chinese character on the computer screen. If I want to write the character "one," I type the Pinyin symbols "yi" ("y" then "i" on the keyboard because they sound like the Chinese character "one"). Then, on the screen, I see a list of Chinese characters with the same sound "yi" (see Fig. 12.1). The character I need is the first character with the first tone. I choose Option 1 and the character appears on my word processing screen. The Pinyin input method eliminates the necessity to reproduce Chinese characters stroke-by-stroke by hand and allows students to learn to write Chinese characters on the computer by building on the skills they have usually developed more readily: the ability to speak (Pinyin input) and the ability to read (character recognition) (http://www.penlesschinese.org).

In this class, although the Pinyin Input Method enabled the input of both simplified and traditional Chinese characters, the students mostly chose to type simplified characters in their online class communication, including chats.

This input method has been widely used among learners of Chinese and is a favorite for learners whose native language is European because Pinyin symbols are Romanized letters. Empirical studies have shown that learning to write Chinese characters on the computer using the Pinyin input method accelerates the learning process significantly (Xu & Jen, 2005). We now review the theoretical literature underpinning the appropriate pedagogy for the use of this input system with chat, because the instructor's goal was to transform the traditional teacher-centered, didactic-learning environment to a more student-centered, constructivist-learning environment.

THEORETICAL UNDERPINNINGS AND LITERATURE REVIEW

Ruschoff and Ritter (2001) stated, "[T]he constructivist paradigm is seen as an important methodological basis for real innovation in foreign language learning" (p. 223). And the core of constructivist learning is that learning is an active process in which learners construct new ideas or concepts based on their current and past knowledge. Emerging information and communication technologies, because of their interactive nature, have provided tremendous interactive opportunities to learners and teachers in the learning environments; as a result, these communication technologies have been changing language learning approaches. The theoretical underpinning for this case study was scaffolding learning, which is within the constructivism paradigm. An introduction to scaffolding learning is presented next followed by literature reviews of the work on social and peer interaction in language learning and online chat in second-language learning.

Scaffolding Learning

According to Gibbons (2002), scaffolding is a temporary structure that is often put up in the process of constructing a building. As each bit of the new building is finished, the scaffolding is taken down. This metaphor of a scaffold, which has been widely used metaphorically in education, originated in Vgotsky's sociocultural theory that learning occurs in the zone of proximal development (ZPD) (Vygotsky, 1978; see also Schutt, 2003). The development of the spoken forms of language is essential for second-language learners as a bridge to the development of literacy (Gibbons, 2002). For heritage learners of Chinese language, their conversational skills with teachers and peers can scaffold the development of reading and writing skills. Online chat may provide a scaffold and may be used in conjunction with other translation tools such as dictionaries.

Social and Peer Interaction in Language Learning

Referring to the computer-assisted language learning (CALL) research of the prior three decades, Johnson (1991) noted the following: "theory in second language acquisition and research in second language acquisition classrooms indicate that the social interaction environments of the classrooms are also crucial factors that affect language learning in important ways" (1991, p. 62). Chapelle (2001) also noted that many CALL researchers advocated study of CALL within its larger classroom and sociocultural contexts. Yates (1996) found that computer-mediated communication is affected by "numerous social structural and social situational factors that surround and define the communication taking place" (p. 46). Because language is a social phenomenon, language learning occurs through social interaction involving teachers and more capable peers (Tharp & Gallimore, 1988; Vygotsky, 1978; Wertsch, 1979, as in Adair-Hauck, Willingham-McLain, & Youngs, 1999). Therefore, social interactions in language learning deserve research.

Anecdotal reports from distance and online learning professionals suggest that although threaded discussions tend to be academic and content based, online chats usually are not content based but instead are very social. But in language learning, especially at the beginning and intermediate levels, the topics the language learners work with are mainly about daily life, which are usually considered social in other subjects. Therefore, it is reasonable to believe that online chats may help language learners develop their target language skills.

Although there has been rich literature on the network-based interaction between learners and native speakers of a language (e.g., Iwasaki & Oliver, 2003; Negretti, 1999; Toyada & Harrison, 2002; Tudini, 2003), little attention seems to have been given to the interaction between peer learners of a target language. The value of peer learning of languages has been under-researched (Lamy & Hassan, 2003). Salaberry (1999) has pointed out that the technology-dependent interaction among learners has been one of the most understudied aspects of computer-aided learning. This interaction, according to Salaberry (1999), should be one of the central research components for CALL in the years to come.

Online Chat in Second-Language Learning

Online chat is synchronous (real-time), text-based, and computer-mediated communication (CMC). An interactionist perspective on second language acquisition (SLA) holds that CMC is beneficial to SLA (Smith, 2003). Smith (2004, pp. 371–372) summarizes many potential benefits of CMC over face-to-face interaction:

... an increased participation-equity-among students (Beauvois, 1992; Kelm, 1992; Kern, 1995; Kim, 1998; Sullivan & Pratt, 1996; Warschauer, 1996a), an increased quantity of learner output (Chun, 1994; Kelm, 1996), and an increased quality of learner output (Chun, 1994; Kelm, 1996; Kern, 1995; Warschauer, 1996a, b). There is also evidence that CMC is viewed by students as being less threatening than face-to-face interaction, which offers results in an increased willingness to take risks and try out new approaches (Kelm, 1996; Kern, 1995; Warschauer, 1996a, 1997). ... Warshauer (1996a), for example, found that students were more inclined to pursue idea-generating discourse and were less inhibited during written production than in oral discussion. Similarly, Munier (1998) noted that students take more risks experimenting with ideas during online discussion. The potential for anonymity may complement this willingness for risk taking as it has been found to create a certain distance between participants that may contribute to an observed atmosphere of critical receptivity. (Kern, 1998), (Smith, pp. 371–372)

In many studies of online chats (e.g., Negretti, 1999; Toyada & Harrison, 2002; Sotillo, 2000; Tudini, 2003), the chat logs were the main or only data resources, and the focus was on aspects of linguistic features of the chats. That is, the studies were oriented to applied-linguistics and second language acquisition, and the research methods were mostly quantitative. Except for the Blake and Zyzik (2003) study exploring the interaction between HL learners and learners of Spanish, little research literature was found that investigated the use of online chat by HL learners who usually command competent conversational skills of the target language but whose literacy skills remain undeveloped when they come to college. Therefore, the use of online chat as a form of text-based virtual conversation by heritage learners of Chinese at the university level deserves research.

THE CONTEXT: IMPLEMENTATION
OF THE TECHNOLOGIES IN THE CLASS

This experimental Chinese language course was specifically designed for heritage learners and was offered for the first time when the study was done. The design and instruction of this course involved collaborative efforts by the first author and the instructor who was a professor in Chinese Studies Program in the Foreign Languages and Literatures Department at the university. The graduate program in which the first author was studying included an important course on faculty technology development. This course prepared the first author to work collaboratively with the instructor in terms of mentoring faculty with technology integration.

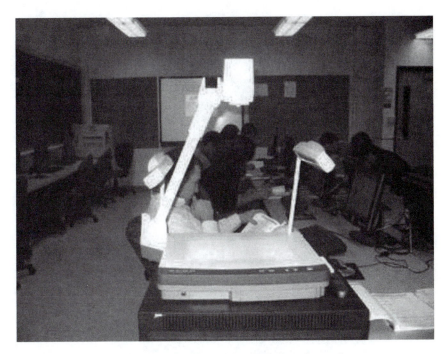

Figure 12.2.   A view of the digitally enhanced
classroom used for the class.

This course was designed to be taught in a technology-rich environment, blending online learning and face-to-face instruction. The technology-rich learning environment for this course consisted of two major parts: a technology-enhanced classroom with a computer for each student and a Web-based managed learning environment (WebCT, 2004), plus a Chinese language chat room on the Web. Therefore, online chat was not introduced as a separate or isolated intervention in this study. Rather, online chats were designed to be part of the class activities in this blended course. Figure 12.2 shows a view of the technology-enhanced classroom used for the face-to-face class sessions. Every student sat in front of a computer. The instructor used an interactive white board (a SMART Board) for lecturing or demonstration of software.

WebCT provided access to the online part of the course. Figure 12.3 shows the homepage of the course revealing the major WebCT tools used by the class. The students logged into this online environment regularly to participate in the class activities such as online chat, discussions, and submission of their assignments. The "Course Content" area served as an electronic mini-library on Chinese language and culture for this class with resources recommended by the instructors or located by the students plus some students' good written assignments. Daily announcements for the

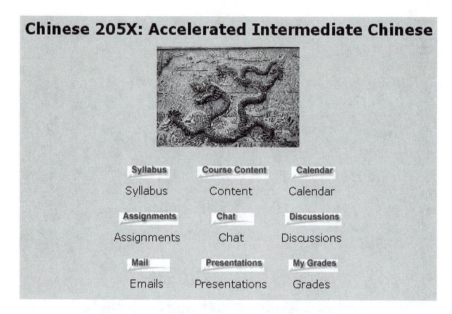

Figure 12.3.   The homepage of the WebCT online
environment used for the class.

class activities and homework were available in the "Calendar" area. The
instructor and the students used WebCT e-mail to communicate on class
related questions and issues. The students' grades were available in the
"Grade" area and the projects were addressed in the "Presentation" area.
The major activities for students in this class included online chats,
threaded discussions, and written assignments.

The Chat Rooms Used by the Class

There were five online chat activities during the fall semester of 2003. The
students chatted twice in the digitally enhanced classroom and three times
outside of the classroom. When the students chatted at a distance, they
were in their apartments, the library, an Internet bar, their office, or the
language lab in the Department of Foreign Languages (according to the
chat logs). The first three chats were in the WebCT chat rooms, in which
the students could only type and chat in Chinese Pinyin symbols. Figure
12.4 shows the menu for the WebCT chat rooms.

The final two chats were held outside WebCT in a chat room provided
free by a professional Chinese online chat service (http://www.bliao.com).
In this chat room the students chatted in Chinese characters. Figure 12.5
shows the header of the Chinese chat room and an excerpt of a chat plus
its translation. The translation of the characters in the header of the

WebCT Chat

Room 1

Room 2

Room 3

Room 4

General Chat for Chin 205X: Accelerated Intermediate Chinese

General Chat for All Courses

Note: Conversations in the following rooms will be recorded:
Room 1, Room 2, Room 3, Room 4.

Figure 12.4.   WebCT chat rooms used by the class.

欢迎光临中文天地！

请文明聊天，勿发布有关色情、反动、黑客等的违法信息。

(03:49:23)[马　　]与所有人说:我不喜欢喝啤酒

(03:50:03)[马　　与陈　　说:陈　，我没有去过新加坡

(03:50:03)胡　　对所有人点了点头:马　　，我和啤酒不是好朋友

(03:50:04)Jon 与所有人说:好

(03:50:05)陈　　与嘉　说:你现在读什麼

(03:50:29)陈　　与柏　说:你现在读什麼

(03:50:30)柏　　与所有人说:你喜欢喝日本花酒吗?智

(03:50:41)嘉　　与所有人说:我听说上海是一个很好购物的城市! 所以,我很想到上海走走!

(03:51:36)柏　　与所有人说:上海人很新潮

(03:52:03)胡　　对所有人点了点头:法国很好玩.

Note: To protect their identities, parts of the participants' names were erased.

Figure 12.5.   Header of the Chinese chat room, Chinese World (plus a transcript of a chat.

chat room is: "Welcome to the Chinese World! Please chat politely. Do not distribute any pornography, anti-government or hacker related information." Chinese World is the name of the chat room. In this Chinese chat room, the students could type Chinese characters in the colors they chose. They could choose to talk to the whole group or ask and answer individual classmate's questions. Every student posting was timed using Beijing Time. (The time data permitted the instructor to assess the students' speed in responding and typing.)

RESEARCH METHOD AND PARTICIPANTS

This study was an action-oriented interpretative case study of chat in a course for heritage learners of Chinese. According to Merriam (2002), the case study is "an intensive description and analysis of a phenomenon or social unit" (p. 8). With a concentration on a single phenomenon or entity (the case), the case study approach seeks to describe the phenomenon in depth bounded by time and activity. As recommended by Merriam (1998) and Yin (1989) detailed information was collected using a variety of data collection procedures over a sustained period of time.

Action research by its nature is very practical and hands-on, because the teacher-action-researcher investigates his/her own practice. This type of research is particularly valuable because it is concerned with everyday problems in the classroom or course, rather than theoretical problems defined by researchers within a discipline of knowledge. Action research tends to be local, specific, and oriented to a specific case (Small, 1995). The aim of action research is always practical: to lead to some kind of change or practical application. Therefore, in this sense, action research is often called applied research—"research with real-world application" (Esterberg, 2002, p. 137). In this action research, the instructor and the authors aimed to implement pedagogical innovations generated by integrating technology with effective HL learning practices.

Decisions about the selection of four participants for the study were very carefully made after the researcher came to know all the students in the class. Based on the typology strategies in qualitative inquiry (Kuzel, 1992; Miles & Huberman, 1994; Patton, 1990), criterion sampling was adopted. This type of sampling is "useful for quality assurance" (Miles & Huberman, 1994, p. 28). Four students in the class met the criteria and were chosen to be the participants of the study: They could speak Chinese but had limited or no reading skills. Two of them were foreign-born American Chinese, one was an American-born Chinese. The fourth one was an international student. Table 12.1 provides detailed demographic information on the four students who were researched. These four focal students were representatives of the heritage learners of Chinese at the college level in the United States such as foreign born and U.S.-born American Chinese, and international HL learners. Although this course was separate and specific to the HL learners, they would rejoin the traditional learners of Chinese as a foreign language in other regular advanced courses in Chinese at this

TABLE 12.1
Profiles of the Four Students Researched for the Case Study

Pseudonym	Tom	Dell	Ryan	Lyn
Gender	Male	Male	Male	Female
Age	21	21	20	20
Citizenship	American (born in Taiwan, immigrated to the U.S. at almost 8)	American (born in P. R. China, immigrated to the U.S. at 7)	American (American born Chinese)	Indonesian (born in and grew up in Indonesia. Entered U.S. for university.)
Previous Chinese learning experiences	Up to second grade in Taiwan	No informal or formal instruction received	No informal or formal instruction received	Two years' private tutoring
Chinese conversational skills	Intermediate-High	Intermediate-Mid	Intermediate-Low	Intermediate-Low
Chinese reading and writing skill level	Read and wrote some traditional Chinese characters	Almost zero	Almost zero	Read very limited simplified Chinese characters
Language(s) or dialect(s) spoken at home	Mandarin Chinese	Mandarin Chinese	Mandarin Chinese	Chinese Fujian dialect
Languages learned	Mandarin Chinese English	Mandarin Chinese English German	Mandarin Chinese English	Indonesian Mandarin Chinese English

university. Despite its great success in the fall of 2003, this experimental course for HL learners won't be repeated until fall 2006 for budgetary reasons. At this point, there is no separate track for HL learners in the Chinese Studies Program on this campus.

The instructor and instructional designer was also the researcher and is the first author of this chapter. The second author is the researcher's research mentor.

Multiple data sources of evidence in this study were gathered and analyzed. Table 12.2 summarizes the data sources for this study. Students' reflective journals, written assignments, chat logs, and threaded discussions were

TABLE 12.2
Sources and Volume of Evidence Used for the Case Study

Source of Evidence	Volumes of Evidence
Chat logs (automatically recorded by the chat tools)	Logs of five chats with two in Pinyin and three in Chinese characters (automatically recorded by the chat tools)
Students' journals (class assignment)	Four participants' four reflective journals and one debriefing journal specifically on chats
Observations	Researcher's observation notes during face-to-face sessions and online chats
Interviews	One 40 minute taped interviews for each participant (4 total) done at a time close to the end of the semester
Interviews and conversations with the instructor	Notes from the informal interviews and conversations with the instructor
Students' summaries of the second Pinyin chat	Four participants' summaries in Chinese of the second Pinyin chat
Activities of the study	Researcher's journal

copied from the online environments of the class. The students' chat logs were all automatically recorded in the WebCT chat rooms and the outside Chinese chat room. In total, the students did three online chats in Chinese Pinyin in the WebCT chat rooms and two online chats in Chinese characters in a Chinese web chat room outside WebCT. Observation was done both during the chat sessions and in the face-to-face classroom. Field notes of conversations between the instructor and designer/researcher, the researcher's journal, and interviews were additional major data sources.

The four students were interviewed in November, 2003 near the end of the course. The interview was mainly in Chinese. Students' relatively strong oral skills in Chinese demonstrated in the interviews were in sharp contrast to their poor literacy revealed in the online chats in Chinese Pinyin and in Chinese characters. This contrast later helped the first author understand students' perception of the use of online chat in the class. Interviews that were about 40 minutes long were tape-recorded. Interviewing gives the researcher the opportunity to more clearly glimpse what the subject is thinking (Esterberg, 2002).

Data analysis was preceded by translation. The researcher first did a word-for-word translation of the taped interviews and any other documents related to online chat. The original and translated data were shared with the instructor to ensure the accuracy of the translation. The data analysis for the case study followed Eisenhardt's (1989) recommended sequence of within-case analysis, cross-case pattern search, shaping hypotheses, and reaching theoretical saturation. A version of grounded theory was used to develop meanings from the data (Strauss & Corbin, 1990) using an essentially two-stage process of coding (Esterberg, 2002). The data analysis started with within-case analysis by analyzing the four individual cases one by one to avoid confusion and bias against one to another. After the within-case analysis, familiarity developed with each of the four embedded cases as a stand-alone entity. Next, the cross-case pattern search was conducted by comparing the results of the four individuals for similarities and differences. The steps of analyzing the data included: open coding, development of themes, focused coding, looking for patterns, and comparing cases. The process of data analysis was recursive and highly iterative. The iterations were repeated as often as necessary until reaching theoretical saturation, the point when the researcher is not discovering anything new, as recommended by Eisenhardt (1989).

FINDINGS AND DISCUSSION

The findings are presented in two parts: HL learners' perceptions and instructors' perceptions. Additional data on the progress of the students is also presented to provide a measure of the effectiveness of chat for heritage learners of Chinese. Several themes emerged from the data analysis that provide the answers that this study sought. From the students' perspective, chat appears to accelerate the learning of Chinese in three ways. First, chat in Pinyin helped the learners acquire Pinyin, which is a fundamental step in producing Chinese characters on the computer. Second, Pinyin was very useful scaffolding in learning Chinese characters. Third, online chat helped the students learn Chinese characters. The faculty perspective provides a discussion of the major pedagogical issues involved in online chat. We start by discussing the students' perspective.

The Heritage Learners' Perception of the Benefits of Online Chat

First, the students perceived that chat in Pinyin helped them acquire Pinyin, which is a fundamental step in producing Chinese characters on the computer. As introduced previously, learning to write Chinese characters by hand is very time-consuming and frustrating for most learners. The Chinese Pinyin input method has connected the Chinese sound system (Pinyin) and the characters, which normally appear to be two different systems to learners of Chinese. By inputting Romanized Pinyin symbols on the regular keyboard, the learners can get Chinese character output on the computer screen. Therefore, solid knowledge of Pinyin symbols is crucial in writing Chinese characters on the computer.

The first chat in Pinyin in WebCT produced unexpected enthusiasm and positive feedback from all the students, including the four learners researched in detail. Ryan wrote in his journal that, "the online chat is a great help towards my Pinyin that is another major weakness I have. I feel that I have improved a lot on my Pinyin on the one chat alone" (October 5, 2003, Journal 2). In addition, Dell and Lyn, two students in this class who had expressed strong fear and frustration in the first several weeks and had wanted to drop the course because of the overwhelming difficulty of learning Chinese Pinyin, decided not to drop out because the chat experience encouraged them to stay in this class. Dell's journal noted "online chat has helped me a lot in learning Pinyin ... We should do more online chats" (October 6, 2003, Dell's Journal 2). Lyn noted in her journal, "I'm somewhat more motivated to learn the Pinyin now because I just realized that it is fun to type in Pinyin and to get the Chinese character output in the computer" (October 5, 2003, Lyn's Journal 2).

Tom, who started the class with the highest literacy level among the HL learners in the class, revealed his very weak knowledge of Pinyin several times during the instructor's/researcher's class observation. She noticed that he was much slower when chatting using Pinyin than in our face-to-face conversations. During the interview, when asked about his unusually slow responses in the Pinyin chat, he said, "I have a poor knowledge of Pinyin. I do not know which symbol is the right one to use" (November 15, 2003, Interview). In his journal, he mentioned that, "my weakness in Chinese is the Pinyin part. I thought chatting in Pinyin was a great way of learning Chinese Pinyin" (October 5, 2003, Tom's Journal 2). In short, chatting in Pinyin helped the HL learners immediately identify their weakness in Pinyin knowledge. At the same time, the chats in Pinyin excited and engaged the learners, and they were determined to improve their knowledge of Pinyin and the Chinese language.

Second, Pinyin is very useful for scaffolding in learning Chinese characters. Because the WebCT chat tool does not support Chinese characters, the students did the first two chats in Pinyin symbols in the WebCT chat rooms. Around the time of the midterm exam, the students asked to chat in Chinese characters instead of Pinyin. Ryan mentioned in class that, "we will ultimately communicate in Chinese characters, not Pinyin" (face-to-face meeting class on October 13, 2003). In addition, Tom indicated in the interview (November 15, 2003) that chatting in Pinyin did not help with their mastery of the four tones of the sound system of the characters. When writing Chinese characters, the knowledge of the tones for the characters is equally as important as the Pinyin symbols. A wrong tone even with the correct Pinyin symbols may still lead to the wrong characters when writing characters on the computer with the use of the Pinyin input system. In the Chinese language, most of the characters have only one sound and one tone.

In the textbooks, every character is marked with the Pinyin symbols and the tone. But the Pinyin input system on the computer only displays the Pinyin symbols indicating the pronunciation of the character and the characters with the same sound. No tone is displayed on the computer. Therefore, the learners have to know the right tone for the character if they want to get the right character. In other words, "the reproduction of Chinese [on a computer] requires precise character recognition; for the precise character to appear requires the accurate knowledge of Pinyin; and accurate knowledge of Pinyin requires correct pronunciation." (Mu & Zhang, 2004, p. 4000). Thus, the learners' solid mastery of the Pinyin is crucial in learning to write Chinese characters. In the interviews, all the HL learners indicated that chatting in characters was more helpful than chatting in Pinyin, but chatting in Pinyin first was helpful and was a necessary preparation step for chatting in characters later.

Third, online chat greatly helped the students learn Chinese characters. Online chats in Chinese characters provided more opportunities for the students to learn. At first, the Pinyin input system exposed the learners to more characters. As explained in the introduction, input of the Pinyin symbols for a character, produces a list of characters with the same sound and with either the same or different tones. Here is an example demonstrating a learning moment technology provides when one student made a mistake in spelling the other student's name in one of the chats in Chinese characters.

A. 新元, 你是汉族人吗? (xīnyuán, are you a Hàn?)

B. 我的名字不是心愿，是鑫源. (My name is not xīnyuàn, is xīnyuán)

Thus, the three different characters "xin" (新, 心, 鑫) and three different characters "yuan" (元, 愿, 源) that the Pinyin input system generated called the students' attention to an important feature in Chinese language—the multiplicity of homophonic characters. These characters are pronounced with the same sounds (yuan) but with different tones. Very naturally, the students get the opportunity to learn more characters. (Note: To protect the student's identity, characters in his name are replaced by other characters that also represent the multiplicity of homophonic characters). This example again illustrates the power of the Pinyin input system as a part of effective scaffolding.

Other opportunities exist when the more advanced students used new vocabulary and the lower level students got to learn the new words. Ryan mentioned that at the beginning of the chats, he usually had to spend much time reading the classmates' conversation carefully, usually with the help of an online dictionary: "I sometimes did not recognize the characters they used in the conversation, but when the characters were repeated again

TABLE 12.3
Students' Progress Shown in Midterm Examination

Student Pseudonym	Number of Characters Produced in the Exam
Ryan	50
Tom	100
Lyn	180
Dell	250

and again, I got to know them. Also, I learned to use them later on in the conversation" (Ryan, interview, November 15, 2003).

The first time the instructor and first author noticed the students' great progress on learning Chinese characters was in the midterm exam. The major examination task in class was to write a Chinese summary of the second chat in Pinyin with at least 50 Chinese characters. All the students in the class met this minimum requirement. To the instructor's surprise, Tom wrote a 100-character paragraph without any errors. Lyn wrote 180 characters in her summary, and Dell wrote the longest summary in the class with a little more than 250 characters. In spite of the errors they made, the instructor could understand what they wanted to convey in their writing. The evidence is summarized in Table 12.3, indicating the length of the students' Chinese summaries of the second Pinyin chat.

Further, the students' confidence and eagerness in communicating in Chinese characters had grown so much that by the time of the midterm exam, they requested to chat in characters instead of Pinyin because in real communication, they would communicate in characters rather than Pinyin. As stated previously, when writing Chinese characters, the knowledge of the tones for the characters is equally important to the Pinyin symbols. A wrong tone even with the correct Pinyin symbols can still lead to the wrong character when writing characters on the computer with the use of the Pinyin input system. Therefore, the first author negotiated the use of a free Chinese online chat room with a professional Chinese chat online service. The students' reaction to the chat in Chinese characters was fascinating. In their debriefing reflective journals, they mentioned many benefits they received from the activity: recognizing more characters, reviewing the characters they had learned, typing characters faster, etc. Here are some of the quotes from participants' debriefing journals immediately after the first chat in Chinese characters:

> I am very satisfied with the chat in Chinese character. I feel that this chat has been very helpful to me. I found that I could type simplified Chinese characters much faster, and, furthermore, I could recognize much more simplified

Chinese characters. In the chat room, I have learned a lot of Chinese characters. I had never had chats in Chinese characters before, but now I sometimes have conversations in Chinese online with my friends. Chatting is really a very good way of accelerating our learning of Chinese. I can see our learning, progress, discussions and reviewing of new characters. I felt that the process of learning Chinese is really enjoyable (Tom, debriefing journal, November 15, 2003).

The other three in this study expressed the same excitement: "I am very happy about it (our first chat in characters) because I could use the characters I had learned to chat with my classmates ... c hatting in characters is more difficult than in Pinyin, but it was much more interesting" (Lyn, debriefing journal, November 25, 2003). Ryan commented that, "with the help of the Chinese chat room, I feel that I have made a lot more progress" (Ryan, debriefing journal, November 15, 2003). Dell mentioned that he was very nervous in the Chinese chat room at first, but later, he gained significant confidence because he found, "I could read some characters. Further, my classmates could understand the characters I had written" (Dell, debriefing journal, November 14, 2003).

The high quality (in terms of the lexical richness, lexical density, syntactic complexity, and amount of language) of the journals and the chat logs in Chinese characters illustrate the power of online chat in helping students acquire Chinese characters. The interviews probed to reveal reasons behind the high accuracy rate in the chats. I found that HL learners were more concerned about accuracy than fluency during the chat and, more importantly, their relatively strong conversational skills helped them assure that accuracy. When chatting, the HL learners used different sources to help them produce the right characters. Lyn mentioned that she used an online dictionary, and that, "the dictionary has been very helpful to me." RIKAI, an online Web site provides instant translation between Chinese Pinyin, characters, and English, was of particular interest to the students: "I used the RIKAI Web site when I ran into characters I did not know. It is a useful secret weapon" (Dell). Ryan and Tom commented in their interviews that they used online dictionaries, translation software, and Web sites:

> I had to use the online dictionary frequently in the first part of the chat. When I ran into the same word and topic again and again, I knew what my classmates were talking about. Then I could join the conversation. But I still need to use the online dictionary when I want to use some new words ... (Ryan, interview, November 15, 2003).

Similarly, Dell reported that before he posted his messages to the chat room, he usually reflected, trying to make sure the sentences were correct. Dell's process was consistent with claims in the literature that oral skills can scaffold the development of the writing skills (Gibbons, 2002).

The great strides Tom, Dell, Lyn, and Ryan made are especially striking when viewed in comparison with students in a regular Chinese 101 class taught in a traditional classroom. The four participating students originally enrolled in the regular beginning level course, which usually meets 5 hours a week. In the class studied, students only met face-to-face 3 hours a week, and the students in the study were able to start with a textbook usually used in the second semester of the beginning level of Chinese class. In addition, in the second half of the semester, several lessons from a higher level textbook for advanced beginners were added. Another mark of the students' dramatic progress was their written assignments. In the summary of an online chat, Dell wrote 250 characters. Lyn's final reflection journal had more than 1000 characters with only a few local errors, which did not affect understanding of her ideas. Ryan wrote his debriefing journal on the first Chinese chat with a length of more than 300 characters. Tom submitted his more than 600-character third journal almost without any error. Usually a Chinese 101 student learns 300 characters in one semester. But the participants in this study surpassed their peers in the regular beginning level courses. They attribute their accelerated learning to their online chatting experiences. As Tom expressed in his journal, "I hope the instructors can keep the chatting as a teaching and learning strategy. I believe it is a very good, effective and fast learning method" (Tom, reflective journal 4, December 11, 2003). He further remarked that, "I sometimes can not believe that I can recognize many simplified Chinese characters" (Tom, chat log dated December 4, 2003). Dell directly stated that, "chatting has accelerated our learning of Chinese" (Dell, reflective journal 4, December 10, 2003).

Although the length of a writing assignment is usually not considered the only indicator of a language learners' writing ability, the length of HL learners' assignments is valid evidence of their learning progress because HL learners have already mastered other common evaluation criteria, including grammar and vocabulary. Table 12.4 illustrates the longest writing assignment each of the four participants completed in the class.

TABLE 12.4
Lengths of the Four Students' Reflective Journals[a]

Pseudonyms	Ryan	Tom	Lyn	Dell
Journal 1	221 w	237 w	340 w	358 w
Journal 2	324 w	439 w	501 w	266 w
Journal 3	230 w/ 48 c	5 w/ 640 c	349 w/129 c	145 c
Journal 4	341 c	343 c	251 c	2 w/ 410 c
Journal 5	93 w/ 68 c	45 w/ 779 c	9 w/ 1093 c	1 w/ 367 c

[a]Students were encouraged to write journals in Chinese from the third journal in the middle of November 2003. Most of the English words in the last three journals were names of places, people, and terms. In the table, "w" indicates English words, and "c" indicates Chinese characters.

In summary, the development of literacy skills (reading and writing) is the most important and often the only learning goal of HL learners, and chatting in Pinyin and in characters was found to be an effective and powerful strategy to enhance HL learners' acquisition of Pinyin and Chinese characters. The participants reported that the first two online chats done in Pinyin helped them acquire Pinyin symbols, and the Pinyin chat was a necessary preparation step later for chatting in characters. But, they believed that chatting in characters was more helpful than chatting in Pinyin in terms of learning characters because chatting in characters helped them practice Pinyin, provided opportunities to review the characters they had already learned, and assisted them in learning new characters in a communicative context. Moreover, chatting in characters addressed their concern about accuracy, and their already acquired face-to-face conversational skills and existing knowledge of Chinese grammar and vocabulary seemed to help them achieve a relatively high quality of accuracy in the chats, based on the observations of the first author and the instructor.

Finally, from the students' perspective, chat enhances the students' motivation and interest in learning Chinese. Online chats provided opportunities for the students to interact socially. This social interaction usually was missing in the regular face-to-face instruction sessions, which were usually filled with content-related academic activities. The students noted the following motivational benefits of the social interaction occurring in the online chats:

- "The chat activity is very good because all of us are having fun, getting to know each other more. Especially for me because I can never attend the class, and I'm curious about my classmates, so this opportunity is very wonderful." (Lyn, debriefing journal, November 25, 2003).
- "I am a person who likes to chat with people. So I really enjoy chatting with my classmates." and "I do not feel I am taking a class." (Lyn, interview, November 20, 2003).
- "They are like our daily chats, very casual." (Tom, interview, November 15, 2003)
- "But in class, we may not ask these kind of questions." and "I get to know my classmates better ... so I feel more comfortable in the class" (Ryan, interview, November 15, 2003).
- "In a small class, it is important for the students to know each other. Chatting helps us know each other and learn Chinese." (Dell, debriefing journal, November 14, 2003).
- "Perhaps the most interesting aspect of this course is the unique atmosphere that allows peer-to-peer interactions. I feel an active participation in learning a foreign language is most important over a plain lecture." (Dell, reflective journal 2, October 6, 2003).

- "The online chat activity was a fun part of the class. You get to know more about other people in the class while learning more about Pinyin." (Tom, reflective journal 2, October 5, 2003).

Thus, online chats provided opportunities for the students to learn and practice the target language very casually in a more comfortable learning environment. As just indicated, the students did not even feel like they were doing a class activity. These findings about the students' positive responses were consistent with the literature in both language learning and distance learning suggesting that CMC is less threatening and encourages learners to take linguistic risks and try out new hypotheses (Kelm, 1996; Kern, 1995; Warschauer, 1996a, 1997), and when there is friendly and open exchanges among students and instructor, a distance learning environment is likely to be more productive than an environment in which exchanges are formal and circumscribed (Gilbert & Moore, 1998; Wolcott, 1996; Zhang & Fulford, 1994).

The findings of this study also confirmed many of Kern's (1996) hypotheses that interaction implemented in a synchronous electronic environment in comparison to asynchronous interaction would generate more opportunities for students to participate, greater language production, more time to develop and refine comments, more collaboration among interlocutors, increased motivation, and reduced anxiety. In this study, the participants did display increased motivation to learn Chinese and little anxiety during the chats using the target language.

Further, in this class, the learners felt comfortable chatting with classmates and found the topics interesting because they used the same textbook and possessed very similar knowledge bases. Throughout all five chats, there was little communication breakdown. The instructor and the authors believe that this ease of communication is very important to beginning level language learners. They need this kind of positive reinforcement to get comfortable with the target language and build the courage to forge on with their language learning. Online chats indeed appeared to strengthen students' interest in continuing to learn Chinese. In his 840-character reflective journal four written in Chinese, Tom stated, "I will keep learning Chinese later on through the use of online chat and other online resources." Lyn expressed the same interest in her final journal: "computer, Internet, online dictionaries, and other resources all help me with my Chinese learning. ... I will not stop learning Chinese." Tom and Ryan made the decision during the Fall semester to earn a minor degree in Chinese. And, Tom, Ryan, and Dell took an advanced Chinese language course in the Spring semester of 2004.

Online chats clearly brought fun to the class and enhanced the students' motivation and interest in learning Chinese. From their initial reaction to the first chat to the comments on the last chat, the participants kept repeating the same words: "I look forward to more chats" and "we should have more chats." The only complaint raised by the students about the use of the online chat was that they were not able to have more online chats because of the time constraint. This was very positive feedback. According to the instructor's previous teaching experience and the literature, many learners of Chinese get frustrated in learning Chinese and quit after one or two semesters of learning. But the HL learners in this class expressed satisfaction with the class, appreciation of the use of Internet and computers, and further interest in learning Chinese.

In an informal, anonymous survey of the course at the end of the semester (December 12, 2003), online chat was ranked as the most helpful class activity by all the students in this class, including the participants in this study. Further, this experimental course was evaluated as a success according to the official departmental evaluation of the course, which the students completed anonymously at the end of the semester without the instructor or designer present in the classroom, as required in the course evaluation. Every item in the course evaluation received an average of 4.5 out of 5 (the highest rating).

Course Instructor and Designer's Perceptions of the Benefits of Online Chat

The course instructor and designer felt that online chat made some valuable contributions to the course, generated pedagogical innovations, and made the instruction much more efficient. Five pedagogical uses of online chat resulted from the analysis. A description of each follows.

Online Chat Was an Effective Tool for Individualized Instruction. The instructor could provide timely individualized instruction to any student during online chats. This individualized instruction is very useful in the Chinese language classes, which usually consist of students with diverse proficiency levels and learning needs (see Kondo-Brown, this volume). Technology has been found to be powerful in providing effective individualized learning (e.g., Fletcher. 2003). Our findings were consistent with the literature.

Online Chat Was an Effective Assessment Tool. In traditional Chinese classes, quizzes and exams are usually used to test students' mechanical memorization of vocabulary and grammatical rules. Students' communicative competence is much more difficult to assess. But, online chat presented itself as a very effective assessment in this class. For both the midterm and final exams, online chat was used as an assessment task. For the midterm exam, the students wrote a summary in Chinese characters of the second chat in Pinyin. For the final exam, the students did a 45-minute online chat in class.

It was realized that online chat challenged students' overall knowledge of the Chinese language, including the sound system (Pinyin), writing system (characters), and grammar system because, as cited previously, "the reproduction of Chinese [on a computer] requires precise character recognition; for the precise character to appear requires the accurate knowledge of Pinyin; and accurate knowledge of Pinyin requires correct pronunciation" (Mu & Zhang, 2004, p. 4000). According to the instructor, "online chat is effective in assessing the students' knowledge of Pinyin, characters, and grammar, and, further, the overall communicative competence. Online chat is a stone that can kill more than three birds. I really like it" (Instructor, semi-interview on December 9, 2003).

As an assessment tool, online chats revealed the students' real proficiency levels by displaying their ability to conduct conversations in real-life situations in terms of correctness of vocabulary and grammar rules, length of the conversation, and appropriateness of the responses to other conversation participants' utterances. None of these elements in language learning can be assessed properly in traditional exams. But, in online chats, all these issues could be assessed. Therefore, we think online chat is an effective assessment tool for Chinese language classes, not only for HL learners but also for traditional learners of Chinese.

Online Chat Logs Were Very Valuable Instructional Materials Tailored to Individual Students' Needs. As just indicated, the online chat was used as an effective assessment tool. The problems and errors revealed in the chats provided very useful and valuable information to the instructor, enabling her to design lesson plans to meet the students' specific needs and offer individualized guidance for each student. For example, one participant in this study kept making the same pattern of errors in two consecutive chats by typing the wrong characters generated by the Pinyin symbols "z." Later, when talking with him, it was found that he had difficulty in differentiating between "zh" and "z," probably because of his early exposure to a Chinese dialect spoken by his grandmother. This student did not realize that it was not correct in standard Mandarin Chinese until the instructor pointed out his errors identified in the chat logs. To make use of the full potential for individual instruction, the instructor usually sent e-mails to or met in person with the students after each chat to review the errors and weakness in their language.

Online Chat Rooms Were Good Student-Centered Learning Environments. The role of the teacher changed from authority figure to facilitator on the side in this technology-rich environment. In the students' online chats, the instructor, instead of being a subject matter authority, kept silent for most of the time during the chats, lurking and reading students' conversations. In two of the chats, the instructor and designer did not participate at all. The instructor was amazed at the smooth flow and rich content of the conversations. Interventions were only made in the chats when important questions remained unanswered, a thread of conversation was getting lost, students needed to be reminded of what they had learned and experienced, or students needed prompting to start a new topic. For example, in one chat, the instructor wanted the students to practice the vocabulary the students had learned in a recent text entitled "dining," so the instructor posted a question to the chat room: "Anybody interested in cooking? We should get together in my house and have an international dinner." Then the students started to talk about their own cooking experiences and their favorite foods. Some HL learners were from families that own Chinese restaurants. These learners were very familiar with the Chinese names of the dishes, much more than from the textbook. Further, by using online dictionaries and the translation Web sites, the students used new words that were not covered in the textbook. Therefore, online chats provided very good opportunities for the students to learn new vocabulary and practice the characters they learned. The students' ability to initiate the conversation topics and to explore online learning aids demonstrated the power of online chats in providing learner-centered learning environments.

Online Chat Enhanced the Overall Quality and Quantity of the Course Instruction. Instead of meeting five times a week as in the regular classes, this class met only three times face-to-face every week. But the instructor found that the students learned much more than those enrolled in a traditional class. One explanation could be that more than one textbook was used in this class, which included introductory chapters about Pinyin in *Integrated Chinese* (Book I, Level I; Yao, 1997), *Integrated Chinese* (Book I, Level II; Yao, 1997), and four lessons from *Oh, China* (Chou, Link, & Wang, 1997), a textbook for advanced beginners (that is, HL learners). The instructor and designer did not originally plan to use the textbook *Oh, China*, but the students' progress and demand for more learning materials led them to look for more instructional materials. In addition to the textbooks, the online resource project done in the class brought a number of student-located and recommended learning resources into the class.

However, a more likely explanation for the exceptional progress of the students is the nature of the online chats. During the chats, specific topics were not assigned to the students. Situated learning theory acted as the guiding principle in designing the chat activities to realize a three-way connection: connect the instruction of the textbook contents with the chat activities; connect the chat activities with real life situations; and use the textbook knowledge in online chats to deal with authentic problems. Therefore, the chat activities were usually carefully scheduled at a time when students had things to talk about in their real life and right after they had learned how to talk about them in Chinese. The chat logs indicated that the topics students covered included the following: their Chinese names, the countries and hometowns they were from, titles of the family members, parents' professions, favorite Chinese dishes, Chinese movies, shopping and traveling experiences, celebrating Chinese moon festival and American Thanksgiving, plans for the winter break, and knowledge about Chinese language and culture. These were all real life experiences and the students could chat about in Chinese. For example, in the last online chat, the students chatted about their Thanksgiving experiences and plans for Christmas. They used most of the vocabulary they learned in the last three lessons in *Integrated Chinese* (Book I, Level II), "Travel," "Hometown," and "At the Airport," and vocabulary they learned in previous lessons. The instructor was pleased to see that the students could properly and skillfully use what they had learned in authentic real-life communicative tasks.

These findings were consistent with at least two of the elements identified by Roblyer et al. (1997) that result from technology-enhanced learning: motivation and the capacity for teachers to create student-friendly materials efficiently. In summary, the course instructor and designer identified a range of innovative pedagogical uses of online chats in a Chinese language class. These pedagogical innovations are likely to lead to further exploration of the potential of educational technology.

CONCLUSIONS AND IMPLICATIONS

Our literature review revealed a scarcity of literature on the use of online chat by HL learners and on technology integration into Chinese as a foreign language classes. A rich research literature exists on the use of online chats in English as a second/foreign (ESL/EFL) and in classes for European languages. However, the studies mainly focused on the aspects of second language acquisition and applied linguistics; therefore, chat logs were usually the primary or only data resources and the linguistic features of the chats were analyzed by using quantitative research methods. This study was process oriented, aiming to explore the perceptions from both the instructor's and the learners' perspectives of the use of online chats.

There are three major findings of this study. First, online chats effectively identified and addressed the HL learners' learning needs; therefore, HL learners' Chinese learning process was greatly accelerated. In this study, the first two online chats in Pinyin helped the heritage learners of Chinese immediately identify their weaknesses in Pinyin and accelerate their acquisition of the Chinese Pinyin symbols and characters in real-life communicative tasks. Further, the order of chatting in Pinyin first and then in Chinese characters worked well in the students' learning process. According to the HL learners, chatting in Pinyin was a necessary preparation step before chatting in Chinese characters. Heritage learners' existing knowledge of Chinese grammar and vocabulary in conversation proved to be valuable in their chats and the overall Chinese learning process. The Pinyin input system, the peer interaction, and the online learning aids were valuable scaffoldings in students' learning of Chinese. These findings are consistent with the literature on scaffolding learning.

Second, online chats added a dimension of social interaction to the class and helped enhance the learners' motivation and interest in learning Chinese. Students enjoyed the casual style of online chats and felt more comfortable in the class because they had got to know each other better during the chats. The comfort and confidence students gained in chatting in the target language contributed to their enhanced motivation and interest in learning more Chinese.

Third and finally, online chats made the instruction more efficient and generated pedagogical innovations. The real daily life topics of the online chats were congruent with the topics and content covered in the textbooks we used. The students had opportunities to use and learn the target language in authentic communication. The instructor could provide timely individualized instruction to the student during chats. Further, online chats were used as an effective assessment tool for the instructor to track the students' mastery of the language, and the chat logs served as invaluable instructional materials. With the initiatives taken by the students, the whole learning process moved from a traditional teacher-centered learning environment to a more learner-centered one. This change challenged the instructor's role as an authority in the class but helped develop the students' learner autonomy.

Implications for Further Teaching and Research

This study has identified the combination of personal, social, and educational elements in online chats that contribute to an effective Chinese language learning environment for both the instructor and the students in this Midwestern university. The social elements of the online chats in a language class deserve further investigation for possible improvement of foreign/second language instruction. To fully explore the promises online chat holds for language learners, especially HL learners, future research should include participants at different language proficiency levels and in different settings. Further, the changing role of the instructor from an authority to a facilitator in technology-enhanced environment may deserve more attention from teacher educators and teachers.

The findings of the study should be considered in light of the study's limitations: the number of the participants and the setting that was limited to one experimental course that has not yet been repeated. However, the findings do give important insights into the issues involved in the effective education of HL learners, which has become an increasingly important issue in the field of foreign language education in the United States. Furthermore, the findings call attention to the issues involved in the effective design of technology-integrated language learning environment and effective evaluation of technological interventions. The information gained in this study may benefit teachers and students of foreign language learners and course designers. Last, the changing role of the instructor to a facilitator in a technology rich environment provides insights for teacher education in the 21st century

ACKNOWLEDGMENTS

We wish to thank the students in the class and Professor Dawn Bratsch-Prince, Chair of the Department of World Languages & Cultures at Iowa State University, for supporting this research. The first author wishes to acknowledge the support of Iowa State University Department of Curriculum and Instruction for a scholarship to support her graduate studies. Grateful thanks to Dr. Aili Mu, professor of Chinese in the Department of World Languages & Cultures for reciprocal mentoring and collaboration in this research and development. Thanks also to Dr. Aili Mu for the first author's assistantship from her Miller Faculty Fellowship grant and the opportunity to collaboratively develop this course. Finally, thanks to Dr. Ann Thompson, founding director of the Center for Technology in Learning and Teaching, for her course in technology and faculty mentoring that prepared the first author for the work with Dr. Aili Mu.

REFERENCES

ACTFL (American Council on the Teaching of Foreign Languages) Proficiency Guidelines. (1999). Retrieved March, 1999, from http://www.languagetesting.com/scale.htm

Adair-Hauck, B., Willingham-McLain, L., & Youngs, B. E. (1999). Evaluating the integration of technology and second language learning. *The CALICO Journal, 17*(2), 269–282.

Beauvous, M. H. (1992). Computer-assisted classroom discussion in the foreign language classroom: Conversation in slow motion. *Foreign Language Annals, 25*, 454–464.

Beauvois, M. H. (1994). E-talk: Attitudes and motivation in computer-assisted classroom discussion. *Computers and the Humanities, 28*(1), 177–190.

Blake, R. (2000). Computer mediated communication: A window on L2 Spanish interlanguage. *Language Learning & Technology, 4*(1), 120–136.

Blake, R. J., & Zyzik, E. C. (2003). Who's helping whom? Learner/heritage-speakers' networked discussions in Spanish. *Applied Linguistics, 24*(4), 519–544.

Bosco, J. (1986). An analysis of evaluations of interactive video. *Educational Technology, 16*(5), 7–17.

Chapelle, C. A. (1999). Theory and research: Investigation of "authentic" language learning task. In J. Egbert & E. Hanson-Smith (Eds.), *CALL environment: Research, practice, and critical issues* (pp. 101–115). Alexandria, VA: TESOL.

Chapelle, C. A. (2001). *Computers in second language acquisition: Foundations for teaching, testing and research.* Cambridge: Cambridge University.

Chi, T. R. (1996). Toward a communicative model for teaching and learning Chinese as a foreign language: Exploring some new possibilities. In S. McGinnis (Ed.), *Chinese pedagogy: An emerging field* (pp. 1–28). Columbus, OH: Foreign Language Publications.

Chou, C., Llink, P., & Wang, X. (1997). *Oh, China!: Elementary reader of modern Chinese for advanced beginners.* Princeton, NJ: Princeton University Press.

Chu, M. (1996). Class plan for teaching Chinese as a functional language. In S. McGinnis (Ed.), *Chinese pedagogy: An emerging field* (pp. 135–158). Columbus, OH: Foreign Language publications.

Chun, D. M. (1994). Using computer networking to facilitate the acquisition of interculture competence. *System, 22,* 17–31.

Clark, R. E. (1983). Reconsidering research on learning from media. *Review of Educational Research, 53*(4), 445–59.

Domuitescu, D. (2000). *Addressing the needs of heritage speakers.* Presentation at the Second Language Pedagogy Symposium; California State University, Los Angeles.

Douglas, M. (2001). *Teaching Japanese as a heritage language at college level: An Individualized curriculum and evaluation of its effect.* Presentation at the Teaching Japanese as a Heritage Language, Southern California Symposium, Santa Monica, CA.

Egbert, J., Chao, C., & Hanson-Smith, E. (1999). Computer-enhanced language learning environments: An overview. In J. Egbert & E. Hanson-Smith (Eds.), *CALL environment: Research, practice, and critical issues* (pp. 1–13). Alexandria, VA: TESOL.

Eisenhardt, K. M. (1989). Building theories from case study research. *Academy of Management Review, 14,* 532–550.

Esterberg. K. G. (2002). *Qualitative methods in social research.* New York: McGraw Hill.

Fletcher, J. D. (2003). Evidence for learning from technology-assisted instruction. In H. F. O'Neil, Jr. & R. S. Perez. (Eds.), *Technology applications in education: A learning view* (pp. 79–99). Mahwah, NJ: Lawrence Erlbaum Associates.

Flottmesch, M. (2000). Building effective interaction in distance education: A review of the literature. *Educational Technology, 40*(3), 46–51.

Fulford, C. P., & Zhang, S. (1993). Perceptions of interaction: The critical predicator in distance education. *The American Journal of Distance Education, 7*(3), 8–21.

Gay, L. P., & Airasian, P. (2003). *Educational research: Competencies for analysis and applications* (7th ed.). Upper Saddle River, NJ: Pearson Education.

Gibbons, P. (2002). *Scaffolding language, scaffolding learning: Teaching second language learners in the mainstream classroom.* Portsmouth, NH: Heinemann.

Gilbert, L., & Moore, D. R. (1998). Building interactivity into web courses: Tools for social and instructional interaction. *Educational Technology, 38*(3), 29–35.

Iwasaki, J., & Oliver, R. (2003). Chatline interaction and negative feedback. *Australian Review of Applied Linguistics, 17,* 60–73.

Johnson, D. (1991). Second language and content learning with computers: Research in the role of social factors. In P. Dunkel (Ed.), *Computer-assisted language learning and testing: Research issues and practice* (pp. 61–83). New York: Newbury House.

Johnston, B. (1999). Theory and research: Audience, language use, and language learning. In J. Egbert & E. Hanson-Smith (Eds.), *CALL environment: Research, practice, and critical issues* (pp. 55–64). Alexandria, VA: TESOL.

Kelm, O. (1992). The use of synchronous computer networks in second language instruction: A preliminary report. *Foreign Language Annals, 25,* 441–454.

Kelm, O. (1996). Applications of computer networking in foreign language education: Focusing on principles of second language acquisition. In M. Warschauer (Ed.), *Telecollaboration in foreign language learning* (pp. 19–28). Honolulu: University of Hawai`i at Mānoa, Second Language Teaching and Curriculum Center.

Kern, R. (1995). Restructuring classroom interaction with networked computers: Effects on quantity and quality and characteristics of language production. *The Modern Language Journal, 79,* 457–476.

Kern, R. (1998). Technology, social interaction and foreign language literacy. In J. Muyskens (Ed.), *New ways of learning and teaching: Focus on technology and foreign language education* (pp. 57–92). Boston: Heinle & Heinle.

Kim, Y. (1998). *The effect of a networked computer-mediated discussion on subsequent oral discussion in the ESL classroom.* Unpublished doctoral dissertation, University of Texas, Austin, TX.

Kondo-Brown, K. (2003). Heritage language instruction for post-secondary students from immigrant backgrounds. *Heritage Language Education Journal, 1.* Retrieved April, 2003, from http://www.international.ucla.edu/lrc/hlj/article.asp?parentid=3600

Kuzel, A. J. (1992). Sampling in qualitative inquiry. In B. F. Crabtree & W. L. Miller (Eds.), *Doing qualitative research (Research methods for primary care series* (Vol. 3; pp. 31–44). Newbury, Park, CA: Sage.

Lamy, M., & Hassan, X. (2003). What influences reflection interaction in distance peer learning? Evidence from four long-term online learners of French. *Open Learning, 8*(1), 39–60.

Lee, L. (1998). Going beyond classroom learning: Acquiring cultural knowledge via on-line newspapers and intercultural exchanges via on-line chatrooms. *The CALICO Journal, 16*(2), 101–120.

Lincoln, Y. S., & Guba, E. G. (1985). *Naturalistic inquiry.* London: Sage.

Long, M. (1996). The role of linguistic environment in second language acquisition. In W. C. Richie & T. K. Bhatia (Eds.), *Handbook of research on language acquisition, Vol. 2: second language acquisition* (pp. 413–468). New York: Academic.

Merriam, S. B. (1998). *Qualitative research and case study applications in education* (2nd ed.). San Francisco: Jossey-Bass.

Merriam, S. B. (Ed.). (2002). *Qualitative research in practice: Examples for discussion and analysis.* San Francisco, CA: Wiley.

Miles, M. B., & Huberman, A. M. (1994). *Qualitative data analysis: An expanded sourcebook* (2nd ed.). Thousands Oaks, CA: Sage.

Moore, S. J., Walton, A. R., & Lambert, R. D. (1992). *Introducing Chinese into high schools: The Dodge Initiative.* Washington, DC: National Foreign Language Center.

Mu, A., & Zhang, D. (2004). Technology accelerates language learning—evidences from a Chinese class for heritage learners. In R. Calsen, N. Davis, J. Price, R. Weber, & D. A. Willis (Eds.), *Proceedings of the 2004 Conference of Society for Information Technology & Teacher Education* (pp. 3997–4002). Charlottesville, VA: Association for the Advancement of Computers in Education.

Munier, L. E. (1998). Personality and motivational factors in computer-mediated foreign language communication (CMFLC). In J. Muyskens (Ed.), *New ways of learning and teaching: Focus on technology and foreign language education* (pp. 145–197). Boston: Heinle & Heinle.

Negretti, R. (1999). Web-based activities and SLA: A conversational analysis research approach. *Language Learning & Technology, 3*(1), 75–87.

Patton, M. Q. (1990). *Qualitative evaluation and research methods* (2nd ed.). Newbury Park, CA: Sage.

Paulsen, M. F., & Rekkedad, T. (1988). Computer conferencing: A breakthrough in distance learning or just another technological gadget? In D. Stewart & J. S. Daniel (Eds.), *Developing distance education*, (pp. 362–364). Oslo, Norway: International Council for Distance Education.

Pellettieri, J. (2000). Negotiation in cyberspace: The role of chatting in the development of grammatical competence. In M. Warschauer & R. Kern (Eds.), *Network-based language teaching: Concepts and practice* (pp. 59–86). Cambridge, UK: Cambridge University.

Peyton, J. K. (1999). Theory and research: Interaction via computers. In J. Egbert & E. Hanson-Smith (Eds.), *CALL environments: Research, practice and critical issues* (pp.17–26). Alexandria, VA: TESOL.

Reigeluth, C. M., & Garfinkle, R. J. (1992). Envisioning a new system of education. *Educational Technology, 32*(11), 17–23.

Roblyer, M. D., Edwards, J., &. Havriluk, M. A. (1997). *Integrating educational technology into teaching*. Upper Saddle River, NJ: Prentice Hall

Ruschoff, B., & Ritter, M. (2001). Technology-enhanced language learning: Construction of knowledge and template-based learning in the foreign language classroom, *Computer Assisted Language Learning, 14*(3–4), 219–232.

Salabarry, R. (1999). CALL in the year 2000: Still developing the research agenda. *Language Learning and Technology, 3*(1), 104–107.

Salabarry. R. (2001). The Use of technology for L2 learning and teaching: A retrospective. *The Modern Language Journal, 85*(I), 115–122.

Savenye, W. C., & Robinson, R. S. (1996). Qualitative research issues and methods. In D. H. Jonassen (Ed.), *Handbook of research for educational communications and technology.* (pp. 1171–1195). New York: Simon & Schuster Macmillan.

Schrier. L. L., & Everson, M. E. (2000). From the margins to the new millennium: Preparing teachers of critical languages. In D. W. Brickbichler & R. M. Terry (Eds.), *Reflecting on the past to shape the future* (pp. 125–161*)*. Lincolnwood, IL: National Textbook Company.

Schutt, M. (2003). Scaffolding for online learning environments: Instructional design strategies that provide online learner support. *Educational Technology, 43*(6), 28–35.

Small, S. A. (1995). Action-oriented research: Models and methods. *Journal of Marriage and the Family, 57,* 941–956.

Smith, B. (2003). Computer-mediated negotiated interaction: An expanded model. *The Modern Language Journal, 87*(1), 38–57.

Smith, B. (2004). Computer-mediated negotiated interaction and lexical acquisition. *Studies in Second Language Acquisition, 26*(3), 365–398.

Sotillo, S. M. (2000). Discourse functions and syntactic complexity in synchronous and asynchronous communication. *Language Learning and Technology, 4*(1), 82–119.

Stepp-Greany, J. (2002). Student perceptions of language learning in a technological environment: Implications for the new millennium. *Language Learning and Technology, 6*(1), 165–180.

Strauss, A., & Corbin, J. (1998). Grounded theory methodology: An overview. In N. K. Denzin & Y. S. Lincoln (Eds.), *Strategies of qualitative inquiry* (pp. 158–183). Thousand Oaks, CA: Sage.

Sullivan, N., & Pratt, E. (1996). A comparative study of two ESL writing environments: A computer-assisted classroom and a traditional classroom. *System, 29,* 491–501.

Tharp, R., & Gallimore, R. (1988). *Rousing minds to life: Teaching, learning, and schooling in social context.* Cambridge: Cambridge University.

Toyoda, E., & Harrison, R. (2002). Categorization of text chat communication between learners and native speakers of Japanese. *Language Learning and Technology, 6*(1), 82–99.

Tschirner, E. (2001). Language acquisition in the classroom: The role of digital video. *Computer Assisted Language Learning, 14*(3–4), 305–319.

Tudini, V. (2003). Using native speakers in chat. *Language Learning and Technology, 7*(3), 141–159.

Vrasidas, C., & Mclsaac, M. S. (1999). Factors influencing interaction in an online course. *The American Journal of Distance Education, 13*(3), 22–30.

Vygotsky, L. S. (1978). *Mind in society: The development of higher psychological processes.* Cambridge, MA: Harvard University Press.

Walton, A. R. (1996). Reinventing language fields: The Chinese case. In S. McGinnis (Ed), *Chinese pedagogy: An emerging field,* Chinese Language Teachers Association, Monograph #2 (pp. 29–80). Columbus, OH: Foreign Language Publications.

Wang, X. (1996). A *view from within: A case study of Chinese heritage community language schools in the United States.* Washington, DC: National Foreign Language Center.

Warschauer, M. (1996a). Comparing face-to-face and electronic communication in the second language classroom. *The CALICO Journal, 13,* 7–25.

Warschaer, M. (1996b). *Telecollaboration in foreign language learning.* Honolulu: Second Language Teaching & Curriculum Center.

Warschauer, M. (1997). Computer-mediated collaborative learning: Theory and practice. *The Modern Language Journal, 81,* 470–481.

Warschauer, M. (1999). *Electronic literacies: Language, culture and power in online education.* Mahwah, NJ: Lawrence Erlbaum Associates.

Warschauer, M. (2000). Online learning in second language classrooms: An ethnographic study. In M. Warschauer & R. Kern (Eds.), *Network-based language teaching: Concepts and practice* (pp. 41–58). New York: Cambridge University.

WebCT (2004). *Web Course Tools Web page.* Retrieved September, 2005, from http://www.webct.com

Wertch, J. (1979). From social interaction to higher psychological process: A clarification and application of Vygotsky's theory. *Human Development, 22,* 3–22.

Wolcott, L. (1996). Distant, but not distanced: A learner-centered approach in distance education. *Techtrends, 41*(4), 23–27.

Xu, P., & Jen, T. (2005). "Penless" Chinese language learning: A computer-assisted approach. *Journal of the Chinese Language Teachers Association, 40*(2), 25–42.

Yao, T. (1997). *Integrated Chinese (level I, part 1 & 2).* Boston: Cheng-Tsui.

Yates, S. J. (1996). Oral and written linguistic aspect of computer-conferencing: A corpus-based study. In S. C. Herring. (Ed.), *Computer-mediated communication: Linguistic, social, and cross-cultural perspectives* (pp. 29–46). Amsterdam: John Benjamins.

Yin, R. (1989). *Case study research: Design and methods.* Newbury Park, CA: Sage.

Yin, R. (1994). *Case study research: Design and method* (2nd ed.). Thousands Oaks, CA: Sage.

Yin., R. (2003). *Case study research: Design and methods* (3rd ed.). Thousand Oaks, CA: Sage.

Zhang, D. (2004). *Exploring the affordances technology provides to heritage learners of Chinese as a foreign language-The case of online chat.* Unpublished master's thesis, Iowa State University.

Zhang, S., & Fulford, C. P. (1994). Are interaction time and psychological interactivity the same thing in the distance learning television classroom? *Educational Technology, 34*(6), 58–64.

Author Index

Subject Index